MURDER FROM THE GRAVE

MARCUS MCGEE

PEGASUS BOOKS

ISBN – 978-0-9673123-1-6

Comments about *Murder From the Grave* and requests for additional copies, book club rates and author speaking appearances may be addressed to Marcus McGee or Pegasus Books c/o Ms. McGhee, P.O. Box 235, Neptune, New Jersey, 07754, or you can send your comments and requests via e-mail to marcus.media@yahoo.com

For the men I have most admired,

My brothers,

> *Richard*
> *Dean*
> *Jeff*
> *Steve*

For a lifetime of inspiration

THE GREAEST SERIAL MURDER ARTIST OF ALL TIME?

While investigating a murder crime scene, San Francisco police find a letter addressed to one of their detectives, the clever and highly-respected Inspector Deuteronomy Saint Claire, who is at odds with the city's top brass for not sharing information over a career of twelve years. The letter is from a serial killer who tells Saint Claire that, despite being dead and in a grave for the last twelve days, he will murder seven people over the next thirty days.

Because the planned murders are interdependent, with each killing setting off the next, the killer dares the secretive detective to either stop him or proclaim his genius to the world.

Former Berkeley criminal psychology professor Saint Claire, convinced the letter is from the same killer who murdered his son, cautiously accepts the premise and the challenge.

By preventing any one of the planned murders, Saint Claire can interrupt the sequence and save lives, but only if the killer's claim to murder from the grave is true. Using clues from the letter and crime scenes, the detective is determined to defeat the killer, and if his instincts prove true, solve the murder of his son.

There is no great genius
without *some* touch of madness.

Seneca
Roman Stoic Philosopher

MURDER FROM THE GRAVE

Marcus McGee

Murder From the Grave

By Marcus McGee

CHAPTER 1

"Inspector Saint Claire?"

"Yes."

"I never knew your first name was Deuteronomy. I don't think anyone knew that."

Suppressing irritation, Saint Claire returned the identification badge to his jacket pocket.

"Not my name."

The young detective presented a zippered plastic bag with a wrinkled envelope inside.

"Well, someone obviously thinks it is. It's got a postmark on it, so we couldn't open it. It's addressed to Inspector Deuteronomy Saint Claire. That's you, isn't it? We found it wedged in a corner under her bathroom sink. Cap'n says you should open it and turn it over as evidence."

The inspector took the plastic bag, folded it and tucked it into his pocket.

"When did this place become a crime scene?"

"Two hours ago. Medical Examiner reclassified the cause of death to murder. She was poisoned. Cyanide."

Saint Claire scanned the periphery, eyes narrowing. If it was a crime scene, it hadn't been contained. There were uniformed officers and at least one desk person he recognized.

"Who's in charge here?"

"You are, now that you're here."

"Good. Get these people out of here. They're in the way. When I'm done, they can come back, but I want them all out now."

Gladys Rosenthal died in the apartment three days earlier. Because she was eighty-three years old, everyone including her son, Superior Court Judge Harold Rosenthal, attributed her passing to natural causes.

But one of the emergency room physicians became curious about her skin, which appeared "cherry-red," and referred the case to the county medical examiner. The medical examiner, noting her lungs were healthy though inflamed, performed initial toxicology tests and two days later indicated death by anoxia resulting from cyanide poisoning. Further tests confirmed the finding.

Judge Rosenthal, on the advice of the San Francisco police chief, agreed to keep the matter low key until a full investigation was underway. The chief and the judge met earlier in the day, and while the judge was anxious to see an inquiry begin, he was confused about why anyone would want to murder his sickly eighty-three year old mother.

For the last twenty-five years of her life, Gladys Rosenthal lived in the magnificent Brocklebank Apartments, at the intersection of Mason and Sacramento Streets. After the death of financier husband Henry, Gladys sold off her residential rental properties and moved into the famous apartment building across from the Fairmount Hotel.

Fifteen years after she moved in, she suffered a mild heart attack. Although doctors assured her the attack was not life threatening, Gladys never recovered emotionally. Whereas before she was known as a feisty and ultra liberal socialite who saw fit to correct neighbor and *Chronicle* columnist Herb Caen *when he didn't have his facts right*, she became withdrawn after the attack. She dropped off the social registers and was rarely seen outside the building.

Saint Claire took his time, eyes scanning and stopping, as he moved from the kitchen to the Spartan living room. Austere though it was, the apartment possessed an understated elegance, much like the woman who had over ripened and wilted in it for the last quarter century. The three furniture pieces—an upholstered couch, a chair and a gold table displaying an ornate, cobalt Bakelite Box with horses and two bejeweled picture frames—reflected the 1940s art deco style of Gladys in bloom.

The glass-encased pictures along the hallway had faded and yellowed over the years. The photographs reflected scenes and characters from a distant and surreal, sepia-tinted age. Saint Claire stopped for a moment, his hands reaching toward a tarnished frame at mid wall, though his fingers stopped just short of touching it. He recognized the face: it was Gladys on her wedding day. Her eyes intense, she smiled at the detective with such intent and cheeky aplomb that he bowed his head, just short of blushing.

The bathroom door was half-closed, but he heard the sound of someone yanking a drawer open and the noise of careless rummaging. The detective pushed the door and stepped into the bathroom. The large, muscular man hunched over the sink had his wide back turned, but Saint Claire could see the top of his head and a quarter-profile in the mirror.

"This is a crime scene, Mister. Would you mind telling me what you're doing?"

The dark haired man ignored the detective, slamming the first drawer and opening another. The detective continued.

"I'm in charge here. If you can't answer me, you can leave with the rest of them."

Saint Claire took a breath to settle his annoyance.

"For the last time, what the hell are you *looking* for?"

The man stopped, raised his head and turned toward the detective. He backed, holding his open palms at shoulders' height, and smiled.

"I'm looking for you. That is, if you're Inspector Deuteronomy Saint Claire."

"Saint Claire."

"I heard it was Deuteronomy. You don't like it? What do you go by? Ron, or maybe Dude for short?"

Saint Claire sighed and glanced askance, his trained eyes scouring the room and the contents of the open drawer. Deliberate, he took a step forward and closed it. Then he leaned forward, examining the shiny golden sink, faucet and handles for irregularities.

"Chief send you?"

"No. What makes you say that?"

The detective did not answer. He was examining the medicine cabinet mirror and its borders. Growing uncomfortable in the silence, the younger man took another step back to get a better perspective of the department legend. He cleared his throat and began.

"The name's Brady. Inspector Tom Brady. You know, like the quarterback?"

No reaction.

"What? You don't watch football? I just moved out here from—"

"Boston. You're Brady from Boston. I read your file."

Brady shrugged, uneasy.

"Right."

"And having read your file, I know you're not here to *assist* me. You're a veteran detective in your own right."

Brady began a half-hearted protest, but Saint Claire continued.

"So the chief sent you over here to watch me. Told you to stick close and share anything I turn up. Right?"

Brady hesitated and sighed.

"Yeah, something like that."

Saint Claire turned toward the younger detective, making eye contact for the first time.

"Of course you realize your admission makes our relationship an antagonistic one from this moment on?"

Brady nodded as Saint Claire began taking prescription medicine containers from the shelves of the cabinet. He tried to get Saint Claire to look up as he began.

"You know, they all respect the hell outa ya up there, over at the department, I mean as a detective, but I hafta tell you, some of them think you're dirty."

Saint Claire opened the first container and emptied its contents into his latex covered hand. Brady leaned forward as the detective studied the yellowish tablets before pouring them back into the bottle.

"The chief said she likes you. She just doesn't trust you. You're a man who keeps secrets, she says. Doesn't think that's good in a detective."

Saint Claire was inspecting the prescription on a third bottle by the time he responded.

"I'm a private person, and I have a right to a private life."

Brady stretched his arms toward the ceiling, his shoulders cracking. Standing a little over six feet tall, he had a well-defined musculature evident through the opening of his jacket. His hair was curly and jet-black, his large face angled, his jaw square.

"Couldn't agree with you more. But as far as this investigation goes, you *will* share anything you discover with me, right?"

He didn't really expect an answer. Brady never really wanted to come to San Francisco. Initially, he stood his ground, but he relented after his wife made plans to move to the west coast without him, and to take the girls with her. As chief financial officer for an investment firm in Boston, she made four times his salary, plus bonuses. So when a larger San Francisco conglomerate purchased the company she worked for and required her to move across the country, his protests were acknowledged and then dismissed.

"That's strange..."

Brady left his Boston regrets and approached the sink.

"What is it?"

"See here."

In his open palm, Saint Claire held twelve seemingly identical white tablets.

"I see. So what is it?"

"Levatol prescription."

"What's Levatol?"

Saint Claire withdrew a handkerchief from his pocket, placed it on the sink and transferred the tablets onto it.

"Beta-blocker. Doctors prescribe it for angina—heart pain, and for high blood pressure. I understand the judge's mother was a heart patient."

Saint Claire leaned close to the counter top, reordering the tablets with his index finger.

"There, and there. See that?"

Brady leaned toward the tablets, still uncertain about what he was observing. He glanced up, non-responsive, as Saint Claire continued.

"Two over here, coloration is off. It seems they're a very pale grey or a faint blue. Hard to tell in this light, but they're different."

Brady leaned even closer.

"Isn't blue the color of cyanide?"

"I see they sent over a real genius. Cyanide salts are *white*, but maybe it's something else."

Saint Claire returned the tablets to the container and placed the container into a plastic crime scene collection bag.

"I'll send it to the lab. If this is the source of the cyanide poisoning, we'll know in a few hours."

He began removing the rest of her medicine from the cabinet, placing vials and containers on the sink cupboard.

"I'll test the rest anyway. I'm sure no one forced Mrs. Rosenthal to take whatever it was that killed her. She took it, thinking it was her medicine."

Saint Claire left the bathroom. Near the foot of her bed, he called back toward Brady.

"I hope I've been forthcoming enough for the chief. I'm leaving, but you're welcome to poke around in there to see if you can find whatever I missed."

When Brady realized the detective was headed out, he hurried after him.

"What about the letter?"

"What letter?'

"The one that was left in there for you. The one with your name on it?"

Saint Claire was already at the front door by the time the younger detective caught up. He answered without looking back.

"Haven't read it and won't read it, for now. I want to arrive at conclusions on my own. If it's from the killer, its purpose is to influence this investigation."

He stopped just outside the door, turning back to Brady.

"I don't play games with killers, so the letter's a distraction as far as I'm concerned. Tell the chief she'll see it when I open it."

Brady forced his way out the door and took a place in front of Saint Claire.

"Wait! Now let me get this straight. You're telling me the killer broke in there and put some kind of matching poison pills in the bottles with her prescriptions?"

"Either the killer did or she did, and I'm betting this was no suicide."

"Yeah, but why would anyone go through all that trouble to murder an eighty-three-year-old woman? She had one foot in the grave and the other on a hockey puck!"

Saint Claire placed his right hand on Brady's shoulder and gripping, pushed the detective aside.

"Rhetorical question? It's an introduction. The killer did it to get us here, or more specifically, to get me here. She died three days ago, on my birthday."

Left hand in his pocket, Saint Claire fingered the plastic bag containing the letter. Brushing past Brady, he strode down the hallway.

After briefing the guard, Brady had to run to reach the elevator on time. Annoyed, Saint Claire pushed the "close" button two times, trying to shut the lift before Brady caught up, but the young detective just managed to get his arm in. The doors hesitated and opened.

"Thanks! Whew, I think I can say I'm officially out of shape."

He stopped panting, drew a deep breath and sighed.

"Well, Happy Birthday anyway."

Saint Claire was monitoring the elevator's progress displayed above the door.

"Yep."

"Can I buy you a birthday drink?"

"Too late."

Uncomfortable, Brady also looked up at the green light moving behind the stencil numbers.

"Getting close to dinner time. Want to go get something to eat?"

Saint Claire reached forward and pulled down the manual lever next to the panel box, bringing the elevator to a sudden stop.

"Listen Brady, maybe you didn't get it when I said it back at the apartment. Your function here is to report on me to the chief, and that makes our relationship adversarial. I'll put up with you to go along with the program, but don't mistake communication for friendship. We will *never* be friends."

The remainder of the elevator ride was silent. When the door opened, Brady watched the detective as he exited, studying the lobby. Eyes scanning the mixed crowd of reporters, police personnel and curious neighbors, Saint Claire spotted his mark near the exit. Brady followed, keeping a distance.

"How long have you worked here?"

"Me, Sir? I been here mosta thirty-two years, since ah was bout twenty-five."

Saint Claire nodded, withdrew a notepad and pen from the inside pocket of his jacket and smiled.

"Career man? I like that. And would you say you know most of the people who live in the building?"

"I would say ah know em all, and mosta everone who come up in here ta visit."

Saint Claire eyed the doorman's badge.

"What is your first name, Mr. Cross?"

"It's Lesta, Lesta Cross."

"Well Lester, consider yourself on break for the next fifteen minutes or so. I need to ask you a few questions."

"So when was the last time you saw her?"

"It was last, I believe it was last Monday morning. She come down here bout eleven, waiting for that limousine that takes her to her hair appointment. Got her hair done every Monday, and then she would go to lunch with the judge. Sometime it be the only time she get out for the week."

Saint Claire could feel Lester's eyes return again to his left ear. In reflex, he adjusted the black felt Fedora downward and continued.

"Was it the only time she got out last week?"

Lester nodded.

"Yep. Far as I can remember, and I was here all week."

"Okay. And while she was gone, do you remember if anyone out of the ordinary came in. Someone you hadn't seen before?"

"I don't know bout not ordinary, but I think Maria came in that day. Mattera fack, I know she did."

Saint Claire turned his head, giving Lester a right profile.

"And Maria is?"

"The maid. She was Gladys's maid. She came on Mondays, when Gladys was gone, and on Thursdays."

Saint Claire stood, his eyes spotting his next interview target at the concierge desk.

"What is Maria's last name?"

"Oh it's one of them Messican's names. Fuentes, I think? Somethin like that. Short, thick woman."

Again he noticed Lester's staring.

"You like looking at my ear, Lester?"

The old man was embarrassed. He shuffled his feet.

"Oh naw, I was just checkin out your *hat*, that's all."

Over the course of questioning, Lester Cross told the detective how Gladys changed after the heart attack. He said she was out to lunch with her friends three times a week and out at dinner and parties almost every weekend before her illness. But then after the attack, she just dried up. She was afraid of everything. She stopped trusting people.

Still, he said she was a very generous person. Gladys somehow pulled strings to help Lester's daughter get into UCLA, and then Gladys helped the girl out with tuition and books until she graduated.

Maria discovered Gladys's body in the apartment on the afternoon of the previous Thursday. When she came running down the stairs, screaming something in Spanish, Lester had to restrain her at the door. After she had calmed a little, she told him, *mi señora está muerta*.

Lester hurried with Maria up to Gladys's apartment and found the old woman on her bed, curled up on the comforter, fetal, her teeth and fists clinched, her face contorted by pain. Lester had seen death before. The Brocklebank building was full of seniors. It was sad, though expected. After a moment of stoic reflection, he called the hospital to pick up the body.

He recalled seeing a few strange faces in the building after Gladys's death, but he figured they were relatives or friends of the family. There was one man in particular who stood out in Lester's mind because he seemed a little odd. He had short light brown hair and he wore small, circular glasses with dark lenses. In Lester's words, the man seemed like more of an East coast person or a European.

Lester said the rumor in the building was that the person who murdered Gladys did so to get back at her son, the judge. He said the judge was not a nice man. The judge had never given Lester "his proper" as a man and looked down on poor people.

The judge wasn't kind to his mother either, according to Lester. He was always impatient and huffy with her.

"It was like he was just doin his duty until she was dead. He was her only child, and he was set up to get alla her money and property after she died."

Saint Claire, by habit, clarified innuendo.

"Are you saying, Lester, you believe the judge might be connected in all this? You think the *judge* killed his mother?"

"I'm not sayin that at all. All I'm sayin is he probably didn't cry too long when he fount out she was dead. He prob'ly popped a bottle of champagne or somethin."

Reflecting on the first time he met Gladys twenty-one years earlier and on how his daughter wept when she heard the news of Gladys's death, Lester got a little teary-eyed and choked up.

"I can't understand why *anyone* would wanna murder that woman!"

The young brunette at the concierge desk had been with the Brocklebank apartments for less than a year, but she remembered Gladys waiting in the lobby for her limousine on Monday afternoons. She said sometimes, when Mrs. Rosenthal was in a good mood, she'd tell interesting stories about San Francisco's past.

"Chloe, is it? Would you say you know most of the people in the building?"

Hands folded on her lap, the concierge shrugged her shoulders and nodded.

"I think so. I haven't been here as long as Lester, but everyone in this place *has* to come by me at some time. And as you can tell, I like to talk a lot."

He smiled.

"Naw! I had you pegged as the *shy* type."

She shrugged.

"More like a flibbertigibbet—that's what my father called me. I stop only to breathe."

He laughed.

"Okay. Can you take a breath for me? Do you recall seeing any strange or suspicious people come through the lobby at any time before or after the murder?"

Chloe's eyes darted up left and returned.

"Ya know, there *was* a strange person! But that was at least a month ago. He was a kinda mysterious man who asked some questions about the building. I didn't think he wanted to live here. He didn't seem like the Brocklebank type. And I wasn't sure, but I think he was wearing make-up."

"You *think* he was wearing make-up? Do you remember what he looked like, under the make-up?"

"Oh, he had kinda short brown hair. I don't remember if he was tall, but he wore a designer watch and had on expensive sunglasses."

Saint Claire looked up from his notes.

"Oh come on! How could you tell they were expensive? Did he show them to you, with a price tag?"

Chloe laughed.

"Mister, when you shop as much as I do, ya get this kinda sixth sense. I think the glasses were Dolce Gabbanas and the watch was a Cartier. It was silver, I think. Probably at least a few thousand dollars."

Saint Claire closed the notepad.

"And he was here just that once?"

She was reconstructing the memory.

"No. Come to think of it, he was here on at least... *two* occasions."

CHAPTER 2

Oro En Paz, Fierro en Guerra. Gold in Peace, Iron in War.
The inscription was etched on the silver face of a wooden plaque
that hung on a wall behind the desk of Sonia Sanchez, Captain
of Central Station, Metro Division, in downtown San Francisco.
Central Station, located on Vallejo Street between Powell and
Stockton, was the busiest division in the police department. The
district comprised the Financial Quarter, Chinatown, North
Beach, Fisherman's Wharf, and three famous hills: Telegraph,
Nob and Russian. Seven of ten major tourist attractions in San
Francisco were located in the Central District.

Sonia was from Oakland across the bay, but she moved
to San Francisco as a college student. After graduating at UCSF
from the school of Criminal Justice, she tried to get into three
prestigious northern California law schools, but she had to settle
for an unaccredited school in Sacramento. Upon graduation, she
took and failed the bar exam twice before joining the San
Francisco Police Department as an entry level officer with a bi-
lingual background.

Over her twenty-five year career, she dealt with
discrimination for being a Latina, sexual harassment and
condescending attitudes from her peers and the public. Some
assholes in the department never took her seriously, even after
she was promoted to captain. The detectives were the worst,
with one standing out in particular.

Minutes earlier, her secretary buzzed telling her
inspector Tom Brady was waiting to meet with her. She had
never met Brady, but she had read his profile. Off the record, she
heard from some of her officers that Brady was a "hunk with a
roaming eye." She had spoken with the chief earlier in the day,
so she knew why he had come.

Sonia stood for a better view as he came through the
door, her eyes falling down the full length of his body. She
extended her right hand.

"Inspector Brady, very nice to meet you. I take it you've
been over at Mrs. Rosenthal's apartment?"

He nodded, his eyes lingering a little too long on her
breasts.

"Captain Sanchez. Yes, I have. I was there when Inspector Saint Claire was going over the contents of her medicine cabinet."

"And?"

Sanchez eased into her black leather chair, assuming a relaxed posture. Brady sighed aloud as he took a seat across the desk.

"Well, there was the letter, postmarked and mailed to him at her address."

She interrupted.

"I probably knew that before you did. Anything *new*?"

"Saint Claire, he found something, something he said was peculiar about some of her pills, the Levatol pills. I think he believes the killer made up cyanide pills to look like the Levatol pills. He sent all her medication for testing, though."

"And the letter? What was that about?"

Glancing at her reflection in the window to her left, she dragged her fingers through her short, black hair. Her preening caught Brady's notice. He flashed a smile and bowed his head.

"He didn't open it. Didn't want it to influence the investigation. Said he'd open it later."

"He's a fucking idiot and a liar! I *hate* that asshole. I told him when I talked to him on the phone he's going to have to open that letter and turn it over as evidence!"

She paused and took a calming breath.

"Did he say anything about motive?"

"He didn't say exactly, but he suggested she was killed to get his attention."

"His attention? Now that's just like him!"

Sonia sighed, disgusted, and leaned toward the detective.

"A word of advice about Saint Claire, since the chief has you working with him: don't trust that bastard. He won't tell you things. He knows a lot. He's got a real fucking PhD. He taught over at Berkeley, so he'll impress you, but he doesn't share."

Brady shrugged, his face skeptical.

"He did tell me what he thought about how she was poisoned. Explained what he was thinking about the killer putting the poison in her medication."

"But he didn't share the letter. Yeah, he shares what he wants you to know."

Although he smiled, she realized he was unconvinced.

"You don't believe me? Ask around. Ask about a detective Joe Curry outa Park Station, Golden Gate Division. He worked with Saint Claire, and now he's dead. Saint Claire was implicated."

"Really?"

His tone was patronizing, and she was in no mood to offer greater proof.

"I swear you detectives really are smug assholes, every last one of you!"

He smiled, flirting.

"You just have to get to know me better. You might be surprised."

Only after she smiled did he continue.

"I don't get it. If this guy's so bad, why do you even *have* him here?"

"I didn't say he wasn't smart. Second year he was here, he sued the department for something he had, some kind of sealed envelope shit. Had the police commission by the balls, and they've been reluctant to let anyone bother him since."

"I heard that, and I also heard that story was some kind of a San Francisco police urban legend. It's been what, ten or eleven years? There's a statute of limitations on evidence. Besides that, the commission's changed over the years."

Sonia raised her hands.

"Well and good, but he's still here. We all hate him, but he'll be here until he's ready to leave, at his own terms."

Brady thought a moment and nodded. In his left hand, he held a report folder, which he placed on the desk and slid toward the captain.

"Yeah, he's obviously got something or someone protecting him."

"And now he's got a killer, sending a postmarked letter, calling him into this by name. I think he's involved somehow."

Brady laughed.

"Whoa! Now *that's* a leap. And just how do you expect to prove that?"

She didn't flinch.

"I don't. Didn't the chief tell you? As of this moment, proving Saint Claire's dirty is your job. That's why she brought you here. Unofficially, of course."

They were more than mere bookshelves. They were a custom feature of the room, the work of virtuosic carpentry. Polished, dark cherry wood shelves from floor to high ceiling, careful numeric etching and lettering on the shelf facing. And the shelves were full of books, thousands of them in different colors, shapes and sizes, many of them dusty and old.

The room smelled of paper, ink, mold and stitch bindings. At its center sat a cherry wood desk with an expansive glossy surface and an intricate woodworked design along the top perimeter. Upon closer inspection, the design was a row of continuous tiny angels, wings extended, palms held together before their chests. The chair at the desk was plain in contrast, a simple hardwood chair with a thin brown seat cushion.

The space was Saint Claire's sanctuary, his asylum. It was the only place where he felt comfortable enough to remove his hat, which he placed on the coat rack near the door. It was where he went to do his best thinking, his most important analysis.

He sat erect in the chair at the desk in the bright room, his posture formal and the notes organized before him. Alone on the desktop was the envelope, now crumpled, with a vertical crease down the middle. Saint Claire sat for fifteen minutes, contemplating it. It was postmarked, meaning the killer had sent the letter to Gladys's address, found a way to get the letter out of her mail before she did, and hid it in the bathroom. Why would anyone go to so much trouble?

And the murder itself! The lab called earlier, confirming the discolored tablets in the Levatol bottle were composed of cyanide salts, matched to look similar to the Levatol tablets. Putting them in place of the legitimate medication would have involved breaking into her apartment on the rare occasions she was away, going through her medicine cabinet to find what she was taking, making up cyanide duplicates and breaking into the apartment a second time to put the poison in her medicine bottle.

The killer apparently had no problem breaking into her apartment. If he had wanted to kill her, he could have done so as she slept. And her apartment held a collection of very expensive trinkets and a cache of jewelry, none of which was disturbed.

It was not Saint Claire's ego. It was logic. The killer hadn't gone to all the effort required to murder Gladys in such a manner because he wanted her dead, and facts indicated he didn't do it to take anything from her. Saint Claire concluded he himself was the point of the killer's fixation, not Gladys, and not the judge.

As an associate professor and member of the core clinical science faculty at UC Berkeley over ten years, Saint Claire taught courses and had written several books on criminal psychology, with an emphasis on serial killers.

He opened the small drawer beneath the desktop and withdrew a keen steel knife with a yellowed ivory hilt, along with a pair of tweezers. Taking the envelope in his left hand, he inserted the knife in the right corner and passed it along the top, opening it. He paused to put on a pair of thin latex gloves.

Holding the envelope at arm's length, he inserted the knife to pry it open. Inverting it, he tapped on one side to check if the contents were covered with white powder, which could contain anthrax spores or some poison agent. No powder fell.

Next, he inserted the tweezers to withdraw a thick bundle of folded paper for visual examination. He put on his glasses, which sat crooked on his face because of the scarring on his mangled left ear. Unfolding the letter, he read.

Thank you, Inspector, for setting this little drama in motion, and with it my resurrection.

Saint Claire bowed his head, regretting he had opened it. Taking a breath, he sat back and continued to read.

I must emphasize the word "resurrection," Inspector, because I am dead. I died over 12 days ago. I am rotting in a grave as you read this letter. In fact, I contrived my own murder, and because I am the most brilliant serial murder artist of all time, I have also contrived my resurrection. Before this drama is concluded, you are going to raise me from the dead, you are going to proclaim to the world that I am (or was) the best and brightest of my class.

Bundy was prolific, but he wasn't bright. Gary Ridgway was a cheap, inbred moron. The BTK Strangler was a barbarian, and the Night Stalker was a pervert. Zodiac, all the others were idiotic, petty, little amateurs who didn't understand what they were. I am in my own class because I kill for the sheer intellectual thrill of playing God. But this eternal blazon must not be to ears of flesh and blood.

Saint Claire opened the drawer and grabbed a magnifying glass. Placing the page on the table, he examined the script: 12-point Times New Roman, italic, printed in black ink by a laser printer.

When I was alive, I killed at will, right under your noses, and no one came close to finding me, except you. Mine is a problem encountered only by the most exceptional of minds. I have murdered so efficiently that I've left no discernable traces, no trail for any of you to follow. I've laughed at the best of you as you've run around in circles like fools in a dark room, too insipid to realize the lights were off.

To call myself a murder artist would be an understatement. I am a genius at killing, a maestro at murder, and like you, a renaissance man besides. To murder without art is an abomination, a criminal act. My work by contrast, is divine.

Saint Claire reread the penultimate paragraph, trying to understand the killer's connection to him. Was this someone he had met or arrested?

And to the point of this letter, Inspector: the fact that I am dead notwithstanding, I am going to commit seven murders over the next thirty days. In other words, I am going to create seven murder crime scenes from right here, where I rot in my grave, and there's nothing any of you can do to stop me. That alone should confirm that I am the greatest serial murder artist of all time, but being the egocentric and psychotic god that I am, I want my work to be appreciated... and admired.

There, Inspector, is where you fit in. That is, if you're up to the challenge. You are, without exception, the most brilliant mind I have encountered in all my killing. You like me, are both smart and lucky. If your luck holds, you have a remote chance of stopping me and saving innocent lives, and I realize that's a motivator for you. You do want to save lives, don't you?

Like interdependently placed dominoes, each murder I commit will set off the next murder, from seven to one. If you can stop one murder at any point in the progression, you save that life and prevent the murders that would have followed in turn, and therefore you win. However, if you fail to stop the murders, you will be forced to tell the world and history about me.

Ah, there's the rub, there's the artistic device that is present in all my work. In irony, the world greatest murder artists, ipso facto, have always rotted within their pathetic graves unknown. And yet from my grave, I am going to murder people at will, and then I'm going to force legendary detective Deuteronomy Saint Claire to describe for all time just who I was and how very brilliant I am. If you don't stop me, Inspector, it is your own lack of luck and intellect that will make me the greatest serial murder artist of all time. And so absent thee from felicity awhile, Professor, and in this harsh world draw thy breath in pain, to tell my story.

Happy Birthday, Inspector

CHAPTER 3

It was true. Forty-nine years and three days earlier, he was born in the backwater town of Thibodaux in Lafourche parish, Louisiana. His father was a cook in New Orleans during the week and a deacon at the church on weekends, and his light-skinned mother was a maid for a prominent white family in town.

He was the third of five children: two older brothers, Pierre and Samuel; a younger sister, Sara; and a younger brother, Henri. When at twelve, he asked his mother why she named him Deuteronomy, she said it was because he was her "special" son, and since the time she was a girl, she had always thought Deuteronomy would be a fine name for a boy.

Until the day she died, his mother, Bernadette, called him her favorite. She and Deuteronomy remained Catholic, though his father, Jacque, and the other children were Baptist.

Deuteronomy resembled his mother's side of the family more than the other children did. His skin was lighter, almost a pecan brown with patches of darker freckles on his face. He was taller, a little over five-foot-ten-inches, and lean. As a young man in college, he competed as a cyclist, and his physique still held traces of athleticism.

From early on, oddities intrigued him. In Thibodaux, he was the only child in the town who dared to visit Miss Annabelle Lee, the reclusive widow who lived on the property going up toward the old sugar plantation. Miss Annabelle was a widow because she killed her husband. She shot him in the throat with his own shotgun. Gossips in town said she murdered his two children as well, but her stepchildren's bodies were never found and the law ruled the homicide self-defense.

As a nervous and excited seven-year-old, he rode his bike over, slipped through the rust encrusted gate and knocked on her door one morning. The old woman was suspicious, since no one from the town had visited her in over fifteen years. Asked why he had come, he was honest. He said he had come to find out if the stories he heard about her were true.

Over time, a cautious friendship developed. Deuteronomy came in the morning to chop wood and perform other outdoor chores in exchange for afternoons spent with Miss Annabelle, listening as she told her stories of her past. When members of the community learned about his weekly visits, they went to his parents. The reverend of his father's congregation warned that something very perverse was happening over at Miss Annabelle's.

Forbidden to visit her, Deuteronomy only became more secretive. He and Miss Annabelle planned regular visits throughout the summer of his eleventh year and well into year twelve, but then tragedy struck.

There was little notice of the hurricane that, moving westward from the Florida Keys, threatened extensive flooding in Louisiana. Deuteronomy's parents drove the family up to Baton Rouge on that September afternoon, but there was little help for Miss Annabelle, who was out of the communication loop. When Deuteronomy's family returned home three days later, he rushed toward her house on his bike, but his way was blocked by floodwaters.

Over the next two days, the bodies started showing up, some of them bloated and floating and others stranded on sandbars or along hillside slopes above the falling waterline. Searching over the rotting bodies, twelve-year-old Deuteronomy found Miss Annabelle's corpse not twenty feet from her front porch.

Two years later, Deuteronomy was an outstanding student at Thibodaux Central Catholic High School, excelling in math and science, preoccupied with finishing first in his class. Monsignor Baudelaire however, advised his favorite student that class rank and grades were not nearly as essential as a well-rounded education.

By his junior year, it was obvious Deuteronomy heeded the advice. At graduation, he was the school's top student in Latin and in English literature and he played accordion in the school's jazz band. He finished second in his class and received a full scholarship to Louisiana State.

"I came to see my wife."

"Her name?"

"Saint Claire. Katrina Saint Claire."

The older woman at the counter left for three minutes and returned wearing a somber expression.

"Today isn't a good day for her. Maybe you could try back tomorrow."

Saint Claire forced a smile and backed a step.

"I see. Okay. Thank you."

In high school, Katrina Scott was a beautiful light-skinned girl with thick, wavy, jet-black hair halfway down her back. Her dark eyes, flecked with hazel, were intense. Some of the religious members of the community thought she was "possessed" and did not let their children associate with the girl.

Katrina was intense about everything she did. She refused to wear anything less than Sears & Roebuck. Her socks and shoes were always spotless and in fashion, her hair pulled back into one neat ponytail, and her fingernails trimmed and painted.

She was fiercely competitive. As a track and field athlete, she never lost a race, even if it meant practicing at the track until 10 p.m. on school nights. She worked hard to achieve the highest scores in her classes, if it meant drinking five cups of coffee in a night to stay up. And sometimes she would take her mother's tiny white pills to stay focused.

No one could deny her intelligence. Her father was a professor of physics at Nicholls State University and her mother taught science and chemistry at a local high school. Katrina gave the commencement speech as school valedictorian and went on to Tulane University in New Orleans on a scholarship. She was the only person who finished ahead of Saint Claire academically. Throughout high school, Kate was always quicker to the point, always a half step ahead.

Outside the brick and mortar building, Saint Claire adjusted his hat and made his way to his car, a dark blue Buick Roadmaster. It was early afternoon, so he still had three hours before he was expected at the station. He was disappointed he missed the opportunity to talk with Katrina, since he needed her advice.

There were two people on the list he still wanted to interview. The first was Maria, the maid. If anyone could provide information about curiosities within Gladys's apartment around the time of the murder, it would be the maid. The killer may have befriended Maria or used her access to get in and out of the apartment as easily as he had.

However, Maria hadn't returned Saint Claire's calls. In each of his three calls to her, Saint Claire spoke to a man who had a heavy Spanish accent. In broken English, the man said Maria worked five different jobs as a maid and was "beezee all the time."

The other name on the list belonged to Gladys's son. Saint Claire had never met the judge, but he knew him by reputation. Judge Rosenthal wasn't a favorite of law enforcement. He was a San Francisco liberal who believed the police department exercised too much discretionary power.

Beyond that, the underpinnings of his legal rulings suggested he believed the police force was abusive, activist and corrupt. He was involved in the city's social scene, attending swank private parties, political fundraisers and rubbing elbows with California's elite. During the winter holidays just passed, the judge toured Europe with the governor. He respected people with money, celebrity or social status and was impatient and condescending with the common public.

Saint Claire scheduled his interview with the judge at 1 p.m. in the judge's private office at the San Francisco Superior Court on McAllister.

Harold Rosenthal wasn't a tall man, but he seemed much more genuine and congenial than Saint Claire imagined he would be. His hair was dark brown, its line receding in the front, with gray at the temples. He appeared to be in his mid-to-late fifties and in good shape, though his shoulders were slumped. He wore a red tie on a white shirt with a dark cardigan. His smile was big and his eyes were warm as he extended his hand, fingers splayed.

"Inspector Saint Claire! It's great to finally meet you! You're the PhD detective, right? Taught over at Berkeley?"

Saint Claire shook the judge's hand, nodding. "They let me *think* I was doing something over there."

"I went to Berkeley, 60s. Protests, anti-war demonstrations, civil rights—people had that fire in the gut passion back then, especially your people. It's all lost with these young people now, all of em. Goddamn shame!"

At a credenza turned bar, he refilled his highball glass. "Scotch?" Cognac?"

He glanced over the judge's shoulder. "You're telling me

you got *cognac* back there?"

The judge laughed.

"Of course I have cognac. What? You think I got no black friends?"

Saint Claire raised a hand.

"Oh come on now. A Rabbi poured me my first cognac, on Purim!"

After twenty minutes, Saint Claire moved to the purpose of the interview.

"Judge Rosenthal, I've been investigating the murder of your mother since yesterday afternoon, and I'm trying to be as thorough as possible. So I'd just like you to share anything you think it might be important for me to know. Did your mother mention a stranger or new person in her life? Any person helping her around the apartment? Any conversations?"

Harold Rosenthal sat on a black leather sofa across from Saint Claire, who sat in a high back black split leather office chair. He sipped the scotch and shrugged.

"You got a mother?"

"I think I *had* a mother. She died a long time ago."

"Sorry to hear that, but my mother—God bless her soul. She did an awful lot of talking without really saying anything. So to answer your question, she may have, or she may not have. I don't remember. Sometimes she'd be talking, and I'd be, I'd be someplace else. Know what I mean?"

The judge craned his neck to see what the detective was writing on the note pad. Saint Claire flipped to the next page, looking up.

"How would you describe the relationship between you and your mother? Would you say you were close?"

The judge reared back.

"Look Inspector, I'm not sure if I like where I think you're going with that question. My mother was eighty-three years old and paranoid. We didn't have a lot in common. She had dementia. She wasn't close to *anybody*."

Saint Claire shut the note pad and returned it to his pocket.

"The dementia, was she diagnosed?"

The judge swigged his scotch.

"No, it wasn't diagnosed, but all her friends were old, the one's that hadn't already died. Many of them were diagnosed, and she was no different than they were. Acted just *like* them."

Saint Claire nodded.

"I see. Well Judge, can you think of any reason why someone would want to murder your mother?"

"In a word, no."

Saint Claire raised the snifter to his lips for the first time, sipping the cognac. His mouth tightened as he swallowed.

"Well, in your career as a defense attorney and a judge, is it possible you made an enemy over the years who would have murdered your mother to get back at you?"

The judge thought a moment and smiled.

"I started out as a lawyer almost thirty years ago. In the time since then, yes, I'm sure I've made some people mad. Most of them just told me to fuck off, and one time I had this deputy DA asshole who busted out one of my car's headlights. So no, I've pissed people off enough to have them call me names and attack my car, but *never* enough to wait around years for revenge, let alone murdering my innocent eighty-three year-old mother to get back at me."

The cognac, as always, was smoother on the second sip.

"You're probably right. You know, seems there's more to this murder than your mother, or you for that matter."

Saint Claire sighed, sipped the last of the cognac and stood, slipping his pen into his jacket pocket. The judge stood in turn.

"Inspector, you've been asking me questions, but would you mind if I asked *you* a question?"

"Go ahead."

"I heard they found a sealed and postmarked letter in my mother's bathroom. I heard it was from the killer and it was addressed to you."

He paused.

"I have to ask, have you *read* that letter?"

Saint Claire had already grimaced before he thought to control his face. Raising his eyebrows, he answered.

"That's a fair question, Judge. Yes, I have read it."

"Is it from the killer?"

"Based on what I read? I think so. But I believe the writer of the letter is psychotic, someone whose contact with reality is seriously impaired. Unfortunately however, the letter doesn't tell us anything about why your mother was murdered or who did it."

The judge called across the room from where he stood, refreshing his drink.

"You should have been a politician, Inspector. I don't give a damn about what the letter *doesn't* tell us. What does the killer say?"

Saint Claire started to make his way to the exit.

"Come on, Judge, this investigation is just getting underway. I'm not at liberty, nor do I have the authority to reveal anything in that letter to you. I'm headed to the station where I have to turn it over as evidence. You know the routine."

The judge stepped between the detective and the door.

"If the letter has anything to do with my mother or me, I believe I have a right to see it."

Saint Claire looked down at Harold Rosenthal's nervous face.

"The letter has nothing to do with your mother, Judge, I assure you. Your mother was an innocent victim, a random murder. The killer had no grudge against her, and this person won't be coming after you. You have nothing to worry about. Now if you'll excuse me."

The judge stepped aside and watched Saint Claire pass.

"I've heard for years about how *smart* you are, Inspector, but I'm a victim here too. Tell me man to man, as a friend. Do you have any idea why my mother was killed?"

In that moment, Saint Claire watched the judge's frame dissolve. In his place stood a trembling little boy who had lost his mother, a child who was just beginning to realize he would be alone, without the constant of his first and most significant human attachment for the rest of his life. A tear stopped on his reddened right cheek.

The detective spoke to console the judge.

"I'm sorry, but I just don't have anything yet. If I get a break or find the killer, I promise you'll be the first to know."

"Haven't you *heard*? His wife's crazy."

"His wife's crazy, my wife's crazy, they're *all* crazy. It's just women! They're all nuts."

Sergeant McCarthy looked at Brady and laughed.

"No, you don't get it. She's really crazy. Ya know, a fuckin psycho."

"I know. You haven't met *my* wife, Andrea. Craziest psycho bitch you'd ever wanna meet. I could tell you some stories!"

Sergeant Sean McCarthy sipped the cloudy brown beer, glanced over his shoulder and leaned closer.

"You don't get it. Saint Claire's wife is certifiable, a whack job. She's in that *mental* facility over on Stanyan. What is it? I think it's Saint Mary's or something like that. Cap'n's been over there. Cap'n Sanchez has *seen* her."

Brady sat silent for a moment, and then he refilled his glass with the dark brew. The room around him felt familiar, though it was only his third time in the pub. It was like being back at home, in Boston. The lights were dim, the tables were low and there was sawdust on the floor. Even the smells brought on nostalgia. He closed his eyes and took a breath of the yeasty, musty, pine dust filled air, exhaling.

"I like this place."

"What I tell ya? Best little Irish pub in San Francisco."

Brady and McCarthy met two weeks earlier on the detective's first day with the SFPD. Brady shook many hands and tried to remember names and faces, but he didn't want to be at Central Station or any other division in San Francisco. If he couldn't be in Boston, a bar was the next best thing. He pegged McCarthy as the nearest thing to a drunk he'd met and got himself invited to the *best Irish pub in the city* on Geary Boulevard.

"Saint Claire's story just don't add up. There's somethin he's not tellin us, somethin he's not tellin anybody."

McCarthy told Brady that Saint Claire left his job as a tenured professor at Berkeley, where he was making at least $120,000 a year plus bonuses and other money for books and lectures. He left that position for a San Francisco detective job where he was only making $55,000 at best. McCarthy said he heard the life change had something to do with Saint Claire's son being murdered in San Francisco.

"The guy's got a lot of that kinda shit goin on, all that mystery shit. Oh I'm sure we'll be readin about him in the paper some day, and it'll be some crazy, weird shit, but ya heard it here first."

Brady sipped his beer, his eyes studying McCarthy's face and manner.

"What is it everyone has against Saint Claire? I mean I've *met* the man, and I admit he's a little uptight, but he's very intelligent. What, is it the black thing? People afraid they might not be as smart as a black man?"

McCarthy laughed.

"Why don't you ask the resta the spooks on the force? They got a hard-on for him more'n anyone else. They don't trust him either."

Brady put his fingertips to his lips to stifle a belch.

"I still don't get it. Has he ever done anything suspicious?"

"There was the Joe Curry incident, but nine outa ten doctors can't be wrong. Everybody up there thinks he's up to somethin. Nobody trusts him. Why do you think that is?"

"Because he *is* up to something?"

McCarthy finished the last gulp of beer, pushed himself away from the table and stood.

"Exactly. Why do you think they brought you here?"

Saint Claire took no offense. It was a game Sonia Sanchez always played. She would schedule a meeting with him, and when he got there, she wouldn't be there. So he sat there, reading. This time it was *Hamlet*, a work he re-read every few years. And yet every time he read it, it was an entirely different play, with a different conclusion.

"Been here long?"

He stood, closing the book.

"Just got here."

"Then you were *late*, Inspector. We'll meet in my office."

Saint Claire watched her walk away before clutching his leather satchel of notebooks and following her down the hallway.

The office was familiar to him, though Sonia modernized it and applied distinct feminine touches. Derrick Slater, the captain of Central Station before Sonia, was a practical man who preferred function to form. The walls of his office were for tacking up notes, his chairs for sitting forward and the messy surface of his desk a platform for strategy and planning.

Slater worked with Saint Claire for ten years before retiring. Under Slater's tutelage and oversight, Saint Claire had distinguished himself as a clever and innovative detective, one who *understood* killers. His success rate was uncanny, and Slater often joked that SFPD should invest more resources to recruit psychology professors from the colleges.

But Slater was the only person in the department who knew what Saint Claire knew, and he knew the story behind Saint Claire's mangled left ear. He was Saint Claire's only friend. Slater's retirement two years earlier left Saint Claire without a liaison, without a conduit to the undisclosed objectives of the department on the case-by-case basis.

Sonia Sanchez sat in the black leather armchair at her desk, her shoulders held back and her manner that of polite disdain.

"Saint Claire, you know why I called you here. Apparently, someone mailed a letter to the Brocklebank Apartments about a month and a half ago, and strangely, it was addressed to you in the care of Gladys Rosenthal. Is there anything you want to tell me about why someone would mail a letter to you at her address a month and a half before her murder?"

Saint Claire thought a moment and shrugged.

"No."

"No, there's nothing to tell, or no, you don't have an idea about the letter?"

"Both."

Discerning from her face that she meant to discuss the matter in excruciating detail, he took a seat in the chair across from her.

"Look, I realize we've had differences in the past about my degree of sharing information, but I'm just as confused by the murder and the letter. I've already shared my suspicions about how she was poisoned, and those were confirmed, but whatever game the killer is trying to play, I don't know it, and I'm not going to play it."

She nodded.

"This person obviously knows you. Do you have any idea about who the killer might be?"

"Yeah, someone who knows me."

Sonia sat forward, putting on her glasses.

"What about the letter? You've read it, I'm sure. What's it about?"

"I've read it."

"I want you to give it to me now. Do you have it?"

He opened the satchel and withdrew a six-by-nine inch clasp envelope with a name and date scribbled on the front. Reaching forward, he placed it in front of her.

"The letter tells us nothing. The writer is a psychopath."

"You would *know* about that, wouldn't you?" She snatched the envelope from the desk. "I'll be the judge of what this letter tells us."

Taking the smaller #10 envelope out, she first studied the typed recipient's address, and then she yanked it open and pulled out the letter. As she unfolded it, her hands shook in excitement.

Cutting a glance at Saint Claire, she bowed her head and began to read. After a minute, she tossed the letter onto the desk.

"Is this it?"

"You read it. That's all there is. Why?"

"There isn't much to it. He's just telling us that he's going to kill seven people in the next thirty days. It's one paragraph! That's *all* there is to it? There's nothing more?"

Saint Claire picked up the letter and scanned it.

"It's a letter from the killer. What did you expect? A confession? A clue list?"

Her eyes narrowed.

"What would be the point of sending a letter like this?"

She grabbed the envelope and reopened it, searching for another enclosed page.

"There's got to be more to it than this! There's something you're not sharing."

He tossed it back to her.

"You asked for the letter. I brought you the letter. I don't know what else I can do. You want me to *add* a few extra paragraphs?"

"Try being honest with me. Try letting me in."

Her eyes searched his face and demeanor for the slightest contradiction, the slightest flinch.

"Look Saint Claire, you yourself just said you thought the

killer was a psychopath based on what you read in that letter."

"Yes, I said that."

"So tell me, what in that one generic paragraph I just read would lead you to such a conclusion?"

He glanced toward the letter.

"Isn't it obvious? He said he was going to murder seven people in the next thirty days. I might be wrong, but I think that qualifies as psychotic."

"Dangerous, yes. But psychotic, not necessarily. Sounds more like a diagnosis. Which leads me to believe there was something else in the letter and you took it out. Or you altered it!"

"Now you're being paranoid."

She took a deep, angry breath through her nose, her jaw tightening.

"Saint Claire, we have before us a singular opportunity. Either we can spend the next thirty days working together the way we should have done it from the beginning, or we can spend the time trying to fuck each other. If we work together, maybe we can catch this killer. If we don't, he wins. It's as simple as that."

He paused, contemplating, and leaned forward, removing his reading glasses.

"And what's it going to take from me in order for me to work with you?"

"You have to share. You have to trust me."

He smiled.

"And why should I trust you?"

"Because you can. Because I'm on your side."

He extended a steady hand.

"You're on my side now? Really? Fair enough for me. Let's give this trust thing a try."

He sat back, taking the satchel into his lap.

"And since we're trying trusting now, Captain, I have a question for you."

She smiled.

"Go right ahead. Ask me anything."

"Inspector Tom Brady? It's his first week with SFPD. What's he doing in the middle of all this?"

The corners of her smile collapsed even before she began an answer.

"Not my call. The *chief* assigned him here. He came highly recommended."

"Yes, from Boston, but he doesn't have a clue about how things work in San Francisco. So do you have any idea why she assigned him here, working with me?"

She was re-reading the letter, feinting equanimity.

"No I don't. I swear if I knew, I'd tell you."

Saint Claire stood.

"Bullshit."

"Excuse me?"

"You heard me. I said *bullshit*. You know why he's here. We *all* know why he's here. So trust goes out the window. In one minute you talk about trusting each other, and the next you're lying to me."

She didn't want to look at him.

"I am telling you the truth. I'm not lying, and I don't appreciate—"

"You haven't been honest with me from the time you got here. Trust isn't just something that comes along with a promotion. It has to be earned!"

He waited for her to look up before continuing.

"You don't earn it by maligning my name and reputation to the chief and you don't earn it by spying on my wife and making a mockery of her condition to my colleagues."

At the coat rack with his jacket draped over a forearm, he adjusted his hat downward over the ear.

"You and the chief brought Brady in here to *discredit* me."

"Now who's being paranoid?"

"He's already admitted it to me, and that makes you a liar."

Her eyes reluctant to encounter his, she had no answer.

"So the next time you feel insulted or discriminated against because someone doesn't trust you enough to share everything, look to yourself."

He opened the door.

"And until I'm sufficiently confident I can trust my captain to cover my ass, I'm just going to have to find a way to cover it myself."

CHAPTER 4

When he realized what they were doing, he was amused by their boldness. They were teenagers, six in all, pants sagging, tied bandanas hanging, and they were stealing the tires off the car that parked three spaces ahead of his car fifteen minutes earlier. Sitting in his Buick for at least thirty minutes, he was watching the dilapidated apartment building on 22nd Street near Mission for signs of activity.

Over time, darkness crept upon the city. This Mission District neighborhood was largely Latino. From windows and restaurants wafted wonderful smells of fried corn tortillas, roasted pork, cooked tomatoes and *frijolies refritos*. The high-pitched whining of a *mariachi* trumpeter trailed from an open door across the street while the repetitive bass beat from the teenagers' boom box vibrated his windows.

They worked with the skill and coordination of a racetrack pit team. One had a large hydraulic jack that he wheeled in behind the front tire on the passenger side. Within seconds, the car was up and his skinny partner shoved a cinderblock beneath the frame. A third teen with an auto-impact power tool wrench removed the lug nuts. And so they worked right around the car. A minute later, four rolled tires away while a fifth dragged the jack. Chrome wheels, they were after the shiny chrome wheels. He laughed.

Twenty minutes later, he observed three women approach and enter the apartment complex he was watching. Because it was after nine o'clock, he was certain she would be among the group. He wanted to be around to witness the car owner's reaction when she returned to her tire-stripped vehicle, but it was getting late.

At the building's entrance, a large muscular man with a gray black ponytail, bare arms and prison gang tattoos stopped him to know his business. He presented his badge, and the suspicious man directed him to an apartment on the second floor.

He knocked on the door. A moment later, a large male face with Indian features appeared in the narrow opening.

"*Bueno.*"

"*Bueno*, is this the residence of Maria Fuentes?"

"Who wants to know?"

He held up the badge.

"Inspector Saint Claire, with the police."

The door closed right away, and the man engaged the deadbolt from the other side. Saint Claire wasn't sure what to make of the reaction, but he could hear the man shouting something in Spanish on the other side of the door. The woman who responded must have been Maria. Listening to the dialogue, Saint Claire understood the man was angry or excited that the police were outside. The detective could hear cabinets being slammed and furniture dragged across the floor. The woman was explaining why *el zambo* was out there and something about Señora Rosenthal.

Minutes later, the door opened again. This time, a short, squat woman stood there, swaddled in a dark pink terrycloth robe. Maria's face seemed tired. It was a round face, dark brown and peppered with freckles and moles. Her short hair was wet and combed back. Looking up at the detective, she shooed him from the door opening.

"You move. I come, I come outside."

He stepped to the right and she came out, shutting the door behind her. She smiled, displaying crooked and stained teeth, two or three rotting in her bottom gum.

"You are *policía*?"

"*Sí.* And I'm here to talk to you about Mrs. Gladys Rosenthal."

"*Mi señora está muerta.*"

Saint Claire nodded.

"*Sí.* She's dead. She was murdered, and that's why I'm here. I'm hoping you can help me find out who killed her and why."

She held pleading hands toward the detective, palms upward, enunciating the words.

"*Hablad más lentamente, por favor.*"

He hadn't realized he was speaking so fast, so he repeated the question, this time much more slowly.

Maria seemed confused about why anyone would have wanted to murder her employer. She said most of Gladys's friends were dead, sickly or very old and Gladys did not trust or associate with many people.

"She had her one son, and that's all."

On the Thursday before she died, Gladys told Maria she felt very healthy. In fact, she coerced Maria to do stretching exercises along with her to an old Billy Blanks Tae Bo workout video.

Maria said Gladys's son the judge was not a nice man. He was impatient with his mother and always in a hurry. He spoke too quickly for Maria and never tried to understand anything she said. Maria still had a key to the apartment because she didn't want to bother the judge in his mourning, and she still hadn't received her final paycheck.

"As far as you can remember, were you the only one besides Mrs. Rosenthal with a key to the apartment? Was there anyone else who came in and out?"

"I had my key, her had her key, but no one else."

"Did the judge have a key?"

"No. He neber come up. He always wait downstairs."

Saint Claire noticed movement in the curtains a second time. The window was open. Someone was listening.

"Was that your husband who answered the door?"

"*Sí*, it was my husband."

"Did he ever go with you into the apartment?"

As he flipped to the next page of his notepad, she seemed nervous.

"No, he didn't go there."

"Where do you keep your key?"

"In my purse, always."

She said she couldn't remember Gladys ever entertaining company at the apartment. According to Maria, excepting herself and Gladys, no one had been in the apartment over the past few years. Lester had gone in after she was dead, but no one else.

Maria said she noticed no strange occurrences in the apartment during her routine cleaning. Her duties involved vacuuming and mopping floors, laundry, dusting furniture and photos, cleaning out the refrigerator and deep cleaning the stove and the bathrooms.

"In Mrs. Rosenthal's private bathroom, did you ever notice any of her medications left out?"

"No."

"Did you ever see her take any medication?"

Again the stirring behind the tattered curtains.

"Sometime. Sometime I see she take a pill for her heart."

"Did you ever *help* her take any medication?"

"No."

"Maria, Mrs. Rosenthal had many valuable possessions. Did you or anyone ever take anything from the apartment?"

"Oh no! I neber take nothing. *Mi señora* give me money, but I neber take nothing!"

Saint Claire closed the book and placed a hand on her shoulder to reassure her.

"I'm not accusing you, but I had to ask."

"I don't steal. Neber."

He presented a card.

"Here is my phone number. If you notice anything odd or unusual over the next few days, please give me a call."

Nodding, she took it. He started to walk away, but he turned back.

"Maria, I'd like to meet your husband. Can you tell your husband I would like to speak with him?"

"He's busy. He's having his dinner."

Badge out again, he tapped it.

"Tell him it won't take long."

Maria bowed her head and slipped back into the apartment. A minute later, the door opened again and a short, skinny man stepped out. He appeared to be in his late thirties or early forties, wearing blue jeans, a black wife beater and an Oakland Raiders cap. There was a tattoo on his neck, a keeled knife with blood droplets, and a skull design on his right shoulder. His left shoulder and forearm were marked with the prison gang symbols *MM* and *SUR*, clearly *Sureño*.

He did not look at the detective.

"Maria say ya wanna talk to me?"

"I actually wanted to introduce myself to you. Inspector Saint Claire with the police."

He extended his hand.

"I came by to ask your wife a few questions and to make sure that the two of you were all right."

Hesitating at first, the man shook Saint Claire's hand. He twitched.

"Thanks, bro. Hector, Hector Fuentes."

"Nice to meet you, bro. As you know, Hector, your wife's boss was murdered, and we don't know why. We do know the killer's still out there, so I was just hoping to put everyone connected with Mrs. Rosenthal on notice. We think this guy wants to kill someone else."

His teeth, Hector's brownish teeth were worn down from grinding his jaw. Probably a crank addict.

"I told Maria to call me if she notices anything suspicious. I'd like you to do the same."

He passed a card to Hector.

"You ever meet Mrs. Rosenthal?"

"Nope."

For the first time, Saint Claire could see Hector's eyes in the light. The dilated pupils led him to believe Hector was under the influence of methamphetamines. That would explain his erratic, paranoid behavior. Maria was nervous too, but she was lucid.

Yet it was obvious she wasn't telling the truth about something. He glanced toward the door. There was a specific reason Hector and Maria hadn't invited him into the apartment. There was something inside they did not want him to see.

Hector's being a drug addict or dealer would supply a motive for the murder. Over the past year, no outsider except Maria had seen the interior of Gladys Rosenthal's apartment. There was no way to account for whatever cash or other treasures may have been there or missing. Her jewelry and other valuables seemed intact, but there had been no inventory taken either before or after the murder.

The killer may have written the letter as a distraction, to lead the investigation away from Maria and Hector. But neither had met Saint Claire, and it seemed neither had the English skills required to write such a letter.

"*Adios* Hector."

"*Adios.*"

Saint Claire checked to make sure his tires were still attached to his car before getting in. Seated, he reread the killer's two-page manifesto by flashlight, trying to glean additional clues. The killer was someone he knew. Moreover, this person had motives beyond those stated in the letter.

By the end of the day, he had exhausted all his hunches, clues and leads with no real progress. It seemed that if the killer was serious about carrying out his plan, someone else would have to die in order to confirm it.

"Nothing is *ever* the way it seems, Ronnie. You know that."

He stared straight ahead, still thinking. Nudging him, she continued.

"Either this killer isn't telling you the truth or he isn't telling you the entire truth. It's one or the other."

His attention swung toward her.

"So you think the killer is a man?"

Incredulous, she exhaled, rolling her eyes upward.

"Oh come on! You already know who *I* think it is."

It was a good day for Katrina Scott Saint Claire. She was alert and in a positive mood. Earlier in the day she composed a poem about death by drowning, and she had written two more pages of her novel.

She skipped breakfast and had fruit for lunch. When the nurse came with her medication, she pretended to take it, only to flush it down the toilet later. She was convinced the purpose of the pills was to keep her disoriented and confused. The SSRIs, or selective serotonin reuptake inhibitors, only seemed to make her more depressed, bordering on suicidal. Somehow, that wicked Haitian woman from back home was behind it all.

Deuteronomy and Katrina hardly knew each other in high school. Katrina attended her proms and special events with polished young men from Nicholls State University, where her father was an associate professor. And although these suitors were older and more sophisticated, she always seemed to dominate them.

She thought Deuteronomy was goofy with his three-row button piano accordion, and rumors persisted about his weird relationship with the older widow, Annabelle Lee. Katrina heard from friends that Annabelle had been a very attractive New Orleans prostitute in earlier years, and some whispered she had taught adolescent Deuteronomy all her sexual secrets before dying in the hurricane, which was a judgment by God.

During high school, Katrina's older sister, Bianca, was found dead on a riverbank in the woods. It was big news in Thibodaux, but the story faded over a few weeks with the local sheriff unable to figure out who was responsible and why. Bianca was a year older than Katrina, not quite as smart, but lighter-skinned and more popular. Her mother, Cora, never recovered. She died less than a year later, still heavy with grief.

Katrina identified with the tragic female figures from the Russian novels she scrutinized, and showed great courage, even after receiving the news of her father's sudden death during her first semester of college.

She looked over at her husband.

"Have things gotten any better for you over at Central Station?"

He sighed.

"Same old, crap. Sonia Sanchez and the chief, still trying to set me up, still trying to get something on me."

"Why don't you quit and go back to teaching?"

"I can't, Kate. I can't leave there. Not yet."

She placed her palm on his cheek.

"You're forty-nine now, old man. You've been over there for twelve years. I know I haven't been there for you, being in here and all, but you have to get back to your real life. You owe it to us all."

Tears in his eyes, he smiled toward her.

"I know. I just think I've been there all this time for a reason, and now it seems maybe I'm finally going to find out what that reason is."

He blinked, wiping his eyes with a white kerchief.

"This killer isn't like any of the others. This is our guy. He has answers, but he's going to make me play his game in order to get them."

Her eyes held gentle concern.

"Don't you have anyone over there you can count on? Doesn't have to be a Derrick Slater, but you need someone you can trust."

Staring straight ahead, he thought for a moment.

"There's a new guy, a Tom Brady from Boston. Chief's got him over there to watch me. His record's clean, but I don't trust him. There's something about him."

"Do you think he's the killer? A lot of cops get off on that stuff. A lot of innate killers become cops, you know that."

"Yeah, that's why *I* quit teaching at Berkeley and came over."

He bowed his head.

"I don't know. It could be the new guy. I'm not sure how much of his coming to San Francisco is circumstance and how much is design. We're just going to have to wait for the bodies to start falling."

Four years of college changed Deuteronomy. His boyish face became handsome, his spindly frame more muscular. His voice deepened, his confidence grew and he seemed witty and charming, at least to Katrina Scott.

They became reacquainted when both were in graduate school at Xavier University in New Orleans. By that time, both were fascinated with the human mind and its manifestations, both seeking Master's Degrees in psychology. Within a year, their friendship had grown into affection and Deuteronomy invited orphaned Katrina back home to celebrate Easter, Thanksgiving and Christmas with his family in Thibodaux.

His mother approved of Katrina. In fact, four decades earlier, Deuteronomy's mother had gone to the senior prom with Benjamin Scott, Katrina's father. Bernadette, in her discreet way, asked many questions about Benjamin and Katrina confessed to Deuteronomy that she thought his mother had never gotten over him.

Late one night as Bernadette and Katrina sat whispering at the table over black pekoe tea and boysenberry cobbler, Johnny Carson shticking on the television in the background, Bernadette reached over and grasped the younger woman's hand, beginning in a barely audible voice,

"Did your father ever tell you about me?"

Katrina had been at the facility for almost twelve years, though to Deuteronomy it seemed much longer. He agonized over five weeks back then, but he had recommended and in due course insisted on his wife being admitted as an acute psychiatric patient. It was a decision he regretted, and Katrina never let him forget he was responsible for her imprisonment and impending destruction by wicked, unseen forces.

On many of the days he visited, she seemed normal. When she was in a good mood, her personality was affable and infectious. But her moods would often reflect the weather conditions in the San Francisco Bay Area.

He sat in a leather chair across from her in the tidy little room. Rain had begun to pelt the barred window. The wind wheezed in through small horizontal openings along the closure.

"When are you going back to New Orleans?"

"I'm not, not at least until I'm able to figure what's going on."

Her eyes hadn't changed over the years. The fire was still there.

"If you go to New Orleans and do what I asked, I'll be able to get out of here, and then I could help you."

His body tensed as he realized what was beginning.

"Oh come on, not this again. Don't do this to me again!"

"All you have to do is bring one back, and I could talk to her. I'll do the rest. There's nothing else wrong with me!"

He turned, reached over and grasped her hand.

"Kate, you're a doctor, you are a licensed psychopharmacologist. You of all people know there is *no* such thing. And besides, you're Catholic."

"Just find one for me, Ronnie. I'm begging you. It's the only way I can be well."

"If you just keep on taking your medication, you—"

She did not let him finish, anger growing in her voice.

"Why? Why can't you just do this one thing for me? Do you want me to be in here for the rest of my life? Is that what you want?"

He remained silent.

"All I'm asking you to do is go down there, ask around and find some old *Voudoun* who could take off whatever shit that bitch put on me!"

"Kate, you're Catholic. You know *Voudoun* isn't real! It can't affect you unless you create it yourself and allow it to affect your mind."

"*Voudoun* is real. I'm living proof of that!"

He sighed, cringing, his eyes moving toward the door as she closed on him.

"I was just fine until that goddamned, old black bitch hoodooed my sister and put this shit on me! You know that! My life was normal. We tried to have a life together, but she wouldn't let us. Don't you remember?"

He rose from the chair, silent.

"What? You're going to stand now? You're going to leave now instead of discussing how you could help me?"

By this time, two male orderlies had arrived, prepared to prevent yet another psychotic incident. Determined to protect his wife, Deuteronomy took a step between the large men and Katrina.

"Kate, I'm going to call Father LaRue. Let's see if he can—"

"*Fuck* Father LaRue! I'm your goddamned *wife!*"

Deuteronomy turned toward the men, hands outstretched, his voice pleading.

"Please, let me handle this. Just give me a minute. She'll listen to me."

He was unprepared as he turned back toward Katrina. To his shock, her clenched right fist caught him in the mouth, the product of a well thrown and landed sucker punch. He staggered backward into the arms of one of the orderlies.

Katrina pressed forward, shrieking, sobbing.

"Yeah, you wanna step up on me? I'm your wife, you goddamned bastard! And you won't help me? You won't listen to me, goddammit!"

The larger of the men stepped around Deuteronomy and rushed Katrina, grasping her shoulders, turning her back inward and wrapping her in his arms. Screaming, she flailed as the second man caught and held her legs. Together, they carried her toward the bed.

Pillows flew in all directions as they searched for the restraining straps.

"Help me, Ronnie! Don't you see what they're doing to me? They're trying to *kill* me! Ronnie help, please!"

Deuteronomy, still hunched over, dragged his left hand from his forehead down his face, his fingers stopping at the bloody opening on his bottom lip. He could only watch as the orderlies restrained his wife.

"Don't you see what she's doing, Ronnie? She's got *you* too, Ronnie. It's only a matter of time and you'll be in this hell just like me!"

A brown-skinned nurse rushed into the room and administered a needle full of sedatives through a peripheral IV line. The effect was immediate.

Eyes glazed over and rolling back, Katrina yielded to the dark magic of the drugs.

"Evil black bitch..."

CHAPTER 5

Yuan Tan. Year of the Rat. The smoky early evening air still smelled of gunpowder. There were cut and smashed oranges scattered about the slanting sidewalk. Before the group, standing in a huge semi-circle around the double door building entrance, there was a dancing lion with a huge head, elaborately painted, tasseled and frilled. It was standing on its hind legs, reaching up for a string suspended above the door. The pace of the large drums quickened and the cymbals crashed nonstop, building to a rolling crescendo.

Minutes earlier, a Chinese city council member began the ceremonies by lighting a fuse attached to ten thousand firecrackers. Rebecca explained on the walk over that purpose of the Lion Dance was to bring good luck, and the reason the dance was accompanied by the firecrackers and loud music played on the large drums, gongs and cymbals was to dispel Evil, since Evil was afraid of loud noise.

Beaming, City Councilman Raymond Lee introduced Rebecca to the crowd and television cameras. He said his homegrown Chinatown neighborhood was honored to have contributed such an esteemed, respected and vital individual from its ranks to the larger San Francisco community.

"This is called *Choi Cheng!*"

Police Chief Rebecca Leong, stunning in a cherry red silk blouse with elaborate hand stitched designs at her shoulders and deep gold Chinese frog closures, had to scream her words to be heard over the drums and cymbals. She continued as the up-stretched lion gaped wide and clamped on the suspended lettuce leaves and red packet tied to a string suspended above the door.

"The lion is blessing the business! He will bring the business abundance and good luck for the coming year!"

After lowering to all fours, the lion continued to chomp on the leaves for a moment before spitting them out onto the sidewalk. The lion repeated the eating and spitting with a plate of orange wedges.

Tom Brady was deaf for a moment when the drums stopped, but he wasn't the only one. People all around him spoke in loud voices as their ears adjusted to the sudden quiet. Rebecca tapped his shoulder, smiling.

"And now we go to dinner."

Rebecca's husband chose a restaurant on the top floor of a building on Grant Avenue. The interior of the restaurant was an escape from reality. To Brady, it was as if he had ventured back to dynastic China. Splendid Chinese art, red silk lined walls, magnificent palace chandeliers and antiques surrounded the long, marble-topped table. From the place he sat, Brady caught just a glimpse of Coit Tower through a grill-framed window.

Rebecca, seated between her husband and Brady, was the ever-thorough guide, explaining the significance of the unfamiliar food.

"Since you are becoming thirty-six this year, you were born in the year of the rat. You have many good qualities. You are clever, quick-witted and charming, but you can also be short-tempered, narrow minded and greedy."

Brady eyed the entrees at the center of the table, his expression sardonic.

"Well, as long as I don't end up chopped up and on some platter, I think I'll be okay."

The majority of Rebecca's guests left after the ice cream with lichee dessert, and her husband excused himself in order to take his parents home, leaving Brady and Rebecca alone at the table in the deserted banquet room.

She shifted her chair toward him.

"I have to ask. After having been here for this short time, what is your opinion of our city and our police department?"

"San Francisco is all fucked up and full of pretentious, arrogant, bloody assholes, but I like it. Your police department sucks because no one trusts each other, but I hate to admit in some ways it's better than what I had in Boston. There, am I fired?"

She shrugged.

"You're entitled to your opinion. I can't fault you for that."

"I really have enjoyed tonight, though. You are an incredible hostess."

She nodded.

"Thank you."

He smiled, peering into her eyes.

"You grew up here, in Chinatown?"

"Born and raised."

She removed a clip from the back of her head, letting the long, shiny hair fall over her shoulders.

"So, do you think our infamous Inspector Saint Claire is up to something more than police work?"

"Hard to say. I don't know him very well. But from what I've gathered, he seems to be an honest cop."

Disappointment showed in her frown.

"You have to admit he's not a team player."

Brady shrugged.

"He's not. So what?"

"Has he ever called you? Has he shared anything with you recently?"

"What do *you* think? The guy doesn't trust me."

She sat back, sipping the oolong tea, her exotic eyes peering over the rim of the cup.

"Have you done any investigation into his background or into whatever activities he's involved in when he's not working?"

Brady looked away, feeling pressure to respond. It was an uncomfortable moment, the first time he had been required to investigate someone he considered his future partner. It just didn't feel right to Brady, to seek a fellow detective's trust only to betray him.

"To the extent that you're asking now, no. But I began a background assessment around the department. I figured it was the best place to start."

"Did you investigate the story about Inspector Joe Curry's death? Unexplained homicide, Saint Claire's gun?"

"I did. Came back cold, that is except for the rumors. Curry's got a daughter on the force."

She leaned forward.

"What have you discovered about Saint Claire's *wife*? Katrina I think it is?"

"I hear she's in the nut bin over at Saint Mary's, but you already know that."

"I heard it was Saint Claire who put her there, and I hear he visits her every day, even after eleven years. Don't you think that's strange?"

Brady sipped his Budweiser.

"Maybe, maybe not."

"Captain Sanchez thinks Saint Claire didn't turn over the actual letter from the killer. She said the letter he gave her was a half page long. Yet, when we interviewed Davis, the officer who discovered the letter in Mrs. Rosenthal's bathroom vanity, she said she remembered it was a heavy, somewhat bulky letter, something that would not be consistent with a one-page letter. What do you think?"

Brady raised his eyebrows and shrugged as he considered the question.

"Based on what I've discovered about Saint Claire, I think he's capable of *not* turning over the actual letter from the killer, but I think the big question then would have to be 'why?' Why wouldn't he turn over the real letter?"

"Well, what is a killer doing sending Saint Claire a letter at Gladys Rosenthal's apartment in the first place? Do you see what I mean? There's something going on between Saint Claire and this killer, and he's hiding it from us."

Setting down the empty beer bottle, Brady pulled the coffee cup front and center.

"Again, the real question is why? Why would a Berkeley PhD and decorated detective of twelve years want to hide his relationship with a killer?"

She placed her hand on his wrist.

"What if Saint Claire *is* the killer? And what if he wrote the letter to himself to throw us all off his trail?"

"Are you kidding me? Why would he do that? Absolutely no motive there."

She withdrew the caress.

"Ego, and in his case intellectual ego. Maybe he's playing games with us and he's trying to prove he's smarter than everyone else. Simple killing isn't enough for these guys. I've seen it before."

She continued, glancing askance.

"Is it the *least* bit odd to you that he knows so much about poisons? He's an expert on toxic compounds. And it was cyanide with Gladys Rosenthal, as you know."

Brady smiled and leaned toward her, practiced flirtation in his eyes.

"I've been doing this for a while. When anything's that obvious, it's leading you in the wrong direction. If you're smart, you ignore it and look for something a little less obvious."

He was too close. She sat back in her chair and checked her watch.

"I think I better go."

Collecting her purse, she opened the leather folder and signed the bill.

"Over the next few days, I'd like you to explore what he does in his off-hours. Check out his wife over at Saint Mary's. Find out exactly why he had her committed."

She looked up, brushing the hair from her face.

"Keep an eye on him. If he's the killer and he's going to murder seven people in the next twenty-eight days, then the pressure's on him to act. We'll just stand back, watch the show and try to get lucky."

He grinned, aware that he had her flushed, a little flustered even.

"*Gung Hai Fat Choy.*"

"How's Katrina?"

No reaction. It was doubtful he even heard the question. He was lost in his thoughts, wandering through a valley of long shadows, dark reflections.

The line separating the visionary and the madman, the revolutionary and the traitor, the savior and the adversary was unclear. Only time and perspective could characterize a difference between one and the other. And yet, time and perspective could make one the other. Thus morality was, and has always been, inconstant.

He was idealistic at the time, and much younger. Had he the opportunity to recast his life, things may have been different. But the decision he made was for the better, even if it doomed her to mind altering drugs, constant supervision and de facto incarceration. It was the right decision.

"Did you say something to me?"

"I said, how's Katrina? Were you able to see her yesterday?"

"I'm sorry. Uh yes, yes I saw her."

Slater's tanned, freckled, liver spotted hands fidgeted, his thumbs in the act of shooting invisible marbles over and over again. He acquired this frustrating mannerism when he got older, and try as he may, he couldn't stop.

"Judging from the size of your lip and you bein all spaced out like you are, it wasn't a good day?"

Saint Claire sighed, rubbing his mouth.

"She still got that wicked jab, or I think maybe it was a roundhouse. Never saw it coming."

Slater cackled.

"I think she kicked your sorry ass."

"I think that's why you haven't been by to see her, because she would definitely kick your rusty, dusty old ass."

Saint Claire visited Slater for dinner every Sunday at Slater's Sausalito home. Saint Claire's former boss had used half his inheritance to build it on a lot on Wolfback Ridge Road. It was a beautiful house boasting 270 degree views of San Francisco, the Bay, the Ocean and the Golden Gate Bridge.

Six months after retiring, Slater also purchased a small bed and breakfast on Princess Street, not far from his home, and married Oksana Ivanova, a Ukrainian woman he met on the Internet. Oksana was twenty-eight and pretty. Her hair was blond and down to her shoulders. Her legs were long and her body was shapely. Even after eighteen months, she didn't speak much English, and it seemed Slater preferred it that way. Oksana had a business degree from the university near Dnepropetrovsk, so it became her job to manage the inn. Shrewd by nature, she hired young Ukrainian and Russian women to maintain the property.

The two men were in Slater's recess, a large, modern room with a pool table, a wet bar, a large screen television and overstuffed brown furniture in *matelassé* slip covers. Oksana was somewhere in the house, but she knew not to bother her husband when the door to the room was closed.

Slater stood behind the bar, bottle of Jack Daniel's at the ready, while Saint Claire sat at a barstool across from him.

"I had lunch with your big boss Rebecca Leong on Wednesday. She told me about the Rosenthal murder and the letter."

Saint Claire leaned toward Slater.

"Did she tell you she assigned a detective from Boston to investigate me?"

"Tom Brady? She told me she brought him in to work *with* you, but we all know better. It's what you get for being so secretive."

Saint Claire smiled, the whiskey stripping his speech of its formality.

"It's what I get for getting involved with an asshole like you. It's that damn Sanchez. I swear she wants to be you."

"An asshole?"

"Exactly."

Slater reached over to pour the shot glass full again, but Saint Claire flipped it face down on the bar.

"What else did she tell you about Brady?"

"Nothin. She knows we do this on Sundays. She doesn't exactly trust me either."

Saint Claire half shrugged.

"So she brings in this import from Boston, and immediately a woman I met only once ends up murdered and there's a letter for me in her apartment. For all we know, Brady's the killer and he's playing some psycho murder game."

"Or he's trying to set you up."

Slater replaced the bottle in the rack and walked around the bar, taking the seat next to his friend.

"How much do you know about Brady?"

"Married, two girls, clean record. Grandfather was deputy mayor of Boston in the 50s, father was a cop, and as far as I can tell, he gets around with the women. Drinks a bit. He's Irish."

Slater nodded.

"That's good, but this is a guy they've got goin after you, so you definitely need to find out where he's comin from. My advice? Let him be your friend. Have a drink with him. Whore around with him if ya have to. Who knows, ya might get laid for a change."

Oksana tapped on the door, indicating it was time to come down for dinner.

Saint Claire managed to relax during the meal with his former boss and Oksana, but the mood in Slater's recess after dinner was much more somber.

"The main reason I'm sharing this with you—*someone's* got to know what's going on, for my protection, and I really don't feel I can trust anyone but you."

Slater raised his eyebrows as Saint Claire proceeded.

"Chief *told* you about the letter?"

"Yeah?"

Saint Claire opened the satchel.

"There were actually *three* letters."

He presented two pages.

"This was the first, the direct invitation for me to play his game."

He let Slater read to the bottom of the page.

"He says if I can stop one of the murders, I save the lives on the other side of it. But he also says if I can't stop him, he's going to *force* me to tell the world about him. So I'm just guessing one of the murders is someone I care about. He won't be able to force me to do anything unless he's got me in a spot, unless he *has* something on me."

The room was silent as Slater finished the second page. Looking up, he crossed his eyes, emoting incredulity.

"Okay, this guy is nuts, but he sounds for real. This could be our guy."

He motioned for the folded sheet of paper in Saint Claire's hand.

"Should I be afraid to read the second letter?"

"Only if you like reading. It's the truncated version, the one he wrote because he knew I would have to turn something over to the department. It says he's going to kill seven people in thirty days, but he leaves out the detail about being dead."

Glasses on his nose, Slater nodded.

"*And* the fact that he is challenging you here. The hairs on the back of my neck are standing up right about now. Think it's him?"

"I turned over a copy of that letter over to Sanchez."

Slater handed the letter back.

"Do I dare ask to see the third letter?"

Saint Claire exchanged the second letter for the third.

"It's not much. It's instructions for the game he wants to play. He says if I let anyone in on what he's doing, I'll have absolutely no chance of stopping him, much to my personal regret. He says I'll get another letter soon, and there are three series of three numbers at the bottom of the page. They're codes for something, a PO Box maybe. And there's that word, *Tepes*. The only thing I can relate it to is *Vlad Tepes*, the original Dracula."

Slater handed the letter back.

"It is a game, and this guy's done his research. Do you think he's really actually dead?"

"I don't know. That's why I'm here. I'm not sure what to believe."

"Well, you've already violated the no-sharing rule."

"What? Are you worried?"

Slater smiled and shrugged.

"Naw. If he really is dead, and he predicted you'd share this with me and he's coming after me, then whatever he's got planned for me is already in the works. I've just gotta keep my eyes open."

Letters returned to the satchel, Saint Claire presented Slater with another envelope containing copies of all three letters.

"Put it in a safe place."

"But if he isn't dead, he knows you're here, and that means he'll *definitely* be comin after me."

Halfway through the second game of pool, Saint Claire's cell phone buzzed.

"Saint Claire."

His expression changed as he listened.

"Really? Where? San Francisco General?"

He was already gathering up the satchel and his coat.

"When did he get there? Is he still alive?"

Saint Claire checked his watch.

"Okay, I'll be there. Give me twenty minutes."

Phone call ended, he turned to Slater.

"That was Brady. He's over at the hospital. Looks like we've got the first of our seven. A man named Hector Fuentes. He was the husband of Gladys Rosenthal's maid."

Slater followed him out the room to the top of the stairs, calling down.

"Do they know the cause of death?"

Saint Claire answered without looking back.

"They don't know yet, but I do. I'll call you."

"Oh, Saint Claire—"

The detective stopped, turning back toward his friend.

"Yes?"

"Thank you very much for fuckin up my retirement."

CHAPTER 6

The emergency room at San Francisco General was crowded, with moaning patients on gurneys lining the hallway leading into the waiting area. All the seats inside were occupied.

Saint Claire found Brady downstairs just outside the door to the morgue.

"You been *in* there?"

"Why? I wouldn't know him if I saw him."

Saint Claire pushed the door open and slipped inside. Brady followed.

"I heard *you* saw him, though. On Friday night?"

Saint Claire spun around.

"I'm just beginning this investigation, Brady. From all indications, it's going to take all the resources I've got to analyze and act on whatever clues are available. I'm trying to save lives here, so the last thing I need is one of your sophomoric attempts to interrogate me on this murder or any other aspect of the case. If you want to know what's going on, follow me and keep your mouth shut. You understand?"

Brady took a breath and nodded.

A forensic pathologist met the detectives inside a second set of doors. She was an older, brown skinned woman with thick gray hair pulled back into a ponytail. She wore powder blue v-neck scrubs and brown leather clogs.

"Inspector Saint Claire, we meet again. Who's your buddy?"

"Inspector Brady, this is Dr. Singh. She's an old friend."

She smiled, amused that Brady had extended his hand, since no one ever shook hands in the morgue.

"He always *says* that, but I'm not actually that old, and I'm single."

She turned, headed for the walk-in refrigerator.

"So, what stiff are you here to see today?"

"Hector Fuentes."

"Just came in. Still warm."

She pulled the vault like door open, exposing Hector's nude body resting on a metal stretcher, a tag on his big toe.

"No one's been by to ID him yet. I—"

The sound of the outer door opening and panicked footsteps stopped her mid-sentence.

"Oops, spoke too soon!"

Maria halted the moment she spotted the body through the open refrigerator door.

"*¡Dios mio! ¡Ector! ¡No! ¡Usted no está muerto! ¡Usted no puede estar muerto!*"

She fell prostrate on the cold, waxed floor, shrieking and pounding the shiny black tile like a child throwing a tantrum. The police officers at either side of her knelt and gently lifted her, helping her move nearer to the body.

"Is this Hector Fuentes, Ma'am? Is this your husband?"

Groaning, she opened her tear-filled eyes and bowed her head, barely able to look. Yet she found the strength to reach her hand toward his face to caress his cheek a final time.

"Sí! Yes, it's him."

Saint Claire and Brady waited outside the morgue as the hospital chaplain inside comforted Maria. In time her sister came by, then her brother and nieces, and then Hector's relatives. Hector's brother said he came down with a cold or flu on Friday night and that it got progressively worse. He said Hector complained about excessive coughing and his chest feeling tight. By Sunday morning, he couldn't breathe. Then at dinner, he threw up a mouthful of blood into his hand before passing out, his head crashing to the table. He was dead shortly after his arrival at the hospital.

Standing with the detectives outside the building while she had a cigarette, Dr. Singh said initial x-rays suggested pulmonary edema, or a building up of fluid in the lungs, which could have been the result of any number of factors.

Brady spoke after emptying his own lungs of smoke.

"When will the autopsy be performed?"

"His wife's against it, but he was a young man and it was an unexplainable death. By law, we don't have a choice. Tomorrow, probably."

Saint Claire stood apart from the smokers, fanning away the fumes.

"Will *you* be performing it?"

"I think so. Why?"

"Well, I'd like to find out what kind of drugs are in his blood right now. Toxicology takes weeks I know, more time than we can afford. Can you get a blood sample tonight, and test it?"

The doctor headed back inside the building, with detectives following.

"I suppose I can. What are you looking for?"

"Presence of methamphetamines, possible presence of arsenic or ricin."

She stopped.

"Presence of ricin?"

"Yes."

"That's weird. I'd ask why if it were anyone else. Well, I'm not a toxicologist, but I do have resources and favors owed. Give me a day, I'll let you know."

It was four a.m. by the time Saint Claire and Brady spoke with Maria. She sat slumped in a chair in the lobby, her head down, her lips whispering orisons in Spanish.

Saint Claire eased into the seat beside her.

"Maria, I'm very sorry about Hector. Now I'm going to talk to you, but you don't have to answer, not until I finish. I'm going to try and make this as brief and painless as possible. Do you understand what I'm saying? You can just nod if you want to."

She did, her eyes showing through puffy slits.

"Maria, I don't believe Hector died by accident. I believe he was murdered by the same person who killed Mrs. Rosenthal. When I came by on Friday and I asked you if you brought anything home from Mrs. Rosenthal's apartment, I was trying to discover a connection outside her apartment. Are you understanding me so far?"

Head turned, she looked into the detective's eyes.

"*Sí.*"

"You don't have to say anything yet, but I know now you were holding something back when I was there. I know for a fact you *did* take something from her apartment. I'm not saying you stole it because it may have been something she gave you, or something you thought she gave you, but you took something home."

Struggling to remain composed, she batted liquid eyes as he continued.

"I don't know what you took, but I believe somewhere in its contents was a container or a bag of white powder, a bag Hector must have recognized. And Hector took that bag of white powder, because Hector was addicted to methamphetamines. Your husband did drugs, right? Crank?"

She closed her eyes again.

"*Sí.*"

"I believe whatever killed Hector was mixed up somewhere in that bag. Whoever murdered him knew he would take the bag and use it. But what I don't understand is how this murderer got you to bring it to him. That's what I need you to tell me."

She was weeping again.

"It was *my* fault then?"

"No, it wasn't your fault. Whoever murdered Mrs. Rosenthal and your husband is a very bad person. This person manipulated you."

"A box. I took the box home."

She sat back, staring ahead, breathing to calm herself.

"Mister Inspector Saint Claire, I didn't steal nothing, but you are right. I took that box to my home. Mrs. Rosenthal give it to me, she leave it for me, and she made a letter that I should give to you."

"Me?"

"Yes. Your name is on it. An if you come to my home tomorrow, in the afternoon, I will give it to you."

CHAPTER 7

The last two months were the toughest, but the prognosis was positive, condition notwithstanding. The hardest part was telling her children. Sonia knew her daughter wouldn't handle it well. Tati would dwell on it, making herself sick in the process. But her son was strong enough for the both. She was so proud of him.

By law, she wasn't required to reveal her condition to her boss, or anyone else at the department for that matter. It began right after Thanksgiving. She had this feeling something was wrong, a distinct feeling that it would get worse if she didn't take action. So she made an appointment, and a week later she got the news.

She took time off work for treatment, telling personnel she needed two weeks for a vacation. Her doctor explained the initial treatment, which would involve combination therapy and vigilant monitoring.

When she returned to the job, the chief had assigned a new inspector, Tom Brady, to work in her department. The addition would help solve a problem that had troubled her from the time she was promoted, a problem that had caused her great stress, thus compounding her personal ordeal.

Sonia was convinced Inspector Saint Claire was dishonest, unethical and praetorian to some perverse end. Years earlier, she heard stories of his intelligence, knowledge in diverse disciplines and insight into the human psyche. In fact, she was excited to have him as a detective in her command.

Actually *working* with Saint Claire proved to be the real disappointment. Early on, she called him to her office and tried to establish the rapport a captain needed to have with individuals in her workforce. He was polite enough, but he would not open up to her. She heard he was very close to Derrick Slater, her predecessor, and while she didn't expect to become instant best friends, a little warmth would have been nice.

It seemed the more she tried to get him to share, the more he distrusted her motives and would not talk. He was always formal with her. Over time, it seemed Saint Claire was avoiding her, reserving the cooperation he extended to Slater because she was a woman, or possibly because she was Hispanic. He seemed to have a problem with her.

She complained about Saint Claire to Chief Tom Donovan, Rebecca Leong's predecessor, but Donovan insinuated she was insecure and was just being a troublemaker. He told her she had to earn the trust of not just Saint Claire, but every officer in her command. After that meeting, she never mentioned it to him again.

Things changed when Rebecca became chief. Rebecca listened to and understood the frustration Sonia was feeling. Rebecca responded, pleased to have an ally among the captains. They had dinner together at least once a week and Sonia had helped Rebecca decorate her new home.

After hearing Sonia's complaints about Saint Claire for three months, Rebecca agreed to call him into her office to determine why he didn't respect Sonia as a captain. Saint Claire was polite, but when he realized the chief had called him away in the middle of an investigation to answer "relationship" questions, he was angry.

He said he had no problem with Captain Sanchez, but that her insecurity was frustrating. Admitting her gender was a factor in the non rapport, he explained because she was a woman, he couldn't go out and get beers with her after work, hanging out into the wee hours of night without tarnishing her reputation. And he couldn't spend the day at her house and have dinner on any consistent basis without starting up rumors. So no, Sanchez couldn't *have* it the way Slater did. Saint Claire explained his formality protected both Sanchez and himself.

Rebecca thought his answer reeked of thinly veiled sexism.

The mounting pressure between Sanchez and Saint Claire often boiled over in the form of a verbal exchange or a redrawing of turf lines, and then all would seem fine for a few weeks. This stressful ebb and flow was uncomfortable, especially for Sanchez.

Frustrated, she asked Saint Claire if he'd be willing to transfer to the adjacent Mission District station under a male captain, but Saint Claire insisted he had no problem working for a woman and wanted to remain where he was. Deputy Chief of Investigations Hartley Hanson concurred, opining Central

Division would be at a great loss without the erudite Saint Claire.

For Captain Sanchez, Tom Brady represented a means to do away with her nemesis. He came experienced and recommended by his chief. He was smart, shrewd and loyal to command. If Brady could get something on Saint Claire and share it with Sanchez, she was convinced she could force the arrogant detective out of Central, or better yet, she could take him down.

He sat in the reception area, reviewing his notes from the hospital interviews while he waited to be called back to the captain's office.

"Inspector uh, Brady?"

He stood.

"Yes?"

"She's ready for you. You can go on back."

It was disappointing to see her in uniform again after spying her in that tight little red dress a few days earlier. Sonia and her son had sat across the table from him at the Chinese New Year dinner. He smiled at her twice, but she seemed preoccupied.

Back in her SFPD captain dress blues, she seemed like a different person.

"You and Saint Claire were at San Francisco General last night. From what I've heard, one or both of you interviewed Gladys Rosenthal's housekeeper? Her husband was the victim. Is that right?"

"Affirmative, and it was Saint Claire who did the interview."

Hours before the meeting, Brady determined he would choose his words carefully, allowing ambiguity no quarter. He would not be a pawn on either side of the conflict.

She sipped coffee from a *World's Best Mom* mug.

"Was he able to establish if or how the two murders might be connected?"

"If? It was the housekeeper's husband. Of course they're related."

She nodded, allowing him to continue.

"The question is how."

She sat back in the chair, placing forearms and hands on the chair's armrests.

"And did the brilliant Saint Claire bother to share with you his theory about how they're related?"

Brady sighed.

"I don't know what's going on between you two, but I have to tell you, Saint Claire has got to be the smartest detective I've ever worked with. It was uncanny. Either that or he's in on something the rest of us don't know."

"Why do you say that? What happened?"

He leaned forward.

"As soon as he got there and saw it was her husband, he figured it all out. He knew what happened and how it happened."

Sonia's face showed confusion.

"What, what do you mean?"

"He told her he knew she had taken something home from Mrs. Rosenthal's apartment. He even knew drugs were hidden in the package, drugs laced with poison. And he knew Hector did the drugs and that's what killed him."

"And he knew all that based on what? Did he say?"

"No. But I think he believes the seven murders are going to all be related, with each setting off a series of events that causes the next. At least that's what he suggested to me."

Her brow furrowed.

"What? Did he *talk* to you about all this?"

"Yeah, we talked. He talks. Thinks the killer used ricin or arsenic. Also thinks the next victim is going to be one of Hector's friends or someone he works with. And it's going to be a man."

Sonia seemed torn, curious about the murders and yet insulted that Saint Claire would rather share his insights with a man he perceived as a threat rather than opening up to her.

"In your opinion, how do you think he knew all that? You think he's in on it?"

Brady was quiet for a moment.

"I don't know. I'm still not seeing what a detective of his skill and stature would get out of killing a random old woman and a drug addict."

"Well, someone's getting something out of it, and whoever it is prefers the poison method. What did Saint Claire guess? Strychnine? Arsenic?"

She raised an eyebrow.

"How much you wanna bet he's *right*?"

For just a moment he wasn't there. For an instant he reflected on a recent defining moment. He thought his mind was funny that way, when it would just go away in the middle of an important conversation. Andrea hated when he did that.

It could be the slightest thing, a word, a combination of sounds, the timbre of a voice or a dappling of sunlight and shadows on clean smooth skin, something general that triggered a specific memory. This time it was a flash of shame and regret.

He and Andrea were having dinner with his mother at a steak house in Old City Hall. A day earlier, Andrea issued an ultimatum, "quit your job and move to California or sign divorce papers." It was manipulative and unfair. It was mean spirited.

His mother knew how much he wanted to remain in Boston. At this dinner, Andrea played the cruelest of all trump cards. She said to his mother, "I'm clipping the apron strings. Tom is moving to San Francisco with his family."

At once, Tom's options were before him, smashing into his face. He could stay in Boston with his mother, a sickly, complaining seventy-four year-old widow with five other children in town, three of them girls, or he could forego certain career success to start a new life in California with his wife and daughters. It was too much to deal with, so he said nothing, emasculated, even as his mother's eyes pleaded for contradiction.

Sometimes it was obvious what triggered such a flashback, but this time he didn't have a clue. Maybe it was Sonia's insecurity and need for control. Perhaps the picture of the captain and her children made him think of his own mother. It was over in an instant.

Returning to the present, he laughed to himself.

"I wouldn't bet against it."

Sonia shrugged.

"Well, there's no denying he's smart, but I'm still convinced he's got something else going on."

Tom cut in.

"Speaking of something else, there was another letter."

"To Saint Claire? Well where is it? Does he have it?"

"Not yet. Fuentes's wife, Maria, she wants him to come pick it up at one-thirty, today."

Sonia was already standing, her right hand cupped over her mouth as her mind raced to plot a way to intercept the transfer. Forty-five minutes. There was not enough time to accomplish it through conventional channels.

"You have to go over there and *get* that letter. You've got to get it before he does and bring it here!"

Brady sat back in the chair, his expression sarcastic.

"What? Saint Claire's not capable of picking up a letter?"

"He'll change it just like he changed the last letter, and we'll have nothing! We have to get the letter first."

Brady stood, turning his neck to crack it.

"I'll be there when he meets her, and I'll try to get the letter. If I can't get it, I'll pressure him to open it so I can read it with him. Okay?"

She smiled.

"You think you can do that?"

"We'll see. He's trying to figure me out, and that means he's got to let me in. He's got to trust me with something."

Shortly after the Great Earthquake and Fire, Abraham Ruef, Mayor Schmitz, all members of the San Francisco Board of Supervisors, the police chief, as well as corporate officers of PG&E, United Railroads and what would become Pacific Telephone, were indicted for graft and bribery.

The mayor and the supervisors had been bribed by these utilities before the earthquake, and former mayor James Phelan and financier Rudolph Spreckels were determined to break this cycle of bribery and graft.

"What are you reading?"

Startled, Saint Claire snapped his head toward the car window.

"What are you doing here?"

"Same thing you're doing here, waiting. Can I get in?"

He didn't answer. Instead, he bowed his head and continued reading. Then he flipped the switch to unlock the car doors.

Settled into the brown leather seat, Brady craned his neck.

"What's that? Looks like an old book."

Saint Claire snapped it closed, tucking it under his seat.

"Little hobby I've had over the past few years—unsolved murders in the city. In this case a major scandal that ended in the murder of the police chief, William J. Biggy."

"Was he poisoned?"

Saint Claire smirked.

"Interesting you should ask that. The thought crossed my mind. Lot of agents they couldn't test for back then. He disappeared off a police boat as it passed Alcatraz. There was only one man on the vessel with him, police officer named Murphy. Biggy's body was missing for fifteen days, and then it was found floating in the Bay near Angel Island."

"And the motive?"

"Corruption."

Saint Claire eyes tracked a short woman exiting a copper colored minivan.

Both detectives watched the woman walk up the sidewalk toward the apartments. Rolling up the windows, Saint Claire removed the key from the ignition.

"There's plenty of evidence and records from the time still around, enough to take a crack at solving the case."

He opened the car door and stood. Brady, standing on the other side of the vehicle, adjusted the position of his weapon and checked his watch.

"So tell me, do you ever get tired of goofing off all your time?"

Maria Fuentes seemed a broken woman. Her nieces attended her inside the apartment, sweeping, vacuuming, fluffing pillows and cooking in the kitchen. The air was redolent with Mayan achiote seasoning and sweet spices. A soulful first tenor intoned the Lord's Prayer in Spanish from stereo speakers on wall shelves, and devotional candles were lit all around the otherwise darkened room.

Maria, slumped on a blue upholstered couch, began weeping again upon seeing Brady peek around the corner. And so the detectives intruded, heads bowed, expressions somber as they sat down in dining table chairs across from the spot where she was seated.

Clearing his throat, Saint Claire offered his handkerchief.

"Maria, I realize you're feeling very overwhelmed right now. But I wouldn't be here if I didn't think it was necessary. Are you understanding me?"

She nodded.

"You remember last night when I told you I didn't think Hector's death was an accident? I told you I believed he was murdered by the same person who murdered Mrs. Rosenthal? So far, the lab has not completed all the testing, but we are certain Hector ingested a toxic element of some kind, and that's what killed him."

She bowed her head, still weeping. Taking a breath, he waited for her to regain composure.

"I also believe that the person who killed Hector and Mrs. Rosenthal will kill again soon, and this person is going to kill someone who is somehow *connected* to Hector, someone Hector may have known."

At once she stopped crying. Her face showed alarm as he continued.

"When I came by to talk with you last Friday night, I was trying to determine who the next victim would be. I thought it would be Hector, but I couldn't get the two of you to let me in. Whatever connection you had to Mrs. Rosenthal, whatever went from her apartment to yours, I need you to show it to me now."

"*Uno momento, por favor.*"

At once she rose and disappeared into her bedroom, returning a minute later with a shoebox sized package. Without speaking, she placed the box in Saint Claire's lap and reclaimed her niche in the couch.

Flipping open the hinged top, Saint Claire found stacks of circulated, unmarked, non-sequential twenty dollar bills, aligned and bundled in blue and white printed wrappers. The killer used need and greed to entice Maria. And yet, before Saint Claire could consider a question, she volunteered an answer.

"I did not steal that money. There was a note on the box, from her. She leave it for me. She *give* to me the money in that box."

"How much is it?"

"Hector count it. Thirteen thousand, five hundred dollars."

Saint Claire removed a bill from one of the bundles, raising it above his face to examine it.

"It's real money. Is this the note you said she left?"

"Yes."

He read the printed words.

"The killer wrote this letter, pretending to be Mrs. Rosenthal. He knew you needed money and that you would take the money home. He also knew you would show it to Hector, who was addicted to methamphetamines. That is why he put the poison-laced drug package at the bottom of the package, where he was sure Hector would find it. The rest is the matter of a drug addict doing what addicts do. He snorted it or cooked it up, ingested it in some way."

He spotted the envelope taped to one side on the inside of the box.

"Not fool proof, but it was predictable. What's this?"

Maria struggled to share a reflection.

"On Friday, when Hector fount out your name was Saint Claire, he get so nervous. He thought you come to take away the money from us. Your name was on that letter in the box."

"And you never thought about opening it?"

"No, because I remember your name. I told him you were *policia*. We were afraid to open your letter. An afraid to spend the money!"

Extracting a utility tool from his coat pocket, Saint Claire cut through the clear tape and removed the envelope from the box, folding it in two. Brady, eyes locked on the letter, moved closer to his partner.

"That's from the killer. Aren't you going to open it?"

He watched the folded envelope disappear into Saint Claire's interior jacket pocket.

"I really think you need to open that."

Saint Claire's glare held a threat.

"Let me do what I have to do."

He turned back toward Maria.

"All the money is yours. You can do whatever you want with it. You can spend it. My first priority is to save the next person from being killed, and you can help me with that by telling me everything you know about people Hector knew."

"What to tell?"

"The names of his friends, the people he worked with, his relatives, anybody he associated with on a regular basis. Take your time. I need you to be as thorough as possible. It's the difference between someone living or dying."

After an hour, Saint Claire had a list of thirty-five names.

"Is there anything else you might want to tell me? Over the past three months, did anything unusual happen to Hector?"

She seemed confused.

"I donno. Like what?"

"Do you recall any new person who may have come around? A Caucasian person? *El gringo* like this guy here?"

Her eyes rolled upward as she strained to remember.

"Maybe one time, but that was very long time ago. He come by here one time."

"Do you remember what he looked like?"

She shrugged.

"Short man. Short hair, blond. Glasses, I think."

Saint Claire stood.

"Thank you, Maria. I have one last thing I need you to help me with. Where did Hector keep his drugs?"

Saint Claire watched her balk.

"You're his wife, and this is not a large apartment. If you know where they are, I need you to collect whatever is still here and bring it to me. Hector is dead. No one will be in trouble. I promise."

Maria sat for a moment with her head down, then rose and exited the room.

Brady stood, eyes scanning the apartment.

"So, you think the killer is white?"

"I think the killer *could* be white."

"Why's that?"

Saint Claire looked over.

"I said could be."

"So he could be black?"

"I didn't say that, but the majority of serial killers are white."

Maria returned with a medium sized tan paper bag.

"This is it. All of everything he had."

Saint Claire took the bag, folding the top over and rolling it into a cylinder.

"Thank you for all your help, and please let me know the time and place for Hector's services. If you think of anything else after we're gone, please call. For Hector's sake, you can help us stop this killer."

CHAPTER 8

"You're nothing like I imagined you to be."

Katrina smiled. "And how did you imagine me to be? Wild? Wanton? A real nut case?"

"No, I was just expecting something a little more uh, off kilter. Maybe a little more wacky, dangerous. I mean, you are in here, in this, this facility."

She crossed her eyes and made a wild face.

"Don't let my temporary sanity fool you. One minute I'm like this, and the next, they're carrying out a corpse. Ask my husband."

Subtle though it was, she detected the eye flinch.

"What? You mean my husband didn't know you were coming here?"

Brady sighed.

"No."

"Interesting. How sneaky of you. So, why are you here, without his knowledge?"

"Curiosity."

She laughed.

"Liar. Wanna try again?"

He wasn't sure how to take her effrontery.

"You have all the answers. Why don't you tell me why I'm here?"

"You're here to seduce me."

Caught off guard, he felt the flush in his cheeks.

"Really?"

"Unsuccessfully. You will fail miserably. You won't fuck me."

"First time for everything. What did I do wrong?"

Seated on the leather sofa, she ran her fingers through her wavy hair and turned toward the window.

"First and foremost, you're a liar, and second, you're *not* a killer."

Brady nodded, still perplexed.

"Okay?"

"You're a detective. You ever work homicide before this assignment?"

"I have, in the past."

She wagged her head.

"Then you should quit. In order to catch a killer, you have to *be* a killer, and you're obviously not a killer. You're out of your league, white boy."

"Okay, so your husband? Is he a killer?"

"A very clever killer. He's so good that none of you suspect him. Think about it. He's got a great cover, San Francisco's most illustrious detective, Berkeley professor, dedicated family man. Who would ever guess?"

No one knew if there was an event that triggered her condition or if she just went mad on her own, but the stories told around the department portrayed Katrina as a raging, crazy woman who was institutionalized not long after Saint Claire left the university to become a cop. No one ever saw Saint Claire in the company of a woman other than his wife, and many of his coworkers and supervisors concluded he was celibate.

For over an hour, Brady had watched the facility from outside waiting for Saint Claire to finish his daily visit with Katrina. Only after the blue Buick pulled off did he enter the hospital.

In a flirtatious conversation with a young nurse, Brady learned Katrina's room number, when she was first registered at the facility, and that hospital records listed her as a paranoid schizophrenic.

"But she's a special case! She's a psychiatrist, a psychopharmacologist actually, so when she's cogent, she understands what's going on in her mind far better that anyone else, and yours too. The hospital has done numerous studies on her."

The nurse twisted the wispy brown hair at her left temple.

"She's very pretty for an older woman. Have you met her?"

"No. Do you think she would talk to me?"

"Probably would, if you really want to do that. I personally would recommend *against* it."

Brady laughed.

"Why's that."

"Because she'll do everything she can to fuck with your head."

Katrina *was* pretty as she reclined on the sofa in the midnight blue silk gown. Her hair was long, pulled back and braided, her eyes outlined, accented with liner and her face was powdered. She avoided eye contact.

"So what are you going to do?"

"About what?"

"Well, if your own partner is a killer or the killer, you can't trust him. Are you going to try and catch him in the act? You going to try to take him down?"

Brady was careful.

"You know it isn't that simple. I have to consider motive, and evidence."

"Fuck motive! It's about being god. It's about being death. You mean you *really* haven't killed anyone before? Tell me the truth. I know you have."

"No."

She sighed, laughing.

"Then what the fuck are you doing here? You won't understand it until you go out there and kill somebody."

"I'm sorry I'm so stupid. Understand what?"

"The exhilaration of power, the rapture of the illicit, the ultimate rush! Murder! Ooh, I'm getting wet. I'm getting turned on just *thinking* about it!"

Frustrated, Brady stood.

"Thanks for talking to me, Ms. Scott. You've been very helpful."

"No, wait!"

She was reaching toward him.

"You said you wanted evidence? I've got evidence."

"Yeah, right."

She shrugged and cocked her head, smiling.

"I swear! I swear I've got all the evidence you need. I've got evidence that will blow your ass away."

Incredulous, he looked toward the door and then back to Katrina.

"Oh really? So where *is* this evidence?"

"Something for something, Inspector Brady. I'll give you all the evidence you need, but you'll have to do something for me first."

He always took the table in the far right corner, diagonally facing the stage, just out of the singer's field of view. It was a second tier of sorts, a darkened area behind the booths. Fifty feet away, a Steinway grand piano sat in the left corner of the dais, allowing an area for the singer, an acoustic guitarist and a drummer.

He hadn't missed a single one of her performances in seven years.

Saint Claire met Gisele Ferreira nine years earlier after testifying against her husband, Stefano Rossi, who was sentenced to death for a series of gruesome murders over ten years. Saint Claire saw her every day for three weeks in the courtroom, distraught, emotional and torn. He studied her pliant face as facts and testimony from the trial transformed her from the role of supportive wife to that of betrayed spouse and heartbroken woman.

At her husband's side for the start of the trial, Gisele was absent for closing arguments, the verdict and sentencing. The detective was intrigued for a while, but he started another case and became consumed by it.

Then he found himself face to face with her at Christmas Eve Mass at St. Patrick's Catholic Church on Mission. Looking down into her face, the universe stopped as their eyes spoke the language of souls trapped by invisible seines, weighted in circumstance, belief and conviction. For a minute they stood frozen, alone in the church. Then Saint Claire shook her hand and backed away.

A week later, he saw an advertisement in a small local newspaper with a large picture of Gisele displayed. Providence, he thought, as he purchased the ticket at the restaurant's box office.

Lights up.

Her first song, *Chega de Saudade*, began the epiphany. As she sang, his world, which had faded over years of solitude to sepia shades of black and white, exploded in one place after another with vibrant color and texture. His son dead, his wife gone, he had consigned himself to a life of public service and structure, sans emotion, sans joy, sans intimacy.

Now, for the first time in years, he smelled perfume. He tasted the mellow *Charentaise* sun in his cognac, the mysteries of creation in his sparkling water. And though he could not understand all the Portuguese lyrics she sang, he was certain he perceived the sense of the song.

Saint Claire sat transfixed through her first set, and then the next two. At the end of the night he approached her. And once again, they were caught in the awkwardness of inexplicable attraction, the awe of bewildering emotion. Words were useless, incapable of expressing in volumes what their eyes and faces spoke in an instant. Questions asked and answered. Hearts unbound.

He didn't see her again until her next show in Oakland, three months later, when he offered to buy her dinner after the performance.

She drank a chilled *Dubonnet* on a stem while he sipped cream sherry. Menu at the ready, he ordered the *Hamachi nigiri* and assorted *shashimi* and offered to order for her, but she declined.

"*Peixe não puxa carroça.*"

"What's that?"

"It's Brasilian expression. *Fish don't pull wagons.* I'm a meat eater. I want the beef steak. Filet, rare"

Both were Catholic. Gisele had not spoken with Stefano since the trial, and still, she would not divorce him. Until the state got around to executing him, she was the wife of a husband. She could not date or keep company with a man. Instead, she became consumed with her boutique, Rio, and her stepdaughter, Carlotta.

Saint Claire and Gisele began talking one to two nights a week over the phone. Gisele, who loved to laugh, found comedy in just about every situation, since "the world is a very funny place, after all," but sometimes, when she was sad and lonely, she cried. She cried that life, and sometimes God, were unfair. She wondered why both had given her so much, why both had given her such a capacity to love, only to mock her.

And Saint Claire shared his pain and loneliness, the story of his life, the painful loss of his son and his agony over watching his wife go mad. Yet in every conversation, however poignant, the words spoken were secondary at best compared to three words that were never spoken, never permitted to breach the threshold of conscious thought. Saint Claire and Gisele were not allowed to love each other, not even to think about it.

They saw each other at performances and at public events, they talked on the phone and wrote emails, but they had never gone to a movie together, never to the beach or to a play, or to a concert where someone else was performing. When greeting each other, they shook hands. They refrained from extending personal compliments. Sometimes it was excruciating, and yet restraint was far better than crossing the line and losing each other.

"Are you sure there is nothing wrong? You seem distracted tonight?"

"No, no not at all! I was just thinking about that first song you sing."

Gisele smiled.

"*Chega de Saudade?*"

He bowed his head, almost bashful.

"Yeah. That was the first song I ever heard you sing. And then you told me what it meant."

"End of sadness, enough of loneliness."

"It's what made that first night was so special. I've never been sad a single day since then."

She bowed her head.

"Thank you, Deuteronomy."

She only used his name when her heart was touched by something he said, so he didn't mind her doing so. He liked the way she pronounced the name.

At dinner after her performance, both sat in silence, fearing the moment when one or the other would have to leave. The green tea was strong and still too hot to sip.

"Any decision on that last appeal?"

She sighed, uncomfortable with the subject.

"Unsuccessful. His lawyer called. I think he is all used them up. No more. The date for execution will not change."

"Is that what the lawyer said?"

She nodded.

"The United States Supreme Court, he said. He can try to appeal it there, but they will refuse to hear it. If the governor does not grant clemency, he will be executed next month."

Silence returned. A minute later, she blotted the tears from the corner of her eyes with Saint Claire's handkerchief.

"When I was little girl and I had something on my mind a lot, my mother always used to say, *fique tranquilo.*"

"And what does that mean?"

"Sometimes there are things you can do to help, and sometimes there is nothing you can do. When you realize you can do nothing, you say, *fique tranquilo.* You have to find your peace. You have to let it go."

CHAPTER 9

"Inspector Brady, I presume?"

"You presume correctly. And you are the legendary Derrick Slater. Boy, if I had a dollar for every story I've heard about you I could buy a damn good bottle of booze."

Slater laughed.

"Well, if you only got paid on the ones that were true, you'd have to settle for an awfully weak beer. Come on in!"

Slater looked down the walkway.

"Where's Saint Claire?"

Brady took a breath, relaxing.

"He's coming. We drove separately. He called at the last minute and said he had to do something on the way. Gave me directions to meet him over here."

Brady stopped, his head snapping toward the doorway where Oksana entered. She had just finished working out in the gym upstairs and wore shorts, a sports bra and tennis shoes. Her blond ponytail jutted from an opening in the back of a 49ers cap. Her smooth tanned skin glistened with sweat. She could feel the weight of his eyes and smiled before disappearing into the kitchen.

Brady looked back toward Slater in disbelief. Slater chortled, shaking his head.

"That's Oksana, my *wife*."

Red in the face, Brady could only laugh at himself.

"Then when I grow up, I wanna be like you. Huge house, hot wife, whatever else you've got goin on here. Or maybe you could just adopt me?"

"Sorry son, but ya gotta get your own. Follow me."

Upstairs in Slater's recess, Brady sipped the Tennessee whiskey, spitting bits of ice back into the glass.

"So you were captain at Central Station when Saint Claire came on? Do you have any idea why he left his high paying professor job over at Berkeley to be a cop?"

"Did you ask him?"

"I've asked him a lot. Maybe it's me, but I get the sense he's not much of a talker, not about his personal life at least."

Slater still stood on the other side of the bar.

"You were in for quite a career yourself back in Boston. Why'd you move here?"

"Cuz my wife's a bitch."

Slater refilled Brady's glass.

"Funny. You don't strike me as the kind of man who can't stand up to his wife."

"You Sir, have never *met* my wife."

"No I haven't, but I'm sure she's got her hands full dealing with you."

Slater settled into a seat.

"It's just that, from an outsider's point of view, your moving to San Francisco and being assigned to unofficially investigate Saint Claire strikes some of us as a bit peculiar."

"So you think he doesn't trust me?"

Saint Claire called, predicting his arrival in a few minutes. Brady could feel precious time slipping away.

"Why does he know so much about poisons?"

"Because his wife is a psychopharmacologist. He helped her get through pharmacy school. Had to study drugs, poisons, all that stuff."

Even upstairs, the men could hear the door chimes and the sound of the heavy front door being pulled open.

"Do you know his wife?"

"Katrina? I've known her for years. I met her at the funeral for their son, Christian."

"Do you think she really *is* crazy?"

Slater began filling a new glass with ice.

"Now there's an intimidating woman. And he swears she's smarter'n he is."

They could hear Saint Claire at bottom of the stairs, in a conversation with Oksana. Slater leaned in and, placing a new drink in front of the empty barstool, he spoke quietly.

"Look, a word of advice. With this killer, you're dealing with one crazy, ruthless bastard. You want Saint Claire to trust you? You *earn* that trust! And just remember, Saint Claire understands these sick assholes. Sometimes you might feel offended. You'll think he's keeping you in the dark, but you'll be wrong, cuz all he's trying to do is *protect* you. You trust him, he trusts you. Got it?"

Thirty minutes later, the three men stood around the pool table, Slater and Saint Claire with cues in hand. The pile of crumpled money on the bar meant the men were playing nine ball, Slater's favorite. Slater was taking their money and talking trash.

"If you ask me, I don't know how you guys do it."

"What's that?"

Steadying his aim, he shot, knocking the cue ball into the four, which rolled across the table, tapping the nine as it passed. The nine edged forward and fell into the side pocket. He stood, triumphant, biting a cigar.

"Work with all them broads. Nothin against your chief and the captain, but there are some jobs and fields that just aren't *meant* for women. Homicide's one of em. It's like balding, a man thing."

Saint Claire wanted to nod, but he didn't. While he agreed with Slater's assessment, he would never make such a thought public. Brady, feeling the whiskey, disagreed for the sport of it.

"I don't know about that. Don't you watch that CSI show on TV, and the other shows? They've got women on there."

Slater was racking the balls for the next game.

"*Tits* reading lines for television audiences. Sells minivans or whatever they sell during those hours. Woman chief, fine, but she should know to stay outa homicide and steer far clear when there's a real killer out there."

Brady laughed.

"I don't believe this! Do you realize how Cro-Magnon you sound? Saint Claire, Professor? You're not blown away by this?"

Returning his cue to the rack, the detective turned.

"I think what the captain is saying is, *women don't make good homicide detectives*. It's instinctive. They feel for victims. They don't identify with *killers*. Some men are able to do that."

Slater cut in, a little offended.

"You know something about killers, Brady? You tell me, how many women killers do you know about?"

"You mean serial killers?"

"Yeah, *real* killers!"

Brady thought a few seconds, sighed and wagged his head.

"Well, none that I can think of."

"That's right. Women are killed by killers. They are not the killers, per se. Women might get depressed and kill their children, they kill their rivals and they kill their sorry ass cheating husbands, but they don't kill wholesale for the sheer joy of killing, not like the men do."

The dinner table was full that night, though it was only Thursday. Slater, Saint Claire and Brady were at the table, sipping from the first bottle of wine, when Oksana's glamorous Ukranian friends, Alonikka and Marusya, arrived. Brady and Alonikka flirted across the table throughout the meal.

When Slater, Brady and the two other women retired to the smoking room after dinner to puff Slater's Cubans, Saint Claire and Oksana remained at the table.

"I was telling you earlier, Saint Claire, that I am worried about him."

"What seems to be the problem?"

"Well, he is changed man. He gets mad all the time, and for nothing! Maybe it's the medication for his prostate, but he shakes a lot and he gets angry."

Saint Claire wrinkled his forehead, thinking.

"And you say this just started happening, recently?"

"Maybe a week ago."

He sighed.

"Okay, I'll watch him tonight, and I'll check on him tomorrow and over the weekend. If you think it's getting worse, definitely call me."

She placed her hand on his wrist.

"Thank you, Saint Claire. You are great man and good friend."

He smiled.

"And you're a saint for putting up with that guy."

"You are single man? Your wife? She never come back, no?"

He thought of Katrina, with regret.

"No."

"My friend, Marusya. She adore you. She is good woman for you. She wants to find her destiny here with good man."

"Well, Marusya is a beautiful woman, but I work all the time. I'm afraid I wouldn't make her or anybody much of a husband."

Still full from dinner, they sat on couches watching
Sports Center on ESPN. Emboldened by the day's familiarity,
Brady called across the room.

"Hey Saint Claire, that letter you got from Maria, why
don't you show it to us? Why don't we work on this together?"

Saint Claire rose.

"I was going to do that anyway. That's why I invited you
here, so the three of us could look at it together before I turn it
over to Sanchez."

"Oh, uh, really?"

Brady was unprepared for the response, but Saint Claire
was unprepared for the next. Slater was standing.

"Goddammit Saint Claire! I told you I'm retired! I don't
wanna be involved in any of this shit anymore. Don't want some
crazy comin after me!"

Brady stood to calm the shouting man.

"Come on now, Cap'n. Calm down, no one's comin
after—"

"What the fuck do *you* know, you fuckin kid? Saint
Claire'll be dead before he'll ever really share anything with you!
Goddamned asshole!"

Slater approached Brady, who backed.

"You know what's wrong with you, kid. You've got a
dick! You think with your dick, always lookin for somewhere to
stick it. You'll never understand killers, cuz killers are men that
in one way or another *don't* have dicks."

Saint Claire said nothing. His friend's behavior did not
make sense. Slater, noticing the detective was watching,
continued in the rant.

"Why do you think Saint Claire's so smart? It's cuz he
doesn't *have* a dick. He probably left it in some coed back at
Berkeley. That's why he understands killers and you don't. But if
he ever decides to grow a dick, he'll be shit outa luck, just like
you."

All at once Slater seemed to realize what he was saying.
As he looked toward Saint Claire's supportive posture and
expression, the fight went out of him.

"I'm sorry."

He raised his hands in surrender.

"I'm sorry, but I just don't know what got inta me. Please forgive me, both of you. I, I just need to be alone. I've gotta go. You guys know the way out."

CHAPTER 10

In order to catch a killer, you have to be a killer. Your pathetic peers are awed by your so-called insight into the minds of killers and your inflated intelligence, but I'm not. Compared to me, you are a worm, a maggot on the battlefield. And do you know why this is? Because at some time during your development, you made a mistake, or worse, your weak mind was dominated or deceived. You have allowed others to impose and imprint irrational values on you, to infect you with a hypocritical sense of morality.

Ah, there's the rub, and therein, Saint Claire, lies your tragic flaw. You never developed into the artist you were truly meant to be. You have understood killers because you are genetically prone to kill. And so, before this game is over, I will unlock your full potential. Here I am the teacher and you are the student. But you are a prodigy. I know you've already figured it out. In order to stop me, you are going to have to realize that here we make our own rules, here there is no morality, and yes, if you are going to stop me, you'll have to be true to your nature. You are going to have to kill someone.

Saint Claire noticed the letter shaking in his usually steady hand. Maybe it was the whiskey and wine from the day before, but it was odd. Maybe it was his nerves. It was six am, and he'd had no more than four hours of sleep.

He reflected on the episode from the previous night. He had never seen Slater in such a state. Over twelve years of sharing gruesome homicide cases, bullshit political pressure from the mayor's office, personal tragedy, bar fights and procedural disagreements, Slater always kept his temper in check.

Outside Slater's house, Saint Claire made an attempt to debrief Brady, telling him what he really had witnessed inside. Brady, recognizing an opportunity to gain trust, assured Saint Claire the incident wouldn't be something he would share with Sanchez or Leong.

Saint Claire rewarded his loyalty. At a coffee shop near the station, the inspector revealed the second note from the killer. Like the first, it was succinct, three-quarters of a page long. While boasting about poisoning Hector, the killer held out the hope that if the next murder could be prevented, six lives would be spared.

The killer asserted Hector was not killed because he was a crank addict and predicted the next killing would prove this point. He said he didn't like cops and courts, the would-be imposers of rules that suffocate and persecute "my people." And then the shocking news: he named Captain Sonia Sanchez among the next six victims.

Saint Claire sipped from the heavy coffee stein at his right, setting it on a royal blue tile coaster on the glossy cherry wood desk. Taking up the letter, he reread the first two paragraphs aloud before moving to the third.

Until the recent pseudo civilization of man, the Homo sapiens gene pool produced individuals of diverse character, disposition and inclination, all purposed to advance human DNA to dominate all other forms of life on Earth.

Within all this genetic variation, several archetypes were isolated. Among these, the martyrs and the prophets, genetically disposed to access the subconscious mind. And there were the leaders, born ambitious, with a physical need to conquer and dominate. Then there were the heroes, the models or genotypes that excelled in battle, resultant from an inborn addiction to adrenaline. Most humans then, as well as now, were genetic place keepers, advancing the DNA from one generation to the next, contributing nothing, while leading basically meaningless lives.

But the greatest of all the archetypes, and the most necessary, were the killers, the assassins. Throughout history, humans have needed within their ranks individuals who could slit throats without giving it a second thought, who could strangle a pleading child or bash open its soft, squishy head, individuals who could disembowel and bludgeon a weeping widow, rape and smother a fluttering little girl, castrate an old man and hack him to pieces, rip out a still beating heart or systematically wipe out an entire village, burning family after family alive.

Yes, the killers were the architects of human history. Every coup or change of power, every succession to the throne, every war and every bloody revolution turned on the capacity of killers to do what they were born to do.

And then so-called modern humans, in their presumptuousness and conceit, began to pronounce their societies civilized, began to forget what got us all here in the first place. First they hired killers to do the necessary ground work, and then they made laws and courts to punish these same killers for doing what they were expected to do, born to do. When they had their wars, they sent killers off to do the dirty work, spurning them when they returned.

And at last came the psychologists, like you, who label killers as aberrant humans, dangerous freaks of nature, the scourges of society. And geneticists, who want to isolate the "serial killer gene" and implant potential killers with microchips so they can be monitored and tracked by satellite. Or they want to perform radical brain surgery and experimental gene therapies. They want to identify fetuses with the gene and recommend abortion to mothers who conceive killers. The leaders and the rest have made war on killers, hunting us down like dogs, or relegating us to captivity or to submissive existence in wars without swords, in butcher shops and slaughterhouses.

When I was alive, I killed for pleasure, but I also realized it was something I was meant to do. And I killed indiscriminately, men, women, children, white, black, Asian, rich, poor, sinners, saints, in America and all over the earth. I lost count after three hundred. But along the way, I had a spiritual awakening.

For the self-actuated killer, killing is an art. While it's true some killers are brutes, lusting blood, commingling the drive to kill with the drive for sex and other weak minded needs, some of us get it right. I stopped killing for killing's sake and began to kill for the sake of art. You've seen my work. I showed at the de Young.

I am the savior. I am the genetic Messiah, born of killers, and my purpose is to forestall the corruption and the extinction of the gene, and by extension, the genotype. By dying and returning in full glory, I also save mankind who, in seeking to exterminate killers, know not what they do.

Saint Claire stopped reading and refolded the letter. It was all he could process for the moment. The passage contained numerous clues, some to move the drama forward, and others to confuse and distract him. Some were direct, while others were more subtle.

He was tentative about his decision *not* to reveal both messages contained within the envelope with Brady. He had concluded Brady wasn't the killer or working with the killer. So involving Brady made sense. After sharing the note at the coffee shop, Saint Claire explained he would disclose as much as he could safely disclose to someone reporting to the chief, for Brady's own good. It was too early to determine if Brady could be trusted.

The more pressing issue however, was the next murder. Saint Claire had spent a decade pursuing serial killers. The megalomania so evident in the letter seemed affected and purposed for shock value, just in case Saint Claire decided to share its contents with supervisors.

Naming Captain Sanchez as a target was part of the game. The killer knew once Sanchez read that passage, her objectivity would be shot to hell. The captain, whose distrust for Saint Claire already bordered on paranoia, would panic, demanding answers and drawing department wide attention to the threat. The killer did it to further isolate Saint Claire from the police and to create chaos.

If the next murder was dependent on Hector's death, then the sequence of events leading to a second victim was already in motion. Unless he could disrupt the progression of these events, someone else would be dead within a matter of days.

CHAPTER 11

"*Gracias*, Senior Brady, for caming. You are very welcome at thees *belorio*."

Brady attended wakes in Boston, but this one was different. The modest chapel was packed with relatives from San Francisco and from Río Grande in Zacatecas, Mexico. There was hardly a place to stand inside or out in the hallway. The neighbors in the apartment next door to Maria were kind enough to pick up and transport the incoming family. Both the chapel and the adjoining hallway bustled with activity.

Inside, older women were seated or kneeling around the open casket, praying quietly or mumbling from small prayer books. A boyish priest sat in a chair nearby, head bowed as he recited the *rosario*. The casket was flanked by candles at both ends. And the flowers, on stands and in baskets, gave the front of the chapel a jungle-like appearance.

Brady spent the afternoon at Kohl Construction, where Hector worked as a framer. He interviewed Hector's boss and fellow employees. Of special note was Hector's locker mate, Julio, who mentioned an odd, unopened box left in the locker.

Brady also went to the YMCA, where Hector played basketball with former high school homies. Hector's friends were shocked by his murder, with one vowing to *fuck up* whoever was responsible. One man, DeMarsario Washington, admitted he did drugs with Hector sometimes and worried that both were being targeted.

Toxicology results indicated Hector ingested a lethal quantity of ricin over the previous weekend. Dr. Singh called Saint Claire on Wednesday and told him the toxin had been isolated and identified in Hector's blood. She had also analyzed a sample of the white powdery substance Saint Claire collected from Maria and found it was laced with the same poison.

The finding meant Saint Claire was right when he predicted how Hector was killed. Brady wasn't sure what to think. Either Saint Claire was a brilliant detective or a diabolical killer, capable of harm to Brady himself, to Sanchez and others in San Francisco.

Saint Claire's wife accused him of being the killer and insisted he had killed many times before. She told Brady Saint Claire murdered a widow woman named Annabelle Lee when he was only twelve. According to Katrina, Annabelle was a pretty fifty-something prostitute in the community who murdered her own stepchildren. She was Saint Claire's instructor in the sexual arts and the art of murder. Katrina said he killed the attractive widow when their perverse love affair became public and the community began to question the nature of the relationship.

She said Saint Claire came from a family of murderers, a grandfather who was hanged for raping and killing six teen-aged girls over a period of three years, and an uncle who murdered for the landowner boss. This uncle threatened or killed sharecroppers and their families if the boss thought they were going to sneak off in the night to set up a sharecropping agreement with another landowner.

Katrina supplied a motive: ego, reminiscent of the reason Sanchez offered. Katrina explained, in clinical terms, that Saint Claire was an "undiagnosed paranoid schizophrenic, with delusions of grandeur." He could only be the brilliant sleuth they knew if he was pursuing a murderer he understood. She insisted he was chasing himself, tracking clues he purposely left behind, and that's why he seemed so intelligent.

Then there was the note from the killer, indicating Captain Sanchez would be among the next six victims. The investigation into the Rosenthal murder suggested the killer did not know Gladys, nor had he known Hector Fuentes. So, to name Sanchez as a victim? It made no sense. If Saint Claire wanted to murder Sanchez, the obvious animus between the two would serve as a motive. But if he really wanted to kill her, why would he warn her and put the whole department on notice? How could any killer be so overconfident and arrogant?

Saint Claire was supposed to make an appearance at the wake and then he was going to meet with Sanchez to share the killer's last note with her. When Brady spoke with her earlier in the afternoon, she seemed uptight and irritable enough already. He didn't want to be anywhere close when she got to the part about her being among the next six victims.

"*¡Tanto gusto! ¿Cómo se llama?*"

Brady knew the voice. It was Saint Claire. Standing by the casket, his eyes examining Hector within, he was scribbling on a notepad, speaking casually with the young priest.

"*¿Sean? ¿E cuántos años tenéis, Sean?*"

Saint Claire wore a long woolen trench coat, charcoal gray to match his ever present hat. Upon eye contact with Brady, he curtailed his conversation with the Father and approached.

"How did it go?"

"I went out to the construction site. Couple conversations I'll have to follow up on in private. I'll do that tonight. And I went to the gym, and I have to follow up on that. Are we still getting together tonight?"

Saint Claire eyed him with suspicion.

"Yeah, after I meet with Sanchez. Your hands always shake like that? I never noticed it before."

Brady looked down at the notebook shaking in his hands.

"No, not usually."

"Well, neither do mine."

Looking down, Brady saw Saint Claire's own hands were uncharacteristically unsteady.

"Let's finish here so I can go deal with Sanchez, and we'll meet at the coffee shop right after. We'll talk."

Spotting Maria, Saint Claire went to her and embraced her, whispering words to her in Spanish and extending hugs and condolences to the other women with her. Turning back toward Brady, he tipped his hat and disappeared into the hallway.

Saint Claire was waiting outside Captain Sanchez's office when he got the call. The place of the meeting had been changed. According to her secretary, he was to drive to police headquarters on Bryant Street and meet with her in the chief's office. He was not surprised.

Captain Sanchez and Chief Rebecca Leong were discussing the murders at an oval table in the chief's office when he arrived. Leong stood and greeted him with a handshake, while Sanchez kept her place at the table, staring straight ahead.

"You're late, Saint Claire. You're always late."

He checked his watch and sighed.

"Sorry I can't always be early like you, Sanchez . I got the message less than fifteen minutes ago and I drove right over."

He removed his coat and hung it on the rack.

"Anyway, it's a good thing the chief will be in on this meeting, Cap'n. I'll be honest. It wasn't a meeting I was looking forward to having with you in private."

He sat, his tone professorial.

"Technically, we've had two murders, but according to the killer, Hector was the first. The killer isn't counting Mrs. Rosenthal. The purpose of her murder was to get our attention."

He placed his satchel on the table.

"He plans to murder seven people in a series, with each murder setting off the next. Hector Fuentes was a crank addict."

He opened the satchel, withdrawing a report, two notepads and an envelope.

"This killer is patient, calculating, but he also has resources, meaning he's probably from a wealthy family. He used Maria's need for money and Hector's addiction to set up the first murder."

He slid the report toward Sanchez.

"Pretending to be Gladys Rosenthal, he gave Maria a box containing $13,500, a gift he was certain she, being traditional, would share with her husband. So he included the drugs, laced with ricin, and let nature run its course. The rest is history, right there in the report."

Chief Leong, not reacting, glanced over at the captain, crossed her legs and leaned back in the chair.

"Thank you, Inspector. As you've no doubt surmised, I spent the afternoon discussing this matter with Captain Sanchez, who herself had a discussion with Inspector Brady yesterday."

Sanchez interrupted.

"And today."

"Yes, they spoke this afternoon as well. Anyway, both Captain Sanchez and I found it a bit peculiar that even before the lab called with toxicology results, you knew the poison used and the probable method of delivery."

Sanchez continued the thought.

"According to Brady, you had that information at the time of Fuentes' death or right after. You described in detail how he was killed when you were over at the hospital morgue, not an hour after he died."

Saint Claire raised his eyebrows.

"Okay. Sorry I was right."

Sanchez leaned forward.

"Would you mind telling us how you knew all that?"

"I'm a detective. It's my job to figure things out."

Sighing to herself, she looked toward the chief.

"See what I'm talking about?"

Leong smiled, turning toward Saint Claire.

"Inspector, according to the record, you visited Hector and Maria Fuentes two days before he died. You went by to interview Maria, but you ended up forcing an interview with Hector as well. Would you mind telling us why you thought it was so important to interrogate Hector and how, based on that exchange, you figured it all out?"

Saint Claire nodded and sat back.

"Well, based on that exchange, I knew he was a meth addict, and I knew he and Maria were hiding something from me. If I had known what they were hiding, I could have stopped the killer right then. It was my best chance. I believed Hector was going to be the next victim, but I didn't know how. It's all in the report there."

Leong looked over at Sanchez, who sat scrutinizing the report.

"Yes, I'm sure it is. Inspector, do you know this killer?"

"No, I don't think so. He knows who I am. I'm ninety-nine percent sure he might be a killer I started after twelve years ago, but no. If I knew who he was, the family of Hector Fuentes wouldn't be over at that chapel tonight."

Leong conceded her objective, pursing a separate line of questioning.

"How did you end up suspecting ricin was used in the killing?"

"Hector's brother described the symptoms. Tightness in the chest, stomach cramps, cold and flu symptoms, difficulty breathing, pulmonary edema. The killer likes poisons, but he also wants to demonstrate how resourceful he can be. Ricin was overkill. In terms of poisoning, it's exotic."

"So you think this guy's the real deal? He's really going to kill seven people in thirty days?"

"Yes, I do."

"And he'll use different, exotic poisons to do it?"

Saint Claire thought for a moment.

"No, I don't think so. I think he wants us to know how intelligent he is, so he won't be predictable. The next one or two might be poison, but after that he'll move on to some other means of killing."

"And what do you think that will be?'

"I don't know. The biggest problem with this killer, we have to wait for the next murder to get the next clue. So unless Brady and I can figure out who'll be next, someone else is going to die tonight or tomorrow."

The chief poured more tea into the cup and sipped, contemplating.

"You've been doing this for a while, Inspector, and you've had time to investigate this Fuentes murder. If you had to guess, who would you *say* will be next?"

He shrugged.

"I don't know. But if I had to guess, I'd look for someone or something out of place."

Just then Saint Claire's face was transformed by realization. It was so obvious upon reflection! Yet the trigger was not in Leong's question, but in his own answer. His own words registering in his mind, his mouth fell open.

Leong placed the teacup on the table. Looking up from the report, Sanchez squinted as she spoke.

"What is it, Saint Claire?"

"The priest over at the chapel, Father O'Brien. He's young and he's white. He shouldn't be there. I'm sure there's a logical reason for it, but it's odd. He's the next victim."

Confusion showed on the chief's face.

"What? Wait a minute, how? What's going to happen to him?"

"I don't know. I just think he's going to be the next victim. I need to get back over to the chapel."

Sanchez slapped the report she was reading onto the table.

"Oh no! You're here for a meeting. You're just looking for an excuse to leave. This meeting isn't over by a long shot, Saint Claire."

His eyes made an appeal to the chief, whose eyes denied the request.

"Maybe you can call Brady and ask him to keep an eye out. She's right. We're not finished here."

Saint Claire's phone rang seconds later with a call from Brady.

"Can you slow down for a second? Now once again, tell me what happened!"

There was silence in the room as he listened.

"Okay, okay, the priest and a little girl? Which one is dead?"

Sanchez began to ask a question, but Leong held her off with an extended palm as Saint Claire continued.

"Just try to keep order. Did you call it in yet?"

A pause.

"Okay, well I'm here with the chief and Sanchez. I'll see if we can get a toxicologist over there, and when I'm done here, I'll be right on over."

Snapping the flip phone shut, he sat. He buried his face in his palms and sighed.

"Crap!"

Leong was standing.

"What happened? Who's dead?"

Saint Claire looked up.

"The priest is dead, and a little girl is on her way to the hospital. He was a kid, only twenty-six years old."

"How'd he die?"

"They don't know. He was sitting next to the casket when he just keeled over. Paramedics think it was a heart attack. The little girl had severe stomach cramping, so the two incidents might not be related."

Sanchez's tone was confrontational.

"You were saying just a minute ago the priest was going to die! How'd you *know* that?"

"I don't know. She asked me to guess, and I said I thought he would be the next victim. He was out of place."

"So?"

Growing impatient, Saint Claire checked his watch.

"Look, this killer, if he's going to make each murder dependent on each previous murder, he's limited himself to a range of victims, especially if the murder tonight has to trigger some future murder."

The captain and chief seemed to be with him.

"I figured if Hector's murder was going to trigger the next, the next murder would involve some ritual or consequence resulting from his death. My first thought was the funeral, so I didn't even consider the wake.

"I was looking for something, something out of place. If the killer already planned these murders and isn't actively involved, then the victims will *always* have to be out of place, or engaged in some activity that's not regular."

Sanchez removed her glasses.

"Okay, I can accept that. But what makes you think all these murders are going to be related to each other? The killer didn't say that in the letter you turned over to me, that is, if you turned over the real letter."

He bowed his head, thinking, before responding.

"You're right. He didn't say that in the letter. It was just a theory I formulated on my own about this killer from our past history."

Leong interrupted.

"And why such a theory?"

"Well, because now I'm convinced this killer's the same killer that Curry, Slater and I were pursuing twelve years ago. He was intelligent. He had vast resources and was ruthless, bordering on sadistic. We came close a couple times, but we never caught him. We figured he either died or moved out of the area to start up someplace else, and we were fine with that."

Sanchez nodded, her face skeptical.

"So is that what this killer from twelve years ago did? Made all the murders interdependent?"

"In the later movements, as the killer described it, that's what happened."

"What? You mean you and Slater talked to the killer back then?"

"No, the killer liked to write, wanted to provide the commentary. He sent us letters."

Sanchez rose to her feet upon that reference.

"And that brings us to the letter you got from Maria Fuentes. You know, I don't like this business about you getting the letters first and then just letting us in on what you think we need to know. You've had that letter for two days now, and we don't know what's in it. The delay is unacceptable."

Saint Claire sighed, answering toward the chief.

"I don't know what to say. I have no control over how the letters come to me. But if the letters contain clues or other information vital to saving lives and I can help, I'm sure as hell going to read them before turning them over. I mean, they are addressed to me."

Leong nodded, glancing toward Sanchez.

"That is true. He does have a point."

Sanchez huffed in disgust.

"Fine. So, you have the second letter? Let's see it."

Saint Claire hesitated.

"I, well I think the chief should read it first, and she should make the determination about what should happen and who should see the letter after that."

"Why's that, Saint Claire? And why are your hands shaking? You nervous about something?"

Saint Claire handed the letter to the chief.

"Just a little tired, a little on edge."

"And what's this about the chief determining who should see the letter? What's the letter about?"

"More of the same. The killer takes responsibility for Hector Fuentes' death and promises six more murders in the next few weeks. It's like I told you, he's calculating, psychotic. He'll try and pit us against each other if he can."

Leong, reading the text of the message, echoed Saint Claire's observation.

"You can say that again, this guy's nuts."

She stopped.

"Oh!"

Sonia's head snapped in the chief's direction.

"Oh, *what?*'

"Hold on. Let me finish."

Rebecca Leong's face flushed as she finished the letter. Refolding the sheet and placing it in her lap, she sat back, putting her fingertips to her lips. Her face held a new concern. She did not speak for a few seconds, and when she did, the words seemed to stick. Clearing her throat, she began.

"In my opinion, the letter tells us *nothing* and provides no clues. It's just the ranting of a madman. Saint Claire and Brady would do better just trying to capture this killer the old fashioned way."

"I don't believe this! Are you thinking you're not going to show me that letter?"

Leong smiled in an attempt to reassure her.

"It's not that, Sonia. I just don't want to give this lunatic a way into our heads. It's obvious what he's trying to do. I need you to trust me here, as a friend."

"I *am* your friend, but I still need to do my job. I'm the captain of Central Division and Saint Claire works for me! That letter should have gone first to me, and then to you. I refuse to be cut out of this. As captain, I demand to see that letter."

"And as chief, I'm advising against it. It'll take us in the wrong direction. It'll make the investigation and the possibility of catching this bastard more difficult."

"You're advising against it. So it is my call to make, right?"

"Yes."

"Then just give me the damn letter! I'm a big girl. I can read a letter."

Saint Claire protested to the chief.

"You're right advising against it. If she reads that letter, it'll compromise—"

Sanchez cut him off.

"Just can it, asshole! I wouldn't be surprised if you and the killer weren't in league, if you two weren't doing these murders together, you sick fuck."

She reached toward the chief.

"Can you just give me the letter, please? As your captain, as your friend, whatever! Goddammit! Can you just give me the letter and let me do my job? Please!"

Reluctant, Leong brought the letter to the tabletop.

"Okay, but I'd like to try to prepare you for this."

"You didn't need preparing, so neither do I."

Sonia reached over and took the letter from the chief's hand.

"Thank you."

Pleased with herself, she smiled as she read, but she slowed at once.

Hector Fuentes suffered when he died. You ever poison someone and watch them die? Watch the eyes express panic, terror and hopeless desperation all at once? I know all the slow, painful poisons. You ever watch a pregnant woman come to the sudden realization she's bleeding from her ears, nose, eyes, vagina and asshole?

Torture is the best part of murder, meaning a quick, painless death is less artful. And so I must apologize in advance, Saint Claire, for the lack of art in the next murder you'll encounter. The reality of my present condition exerts obvious limitations, but I promise at least two honorable mentions and one real masterpiece over the next six murders.

I've murdered in all the great cities, New York, London, Moscow and even your native New Orleans, but San Francisco is my all time favorite. It's the diversity, the complexity of life here. The possibilities are endless.

My victims have always been random, but just to make the game more interesting, I've decided to change the rules this time. Of the next six victims, at least one will be someone you know very well, and believe me, I'll be doing you a favor.

One of the next six will be that bitch you work for, that bitch Sonia Sanchez that you hate. I'll be doing you a favor because I'm sure she's getting in your way. I'll also be doing her a favor and a favor for Rico and Tatiana, saving them years of pain and anguish.

Because Sonia Sanchez was going to die anyway. She's HIV positive. Check the mini refrigerator in her bedroom, bottom cabinet, second shelf up on the left. Those are antiretrovirals and protese inhibitors, not your typical cold and flu medicine. So it's either me or AIDS. With AIDS, who knows? With me, it'll all be over in a few weeks.

Sonia stopped reading and crumbled the letter in her hand.

"Is this your sick fuckin idea of a joke, Saint Claire? What did you do, break in my fuckin house?"

He recoiled.

"I would never do that."

"Or did you figure that by revealing my condition I'd quit and I'd be out of your way?"

"No!"

Sanchez glanced toward the chief, who was uncomfortable, her head bowed.

"You know, it doesn't matter, cuz I'm not gonna quit! I am not gonna quit!"

She looked to the detective.

"What? You wanna kill me, Saint Claire? You wanna kill me? Why don't you just fuckin shoot me?"

Raising his hands, he walked toward the coat rack and retrieved his coat.

"Look Sanchez, I'm sorry you're being threatened and I'm sorry certain things came out in that letter, but I'm on your side. Believe me, if this killer can be stopped, you and I are going to have to start working together to do it."

CHAPTER 12

It happened right before his eyes. Brady was sitting in the chapel, speaking with Hector's pretty niece Leticia, a flight attendant from Houston. From the corner of his eye he saw the priest stiffen. Snapping his head toward the casket, he watched the young man fall sideways off the seat. Bolting up, he watched young Sean O'Brien take a final strained breath.

Pandemonium ensued. Then, on the other side of the chapel, a little girl screamed and went down, producing a wave of panic and an ugly scramble toward the door. Young men leapt over chairs, crying children were dragged across the slick floor and an older woman was trampled.

Two ambulances arrived after fifteen minutes. By that time, the little girl was on her way to the hospital by car. Leticia stayed with Brady until two Spanish-speaking detectives arrived to begin interviewing witnesses outside the building.

Saint Claire called just as Brady was leaving and wanted to meet him at Central Station an hour later. Still shaken by the events at the chapel, Brady accepted Leticia's offer to have a drink in her room. She was staying downtown, at a hotel on Union Square.

Leticia was no more than twenty-two or twenty-three. Her hair was black and curly, flowing down her back. She was brown and smooth, with a pretty face and a firm young body. Brady knew her type. She was his usual mark.

Pretty women at that age were infatuated with their own sense of power and independence. It was a rush to be able to come and go at will, to choose what to do, where to eat, whom to spend time with and whether or not there would be sex. It was fascinating to realize that playful flirting, evincing even the slightest indication of interest, was enough to rattle most men, regardless of their station in life.

Half-full flutes of sparkling wine on the nightstands flanking the bed, he kissed her neck and shoulders while his careful fingers aroused her below. He knew from experience it was all about blood flow. Enough blood to the pelvic area, and sex was a foregone conclusion.

He was supposed to meet Saint Claire in thirty minutes, so he hurried, combining fast and slow, gentle and forceful, shallow and deep, full and void. She moaned aloud and shifted her body, directing him, driving him, exciting him, *Animato, Ostintato, Crescendo*, until a sudden, abrupt ending.

He hardly *felt* it. Usually it was explosive, but this time it was just a twinge, a flutter. He wanted to try again, but he was out of time.

"What's wrong?"

"Nothing. I've just gotta go. Gotta work."

In a way, he was embarrassed. He couldn't understand why he hadn't performed better! But she was just another body. He would probably never see her again.

In the station, Brady waited at his desk, playing solitaire on the computer. Five minutes. Contrary to Sanchez's complaining, Saint Claire was usually punctual. Brady wondered how the meeting had gone, with Sanchez reading the letter. Whatever happened, the relationship between his partner and his captain had gone to the next level.

When the phone at his desk rang, he knew it would be Saint Claire. The detective seemed tired, but there was a degree of desperation in his voice. He asked Brady to go over to his desk and retrieve a stack of unopened mail. Brady flipped through the letters, reading the senders' names to Saint Claire on the phone.

"Stop!"

"What? What is it?"

"No, go back. You said there was one from Derrick and Oksana?"

Brady flipped back three letters to the item in question.

"Yeah."

"Open it, but be careful."

Brady put all the other letters aside and, taking a pair of scissors, inserted the blade and slit open the envelope. Holding it out, he peeked inside.

"Looks like a card."

Reaching in with two fingers, he pulled it out.

"It is a card. Want me to read it?"

"Please."

"It's a *Thank You* card. It says, 'Thanks for the case of Jack Daniel's. You are always so very sweet!'"

"Oh no." Saint Claire's voice broke.

"What? What's wrong?"

"I never sent him a case of Jack Daniel's. Look, instead of meeting at the office, we need to go over to Slater's. I'm headed there right now. Hurry your ass!"

It was after midnight when Brady arrived at Slater's house in Sausalito. He didn't see Saint Claire's car in front of the house, but he approached the door and knocked. Oksana answered, though she did not invite him inside. He stood for a minute before Slater's face appeared at the door crack. His graying hair was frazzled and his face grizzled.

"Brady? What the hell are you doing at my house at this time of night?"

"I'm meeting Saint Claire here. What, he didn't call you?"

"Saint Claire? No. What's going on?"

Brady thought to mention the case of Jack Daniel's, but wasn't sure of its significance. He'd let Saint Claire explain.

"I don't know, but it sounded important. Can I come in?"

Slater didn't answer, but he pushed the door open as he turned, signaling Brady to follow. Downstairs, Slater told Oksana to send Saint Claire up when he arrived and invited Brady up to the recess.

"Can I pour you a drink, Brady?"

Brady eyed the bottle in Slater's hand.

"No, thanks. I think we *both* better hold off on the drinking until he gets here."

When Saint Claire arrived ten minutes later, he carried a black leather medical bag. Placing it on the bar, he went over to his old captain and shook his hand, unable to disguise the fact that he was scrutinizing Slater's handshake, his face, his eyes and his voice.

"Did you send the *Thank You* card?"

"What *Thank You* card?"

"For the case of Jack Daniel's. Did you send that card?"

Slater sighed, remembering.

"Oh that card! And the tickets to the recital? Hell no! You know I don't do that shit. I would have just called ya if I had thought about it. Oksana sent that goddamned card. She does that kinda stuff."

Saint Claire placed his hand on Slater's shoulder.

"Okay, now this is going to sound crazy, but I never sent you a case of Jack Daniel's."

"Then where'd it come from?"

Slater stopped. He knew.

"Jesus Christ!"

"Where's that case now?"

He motioned.

"Behind the bar. Thank God I was well stocked when I got it. I think I've only gone through two bottles. What are you thinking?"

Saint Claire opened the medical bag.

"Well, my hands have been shaking all day, and I noticed Brady's were doing the same. That's not normal for either of us. When I talked to Oksana the other night, she said you were shaking, and you were even more an asshole than you normally are. Too big a coincidence."

He withdrew a plastic case from the bag.

"So I started thinking. If there is some chemical or drug in our systems, it must have been introduced at a time when the three of us were together. Oksana's fine, so it wasn't at dinner."

Going behind the bar, Saint Claire ducked and reappeared, placing the case of Tennessee whiskey atop its surface.

"And then I vaguely remembered getting a piece of mail from you and Oksana. It felt like a card, something I wasn't used to getting from you. I was going to open it, but I just never got around to it."

He took a swab from the kit and grabbed a bottle of the whiskey and a glass.

"My first thought was arsenic, but arsenic salts aren't soluble in alcohol, so we would have seen the arsenic crystals in our glasses, or tasted the difference. But then I thought of our killer and how he bragged about slow, wicked poisons—that along with the fact that all three of us were experiencing tremor and a range of other poisoning symptoms."

He poured the alcohol, swirling it in the glass. Then he dipped the swab, which turned purple when exposed to the air.

"So my next guess was mercury salts, which actually are soluble in an alcoholic drink. The test I just performed indicates

I was right. The whiskey we drank that night, the whiskey you've been drinking, Slater, was poisoned with mercury."

Brady's eyes widened.

"So what does that mean, Saint Claire? What, is it going to kill us?"

Saint Claire smiled.

"I'm sorry, Brady. You had at least five shots. That's a lot of mercury. You might as well be a rectal thermometer."

Brady didn't find anything funny about Saint Claire's joking.

"No, I'm serious. Is this poison going to kill us?"

The detective shrugged.

"No, at least not all at once. It's a cumulative poison that collects in the body. Depending on the amount of exposure, it'll kill you in about three months, but first it'll steal your intellect, make you a shadow of your former self. It'll make you crazy."

He looked toward his old friend.

"Slater, you need to get immediate medical help. Some of the symptoms of mercury poisoning are irreversible, but I'm sure the doctors over there can do something for you. You can't afford to waste any more time. Oksana's downstairs waiting to take you to the hospital."

Brady stepped up.

"What about me? What do I do?"

"You're a young man. You'll probably get over it. How many drinks did you have that night?"

Brady looked ill.

"Maybe six, or seven throughout the day."

Saint Claire wagged his head.

"You'll be fine. You'll probably suffer from *erectile dysfunction* for the rest of your life."

He relaxed his wrist and shook a dangling hand.

"It'll be limp, but it's better'n dying. They got pills that might help you get it up."

Saint Claire stared into Brady's eyes for a moment before yielding to a smile.

"I'm joking. You'll be all right. You've got to stay here to help me test the rest of the bottles. I want to try and get idea of how much mercury we're dealing with."

Brady eyes were fixed on his own extended hands, still trembling.

"I don't know. Maybe I should go with Slater. I think I should go."

"Those tremors'll go away in time, and tonight I'll give you some DMSA. It'll bind with the mercury to help draw it from your blood. Don't worry. You'll be fine."

He headed back toward the bar.

"Now let's get to work, droopy."

CHAPTER 13

"Does your husband know we're meeting?

"He doesn't need to know. Do you think I know where he's at when he's missing two or three nights a week? Look, if you had a problem with this, you should have told me that over the phone."

Saint Claire took a breath, relaxing.

"No, I'm fine. It just feels a little surreptitious."

"It is surreptitious. He can never know that we've gotten together like this. He's very jealous. I'll never tell him, and I imagine you probably won't. He carries a gun, you know."

Saint Claire was beginning to realize she shared her husband's dry sense of humor.

"That's all right. So do I. Only mine is much larger."

"Oh, I've always been a believer in *the smaller the gun, the better for fun*. Big is primitive, barbaric."

"Well then, your husband's a real gentleman."

To his surprise, Andrea Brady called and introduced herself that morning, asking if he had time to meet her for a late breakfast or early lunch. Curious, he accepted and the two agreed to meet at quaint Italian place in the Financial District on Sacramento Street.

She was older than he imagined she would be, but what she lacked in prettiness, she more than made up for in charisma.

"How's your friend, Slater?"

"In the hospital, where doctors think he'll recover. Personally, I won't mind if he's forgotten half the one-liners and lousy jokes he's been telling me all these years. Why did you want to meet me?"

"To see you, or at least to find out what you were like. You know, it's not often my husband is so impressed with another person, especially another man. If I didn't know any better, I'd think he admires you."

"But you know better?"

She laughed, sipping *Pinot Grigio* from an oversized glass.

"I think he respects you for your intelligence, but you're a mystery to him."

"Why's that?"

"Because you're black."

He tried to steady the wine glass in his shaking hand.

"It's hard to believe he never ran across any black people in Boston."

"Oh he did. It's just he's never really been especially crazy about black people."

"Meaning he's a racist?"

She laughed.

"No, though he has let the notorious n-word slip out on occasion, but lately it's only been when he's watching sports and his team's losing. Race was more an issue in Boston because it's Boston, especially on the police force. For him over there, it was us-against-them, with them being the blacks. So, to answer your question, he's not a racist. He's just a little prejudiced about some things."

Reaching over, she touched the back of his hand.

"But aren't we all?"

He eyed her pale, manicured hand atop his. The contrast was profound.

"I suppose we are. Does your husband talk to you about his work?"

She sat back.

"Enough to understand you don't trust him, but just so you know, Sanchez doesn't trust him either. She thinks he'll end up being more loyal to you than her."

"And *you* think I should trust him?"

"I think over time you'll end up trusting each other."

Saint Claire sat back in the seat, still curious.

"Okay, you came out to see who I was. Well here I am. So that's it?"

"I don't want my husband working homicide."

"And why's that?"

She looked away as she answered.

"Well, look at you. *You* work homicide."

"Yes."

"Where's your family? Where's your wife?"

He let her continue.

"Look Professor, I'm not judging you. It's just you homicide people don't do well with families. It's the nature of what you do. You're brooding all the time, you keep odd hours, you're suspicious of everything and everyone, you have problems with intimacy and you don't share. Not exactly great qualities for a husband or father."

"Okay."

"I know Tom cheats every opportunity he gets. You don't have to say anything, because I know he does. I'm older, and I don't dress provocatively. He likes em young, pretty and kind of slutty, which is not me. We miss on that, but in every other way, things have been good between us. He's a loving husband and a great father to our girls."

He smiled.

"Gives me a little insight about your husband, but you still haven't told me why we're here. Is there something you want me to do?"

She spooned a dollop of the creamy *foie gras* from the terrine onto a slice of *brioche*, spreading it with a small knife.

"He tried homicide before, when we were in Boston. His partner was older, the hard-boiled type, alone, the typical detective. He was tough on Tom. He told him he didn't have what it took, told him he wasn't smart enough."

She passed the knife to Saint Claire as she continued.

"Tom took that as a challenge. Determined to prove he was smart enough, he buried himself in the cases they were working on. He lived and breathed those cases, and before long, he was solving them. The old guy was jealous and wouldn't teach him anything, but Tom stuck with it anyway."

"And there was something wrong with that?"

"Our family suffered. He was hardly ever home, and when he was, he was brooding and short-tempered with the girls and me. It got to the point that we didn't even want him home. And that's when I took a hard look at the job. It wasn't just him. It was all you homicide detectives. So I went to him and told him to choose: family or homicide."

Saint Claire took a bite of the shaved raw *Ahi* from his salad, nodding approval.

"So he quit?"

"No, he chose homicide. He moved out on us. He was gone for about a year. And then there was a big shooting incident that changed everything."

Saint Claire stopped, confusion registering on his face.

"I read his record from over there. It never mentioned any shooting incident."

"And that took some doing. Ultimately, a judge friend of the family sealed the record so there was nothing to report, and nothing went on his profile."

It was all coming together. He didn't even have to guess.

"Who'd he kill?"

"Black kid, fifteen years old."

His instincts had betrayed him. In his scrutiny of Brady, Saint Claire never sensed he was a killer. Circumstances aside, this man had taken a life, and more than that, the life of a child.

"Self-defense?"

"Well yes, but the kid wasn't armed. Tom thought he was, though."

Brady was more complex than he appeared. Saint Claire knew about secrets, and there was nothing immoral about having them. But the shooting wasn't just a secret. It was a cover-up. It didn't help Brady's case to know there had been an existing animus against blacks, an "us-against-them" mentality at the time he pulled the trigger.

"Why are you telling me all this? What do you want?"

"I said it earlier. I don't want my husband working homicide. When Tom told me about you, he had this sanguine look in his eyes, so I got nervous. I think he does admire you. And I get the sense he wants to be a crack homicide detective just like you or alongside you. I'm counting on you to discourage that."

"Why?"

She bowed her head.

"I guess you wouldn't understand. It's for our family. We lost him once. We need him and we don't want to lose him again."

Saint Claire thought a moment.

"What about what he wants?"

"He doesn't want to be a homicide detective. He might think he does, but he's not made from that stuff. He has a family. He loves his girls and they love him. He loves life, not death, not like you do."

"Excuse me?"

She didn't blink.

"I don't know what you were like before, when you were a professor, but I know you were married to a beautiful woman and you had a son. And I don't know why you gave up your

Berkeley job to become a cop, but whoever you were in that other life died when you decided to be a homicide detective."

Brady was sharing his suspicions with his wife.

"Your life is consumed with death and treachery, Inspector, so when do you ever have time to love and live? You'll never be able to truly love again until you give up death or murder or whatever you're chasing. And if you ever loved your wife, you'd help her because you loved her, and it wouldn't matter whether or not what she wanted was logical to you."

Sensing she had said too much, she backtracked.

"I mean if you loved *any* woman. All I'm trying to say, Saint Claire, is that being a great detective like you are means selling your soul. You could probably regain it if you quit, but you can't. You're not alive in the sense the rest of us are alive. You're more like the killers you chase. Now Tom isn't perfect, but I love my husband. I'm just trying to keep him alive, for me and the girls. I'm sorry. I didn't come here to judge you. I just wanted to ask you to help me."

He tried, but he was unable to mask the injury to his ego.

"I understand. But if I'm the monster you say I am, why would you think I would want to help you?"

"Oh you've got me all wrong, Professor! I don't think you're a monster. You're a decent man doing a job most people aren't capable of doing, and you're doing it at great personal sacrifice. I respect that, but my daughters and I don't want it for Tom."

Once again, she placed her hand atop his.

"Can you please just try to understand that?"

He nodded.

"I won't campaign against it, but I'll do what I can."

"Coming from you, I couldn't ask for anything more."

The arrival of entrees and a bottle of Luigi Coppo Reserve Chardonnay from *Piemonte* lightened the conversation. Over lunch Saint Claire and Andrea discussed Boston and the move, Andrea's job, the stalled rebirth of New Orleans and restaurants in San Francisco. They were amazed at how compatible their tastes were in food, wine, art, music, dance, religion and history.

"I was wrong about you, Saint Claire."

"Wrong about what?"

"You're a Renaissance Man. You have such an incredible capacity to fully enjoy life, only you're obsessed with not living. You're obsessed with death. You're worse than I imagined."

He laughed and thought of Gisele.

"I suppose I am."

"Why? Why don't you quit murder and begin to live?"

"I will, but I'm waiting. It probably makes no sense to you, but I have unfinished business that won't let me move on. When I finish it, I'll quit, just like that."

Andrea looked into his eyes.

"When's that? Never?"

"Well, if this killer I'm after is the killer I started with, within the next thirty days."

The meeting with Dr. Singh had to be pushed back three times, once because test results hadn't come back, and two other times to accommodate the forensic pathologist's schedule. Her lab wasn't in the San Francisco General main hospital but almost two miles away, on a side street cluttered with small medical support private businesses and extensions of the hospital.

After having paid for parking three times at a nearby lot, Brady left his car at the hospital parking structure and caught a cab over for the tentative meeting. He found Saint Claire seated in the reception area when he arrived. He was reading, as always.

"Meeting pushed back again?"

"No, she's almost ready for us. Have a seat."

It was the same old book about the murder of San Francisco Police Chief Biggy.

"Solve that murder yet?"

"No, but I think I know who did it. At this point I'm just trying to figure out how."

"Lotta corrupt cops back then?"

Saint Claire laughed.

"Lotta corrupt everyone. But San Francisco politics have always been ugly."

Brady checked his watch a second time, chose a magazine from the table and eased into the chair next to his partner.

"Boston's probably even uglier. Lived my entire life there. And I love Boston with all my heart, but in some ways I don't miss that place."

"Left a few demons back there?"

Brady's eyes were distant.

"Yeah, a few."

Dr. Medha Singh's expression was grave as she greeted the detectives and escorted them back to her private office just off the main lab. Her office was neat, though littered with books. There was a bookcase behind her desk, another along the wall opposite the door and several stacks of magazines and manuals, spines out, in strategic places throughout the room.

Seated at her desk across from the detectives, her tone was reproachful.

"Okay, I've seen a lot of weird shit in my time, but what's *really* going on here?"

"I don't know. You tell us. The priest fell over dead at the wake. You know what killed im?"

"Batrachotoxin."

Brady cut in.

"Batra-what?"

"Batrachotoxin, it's an extremely potent cardiotoxic and neurotoxic steroidal alkaloid. Your priest never stood a chance. I'm just surprised more people weren't killed."

"What is it?"

Saint Claire answered.

"Frog poison?"

Singh perused the report.

"The most deadly toxin on earth, about ten times more potent than tetrodotoxin from the puffer fish Comes from a poison arrow frog of the genus, *Phyllobates*. Kills fast. We found it in his system and all over the rosary beads he used at the wake."

She placed the report on the table and sipped from her coffee.

"As far as we can tell, the toxin entered his body through his fingertips or he touched his eyes or lips after having transferred the poison to his hands."

Saint Claire reached over and took up the report.

"So you think the priest's rosary beads were coated with the toxin?"

"I think? It's exactly what happened. And if, before he died, he had touched *other* people, as priests sometimes do, they'd all be dead too. Some might still die."

"I don't get it. Anything that deadly, it wouldn't be just lying around. Where would someone get that poison?" Brady asked.

Singh shrugged.

"Collecting poison arrow frogs is a growing hobby in this country. The relative toxicity in the frogs is derived from their South American diet: primarily toxic ants, mites, and beetles. The toxins are passed from the arthropod to the frog, and then sequestered in glands on the amphibian's skin."

She passed a second copy of the report to Brady.

"So frogs brought from the wild into captivity and fed a regular captive diet, usually fruit flies or hatchling crickets, eventually lose their toxicity."

Saint Claire thought aloud.

"With adequate resources and a little motivation, our killer could have gotten a fully toxic frog from South America, or perhaps through an exotic pet dealer?"

"Apparently something like that happened. One of the paramedics touched either the rosary beads or the Father's hands. He died in the ambulance on the way to the hospital. Like I said, I'm surprised it wasn't worse."

Brady examined his own hands, causing the doctor to chuckle.

"Don't worry. We'd all know if you had touched the poison. You'd be dead."

She checked her watch.

"But a dead partner is the least of your problems now, Saint Claire. I had a reporter from the *Chronicle* come by today. A dead priest, a dead paramedic, both poisoned, at the funeral of a man poisoned, whose wife worked for an old woman poisoned! And we've got cyanide, ricin and bactrachotoxins being used. Exotic shit! It's only a matter of time before they sense there's a big story here."

Saint Claire's face held concern.

"What did you tell the reporter?"

"Nothing. I don't get paid to talk to that vermin. So again my friend, what's really going on here?"

Saint Claire looked over at Brady, stood and closed the door.

"This killer, I think I know him. Not by name or anything tangible. I know him because I've been after him for a dozen years. He's very dangerous, and he's just getting started. The priest, Sean O'Brien, was just the second of seven murders he plans to commit this month. As you are aware, he has a sophisticated understanding of poisons and he's an elaborate planner."

Brady nodded. "Not to mention the fact he's got resources."

"Right. My best guess is the killer visited the chapel after determining Hector Fuentes would be the first victim. What would follow naturally from that murder would be the wake. He somehow determined when Father Gonzales, the regular parish priest, would be away visiting relatives in Santa Fe. Knowing as much, he chose Father O'Brien, who would have to fill in for Gonzales, as his second victim."

Singh raised her eyebrows.

"Sounds complicated."

"We're just scratching the surface. Think about this. If Gonzales's vacation determined the day of O'Brien's murder, then working back, it determined the approximate date of the Fuentes murder, which in this elaborate scheme would have had to determine the exact date of the Rosenthal murder, which was to happen on my birthday."

"Like dominoes?" Brady asked.

"Yes, working backward. And from where we stand, it means some future event or circumstance related to the next murder was used to determine the date of this one, the date of which will be determined by the murder after that."

"And so it goes right on up to the seventh murder?"

Saint Claire nodded.

"I think so. But what I don't understand yet, is why it happened at the wake and not before. Father Gonzales had been gone for five days. O'Brien served at the chapel for that entire week. He must have prayed the rosary during that time, so why wasn't he dead before?"

Brady shrugged.

"Maybe he had special rosary beads he only used for special occasions, like wakes."

"That makes sense. You want to check that out?"

Dr. Singh was still standing, her arms crossed and sweaty fingers clutching the lab jacket.

"So you guys are telling me I should expect five more bodies rolling in here, poisoned?"

Saint Claire held up his hand, palm outward.

"Maybe not. For the moment, we're helpless to stop him, but so far he's had an unfair advantage, and he knows it. If he wants to prove how clever he is, his tactics have to change. At some point he's going to have to level the playing field, and when he does, we'll have the opportunity to prove how smart we are."

CHAPTER 14

"So, what's the prognosis?"

He took a deep breath and sighed.

"It was a big scare, but they're tellin me I'll recover."

"That's good."

It was an awkward conversation from the beginning. Sonia resented having to live in Slater's shadow. There had been perhaps two conversations before, no less uncomfortable. Not that he ever said anything disparaging to her, but there was a degree of arrogance in his attitude, and it bothered her. He was such a man's man.

The entire force was abuzz with news of his poisoning and rumors about a deranged serial murderer. Sonia Sanchez's emotions ran the gamut from impudent to angry to paranoid over the last forty-eight hours. She hadn't slept well, if at all, for two nights. Physically, her body was weary. Psychologically, her spirit was compromised.

Forcing a smile, she placed her hand on his shoulder.

"Do you feel up to talking?"

Saint Claire came by the hospital the first night and twice the next day. He said he had performed tests on the remaining bottles of Jack Daniel's. The killer dissolved mercury salts into only six of the twelve bottles, and arranged the poisoned liter bottles in a checkerboard fashion within the case. The shiny, shrink wrapped black plastic seal on the corrupted Jack Daniel's liters was an exact match to the original. It was something anyone could purchase online for next day shipping. The only surprise involved the relative ease of such tampering.

Test results from bottles in the recycle bin indicated the first bottle Slater opened was probably unspoiled, but the second contained the quicksilver compound. Slater consumed the entire second liter, save ten or eleven shots he poured between Saint Claire and Brady. The third bottle in order was untainted, but the fourth from the bar well showed measurable levels of dissolved mercury salts. This bottle was nine-tenths consumed, mostly by Slater, though Saint Claire had drunk three modest shots and Brady seven.

The killer's intention was not to murder Slater outright, but to poison him slowly, bringing on a madness that would resemble Parkinson's disease or Alzheimer's. The concentration of mercury in his body would have killed the ex-captain after a few months, and therein was the divinity of the plan. Δεν βρέθηκαν λέξεις.

But the mercury poisoning would not have killed Slater within thirty days of the Rosenthal murder, meaning the killer was not counting Slater among the seven. With Slater, it was personal, especially if the killer was the same murderer from twelve years earlier. Destroying first Slater's mind and his dignity would indicate ultimate mastery.

Both were certain the killer understood Saint Claire drank with Slater, but Saint Claire believed the killer intentionally tipped him off about the poisoning. All else aside, ego was driving the plot forward. The killer needed Saint Claire alive and in command of his mental faculties in order to establish superiority.

His speech was slow and slurred.

"You're the last person I expected to see here. What? Did you come to pull the plug on the machine keepin me alive?"

She forced an uncomfortable smile.

"Not at all. I actually came to see how you were doing."

"And?"

"And what?"

He batted his eyes in an attempt to clear his vision.

"Sonia, let's just cut to the chase. You need information from me or you need me to do something for you. Which is it?"

She took a deep breath and shrugged.

"Both."

"Let me guess. You don't trust Saint Claire."

She was defensive.

"I don't know if I trust him. You trusted him, and look what happened to you."

"Wasn't Saint Claire who did this."

"How do you know that?"

She continued before he could respond.

"I mean, don't you think it's at least possible he's the killer? It wouldn't be the first time a cop crossed over to the dark side. You ever wonder how he knows so much?"

"He's super intelligent. At least that's what I call it."

"No one's that smart."

Sonia tried to find communion in his eyes, but they seemed glassy and unfocused. She leaned in.

"Has he told you anything?"

"Not lately. We were talking, but after this mercury-poisoning incident, he hasn't said much. Asshole decided he wanted to keep me on the outside, for my safety. Wish he had decided that a month ago!"

She nodded, acknowledging his frustration.

"I understand. Has he said anything about me?"

"No. Why?"

Rare vulnerability showed in her facial expression.

"Well, according to the last letter from the killer, I'll be one of the upcoming six victims."

Slater tried to sit forward, but the attached medical equipment and muscle stiffness in his back, thighs and abdomen held him in place.

"What? Did the killer name you in person?"

She bowed her head, trying to hide her angst.

"Yes."

Bingo. That's why she had come. She would never admit it, but Sonia was afraid. Slater understood her fear because he had lived it over the last week. He lived with the fear the killer might target him owing to his relationship with Saint Claire. What was coming? Ricin, frog poison, an axe, a bullet? When, where, why? Was trap already set? Would it be sudden? The vexation was overwhelming, especially when he was alone. But with Sonia it must have been much worse, knowing the killer called her by name.

And as much as she resented Saint Claire, she must have known that, if he wasn't the killer, he was the one person smart enough to save her. It's why she drove to the hospital to speak with the person who knew Saint Claire best.

"Did the killer say why you would be a victim?"

"No, but he said I was a bitch."

He wanted to say it. He almost said it, though he stopped himself. But then it became just too irresistible.

"Sonia, you *are* a bitch."

He smiled.

"But you're a woman with power. You're all bitches. What else was in the letter?"

"That was it."

She batted back tears.

"So Saint Claire never said anything to you about the threat?"

"No, but for the last two days I have been through an ordeal. We haven't had much of a chance to discuss anything."

He reached over, placing a hand on her forearm.

"I know what you're goin through, and I know you're feelin a little desperate about now. It's why you're here. I'll level with ya. Saint Claire's my friend. We've been friends for almost thirteen years now. I'll admit I've had my doubts about him, about his secrets, about why he doesn't share everything he knows. And when I thought the killer might be comin after me, the thought did cross my mind he could be the killer. But that's because I was thinkin this killer in some ways reminded me of Saint Claire. They've always thought alike. They're both so smart."

Judging from the reaction on her face, he realized she was misinterpreting his unguarded admission.

"But that was just my paranoia gettin the best of me. I was wrong. He saved my ass, as you can see."

He sighed, growing weary of talking.

"If this is the killer we were after before, he's smarter'n the rest of us, but he ain't smarter'n Saint Claire."

Slater closed his eyes, signaling a conclusion to the conversation.

"Like I was sayin, I've known him for twelve years, and he's a little weird, but he's not a killer. So if your ass can be saved and if anyone's gonna save it, it's gonna be Saint Claire. Trust me, Sanchez, you're better off with him on your side."

Gisele closed the boutique at six on weekdays. Saint Claire always waited thirty minutes before he called so she could z-out the registers, complete the computer updates and restock. Their Tuesday and Thursday conversations were brief, so calling at six-thirty when she was free assured he would have her undivided attention.

He hadn't told her about the killer and she hadn't asked.

Seated in his car outside the hospital, he adjusted the cell phone to speaker mode. It rang three times before she answered, her Portuguese accent making music of her voice.

"Massage parlor. What can I do you for?"

"How was your day?"

"Oh so busy, but I have funny story for you."

He was already laughing.

"Okay, let's hear it."

"Okay, this lady come in today after lunch. Regular lady, not too fat, not too small, but she ask me, 'Are you owner of this store?' and I say, 'Yes, I am.' So she point her finger right in my face and she say, 'You lie! You are *not* owner, you are owner's girlfriend. I know his wife and I will tell her.' Then I say, 'What store did you come to?' and she say, 'This store, *Roma*, I know where I am!' So I say, 'Sorry you miss your boat. This is *Rio*. You ain't in Roma taday!' Can you believe that?"

He smiled.

"I think she had too many martinis at lunch."

She laughed.

"That would explain everything. Oh these people, they make me crazy!"

After a pause, Saint Claire cleared his throat, the way he always did before making in announcement.

"I just got news about an hour ago that my brother died. He had a heart attack back uh, back in New Orleans."

"Oh I'm *so* sorry, Deuteronomy. What can I do?"

"Nothing. I think I'll have to go back there though, probably next week. I'll still call you at our regular times."

Gisele tried to convey the emotion welling from her heart.

"If I were with you, I would hug you. I would give you great big hug."

"Thanks. I can feel it."

Talking to Gisele always made him feel better. She was always so positive. She joked, she laughed aloud and she sometimes described in minute detail the delicate fragrances of the roses he sent her on occasion. She was so colorful and alive.

"Stefano's lawyer called. The state of California is going to kill him in two weeks. This is my last chance to forgive Stefano. He tells me if I do not visit him he will choose death by the gas chamber instead of the lethal injection in order to punish me."

And now Gisele! Indirect though it was, he had even brought death to spoil her life. It was as if he left the stench of death on everyone and everything he touched. Saint Claire was, in fact, on the list of those invited to witness the execution.

"How old was he?"

"Who?"

"Your brother that died. He was older than you?"

He returned to the present.

"Oh, my brother. Yes, he was older than me."

"What was his name called?"

"His name was Sam. He was fifty-nine."

Voice taking on a reverential tone, Gisele began.

"Ó Deus Eterno, em quem a Misericórdia é insondável, e o tesouro da compaixão é inesgotável, olhai propício para nós e multiplicai em nós a vossa Misericórdia, para que não desesperemos nos momentos difíceis, nem esmoreçamos, mas nos submetamos com grande confiança à Vossa Santa Vontade, que é amor e a própria Misericórdia. Amém."

Closing his eyes, Saint Claire concluded.

"Amen."

"So Sam's dead? How very convenient for me. While you're in New Orleans for the funeral, you can locate a *Voudoun* and pay her to come back here to take this shit off me."

Katrina was seated on the leather couch with her feet, toenails freshly painted, extended onto an ottoman. She wore a long scarlet silk robe and matching silk marabou slippers. Her face was powdered and her shiny black hair hung in perfect ringlets down her back. In her hands she held a teacup and liner. Cup up to her lips, she blew across the rippling surface of the steaming light green liquid.

"You decide on when you're leaving?"

He shrugged.

"No, I haven't. I just got the news less than two hours ago. I have no idea what I'm going to do, or if I'll even be able to go. I'm in the middle of a major investigation."

She laughed.

"You're not a good liar. Of course you'll go. He was your brother."

Saint Claire eased down into the leather chair.

"I didn't say I wasn't going. I said I'm just not sure how it's all going to work out."

He continued with a measured carefulness.

"And I don't think I'll be bringing back a *Voodoo* priestess."

She sat forward, placing the tea assembly on a table next to the sofa.

"You don't care about me! You have never cared about me!"

He raised a hand forward in protest.

"Of course I do. That's why I'm here every day. That's why I've been here for you."

She sighed.

"Oh it's such a burden, isn't it? And you're such a saint. Poor little Deuteronomy Saint Claire! He has a crazy wife and he's so dedicated that he has to go by to check on her psycho ass every day. Poor man! Well, I'm sorry I'm such a burden to you!"

She leaned forward.

"But did you ever think that if this *Voudoun* could cure me you wouldn't have to waste your time visiting me every day? That I'd be out of this place, out of this prison!"

She watched for a reaction. None came.

"But oh, I forgot. You want me here. That's right. It was you who got me labeled a certifiable lunatic in the first place! You put me here."

Taking a breath, he spoke.

"You belong here. We both know that."

Her practiced smile and the pause indicated a change in tactics. She stood and approached her husband, taking a seat on the chair's armrest.

"But what about where *you* belong, Ronnie?"

She took his hand and placed it on her firm thigh as she opened her legs. She drew her face close to his, her nostrils flaring, her hand directing his hand closer and closer to her center. She licked her lips.

"Do you remember how good it was, Ronnie? Do you remember how wet and tight I made it for you? Just imagine how hot and tight and juicy it would be for you tonight after all these years."

Her hand slid upward along the inside of his thigh. Though he attempted non-reaction, she worked upward, exploiting his vulnerability. Involuntarily, his breathing grew shallow and the blood vessels in his groin opened. He grasped her wrist to halt progress, but her warm hand clenched the animated object of her attention.

"Ah, there it is! There's my friend."

She tightened her grip.

"Sometimes you're my friend, Ronnie, but this is the one friend I could always count on."

He grasped tighter as her hand began to simulate the motion of intercourse.

"What are you doing?"

She laughed.

"How long has it been since you've had it? Twelve, thirteen years?"

She yanked the tie at her waist and let the robe fall open, exposing a scarlet, lace-trimmed matching bra and panty set. Her full breasts were pushed upward to exaggerate their voluptuousness. Her stomach was flat and toned, her legs were shapely and silky smooth as she teased him, tempted him. She whispered.

"Remember how I used to make you beg for it? And how when you finally got it, how deliriously intense you'd get, the delicious fantasies and appetite you'd indulge. And I'd let you take it over and over and over again, until there was nothing left in you."

She sat onto his lap, grinding, gyrating her hips.

"You can have it right now if you want it. All you have to do is want it bad enough."

It wasn't the first time she had used the allure of sex in an attempt to persuade her husband to work toward her release from the facility. From the day she was committed, she blamed him for testifying at her hearing, for revealing and skewing information proprietary to their marriage. To her, that breach destroyed the bond.

She did not speak with him or entertain his visits for the first six months, insisting that was malicious and had come to gloat, declaring his own righteousness. But eventually she became lonely, longing for companionship and intellectual intimacy. Over time, she realized he was the only person she knew who ever gave a damn about her, and as she softened, a new though guarded relationship developed to replace what had been lost.

Katrina made peace with her husband, and yet the first time he attempted physical intimacy, she exploded in anger, swearing that as long as she remained in the facility, conjugal rights or no, he would never enjoy sex with her.

Sometimes when she felt especially cruel she would seduce him to the point of begging, only to deny him consummation. In time, her amorous overtures became ineffective, but this night was different.

He hesitated.

"You tell me. How bad do I have to want it?"

"You don't have to do anything, Ronnie. All you have to do is tell me you'll look for the *Voudoun* and it's yours, right here, right now, tonight."

He was a man of his word. Both knew any effort on his part would be expected to yield results. Any concession meant committal.

Removing her hand, he lifted her from his lap and stood.

"I can't do it, Kate. You know why I can't do it."

Her anger was immediate.

"Fuck you!"

He looked toward the door and responded without turning.

"My brother just died. I don't need this!"

She let the robe fall off her shoulders to the floor.

"I'll tell you what you need. You need to know the truth."

She waited for him to look at her before she began.

"Do you think I've been waiting for you all this time? Do you think I've gone thirteen years without getting laid on a regular basis? Is that what you think?"

She laughed.

"No, I vowed you were never going to get any of this, but I didn't say it wouldn't be enjoyed. I never said *I* would go without."

Studying his reaction, she knew she had his attention.

"Oh, but I'm not a whore. I've been selective. Do you remember Dr. Turner from that first year?"

She let his mind slip back to the time.

"Hot and heavy. At least once a week, but it only lasted a year. And then there was Jonathan Hébert, the Creole man I told you was my cousin?"

She smiled.

"Well, he wasn't my cousin. Not by a long shot. You're a detective. You should have known better."

As a psychologist and detective, he was suspicious of her motive. But as her husband, a feeling of betrayal began to overwhelm him.

"My personal favorite was your old partner and friend, Joe Curry. He was just so in tune with what I needed. It was as if he could read my mind. I was devastated when you killed him, but I figured you found out about us."

He started to react, but he decided he would dignify the allegation with a response. Instead, he took a breath, listening as she continued.

"And Kain, Christian's friend? Of course you remember Kain! Or should I say Michael Rad, your student and self-described nemesis? Michael Rad was obsessed with either defeating you or becoming you? He was here just last month, you know. I've been seeing him off and on, for years."

She smiled.

"But your new partner isn't bad. Oh yes, Tom Brady? Nice tight ass, big shoulders, square jaw. Of course you know *he* came by to see me. Did he bother to mention that to you?"

"He didn't mention it, no."

"Of course he didn't. He couldn't mention it without risking you'd find out. He's a good liar, but he knows how skilled a detective you are. He was worried you would see through his story and discover the truth."

She had created a question in his mind, but he chose not to ask it. Stretching out on the sofa, back arched, she crossed her legs, teasing him.

"He doesn't want you to know he *fucked* me that day, right here on this couch, and then we moved to the bed. He was here for more than an hour."

She turned over and rose to her knees and hands, her hips gyrating.

"He has a big gun, Ronnie, even bigger than yours."

"You're lying."

"About the size of his gun or about the fact that he fucked me?"

He looked away.

"You're just playing another one of your games."

"You think so? Well, you have to know I'd *do* him just to spite you. I'm capable of that, you know it. And I can be very persuasive when I want to. So it all boils down to one question: do you trust your new partner who hooked up with your wife behind your back? Ask him and study his reaction. You'll know."

"I don't have to ask. I don't believe you."

She laughed.

"It doesn't matter. I've already created the question in your mind. I've put the thought there. And next will come the image your own mind will create of Tom Brady's shivering body tensed on top of me, his back arched, his face and body sweating, his pelvis humping between my open thighs, pounding me, my fingers digging into his ass as I moan aloud the way I used to moan for you."

On her feet, she took a place between her husband and the door.

"You can deny it all you want to, but that image in your mind will be there next time you see him, and every time after that. The only way you're really going to know is to ask him, but you're too arrogant for that."

She put her arms around him, her head against his chest, her hands clutching his butt.

"Now you have to live with the torture of that thought, Ronnie. It's cruel of me, isn't it? But no more cruel than a husband locking his wife away in an institution and throwing away the key."

She opened the door, her composure breaking as she began to weep.

"If you ever loved me, you would help me. This is not me and you know it. I want to be well. Bring back the *Voudoun* to cure me, please! I'll die if I don't get out of here soon."

CHAPTER 15

"Hello Sweetie!"

She kissed his lips.

"Who's your friend?"

"Brigitte, this is my good friend, Sergeant McCarthy. I brought him here to get him laid tonight. Do you know of anyone who might be willing to take care of him?"

During his first few weeks at SFPD, Brady spent four or five nights a week out drinking in local bars and brewpubs with McCarthy, but the relationship gradually changed. McCarthy still invited him for drinks after work, but Brady scaled the outings back to one night a week. McCarthy was a nice guy, but he was a guy, and Brady preferred female company.

He tried a number of massage parlors, erotic venues and strip clubs before he happened on *Casanova's* three weeks earlier. Upon entering, he met Brigitte, and he slept with her that first night. She was very pretty, Playmate material. Her legs were long, her breasts were huge and her face was flawless, but she was just decent in bed. She did everything, though nothing exceptionally well. It was the problem with pretty young women. A lot of them just wanted to lay there with their legs propped open, looking sexy, but they weren't willing to put forth the effort. And she didn't have the best ass.

Spirit, one of the other girls at the club, a redhead, was much better. She wasn't nearly as attractive, but she was a little spitfire in the bedroom. New at *Casanova's*, she was still saving up money for the boob job and other surgeries. Naked or otherwise, she had a black girl's butt. Spirit knew she wasn't the only one sleeping with Brady and she couldn't have cared less.

During Brigitte's stage performance, Spirit plopped down on Brady's lap, looked over at McCarthy and laughed.

"Honey, I'll never have sex with you because you're an old, freaky pervert. Maybe you should try that massage parlor on Broadway with the tired-out hoes your own age."

Sobered by rejection, McCarthy turned his focus to departmental gossip.

"Say, what's this about the killer havin Sonia Sanchez on his list? Where is she in this backward order that's supposed to be going on?"

"Don't know. Saint Claire thinks one of the reasons the killer mentioned Sanchez's name was to stir things up at the police department, and so far it's been pretty tense between those two."

McCarthy shrugged.

"They're both loopy if you ask me. A damn broad and a black!"

He hesitated, attempting to gauge Brady's level of trust in his new partner.

"You *have* heard what a lot of em are sayin about Saint Claire, haven't cha?

"That he knows more about the killer than he's telling?"

"That he is the killer. That he tried to murder Cap'n Slater. And you."

Brady sat back, sighing in disbelief.

"Now that makes totally no sense. Slater's like his best friend. Why would he kill Slater?"

"Cuz Cap'n Slater knows a lot about him. He knows all Saint Claire's secrets. He knows why Saint Claire became a cop, about the son's murder, about Joe Curry's death, the story about his messed up ear and probably some worse things. Maybe Saint Claire thinks he'll get senile and start talking."

"Saint Claire saved his life. Slater will tell you that. It was Saint Claire who discovered the mercury in the Jack Daniels bottles."

McCarthy nodded.

"Yeah, but how do you think it got there in the first place? Who sent that case of booze to the Cap'n's house? It was Saint Claire!"

"It was the killer."

"They're one in the same."

McCarthy raised his hands, conceding the night.

"Look Brady, you're free ta believe whatever you wanna believe, but I'm warnin ya. Don't trust Saint Claire. There's somethin about him that just ain't right, and it don't take a genius ta figure that out. Watch your back."

There was something in McCarthy's voice that caught Brady off-guard. Maybe he knew something.

"Okay I'm listening. Why are you so sure Saint Claire is the killer?"

McCarthy pointed a finger at Brady.

"That theory you had, the one about the killer workin backward in these murders from the end ta the beginning? Where'd that come from? Was that your idea, or was it Saint Claire's?"

Brady glanced up as he thought to remember.

"It, it was both of us. We came up with that theory together."

"Bullshit! Saint Claire led you down that road. He let you think it was both of you, but it was his idea. Come on, he's a fuckin psychology doctor workin as a cop! He's the killer, and he's leadin us all on ta believe what he wants us ta believe. Why? I don't know."

Brady paused, lowering his guard.

"How can you be so sure?"

"Just look at the killer's profile. He's a genius like you said, he knows about poisons, he knows how we cops operate, he's got money, he's manipulative, he's this detailed planner and he's more patient than any of us could ever think ta be."

McCarthy paused for effect.

"Does that sound like anyone you know or work with?"

He took Brady's silence as an answer.

"Yeah, it's Saint Claire. He's the killer. He's the only one anywhere on the scene who could be that smart."

CHAPTER 16

You understand the human mind, Professor. You know how it creates manifestations, paradigms and symbols to cope with concepts it determines as inconceivable. And so the human mind is able to conceive of murder, specifically within the context of reason and motive. Morality aside, humans and societies over time have been able to justify wholesale murder by creating wars, launching crusades and inventing causes, and they've sent us to do their dirty work.

But when we've returned from doing what they couldn't do, and we've continued to do what we naturally do, there has been panic and hysteria as human societies have struggled to determine reasons or motives where none have existed. We murder because it is what we do. We must feed.

Vlad Tepes was a man. He was one of us, but society made him a monster, a creature of darkness, the personification of evil. Thus the vampire is society's exaggerated manifestation of the killer. The collective human mind has fashioned an unholy creature who, though it lives, is without a soul, an immortal evil that stalks them nightly, seeking to fill a boundless void, a hunger that can never be sated.

It was four a.m. when he finally figured out one of the clues and understood where it pointed. At the bottom of the first letter were three series of numbers, a Greek expression, Δεν βρέθηκαν λέξεις, and a single word, *Tepes*. Vlad Tepes, son of Vlad Dracul, was the sadistic Wallachian prince who had put between 40,000 and 100,000 people to death, mostly by impalement.

Saint Claire turned on the computer, searching for a connection. In order to impale a victim, the prince attached horses to each of the victim's legs so that as the animals inched forward, a sharpened stake was forced into the body. According to records, the end of the stake was oiled and care was taken that the stake not be too sharp, lest the victim should die prematurely from shock at such extreme pain.

The stake was inserted into the body through the anus and was forced through the body until it emerged from the mouth. In other instances, victims were impaled through other body orifices or through the chest. Babies were sometimes impaled on a stake forced through their mother's hearts and out their chests.

Then Vlad would have the stakes erected and arranged in geometric patterns, often concentric circles. He left the gory bodies to rot for months, clotted blood oozing and yellow-green phlegm trailing down the stakes as bowels erupted or exploded from the accumulation of gas. Sometimes Vlad would command a feast amongst the forest of impaled corpses, and he would force noblemen and wealthy merchants to join him to partake in this gruesome banquet. Those who declined his invitation or complained about the stench quickly became additional timbers in his carnal forest.

The prince would impale thousands at a time, and on one occasion, he impaled ten thousand in the Transylvanian city of Sibiu in 1460. Yet despite the grandiosity of his public work, he tortured and killed thousands privately, employing creative methods, which included driving metal nails through the tops of heads, cutting off limbs, blinding, strangulation, cutting off noses and ears, the mutilating of sexual organs, scalping, skinning and burning alive.

Vlad was a killer who murdered without reason, without motive. In him killing was an abiding hunger that demanded blood. In the darkness that overtook him daily, he killed for the sheer need and impulse to kill. He fed on blood and death. Unable to conceive the genetic predisposition and depth of his irrational blood lust, society created the vampire myth to explain the behavior of the killer genotype. Thus Vlad Tepes, or Vlad *Dracula* became the first vampire.

In college, Saint Claire was fascinated with Bram Stoker's work, and he spent one of his winter breaks researching the prince and his vampiric legacy. Many years passed since that investigation, but when the detective saw three series of numbers and the word *Tepes* typed at the bottom of the first letter, he understood the latter reference. His profound challenge however, was to determine where the killer was trying to direct him next.

He studied the letter each night since he first read it, examining the numbers, searching for algorithms, experimenting with matrices and applying decoding techniques, but to no avail. *04:14:34, 09:02:06* and *40:11:27*. The numbers obviously meant something, but he spent himself trying to decipher their code, without the slightest success.

Tired of the numbers, he examined the typed word in both literal and non-literal contexts. He went to the Internet to re-research the life of Vlad Tepes and his methodology as well as recent scientific/psychological/social arguments concerning the *MAOA* genotype and theories about Natural Born Killers.

In the second letter, the killer referred to himself and other killers as a genetic archetype, as a genetic variation within the human gene pool, with a pronounced bloodlust and the unique ability to kill without compassion. Almost condescendingly, he called these killers the unacknowledged architects of human history.

By contrast, many genetic researchers argued against the existence of a distinct genotype. Others conceded that, while a predisposition for killing exists in some individuals, environmental factors probably influence whether the person becomes the soldier, who kills and commits atrocities for his county, the butcher, who hacks apart bloody corpses on a daily basis for his community, or the sociopath who begins a life of serial murder.

But it wasn't the musing about a *killer gene* that started Saint Claire up from sleep at four in the morning. It was a consideration of the killer's *modus operandi*, which included breaking in and entering homes to case his victims.

Saint Claire knew the killer slipped past security and through locked doors to enter Gladys Rosenthal's apartment on at least three occasions. And the revelation about Sanchez's medical condition from the second letter was evidence the killer had explored her bedroom.

With this in mind, Saint Claire wondered if his own home security was breached. When the detective discovered the mercury poisoning in Slater's home, he realized the killer must have examined bottles in the former police captain's bar in order to determine drinking habits. And when the detective saw the pre-printed return address label from his own desk on the Jack Daniel's case, he knew the killer had been in his library.

Fatigue was a factor. If Saint Claire's mind had been fresh, he would have correlated the clues sooner. As soon as he saw the label, he would have determined the killer *wanted* him to recognize the intrusion.

His mind rested, it came together at four a.m.: the killer in his library, and the word *Tepes* at the bottom of the first letter. Bolting from the bed, he went to his desk and got his glasses. It had been years since he saw the book, but he knew it was up there, high up on the left side of the room, on one of the shelves containing his classics collection.

Standing on the ladder, he tilted his head sideways as he strained to read titles from the book spines. Past Goethe, past Poe, past Stevenson, past Shelley and there it was, just out of his reach. So grasping a vertical bookshelf support, he pulled himself along on the rolling ladder toward the book.

At his desk, he blew the dust from the top of the book and placed it at desk center. Viewing the book from the bottom, he noticed a barely perceptible gap in the pages. Employing his letter opener, he flipped the book open and discovered the shiny, unsheathed CD-Rom. The killer had placed it within the pages of Bram Stoker's *Dracula*, at page 187.

CHAPTER 17

Of course if you're reading this letter, Professor, you know I've been in your home. If I wanted to kill you, you'd be dead. The first two letters were to set the stage, and for that reason I forced or cast the esteemed and illustrious Inspector Deuteronomy Saint Claire to deliver the prologue to my theatrical work of art to the police and public. But a necessary segue before the plot thickens.

Certainly you must have questions about me. The father in you wants to know who I am, the professor, what events in my childhood made me a killer and the detective a clue about how to stop me. This third and final letter to you will answer only two of your questions, but you'll discover the third at a price.

By now you realize I'm not your garden variety serial killer. Most of them I feel sorry for, because they're weak and have no idea what they are and why they do what they do. And just as it is with the other archetypes, some are mentally unstable, but because they kill, their behavior only intensifies their instability.

I am the Messiah because I have the vision to see the complete picture, backward and forward through time. I understand the archetypes, whether they are god-ordained or a necessary result from the diversity needs of evolution. Like Moses and Jesus, I was born to save a people. My death marked the beginning of a new understanding, a new era.

Saint Claire sat at his desk in a midnight blue cotton robe as he read the letter on the laptop screen. His hands were shaking as he scrolled down the page.

As you have no doubt have surmised, my creativity is somewhat limited by my current state of decomposition. So before you dismiss me as a purely intellectual killer who employs poisons because he eschews blood and violence, let me assure you I've tasted my share of blood, literally. I was as skilled with a knife, a piano wire, a razor and an ice pick as I was with poisons. I've shot, stabbed, bludgeoned and strangled my share of men, women and children. Never forget that I'm a killer. But then, so are you.

And now let me demonstrate how by divine providence you and I are engaged in this most necessary exercise. We will ultimately meet in the Garden of Gethsemane and you will have a destiny to fulfill, son of Simon. But for now, here's a gift.

Saint Claire's eyes flicked down to the bottom left corner of the screen, checking to determine the length of the file. Twenty-two pages. There were clues and references in the letter, and he realized he was so excited that he was reading past important details.

Taking a breath to calm himself, he determined he would read the letter through without stopping the first time, and later he would slow down to analyze it page by page, paragraph by paragraph, sentence by sentence and word by word, if necessary.

Eleven months ago, you were working on a case involving a killer who was stalking young men. His victims ranged between 17 and 23, and they were usually good-looking and muscular. The killer found them at raves and in dance clubs along Folsom and lured them away from friends and the crowds with the enticement of free alcohol, drugs and group sex orgies.

Indicative of your ineptitude, this killer had already murdered nine young men before you and the police were willing to recognize you had a serial killer on your hands. By this time, he had come to the realization that you all were bungling and ineffective, which you were. So he grew more bold and confident, and he began killing at least once every two weeks.

Do you realize, Professor, that San Francisco is a killer's paradise? According to your own statistics, the incompetent San Francisco police catch the killer in only half of the city's murders. So if you murder someone in this city, you stand a 50/50 chance of getting away with it. Those aren't bad odds. But that number is skewed even further if you decide to kill a black man. Odds get much better. You'll "most likely" get away with it; in fact, you've got a 70% chance of getting away with it.

That's where you and the police went wrong in the case of the so-called "Pretty Boy Slayer." Of the first five killings, four of the victims were black. I believe your moronic Chinese chief of police suggested the killings were gang related. But in the next four murders, three of the victims were white, and only then did the city begin to mount an investigation in earnest.

The victims were all found bound with clear duct tape and gagged with ping-pong balls in their mouths. All had been raped and tortured. In the later stages the killer mutilated or castrated the boys. He photographed his drugged victims in women's clothes and left an 8"x10" computer digitally printed picture beside each of the bodies.

In the newspapers, you said the killer was targeting "straight acting gay and bi-sexual males." I think you called them "down-lows" or something similar. You said it was the killer's way of "outing" these good-looking young men who were playing it both ways. You never mentioned the mutilations publicly or the fact that the boys were dressed in women's clothes in the photos, but you knew it was all the work of a single killer.

The pretty boys were dispatched with a single wound from an ice pick, placed on the back of the neck at the base of the skull. The upward path of the weapon usually severed the spinal cord and caused massive damage to the brain stem. In two of the later killings, the tip of the ice pick emerged through the left eye sockets of the victims, indicating the killer was right-handed.

The police, as always, assumed a purely reactionary role—managing crime scenes, mock-responding to community concerns, speculating about motive and ultimately hoping the killer would tire or move on to another city. But he didn't. He continued to kill right under your noses, and you couldn't catch him.

When he reached twenty-two murders, I turned my attention to Mr. Pretty Boy. For even natural killers, the first few are memorable. The first one or two are the most exciting, and that's because early on, our nerves are on edge, we're worried about being caught, the adrenaline rush is new, like that first hit from a crack pipe. Every killer remembers his first. But as the body count rises to ten, fifteen, twenty, we change as killers, especially if we've established a personality or reputation in the community.

In an attempt to re-live the rush and fear from that first time, we challenge you our antagonists in this drama. And the smarter you are and the more you are into us, the better. We want you to know us, we intentionally leave you clues, we seek to both impress and humiliate you.

There are few purists in the world, those who've distilled their art to its essence, and who by doing so, become divine beings. As such, we execute divine judgment and justice. All humans, being born in sin, are deserving of death. By one man sin entered the world, and death by sin, and so death passed upon all men, for that all have sinned. Thus every person born is destined to die, and mine is a necessary work.

The truth is, Professor, that God only can judge; and in his patience he intends to show that the judgment of men is worth little or nothing; if I've killed seven hundred, I've killed no one. I've made no difference in the world. I have done nothing yet.

Saint Claire paused, confused, and reread the last paragraph. He wasn't sure how literal the killer was being in the letter. Was he really dead? Had he killed seven hundred people or was the seven another Biblical reference? What was the object of this game?

It took me less than a week to discover the identity of your Pretty Boy Slayer. While in obtusity the police sought him in the nightclubs all along Folsom, I found him in a café on Market, at a place where the pretty boys went for late night breakfast after partying in the clubs. From the moment I made him, I noticed he was obviously not bright. He stood out because he was older and not so pretty.

When I slid into the seat across from him and peered into his soul, I saw a little boy, perhaps nine or ten, a little boy who had no father. The boy's mother was a drunk, and when drunk, a "take-home-and-bang-her" drunk who spent her weekends in bars.

She was a mean-spirited woman who belittled the boy both in private and before the random men who spent time in her room, the men who made her moan and cry out in the bed just on the other side of his bedroom wall. When he was young, he thought his mother was being hurt in there, so he would sometimes open her door and watch.

One time when he was thirteen, his mother came home and caught him in her room, trying on one of her bras, a mini skirt and a pair of her high heels. Livid, she beat him with a broom stick and called him a fag. She told him he was going to die and burn in Hell.

From that time on, she referred to him as her "immoral little freak show." When he was 16, she moved out of the apartment to shack up with a new boyfriend. She continued to pay rent for three months and came by with groceries once, but that was the last he saw of her. She died of a heroin overdose on his seventeenth birthday.

The Pretty Boy Slayer, whose actual name was Donald Lazarus, committed his first murder at age 19. He was seeing a beautiful 15-year-old boy with wavy black hair and striking green eyes. He helped young Austin discover the power of his sexuality, but all the while he knew Austin was destined for someone better, someone more handsome than himself.

Besides that, Austin came from a strict religious family that would never approve of their son's lifestyle experiment. As a result, Austin was very careful to hide all aspects of the relationship. He would never see Donald in public, he didn't want Donald to meet or know any of his friends and he didn't want to know Donald's friends.

It was easy. He got Austin drunk and high one night, and then he strangled him in his sleep. Donald almost lost his resolve when the boy's eyes opened as he gasped, dying. It was difficult for him to dress Austin's dead body, but he put him in a dress, taped his wrists together, his ankles together and left him at the entrance of his high school where he was found the next morning.

He didn't kill again for a year and a half. During that time he had a job at a computer software company. He tried to fit in. He even tried to have a girlfriend, but she ended up being like his mother. His asshole supervisor had it out for him, constantly harassed him and finally found a way to fire him.

Frustrated, he began to drink heavy, and within weeks after being fired, Donald had murdered a second victim. Now because the first murder set the standard, he tried to make the second match the first, only with slight improvements. He placed a ping-pong ball in this pretty boy's mouth and taped the mouth shut with the clear duck tape.

In subsequent murders, he added the digital photographs printed from his computer. And later he began with the mutilation and the castration, but he castrated the boys only so he could save the severed penises, testicles and nipples pickled in formaldehyde in his Mason jar collection.

Now I know all this because he told me about himself in slow detail before I killed him. When I murder serial murderers, I go to great lengths to kill them in the exact way they dispatch their victims. So ironically, the police mistake the murdered serial murderer they've found for just another of the serial murderers' victims. You no doubt remember Donald Lazarus's name. He was the slayer's last known victim.

The FBI estimated two years ago that there were about 60 serial murderers operating within the United States. If their numbers were accurate, then I've personally cut that number in half since that time. Not because I'm on your side, but the culling of the weak is a necessary work. Killing a killer has a special rush for me, like a vampire latching onto another vampire and sucking him dry, absorbing his power. I've traveled the country, systematically eliminating killers who've succumbed to base perversions and others who dishonor the genotype.

Isn't that a little ironic, a serial killer whose victims are serial killers? But I'm the best there's ever been. I'm alone an artist in the company of mere technicians. I am the savior.

Sensing my divinity, Donald submitted to me, weeping. I taped his wrists together and his ankles together. I put the ping-pong ball in his mouth and taped it shut. Taking his ice pick, the same he had used to kill his victims, taking that ice pick in both my hands, I pulled him up to his knees, his head into my lap, his face forward. Then aligning the sharp tip at the nape of his neck, just above the spinal cord, I stabbed, pulling the pick upward toward me through his brain, favoring my right wrist, adjusting so that its tip exited his left eye.

CHAPTER 18

Sonia made Rico's favorite dinner and bought her daughter's favorite dessert. The *carnitas* were seasoned and roasted in the way *Abuela* taught her to do it, and the *pico de gallo* was prepared with fresh, redolent cilantro, spicy green chilies, overripe limes and sweet savory tomatoes. After roasting the pork, Sonia shredded it so it could be placed in the white corn tortillas she had made herself from a recipe passed down over five generations. Spanish rice and frijoles *negros refritos* balanced the plate.

For dessert, she served a fruit basket cake, a light yellow four-layered cake with whipped cream, kiwis, strawberries and bananas from her friend Ingrid's bakery. Tati first had the cake at her cousin's *Quinceañera* and requested it as often as she could have it.

After dinner, Sonia sat the children at the kitchen table, issuing a warning that she had something important to discuss with them. She could sense both children were alarmed, so she tried to be direct.

"I'm not going to bad talk your father, so this isn't like that."

She looked into their eyes.

"This is something we have never discussed, but I think you children are aware that Antonio likes, well he likes other *men*. Your father is gay, and he was even when we were married."

She blinked back tears, trying to be strong for the kids, who nodded.

"Well, he married another man when the city was allowing it, and right after that called me and told me he was HIV positive. He said he was exposed to the virus, but he hadn't developed AIDS."

Tatiana guessed.

"Dad has AIDS?"

Sonia bowed her head.

"Yes."

"Is he going to die?"

She shrugged, resolve shaken, not wanting to continue.

"He's taking medications. They have a lot of new drugs that help."

Rico knew his mother. He sensed it. Taking Tatiana's hand in his left and Sonia's in his right, he sought to help his mother.

"Tati, I think what Mom's trying to say is she has AIDS, too. Right, Mom?"

Sonia's face was hidden as she bowed, weeping. She could only nod while clasping her children's hands at each side.

Tears began to stream down Tatiana's face.

"Are you going to die, Mom? I don't want you to die!"

Sonia put her arm around her daughter, pulling the girl to her bosom.

"No, no Tati, I'm not going to die, not any time soon. I don't have AIDS, but I am HIV positive."

The vision of his mother and little sister crying became too much for Rico who closed his eyes, trying to control his emotions, tears running down his cheeks.

Sonia spoke to comfort the children.

"The drugs are helping. I'm feeling very healthy."

She pulled Rico close, massaging his slight shoulders.

"You know that basketball player, Magic Johnson? I think he's been HIV positive for over twenty years, and he's still alive. Because of the drugs, a lot of people never get AIDS. Thank God I was diagnosed early."

Telling the children about her condition was the most difficult thing she had ever done, and yet there was more.

"You guys, you know how when I made captain I promised I'd always be honest with you, no matter what?"

Rico nodded and Tatiana sniffed twice in acknowledgement.

"Well, I'm going to have to ask you move into your Tia Rosie's house in Vallejo for awhile, for just a little while."

"Tia Rosie's? I don't wanna go there! I wanna stay with you. And what about my school?"

"I'll have to work that out. Rico, maybe you could drive her?"

He seemed confused.

"Of course I can, but what's going on?"

She stood, crossing her arms, not quite sure how to begin. She took a deep breath.

"There's a killer we've been after, and he's very bad, he's a real creep. But he knows who I am, and he's threatened me."

Rico put an arm over his frightened sister's shoulders.

"How? How did he threaten you?"

"Well, he's been in this house, and he knows about you and Tati. I just don't want anything to happen to either of you."

"Mom, you didn't answer my question. How did he threaten you? What he say?"

As she looked toward her worried children, withered before her at the table, she never imagined it would have come to this. When she married Antonio two decades earlier, she was sure they would be together forever.

Rico looked like his father, dark with a Spanish countenance. Yet his eyes were light colored and soft like his mother's. He dressed well, kept his moustache neatly trimmed and always wore clean smelling cologne. He would turn twenty-two in a few weeks.

Tatiana was younger, and a little overweight for her height, but a nice looking girl. There were complications during her birth, and though doctors assured Sonia no damage had occurred, Sonia secretly worried her daughter was a little mentally challenged. Tati was empathetic and sensitive, but she didn't walk, speak or read as readily as her brother did, and sometimes she was slow to respond to comments or instructions. Feeling guilty, Sonia always indulged the girl.

Sonia and the children had been through so much together, and before them was perhaps their greatest challenge yet.

"Mom? What did he say to threaten you?"

She looked down, determined to be honest, though aware that the words would hurt her children.

"He said he's going to kill me within the next three weeks."

CHAPTER 19

"The chief is forcing me to take the next two days off. I tried to stay on the case, but you know how this department is. They won't let anyone work overtime. Come on, I've got nothing else to do! I'm going with you."

Saint Claire did not react, though he looked up from his reading.

"You have a wife and daughters. You need to be spending the time you have off with them."

"It's two days. They won't miss me. Besides, the trip will give us a chance to get to know each other better. Who knows, we might even be able to figure out when and where the next murder will be."

"Hey, I'm taking this trip and these two days off partly to get away from you. And I'm sorry, but I don't want to know you better. I'm going there because my brother's dead. Maybe you see New Orleans as a chance to whore around for a couple days with a pretty Creole girl or two, but not at my expense."

Brady sighed.

"Exactly my point. I don't know who's been filling your head, but I'm not like that. If you let me go, you'll get a chance to see who I really am."

"I'm a psychologist and a detective. I already know who you really are."

Saint Claire sensed the resentment he felt for Brady. Though he determined he would not allow Katrina's words to affect him, the images she spawned were there in his thoughts. He had been avoiding Brady's calls and making himself busy preparing for the trip so he didn't have to meet with his partner. Taking a breath, he resolved to overcome Katrina's spell, and yet not to overcompensate.

"I'll be busy with the funeral the whole first day."

"That's fine. I'll find something to do, or I could go with you if you let me."

"You ever been to a black Baptist funeral?" He laughed to himself. "Of course not, you're a white boy from Boston!"

Saint Claire looked over at Brady.

"I just think I'd rather go alone. Nothing personal"

Brady interpreted the eye contact as a break.

"What if I were to tell you the chief ordered me to go to New Orleans with you? To watch you and report what you're up to?"

"I'd tell you she ordered me to send your ass packin back to Boston. And said to take McCarthy with you."

Saint Claire turned toward his partner.

"But when it comes right down to it, you're a grown man. You don't need my permission to go to New Orleans if you want to pay for a ticket and go. You can do whatever you want. So why are you asking me?"

"Out of respect. I already bought my ticket, but I won't go if you don't want me to."

Saint Claire remembered he was beginning to like Brady, beginning to enjoy the idea of having a partner again.

"All right, you can go. But it's a *black* funeral. People *dance*, and I already know you've got no rhythm. Don't embarrass me."

Deuteronomy Saint Claire and Tom Brady sat in a terminal at San Francisco International, awaiting a flight into Louis Armstrong International Airport in New Orleans.

Brady was restless. He watched Saint Claire review his interview notes for a few minutes before interrupting.

"You nervous?"

"Why should I be nervous? It's a funeral, and it's my brother's, not mine."

"I don't know. With everything going on, have you thought that maybe this killer might have something to do with your brother's death?"

Saint Claire closed the folder.

"The thought crossed my mind. I'll check it out, but it just doesn't seem likely."

"Why's that?"

"Because New Orleans is too disconnected. It's too remote. All the killer's murders are interdependent, leaving me to conclude they'll all have to occur in San Francisco. It'd be too complicated to leave here, take a murder there and come back here."

Brady thought a moment.

"Yeah, but what if the killer's changed his mind about making everything so connected? Maybe he's thinking to change his tactics."

"He can't."

"Of course he can. What do you mean he can't?"

The time had come. Saint Claire decided over the last four hours that, if the killer intended to set him up for one or more of the murders, his reliance on Slater as a confidant and advocate was precarious at best.

When Saint Claire visited Slater earlier that afternoon, he'd recognized for perhaps the first time that the incident had exacted a toll on his former captain. Slater's complexion was wan, his breathing shallow. The flimsy hospital robe provided glances of his sagging naked genitals and bald, wrinkled backside. His desiccated feet were bare, his hair was thin and matted while coarse white whiskers jutted from his cheeks and chin. He seemed withered. In the matter of a week, his friend Slater had become old and vulnerable. It would be easy for Internal Affairs to dismiss the former captain as mentally traumatized and unstable after his ordeal.

Sitting there, Saint Claire decided to place greater trust in Brady. Brady was a womanizer, insensitive and possibly even a racist, but he had proven himself. He never lied to the chief or Sanchez, but he protected several quiet details about the case that Saint Claire had shared with him. Brady's loyalty notwithstanding, there was no one else Saint Claire could trust.

"The killer's dead, or so he claims. According to his first letter, he was already dead ten days before Gladys Rosenthal's murder."

Brady furrowed his brow and shook his head.

"That's impossible! What do you mean *dead*? Dead, like in the ground?"

"In the grave."

Face contorted, Brady leaned forward, whispering.

"But this guy's still murdering people! How can he do that if he's dead?"

"He says he set up the murders before he died. Each murder sets off the next one in the series."

Saint Claire sighed, continuing.

"So far, it's at least possible he's committing these murders from the grave. Just can't be sure yet."

Brady was trying to think back, still sorting through the details of the murders.

"He wrote you this in a letter?"

"That and other things. I'll show it to you when we get to New Orleans."

Brady thought further.

"Wait. We already know this killer knows you, and he knows Slater, but if he was dead more than what, twenty-five days ago? He can't possibly know me."

"Makes you a *wild card*. That is, if he's really dead."

Brady nodded.

"Yeah."

The woman at the terminal gate welcomed travelers flying to New Orleans and announced boarding for first class passengers. Zipping his bag, Saint Claire stood.

"Guess you'll get on later?"

Brady was still rapt. He stood.

"You're the smartest guy I've ever met. So what do you think?"

"About what?"

"About the killer being already dead. You think he's telling us the truth?"

Saint Claire withdrew the boarding pass from a jacket pocket.

"It's possible. He's a megalomaniac. He wants to be the greatest killer of all time. But I don't necessarily trust he's telling the truth."

"Why's that."

Saint Claire smirked, shrugging.

"He's a killer. He gets his thrills tricking and hurting unsuspecting people. And I'm supposed to believe what this guy says? This is the bastard who murdered my son! No, I hope to *God* he is alive. Maybe I'll end up going with him, but if I have my way, I want to be the one to send his ass straight to Hell."

CHAPTER 20

He hadn't visited in the last four years, not since a couple years before the hurricane. Normally he didn't mind traveling, but there was no direct flight between San Francisco and New Orleans and the convoluted itinerary had always been vexing. He was anxious to get back to Louisiana.

New Orleans always held an inimitable place in his heart. He was born and raised in Thibodaux, and yet upon his first visit to the Big Easy at seventeen-years-old, he knew he was home. From the beginning, the city was within him. Even after he moved away, he could feel the sultry streets pulsing, traversing his body, the spirit of its inhabitants in his blood, coursing, dancing. His heartbeat was the faint rhythm that set its life in motion. And when he drew a breath, the very city breathed with him.

It was why the hurricane was such a blow. Even in San Francisco, he felt it coming. He knew there would be death and devastation long before the federal government realized its own shortsightedness. And he knew a hurricane dubbed Katrina would have a special significance in his life.

His wife insisted the storm was her own spirit striking a blow at the *Voudoun* who had hexed her. After the storm, Katrina claimed the *Voudoun* was dead and the spell could finally be lifted. And so began the pressure to bring a *Voudoun* to San Francisco who could lift the curse.

Deuteronomy had watched the news reports on the storm, uncertain of what he should do. He wanted to get on a plane and fly down to help, but the city and everyone on the ground there, inhabitants and rescuers alike, were at the mercy of nature, poor planning and bigotry. He felt helpless waiting, and though he lingered in California for a cue to go home, it never came.

Bracing himself in the seat, he heard the jet's tires screech on the tarmac as the engines reversed and wing flaps opened, wind plowing through them. At last, he was home. He sat lost in thoughts of his youth, remembering an old song. He knew what it "means" to have missed New Orleans; he missed it each night and day, the longer he stayed away.

The moss covered vines, the tall sugar pines, where mockingbirds used to sing, he wanted to see the lazy Mississippi a hurryin into Spring; the Mardi Gras, the memories of Creole tunes that filled the air, he had dreams of oleanders in June, while wishing that he was there.

"Hey Mr. Elitist, you going to sit there all night or are you going to get off this plane?"

Brady had a black leather carry-on bag strapped to his shoulder.

"You're sitting up here sipping wine and having a meal while I had a little boy next to me with his toy gun in my ear. They gave me peanuts. You coming or what?"

Saint Claire stood, taking a breath.

"I'm home. I could stay here and never go back."

The nighttime shuttle ride from the airport to the hotel was silent as he compared images in his memory with the scenes along the way. He steadied his breathing to calm himself. The air was warm and familiar. Brady nodded, struggling to stay awake.

Because it was Brady's first visit to New Orleans, Saint Claire made reservations at a hotel on *Rue Toulouse* in the *Vieux Carre* within the French Quarter, where his partner would have better access to the city and its attractions. Saint Claire directed the driver to take a detour down *Rue Dauphine*, running parallel to *Rue Bourbon*, in order to give Brady intersection glimpses of the most famous street in the South.

The lobby area of the four-star hotel was elegant, a mélange of 19th century design and decor with modern touches that were uniquely New Orleans. Saint Claire booked adjoining rooms, each decorated in soft cream, beige and gold furnishings. Both had balconies framed with intricate wrought iron designs overlooking a beautiful inner courtyard.

Downstairs at dinner, Saint Claire smiled when offered libations from the bar.

"My friend here will have a Jack Daniel's on the rocks, and so will I."

Food and alcohol in their systems, the men returned to conversation.

"Thanks, Saint Claire."

The detective laughed.

"Why? Did someone *improperly* inform you that I was picking up the tab?"

It was the first time he could remember seeing Saint Claire really smile.

"No, I mean for letting me come here with you. I'm sure it must be hard losing your brother and all, and I kinda just invited myself along."

"No, I'm actually glad you came. It'll give us a chance to talk. And being away will probably give us both a little better perspective on the case, you know, detach a little. Because I have a feeling the worst is ahead of us."

Saint Claire took the bill and placed his credit card in the folder.

"Come on. Let's go have a cigar."

Thirty minutes later, both men sat at the outdoor table, brandy filled snifters on hand. The smoke that ascended from the cigars, like a burnt offering, brought a sense of appeasement and ease to the men.

Brady sighed, settling back into his seat.

"So did you find out from anyone how your brother died?"

"Hurricane. Katrina hurricane."

Brady squinted.

"How's that?"

Saint Claire nodded.

"Sam, my brother, was living in Lakeview when the storm hit. His wife said the evacuation was going slower than it should have because her bed-ridden mother lived with them and arrangements were being made to transport her out."

He sipped the brandy and continued.

"They lived in a two story house, so they figured the upstairs wouldn't be affected in a flood. My brother was in the process of moving all their household belongings upstairs when the water broke through the floodwalls of the 17th Street Canal, not far away."

He crossed his arms, drawing a breath.

"Within minutes, the whole area was flooded, fourteen feet deep in some places. Up on the second floor, Sam's family and all their possessions were safe, but the downstairs was completely flooded. They were rescued after five days."

"Okay, so how'd he die?"

"Mold. When the water receded, he started scraping up the mud and gutting the bottom floor, but there was some kind of mold thing that happened down there. It caused respiratory problems for him that affected his heart. Died of congestive heart failure. So when it comes down to it, he was just another victim of Katrina."

Brady nodded.

"Indirectly, I guess."

"Makes you wonder how many people that hurricane really killed."

For a minute neither man spoke.

Fireflies blinked in the flowering trees like Christmas lights. The nighttime air was warm and flowing, with jasmine breath. A jazzy, syncopated, staccato trumpet solo pitched and fell above the faint clamor of Bourbon Street revelers heard in the distance.

Saint Claire closed his eyes, taking it all in, savoring the return of so many cherished, nearly lost memories. His heart reached back, across time, distance and even death to find his mother, young and pretty, his father, still principled and solemn, and his big brother Sam, a teenager, grinning with pride on the day he received his driver's license. Now Sam was dead, at fifty-nine. He was too young to just die.

Tom Brady's eyes wandered through the trees in the courtyard, unremarkable trees except for the fact that many were laced with beads. All over the trees and balconies there were beads, some glistening in the nighttime lights, others after having hung there for a few seasons through sun and storm, had lost all luster. There were thousands of beads, young and old, intact and broken, bright and moribund.

The thought of his grandfather struck him. *Governor*, that's what people used to call him. Tom always wondered why. Jack Brady had been the deputy mayor of Boston for two terms, but he had never aspired for any statewide office. In fact, he warned Tom never to run for office. Instead, he predicted his grandson would one day become the police chief, a leader with the right principles, fighting the bad guys from that station.

Tom felt ashamed for selling out the hopes Jack Brady had for him. He felt like a cheap whore. Yet as much as he wanted to blame Andrea, he knew deep inside that she had been honest with him all along. It wasn't her fault. It was his own, for his being weak.

There still was a trace of hope, but it would involve taking on his wife, and more than that, his own inner demons. The thought of such a conflict always induced him to the first of two convenient defaults, which was drinking. And the first usually led to the second, which was "women."

He swigged the last of the brandy and looked over at his partner.

"So are we gonna to hit the town or what?"

Saint Claire checked his watch.

"No, you go. I've got a busy day tomorrow. Bourbon Street is just a couple blocks away. Follow the sound. I'm sure you'll get along over there just fine without me."

Just then, Saint Claire's phone rang. Feinting disinterest, Brady studied Saint Claire's animated reaction to whoever was on the line.

"You really went in there and visited him? Are you okay?"

Glancing over, Saint Claire recognized he was being watched.

"Hey, I really want to talk to you about this. I'll call you from my room. Give me five minutes."

"Who was that? Your wife?"

Saint Claire felt no need to lie.

"No. A friend. Just a friend from back home."

CHAPTER 21

"So, you *have* heard they both went to New Orleans for the brother's funeral?"

"I have. That either means Brady's putting in a convincing performance in order to gain Saint Claire's trust or he's been won over."

"Of course he's been won over. Men will *always* side with other men. It's why we're always getting fucked!"

Sonia Sanchez had just finished having a light dinner with Chief Rebecca Leong and her family. Rebecca's private study was on the far north side of the house, away from the bedrooms and all other activity. In the room were a desk and computer, a wood carved Buddhist temple, facing east, and a gym, consisting of a treadmill, an "abdominal crunch" machine and a rack of weights. The women sat just outside the door on a patio, each puffing a cigar.

"Oh I wouldn't be too sure about that, Sonia. Brady's smarter than he comes across. And from what I've heard from reliable sources, he'll do what's right. If Saint Claire's the killer, or if he has anything to do with this killer, Brady'll help us take him down."

"We'll see. Am I being paranoid not trusting men?"

"I don't know. I can't imagine how I'd feel in your place."

Sonia sighed.

"Brady seems all right. Have you seen his wife?"

"Yes?"

"I don't get it. Does she seem like his type?"

Rebecca leaned closer, shivering in the cold air.

"I don't know. Does my husband seem like *my* type?"

Sonia looked toward the other side of the house in the direction of the family.

"No, he doesn't, and I'll leave it at that."

Five days earlier, the women's relationship had been much different. Rebecca did not react to the killer's revelation that Sonia was HIV positive, but she became more and more perturbed in the days that followed. She avoided Sonia, and when she reluctantly agreed to Sonia's request to have lunch and talk, Rebecca attempted to cancel. Sonia however, was insistent.

During lunch, Rebecca was slow to share her feelings and opinions, but she finally let go. News of that magnitude was supposed to be *shared* between close friends. Friends shared their burdens, their joys, their pains and their fears. Rebecca told Sonia it felt like a slap in the face to find out the way she did, in a killer's letter.

Sonia countered that she was distraught and afraid. She asked Rebecca to consider her situation as a single mother. And she didn't want to put Rebecca in the awkward position of deciding about whether or not to take administrative action on the matter or to maintain the confidence. After two hours of talking, their friendship emerged stronger.

Cigars extinguished, they re-entered the house and sat in the lounge area of Rebecca's study.

"You know what I'm curious to see?" Sonia asked.

"What's that?"

"If the killer strikes while Saint Claire's away in New Orleans."

CHAPTER 22

He was up at first light, curious to see with his own eyes if the stories and televised images were true. He walked along the narrow *Rue Dauphine*, peering down alleys and up balconies in the slanted light. He could see where construction crews made repairs here and there, but this was the French Quarter. He didn't expect to see any real damage until he reached Canal Street. He wanted first to see New Orleans East, where he heard the earliest flooding had occurred.

He hired a cab on Canal Street to drive him up I-10 toward the Ninth Ward. He knew the area well because he had an apartment in Edgelake when he was at Louisiana State for undergraduate studies.

Volumes of descriptions and photographs could have never prepared him for the devastation he saw when he crossed the Industrial canal and got on Claiborne Avenue.

Before going back to the hotel, he asked the driver to take him through Lakeview, where his sister-in-law still lived, and through Metairie, where his niece had a house. By 11:30, he was overwhelmed. Something was still very wrong in New Orleans.

He got back to the hotel a little after noon. The funeral was at 2:00, and he wondered whether Brady was up. Somewhere in the early morning he thought he heard Brady's voice along with a woman's. Births and funerals waited for no one. He knocked on the door.

After almost a minute, Brady opened the door, tying his robe.

"It's you. Good morning. What time is it?"

"Bout 12:15. Morning's over."

"What time's the funeral?"

A half-naked, brown-skinned woman hurried past in the background, gathering clothing. Saint Claire hesitated, but he suppressed an impulse to comment.

"It's at two, but we'll have to leave by 1:30."

"What are you doing for breakfast?"

"It's lunchtime. House of Blues. Girl at the desk said the jambalaya's worth the trip."

As promised, the food was wonderful. And yet, Saint Claire was in a daze through most of lunch.

"You seem sad. Is it the funeral?"

Saint Claire looked toward Brady, almost laughing.

"No. As you'll see, funerals here in New Orleans are anything but sad."

And yet melancholy overcame his expression.

"It's not my brother's death that's bothering me. It's the death of the New Orleans I knew and loved. I was out there. It felt like the end of the world."

CHAPTER 23

The after-funeral repast at Sam Saint Claire's house was for family only, but Brady was invited by Mignon, Sam's middle daughter and Deuteronomy's favorite niece.   Initially, Deuteronomy thought she extended the kindness because Brady was her uncle's guest, as a token of respect. But when he noticed her eyes trained on Brady as he came through the door, and then the giddy sense of curiosity in her smile, he realized Mignon was intoxicated, either from alcohol or from the charms of Tom Brady. He would make sure it wasn't Brady.

"He's married with two daughters in San Francisco. Besides that, he's not your type."

Mignon laughed.

"How interesting you should provide such specific information, Uncle. Until two hours ago, I had never met Mr. Brady."

Brady smiled and shrugged.

"I don't know, but I think he's trying to protect you."

Mignon leaned over and kissed Saint Claire's cheek.

"I love you, Uncle, but I am thirty-five-years-old. I've *been* out there in the big bad world for a few years now, so if you feel the need to protect someone, protect him."

Mignon was a light-skinned, pretty woman who dressed stylishly and exuded confidence. Her maternal grandmother was half Choctaw Indian, and it showed in Mignon's high cheekbones and long, wavy, jet-black hair. She worked out long hours to keep her stomach firm, her waist small and her legs toned, but it was her well-shaped butt that stood out in just about anything she wore.

She married young and had a thirteen-year-old son, Louis. She had been widowed eight years earlier when her husband was shot to death by the gang members who robbed him and stole his Escalade. After her husband's death, Mignon did not date because her son was young and she made ample money to live without spousal income and interference. However, since her son was older, she was more inclined to date.

The bottom floor of the Sam's Lakeview home was still incomplete, but the kitchen, always the most important room in that Saint Claire home, was equipped and functional. Neighbors had dropped off rum cakes, pecan pies, fried chicken, gumbo, catfish, collard greens, fried soft shelled crabs, Creole rabbit, crawfish *etouffee* and oyster stew.

While Deuteronomy and his brothers Pierre and Henri sat upstairs and drank a cognac toast to their departed brother, the laws of attraction drew Brady to Mignon and her to him. The two sat on the porch swing outside the front door.

"So you're married? That's too bad."

"Meaning you would date me if I wasn't?"

She smiled.

"I suppose I would."

"Can I hold you to that? Give me your word?"

She sighed, half-laughing, pausing.

"Yeah, go on a date with you. Can't promise anything else, though."

"I'm divorcing my wife as soon as I get back."

She looked back toward the door.

"Mr. Brady, you have no idea how many times I've heard that line."

"I'm serious. Has nothing to do with you. It's something I've needed to do for years. I just never..."

He hesitated, shocked by his own frankness.

"I never had the balls. I just went through the motions because I didn't know what I wanted. I tried, once."

"And you know what you want now?"

He leaned toward her, peering into her eyes.

"I think I do. And I know what I don't want. That whole marriage was a lie, all for her benefit. I'm moving into my own place once I get back to San Francisco. And then I'll call you."

Mignon sat back, sipping on her *mojito*.

"I won't hold my breath, Mr. Brady. But if you call, I'll definitely answer."

"Can I come in?"

Saint Claire hesitated, uncomfortable.

"I have to return a phone call in a few minutes."

"I won't be long. I promise. I just need to ask you something."

A half-full cognac bottle and a glass sat on the desk in Saint Claire's hotel room. Next to the desk sat two leather armchairs with a small glass topped table in between. Brady took a seat in the chair on the left.

"Can I have a drink?"

Saint Claire wagged his head, resigned.

"It's a serve yourself bar."

He sat in the other chair as his partner tilted the bottle.

"And while you're at it, pour me one. It's been a long day."

After a few minutes of silent sipping, Brady began.

"You know, I was sitting in my room thinking about the killer and I got an idea."

"Congratulations. I had given up on you. Go on."

"If he's already dead like he says in the letter, and the murders are interdependent like you said, who's to say something hasn't miscued on its own? I mean we're two weeks in and there've only been two murders. Maybe someone did or didn't do something and his whole series of killings has already been disrupted without our help. You ever think about that?"

Saint Claire nodded.

"I have, but it's just wishful thinking. You have to realize our killer is the consummate planner. As more and more time passes, he'll leave less and less of this to chance."

He sipped his drink.

"If there've only been two killings, it's because he wants the finale to be spectacular. Make no mistake—the next two weeks will be murder."

Only after a third cognac pour did Brady work up the nerve to broach the subject.

"So your son was murdered? What happened?"

Saint Claire's glare was contemptuous, angry.

"I think you've mistakenly assumed that we're somehow friends because I let you come here. You're way out of line bringing up my son. See the door?"

"Why? What's the big secret? Look, I'm sorry your son was murdered, but I didn't do it. You're a psychology doctor! You know how it works. Maybe if you just talked to someone about it, it wouldn't be such an uncomfortable subject."

Saint Claire stood.

"I think you should leave!"

"How about this? I'll tell you something personal about me, and if that helps you trust me, then maybe you'll open up and share something about yourself."

Brady stood, approaching Saint Claire.

"My wife is a *lesbian*."

"You mean bi?"

"No, not bi. She's a lesbian. We don't have sex at all. It's been that way from the start."

Saint Claire seemed uneasy, but as he thought of Andrea, his natural curiosity was irrepressible.

"So when you married her you knew she was?"

"Yeah."

"So why'd you marry her?"

Brady took his glass and poured another drink. He sat.

"The simplest questions always have the most complicated answers. You ever wonder why that is?"

"Maybe it's because the simplest people always somehow manage to create the most complicated situations? You're saying you, with full knowledge beforehand, married an avowed lesbian?"

Brady nodded and took a big swig of the cognac.

"We had an arrangement. She was an up and coming executive with a conservative company and she needed a husband. I was a playboy who thought having a rich wife who wasn't jealous would be ideal. So we just agreed to get married for appearances. And it offered certain social advantages. She's always had female partners and I've been allowed to do my thing."

"And you've never had sex with her?"

"Are you kidding? The thought of a real penis going in her would totally gross her out. With the girls in both cases it was artificial insemination *á la* turkey-baster. She supplied the *Hustler* magazines and the beakers."

Saint Claire poured a drink and sat in the chair across from Brady. He regretted he had asked the personal questions he did because, on a *quid pro quo* level, he knew it entitled Brady to pry into his life. In for a penny, in for a pound.

"So you've spent the last fifteen years in a false marriage?"

"Yeah, but it's not as strange as it seems. At least I'm real about it, but there are a lot of men out there just like me. They just don't know it."

Saint Claire considered his own marriage. Looking over, he shrugged.

"You're probably right about that."

He paused before continuing.

"I guess a guy like you, a playboy, doesn't believe in being loyal to someone and honoring commitments, right?"

"That's not true. I want those things. That's why I'm leaving my wife when I get home. I want to find a person I can love and have something real with. If nothing else, this trip taught me that."

Saint Claire understood the inference. He saw Brady laughing and flirting with Mignon earlier.

"It's been an emotional day for me."

"I can understand that. I'm sorry about your brother."

Saint Claire bowed his head.

"Yeah Sam, he was always my hero growing up. More like a father to me than a brother."

After a moment, Brady broke the silence.

"I know we haven't known each other long and I understand you don't consider me a friend, but I admire you. I have from the first day. And I hope someday you *will* consider me a friend."

Saint Claire could only nod.

"What happened with your son?"

"He was murdered."

Brady remained silent, placing the onus on Saint Claire to continue.

"This was thirteen years ago. I was teaching over at Berkeley then. I had a busy schedule. My son, Christian, was in his freshman year at USF. He was living on campus."

Saint Claire glanced sidelong at Brady and continued.

"He was a bright boy. Always top of the class, model student. I was just so busy back then. The last time I talked to him we argued about a personal matter, after he moved out. He thought I was being dogmatic and judgmental and I thought he was being selfish and irresponsible. It was a heated argument, a battle of wills, and it ended on a... negative note."

He bowed his head.

"Two days later I got a call from the San Francisco Police Department. They told me my son had been murdered, the most recent in a series of murders where the killer stabbed victims to death, wrapped them in heavy wool blankets soaked in lard and burned the bodies. They called it the wick effect."

He sipped the drink.

"High temperature burn, low flame. The killer put his victims in the bathtub and lit the blanket with charcoal starter. After burning for hours, everything was gone, bones reduced to a grey powder. Only way they identified most of the victims was through dental records, and that was if they could get those. But this killer had a trademark. He always cut off his victims' pinkie fingers so they could be identified. All that was left from my son was his pinkie finger."

"Sick fuck! They ever catch the bastard?"

"No, not even after he killed three more boys. That's when I got fed up. I didn't think the cops were even trying to find the killer, so I started investigating the murders on my own. I read the cases and I studied whatever evidence was available. After about six weeks I was onto him, and I almost got him."

He sat back in the chair, straightening his knees to extend his legs.

"That's when I met Derrick Slater. He was there because one of his detectives back then by the name of Joe Curry had been trailing me. It was strange how it happened, but Slater shot the killer in the shoulder. The guy went down, but he managed to get up and get away. He saw me. He saw my face and somehow found out who I was, because after that I started getting the occasional letter from him. In some he taunted me and in others he challenged me."

"And that made you quit your job at Berkeley and join the police?"

"Not exactly. Curry and I became friends after that, and working alongside him for a few weeks, he asked if I wanted to join the force where I'd be in better position find the killer. I figured there I'd have the support of the police department and all its resources."

Brady was engrossed.

"Did you get him?"

"He finished out his series of seven, and then he changed his MO. And when we started closing in on him that time he changed again. He's been killing in the city for years. He takes breaks, once for three years, another time for two, but he always comes back to San Francisco. You read the letter. He said it was his favorite city."

Brady recoiled as he realized what Saint Claire was intimating.

"It's the same killer? You think the guy we're after is the same killer who murdered your son. That's why you know him so well? That's why this is so personal for you?"

Saint Claire shrugged, nodding as he turned toward Brady.

"Yes. That's why it's personal."

"So if he's really dead, this thirteen year episode's almost over for you! In two weeks he disappears forever and you can get back to your life."

Saint Claire's expression was morose.

"You know, after all these years I don't know if I have a life to get back to. For thirteen years, my life has been about tragedy and death and I don't know if I can escape it. If I can't, maybe I'll just come back to New Orleans."

CHAPTER 24

Schwa Vang came to America in 1976 when he was eight years old. He watched the Laos government murder his grandfather, several uncles and his older brothers. He initially came to Green Bay, Wisconsin, with his remaining family because of efforts by Catholic Charities and Jewish Social Services. Schwa's father, Chong, his mother, three remaining brothers, sisters-in-law and four sisters arrived in the city of Appleton during early summer of 1976 with nothing more than the clothes on their backs. They were given a small house to stay in, some cash and immediate welfare benefits from the county.

By the late 1990s, Paul owned six homes in Fresno, which he sold for huge profits in the early 2000s. From the time he came to America, he always dreamed of living in San Francisco. Thus with the proceeds from his sales he bought two "painted ladies," two elaborately refurbished Victorian homes on Franklin near California. He, his wife, infant daughter Beyoncé and his wife's parents lived in one while he rented out the other.

Paul operated his real estate business out of the first floor his own Victorian on Franklin. The office was modern, with Asian touches. Paul was a short, stocky man with creamy tan skin and a round, puffy face. He dressed in dark designer suits, except for on Fridays, when he wore his 49ers spirit wear. He loved to joke and laugh.

He met Sean O'Brien after the young priest had already moved in. Kaohly, Paul's young wife, selected the lessees and collected rents while Paul performed all maintenance duties, which were minimal, since Kaohly screened for long-term tenants.

Mr. Radionchenko in the first unit had been there seven years. Likewise, Miss Bessie P. Macintyre's lease agreement extended years back to contracts with the former owners. She had been in the third unit for thirteen years. The couple who had been in the second unit before Sean O'Brien came had leased for five years before the wife got pregnant and they had to find a larger living space.

Young Father O'Brien had been in the unit for twenty-one months before he fell over dead in the chapel during the Hector Fuentes wake. Two days later, police detectives came over to the apartment and inspected it for more than four hours.

The black cop spent most of the time in the unit while the white guy searched the outside of the house and interviewed Miss Bessie, Mr. Radionchenko, Kaohly and Paul. Both seemed suspicious, or paranoid.

Father Gonzales came by the next day. He asked Paul if he could enter the apartment to collect church documents and other diocese property. He explained that Sean's family in Ireland had arranged to ship his body back home. Sean's wealthy father had pre-paid the entire three-year lease and his mother spent thousands of dollars decorating and furnishing her only child's apartment. Father Gonzales said one of the church charities would come by to pick up the furniture and other valuable belongings on Friday.

When Paul entered the empty apartment on the weekend, he first noticed the drywall damage. There was a softball-sized hole in the wall that was covered by the bed's headboard and a much larger hole in the wall that was behind the chest of drawers. There was a small hole in the living room where the couch sat and another in a corner next to a plant the movers had left behind. There were additional holes behind hung pictures.

Before leaving, both detectives stressed to Paul and Kaohly that a killer might be lurking near. They warned Paul to contact the police right away if he noticed anything odd or out of place. But when Paul saw the holes in the walls, eight in all, he was too angry to recognize them as suspicious. Fuming about the holes, he phoned Father Gonzales and told him he was keeping Sean's $1,500 deposit for damages and flew out of town the next day for a six-day trip to Minneapolis for his sister's wedding.

Paul came home eager to get the apartment ready for the first renter on the waiting list. He and Kaohly were concerned they already lost a week and a half of rent. He hurried to the Home Store to buy drywall, but the drywall knives, saw, compound and sander were already a part of his maintenance inventory.

It had been at least a year since he had to make a repair, and the rusty lock on the room under the house was stuck on the first two attempts in the cold morning air. Pulling the doors to the room open outward, Paul steadied the flashlight beam with his left hand while aiming the keys in his right. Pushing the dripping cobwebs aside with his left forearm, he made his way to the tool closet. Scraping the dust and webs from the keyhole with the key tip, he fumbled for a moment before inserting the key and turning counterclockwise.

The grimy white doors of the closet were held closed behind two aluminum lever-like handles in the center. The handle on the left was fixed, but the handle on the right with the keyhole could be lifted to unlatch the doors. And so, gripping the left handle with the free fingers of his left hand, he raised the right handle with his right. Pulling with both hands to open the doors, he met with an initial resistance, and pulled much harder on the second try.

Tw-twang! He felt the tight gripping pain in his throat even before he heard the muted twang. Stunned, he staggered backward, the flashlight tumbling to the concrete floor. He tried futilely to inhale, and though his body heaved, he could take in no air. Searing pain knifed down from his throat to the pit of his stomach.

He tried to call out, but the aching and tightness in his throat was unrelenting. Finally, he fell to the floor, lungs burning as he crawled toward the door. His shaking right hand reached for the threshold while his left investigated his bloody chest and then his neck. First one, then two!

In a state of oncoming shock, Paul's fingers detected four wooden stakes or sticks, about the size of pencils, lodged deep in his throat, one directly through his windpipe, a fifth stake in his upper chest, just below his clavicle.

He tried to pull one out, but the pain was horrendous. He became dizzy as his eyes rolled back. In one final desperate moment, he lunged forward to get his arms and head out the door. Rolling onto his back, he fixed his eyes on the sun, muscle spasms actuating his cheeks and the corners of his blood-filled mouth. His gaze fixed, in a final vision he beheld something in or beyond the sun that filled him with great terror. His body tensed violently and relaxed.

When he didn't come back to the house for lunch, Kaohly began calling his cell phone. Then she took the baby up to her parents' room and went to check for him at the apartment. She asked at Mr. Radionchenko's and Miss Bessie's, but neither had seen him.

Then she remembered he was going to repair the

drywall. She checked his usual workstation on the side of the house, but he wasn't there.

As she rounded the corner she stopped in her tracks, her eyes fixed on his bloody left hand and then his arm extending back beyond the room under the house. Easing forward, she could see his right hand and then his tangled hair. Maybe he had accidentally hit his head and had just knocked himself out. She stopped at the door, holding her breath before pulling it open wider.

Kaohly screamed so loud that the whole neighborhood paid attention. A mail carrier passing by looked over and began to shriek as well. Construction workers, repairing a house across the street, rushed over to see what was wrong. Within minutes, more than a dozen people crowded around, eyes unable to divert from the gory scene that lay before them. And sickly Miss Bessie, startled by the terror of Kaohly's initial cries, had a heart attack and died in the ambulance on the way to the hospital.

"Thank you for taking the time to meet with me, Chief Leong. I realize you must have a very busy schedule."

The ladies sat.

"No, it's always been good policy to hear comments from concerned family members. And I understand you wanted to share some thoughts with me?"

"I'd rather we had a simple discussion, woman to woman. Of course it's been no secret that I have a problem with my husband working homicide."

"Yes, I've heard as much."

Andrea Brady reached across the table, stroking Rebecca's forehand.

"I'm certain you know of the incident. About a week ago, Tom was somehow a victim of *mercury* poisoning. Mercury! Not your run of the mill work hazard, but ever since, he's not been himself."

"And what do you mean by that?"

"He's been confused, disoriented, just sort of distant from me and the girls."

Rebecca suppressed a smile. She was well aware of Tom's reputation as a playboy.

"And you believe this is a result of the mercury poisoning?"

Andrea studied Rebecca's face. The question carried a subtle patronizing tone. She was already beginning to dislike the chief.

"I understand you have licensed psychiatrists who work for the department. For his own good, I think my husband's mental health should be tested to insure his being poisoned doesn't pose a further threat to him or to anyone else."

Rebecca resented the unmistakable condescension in the comment.

"That would be my call to make."

"Of course it would. I was merely hoping to provide a bit of insight, from a duly concerned wife's perspective."

Rebecca nodded.

"Understood. Was there anything else?"

"Are you married, Chief Leong?"

Rebecca hesitated.

"Yes."

"Children?"

"Two."

Andrea showed her professional smile, sitting back in the chair.

"Then certainly you understand. Our girls are still young. They worry about their father. Are you aware he recently went on a trip to New Orleans with Inspector Saint Claire?"

"I heard about it, though what my detectives do when they are off duty isn't really my concern."

"Oh really? Is that why you specifically assigned Tom to investigate Saint Claire's personal life, which includes secretly following him around town and a visit with his ex-wife at the hospital?"

Rebecca shot a sinister look across the table.

"That's police business, and you would do well not to interfere."

Andrea raised her eyebrows.

"I don't know. I came to talk to you about business important to *my* family, but you haven't seemed to mind interfering there. In fact, you encouraged Tom to go to New Orleans."

Sensing the strength of Andrea's resolve, Rebecca

abandoned the barbed exercise.

"What do you want?"

"Once this case is over, I'd like Tom assigned somewhere other than homicide. Is that too much to ask?"

Rebecca sighed.

"I have a police department to run, something I'd never be able to do if I had to subject my decisions to the worries and whims of the distraught wives and children of my officers."

Andrea raised her hand in a halting gesture.

"Make no mistake, I'm not distraught. I'm simply trying to protect my family, just as you would no doubt protect yours."

She leaned in, her voice softer.

"*And* I didn't come empty handed. I would never ask anything of you if I wasn't planning on giving you something in return."

Rebecca rolled her eyes.

"I'm almost afraid to ask. What?"

"I can tell you something about the murder case they're working on that you don't know."

"Probably not. But try me."

Andrea paused for effect.

"The killer they're after... is already dead."

She smiled as she watched the confusion show on the chief's face.

"He was dead before the first murder. At least that's what he told Saint Claire. He planned all the other murders in advance, before he died."

Nodding, she helped Rebecca's thought processes along.

"Think about it. With the Mexican man and with the priest, the murderer wasn't an active participant in the killing, not to mention the old Jewish woman."

She smiled and drove home the conclusion.

"You know, it's more than possible this killer is committing these murders... from the grave."

CHAPTER 25

"Okay, okay. Now step back! You all need to step your asses *back*! Police inspectors coming through!"

The reluctant crowd parted, allowing Saint Claire and Brady access to the area inside the yellow *Police Line* tape. The body was still sprawled supine on the ground, glazed eyes still fixed toward the heavens.

Approaching a still-bleeding, dead body was always unnerving for Brady. He hesitated three feet away as Saint Claire knelt, studying the four small wooden stakes embedded in Paul Vang's neck and the one in his chest. Eyes open, they were dried-out and dark. Next to Brady, the police photographer snapped pictures from varying angles.

Along the perimeter, the crowd swelled to more than seventy or eighty persons, including at least one reporter. A large, dark vehicle from the San Francisco Chief Medical Examiner's Office sat at the curb, awaiting Paul's body.

Kaohly was in the house, attended by her brother and sisters, in-laws, parents and other relatives who streamed in. Grizzled, gray-bearded Mr. Radionchenko sat in his rocker on the porch, speaking to himself in Russian, making wild gestures toward the sky in frustration. Laquisha Winters, the stepdaughter of Miss Bessie, was also on the porch, watching as Saint Claire studied the body.

Dark brown dried blood formed crusted circles around two of the small wooden stakes in Paul's neck, while the one on the left oozed still moist blood. There was evidence he tried to pull out the stake farthest right. Protruding more than an inch above the others, its crooked base was the source of a gore trail that fed the dark, strawberry jam-like pool on the ground.

Upon closer inspection, the stakes appeared to be sharpened wooden dowels, pine or possibly birch, one-quarter inch thick in diameter. And judging from the girth of Paul's neck verses the length of the stakes extending outside, Saint Claire estimated they were each six inches long.

Leaning still closer, he could see the killer had notched the back end of each of the stakes, which indicated they had been launched by a bowstring of some kind at great velocity. The fact that four of the five had found their mark meant they were fired at point blank range.

Saint Claire seemed fascinated by the sticky blood still oozing from Paul's neck. Standing, he stepped over the body to enter the space under the house. He motioned for Brady to follow. Inside he spied the tool cabinet, its doors ajar. With a three-foot long two-by-four remnant found on the floor, he stood to the right of the cabinet, prying first the left and then the right door open as Brady cringed on the other side, clear of a possible second trap.

Apprehension fading, Saint Claire stood before the cabinet, looking in. Six miniature handmade bows were mounted on a metal base, attached by metal screws to a shelf top in the cabinet. Three on each side of the vertical metal divider in the center of the cabinet, they were each aimed inward at complimentary angles.

Saint Claire stopped. The bow farthest right had failed to fire. Slipping back to the outside of the right door, Saint Claire pulled it open wider. A sharp twang was followed by the sound of the sixth stake forcefully striking the front wall.

Brady recoiled.

"Goddammit! Saint Claire, what the *fuck* was that?"

"Last one. Victim didn't open the right door wide enough to trigger that last bow. It's safe now. Come see this."

Brady stood, still uneasy as he approached the tool cabinet.

"What is it?"

"Some kind of a booby trap. When the guy out there opened these doors, that string going across right there triggered those three bows on the left, and this here string triggered the ones on the right. See how the bows are all aimed inward? Victim would have naturally been standing in this exact place when he opened the cabinet."

Saint Claire crouched to get an eye level view of the shelf.

"And see how he made the height of the base adjustable? Killer must have known exactly how tall he was and where his neck would be positioned."

"Okay, but how would the killer know that guy was going to come down here and open this dusty cabinet within his thirty-day time frame?"

"I'm not sure. But that's why we're here, for the second time. We obviously missed something the first time we came."

Saint Claire received the call from Captain Sanchez at eleven-thirty that morning. He had filed a request with dispatchers a week earlier, asking to be notified of any suspicious activity or events occurring on Franklin near California or near Sean O'Brien's former apartment.

Sonia had been monitoring murders reported in the city for the last ten days. With every day that passed, she grew more anxious. So much time had passed since the priest was killed. Maybe the killer changed his mind. Maybe he got caught. Maybe he would be waiting in her house when she got home.

She had talked to Saint Claire when he was in New Orleans, and to her surprise, the conversation was civil. He seemed concerned about her and sympathetic when hearing her fears and suspicions. He recommended a two-week vacation away from San Francisco, throughout the completion of the killer's announced time frame, but she refused. She did not want to yield to this blatant attempt at intimidation.

Saint Claire promised he would check her apartment to ensure she would be secure at home, and he hinted he would keep an eye on things for her outside, even if he had to do it during his off-time. She smiled as she ended the call. If they could just make it through the next two weeks, she thought she and Saint Claire could end up being friends after all.

"That was ma *nigga*, dawg! Some sick-ass fool done kilt ma nigga!"

Peter Thao slammed his fists into the wall and then banged with his forehead.

"Paul was ma nigga. He was good folks. Come here!"

He extended his arms, embracing his sister. He was crying. She was crying.

"You all right?"

Kaohly just whimpered in his arms, her body sagging.

"Yo, you got family, girl. We gonna take cara ya."

He looked toward the door, noticing the detectives for the first time. Stepping between his sister and the non-family members, he cocked his head.

"Y'all popo?"

Saint Claire stepped forward, answering.

"Inspector Saint Claire with the police. And this is Inspector Brady. I realize this is a bad time for the family. We're very sorry you have to go through this, but Mr. Vang was obviously murdered, and we'd like to try to catch the person responsible. Would you mind if we asked Mrs. Vang a few questions?"

"I mind, but maybe she don't. I just know if you're tryin ta catch the nigga who kilt Paul, it ain't cuz ya wanna ta help us."

"Hey, watch the language!"

Brady had stepped forward to challenge the short, stocky young man, but Saint Claire gestured, his eyes insisting Brady back off and calm down. Clearing his throat, Saint Claire smiled to reassure Kaohly.

"Mrs. Vang, do you have a few minutes to speak with us in private? We really would like to track down the person responsible for your husband's death. We'd like to catch him before he kills someone else. Five minutes?"

Kaohly nodded in the affirmative.

"We can speak in the living room."

Whether it was Paul, Kaohly or a paid professional, someone with a detailed understanding of interior design had decorated the space. The dark cherry wood motif of the floor resurfaced in the crown molding that encircled the room where the walls met the ceiling. Lime-painted Venetian plaster covered the walls and ceiling, creating the effect of age. And a large, embroidered, hand-woven, richly-colored Persian rug covered most of the floor, with tints and themes echoed in the rust and burgundy hued draperies that hung from burnished brass looms suspended from the walls.

The cream-colored, soft Italian leather sofa sat next to a huge bronze planter with a luxuriant palm. Brady sat on the couch at the end opposite Kaohly, while Saint Claire took a seat facing both in a matching leather armchair. Setting his pen and notepad on the glass-topped table before him, he sat back.

"How do you say your first name again?"

"Just call me Mary."

"Okay, Mary. Let's start with the obvious. What did your husband need from that tool cabinet and why was he down there?"

She wiped a tear trail from her cheek.

"He had to fix the walls."

"What walls?"

"In the apartment. There were holes in the walls, where the priest lived, two of em pretty fuckin big."

Saint Claire looked toward Brady.

"Did you see any holes?"

Brady shrugged.

"I didn't see any holes."

"There were holes. Y'all just missed them. I'll show ya."

Brady figured that Paul married Kaohly after he became successful. She had to be at least twenty years younger than he was and in *Sean John* jeans, suede *Fubu* tennis shoes, a *Baby Phat* tee and her long black hair pulled through the opening in the back of a black Raiders cap, she seemed out of place in the ornate room. When Brady interviewed her following the O'Brien murder, he told Saint Claire he was surprised she was married to Paul, despite his wealth.

But during that interview she was dressed very differently. She had on a silk red designer dress and her hair curled as she was on the way out to have martinis in the Financial District with hot girlfriends. Still weeping, she seemed a different person as she rose from the couch.

All eyes were on Kaohly as she walked with the detectives down the street toward the rental property. But with Paul's body now removed, the crowd had begun to dissipate. Kaohly ascended the stairs and opened the front door with a key on an elastic band around her wrist. Turning right, she opened the apartment door and led the detectives in.

Saint Claire stopped, confused. How could he have missed something so obvious? Kaohly knelt next to the largest opening.

"The couch sat here, so unless you moved the couch, you wouldn't have seen it."

She stood, going to the wall on the opposite side of the room.

"And this one was behind the mirror. That one over there was behind a painting. There were at least eight holes in the walls here."

Brady looked toward his partner.

"Are we that stupid, or is this killer that smart?"

Saint Claire sighed.

"How were we supposed to know? We weren't looking for hidden holes in the walls or behind the furniture, and we probably wouldn't have understood what they meant if we had found them. This killer isn't that smart. He just has the advantage of action while we've been forced to react. It isn't genius, it's cowardice!"

Kaohly had her fingers in one of the jagged openings.

"Are you sayin that priest didn't make these holes, man? You sayin someone else did because they knew Paul was gonna try'n fix em, and they set im up?"

Brady answered.

"The killer had to know enough about your husband to predict he would open that tool shed today."

He stopped.

"Waitaminute, Mary. The young priest died over a week ago. When did everything get cleared out of this place?"

"A week ago, Saturday. Why?"

"From what I remember about your husband from our interview, he was a type A personality. He got everything done in a hurry. You're sayin a whole week went by? Why'd he wait so long to start the repairs?"

She paused and bowed her head as the tears returned.

"He woulda started it last Monday, but we had to fly out that day to go to his sister's wedding in Minnesota."

She stopped.

"So this was gonna happen a week ago if we didn't go to that wedding?"

Saint Claire seemed angry and frustrated.

"I pulled the couch out! I saw that gouge in the wall. I just didn't connect it to anything else. If I had known about the rest of the damage, maybe I would have figured it out. I asked both of you to call me to report anything suspicious. Why didn't you call me?"

Kaohly reacted.

"Hey, they were just holes in the wall! Alotta time when people move out there are holes in the wall. The carpet had a brown stain. Nigga please! Was I supposta call you about that too?"

Saint Claire took a breath, calming himself.

"Look Mary, I'm sorry. I'm just angry with myself because I was in this apartment with the clues right here, and I wasn't able to save your husband's life. I'm frustrated I couldn't save him, but Paul didn't die in vain."

At the window, Saint Claire looked out at the city.

"If there's a clue here that leads to another murder or the killer, I'm going to find it and stop him. He's played three of his seven cards. The game always turns on the fourth. If he wants to continue, he'll have to sport his hand, and when he does, I'll be there to put his ass to rest, one way or another."

After Mary left the room, Brady couldn't wait to broach the subject.

"I don't get it, Saint Claire. All these young, off-brand *Asians* get to use the N-word now? And that's all right with you, but *white* people still can't?"

CHAPTER 26

Her guest inside, Katrina peeked around the door into the hallway before shutting it. She was so excited she wanted to scream, but closing her eyes, she breathed, filling her lungs, slowly relaxing. Thirty-three years, she had waited that long for the moment to arrive. Thirty-three years!

She resented the way people in town had looked at her after the event, the way some of them whispered suspicions and gossip behind her back. Others made cruel, mean-spirited insinuations right to her face. They had no idea. Yet if they had seen the truth with their own eyes, they would not have believed it.

Growing up pretty and light-skinned had its advantages in a community that based the worth of a person on skin shade and hair texture, but it was also a trap. The same social standards that adjudged light-skinned girls more desirable than their dark-skinned counterparts made them inferior to their fairer-skinned sisters.

Katrina Scott was so light she could be mistaken as white, but her sister Bianca was lighter with straighter hair. In fact, Bianca's hair was brown with blond highlights and her eyes were blue. Throughout childhood, the community always treated Bianca as the prettier, smarter, and more charming of the sisters, but Katrina knew better.

Bianca was not as shapely, her grades were never as good and she was a spoiled whiner who always played up her white features, hair texture and skin color. Clearly their mother's favorite, teenaged Bianca was invited to social events and gatherings while Katrina was left at home. The community downplayed Katrina's achievements and made her feel second-rate.

She heard about the evil woman late one night when she was eavesdropping on her parents, relatives and friends at a gathering at the house. They said the old black woman, Madame Toussainte, lived over by the river. According to one of Katrina's aunts, this woman could grant any wish or desire, but she warned that the woman was a trickster who could "cheat, lie and cuss just like the Devil himself."

The grown-ups called it *Hoodoo*, and while most seemed to agree it came over to Louisiana from Africa, Madame

Toussainte was an African from Haiti who spoke French, English and African. She was a *Voudoun*, a voodoo priestess.

They said she was seventy-years-old with no teeth in her mouth, and sometimes when she spoke, her eyes rolled back in her head, turning white. Her hair was long, knotted and gray. She reeked of herbs, drank the warm blood of chickens and had an evil eye so powerful she could use it to kill or make a man kill himself or other people. Fifteen-year-old Katrina was fascinated by the thought of this woman. Late one afternoon two weeks later, she went down to the river to spy on her.

The old woman lived deep in the woods, in a place few people ever ventured, especially white people or the law. Her house was a little shotgun wooden hut with a room on one side, a kitchen on the other, a wood-burning stove in the kitchen and a fireplace in the room. There was a porch out front with a rocking chair, where Madame Toussainte would smoke her pipe or dip snuff.

She was black all right, as black and ashy as a shoe boot, but she didn't seem remarkable in any other way. Katrina had seen poor old black women of her sort before. The woman was short and lean, with unmistakable vigor and determination. She had chickens, maybe a hundred chickens, some black and some frizzled black, with a few guinea hens.

She lived alone and chopped wood like a man. In the yard next to her house, she always had a huge iron pot, a steaming caldron suspended above a fire. There was also a small copper whiskey still set up in the back of the house.

Katrina spied on the ugly woman three times before she realized the woman knew she was out there the entire time. Looking up, the woman spoke, summoning her.

"Come'ere, gurl. Come outa da hidin and tell Madame Toussainte fa what ya been lookin ta see."

Reluctantly, Katrina came out of the bushes and approached the old woman's porch. Madame Toussainte drew from the pipe and blew a great gray billow of smoke into the air.

"Such a pretty gurl. But dere be some otha gurl out dere ya want fa me ta put da big hurt on, don't cha?"

"Yes."

"Who dis gurl?"

Katrina lowered her eyes.

"My sister."

Madame Toussainte told Katrina she would have to take some of Bianca's personal effects, hair from her brush, fingernail or toenail clippings, a pair of freshly worn panties and a soiled sanitary napkin and bring them to her. It took weeks to collect the items, but Katrina brought them to the Voudoun's house with great trepidation.

"Dis everting ah tol ja ta brang, cep fa wha cha ya gotta pay me."

Of course she would have to pay! Katrina was angry with herself for being so naïve.

"Ah wan alla dat pretty hair, gurl. Gimme dat, and ya don't gotta gimme nothin else."

In the surreal summer sunlight shining through a dust-covered window, she watched as the old woman sliced her hair with a pair of shining silver scissors.

"Ah put er on da riva. Ya don't gatta worry bout dat gurl no more."

Donning a hat, Katrina went to her mother's beauty shop and bought a wig with money she had been saving for a stereo record player. When she got home, Bianca was awaiting her arrival. In all the intrigue, Katrina had forgotten about their Wednesday night dance practice. When they said goodnight and went to bed, Katrina had no idea it was the last time she would ever see her sister alive.

She didn't expect anything would happen so soon, and she never imagined it would be so drastic. Cora Scott, the girls' mother, startled the family awake at 6:00 a.m., frantic that Bianca was not in her bed. Bianca's robe and house shoes were missing.

Concerned Bianca might have gone to see a boy, the family waited until nine before alerting the community and the local sheriff. While the community was quick to put together a search team, the sheriff department did not mobilize, insisting Bianca was just having a night with a secret boyfriend. She was almost seventeen, after all.

When night came and a next day, Katrina was the most panicked of all. Stupid old black woman! Nigger bitch! Katrina wanted her to humble Bianca, to make Bianca's hair fall out, make her skin turn darker, or make her fall in love with an ugly, dark-skinned guy—not have something really bad happen to her, not for her to be missing!

By Saturday, Katrina was barely able to move or breathe. Her entire body's energy was concentrated in the pit of her stomach. She sat in the darkened bedroom they shared, head buried in the pillow, puffy eyes weeping, aching heart longing for her sister, troubled mind remembering how profoundly she loved Bianca and how much fun they had together.

She imagined Bianca coming in the house, her shrill voice telling silly jokes the way she always did, but hour after hour went by with no news. She could hear her mother crying in the living room and the desperation in her father's voice as he tried to comfort her. With the fading of the late afternoon sun faded the hope of a happy reunion.

On Sunday morning, the sheriff came by and asked Benjamin Scott to come outside the house. Peeking from the corner of her bedroom window, Katrina watched her emotional father get in the car with the sheriff and saw the car drive away. When they returned two hours later, Benjamin's usually broad shoulders were slumped. His spirit had deserted his body. He and the sheriff walked up to the door and entered the house.

Seconds later, as Katrina listened to her mother's guttural screams, she knew. Bianca was dead. She was never coming back. Leaping from the bed, she locked her bedroom door and shoved the chest of drawers in front of it. No one was going to tell her Bianca was dead.

On the bed, she rocked back and forth, pillows to her ears, breathing deeply. Her mind raced and she felt pressure bearing down on her, taking her breath away, a wicked spirit, threatening to suffocate her. She struggled even harder for air, breathing fast, her chest heaving, her mouth gasping.

She first felt a tingling in her fingers and toes, and then her limbs and head felt light. She wasn't sure when she passed out, wasn't sure when the real world around her became fluid and fused with the distorted walls of her room flowing by. She couldn't tell if she was dreaming or merely asleep. And then she saw bright light at the far end of a long corridor coming closer, closing in, and in that light she saw Bianca's smiling face, then her shoulders and finally Bianca's arms reaching toward her.

"You don't know how happy I am that you decided to come to help me. What... what should I call you?"

"If you were older than me, you'd call me Matilda, but since ya aren't, Mama Jezebel will do."

Katrina was skeptical.

"And you're a *Voudoun*?"

"I'm a medical doctor, gynecologist graduated from Meharry, but yes, I am also a root worker and a Voodoo priestess."

The sophisticated older woman placed a black medical case on the table.

"Come, touch my hands."

Katrina hesitated.

"You don't look like a *Voudoun*."

Mama Jezebel was thin with an oddly attractive face. She wore her gray hair short, but styled smartly in tight curls. Katrina recognized the brand of her classy twill pantsuit, definitely *Albert Nipon*. She couldn't guess the maker of the expensive brown boots the woman wore, but something about this Mama Jezebel seemed wrong, something seemed out of character for a *Voodoo* woman.

"Would it make you feel better if I went out and came back in with my breasts exposed, maybe with an animal loincloth at my waist and a bone in my nose? I tell you now, you're too caught up in the look of a thing. That I know that without touching you."

She sat on the sofa, extending her hands again.

"But when I touch you, I'll know you. And when I know you, I can help you. Now come."

Katrina approached, sat and placed her hands atop the woman's palms. Grasping Katrina's hands, Mama Jezebel tilted her head back, the pupils of her eyes disappearing. After a moment, she loosened her grip and found Katrina's eyes with her own.

"You have a husband who is a decent man, but he doesn't trust you. He wants you to stay in this facility. He believes this is the best place for you."

She closed her eyes, tapping her gift.

"Yes, you have a husband and a son, yes, and you are the keeper of two big secrets, yes, one for the husband and one for the son."

Katrina nodded, intrigued.

"You had another child, yes, a daughter that died young. It was a very painful experience for you. Ah yes, and you had a sister. There is great pain around this sister as well. It follows you."

Mama Jezebel stopped, suddenly releasing Katrina's hands. Now there was a familiar accent in her voice.

"A bad, very bad woman's got you all crossed up. She's got a jinx on you."

Katrina's shoulders slumped at the confirmation of what she already knew.

"Her name was Madame Toussainte. Do you know her?"

Mama Jezebel took a breath and nodded.

"A bad woman. Very powerful she was. If she crossed you to teach you somethin, I might can uncross you, but if she crossed you to damn your soul, then there can't be no uncrossin."

By Sunday afternoon, it seemed the entire community crowded around the Scott home, offering condolences and expressions of comfort. Miss Renee Williams, Cora's cousin and best friend, stepped in to run the house while Cora wept in her bedroom. Miss Renee took in food and gifts, answered questions and buffered the family from well-meaning but nosy and gossipy neighbors.

According to Miss Renee, Cora was such a good woman that the Devil took notice of her, as he sometimes does. She explained that sometimes God allows the Devil to take precious things from good people to test their faith. She assured neighbors that Cora's faith in God remained strong, despite the tragic loss of her sweet daughter.

Speaking to the gossipers, she reaffirmed Bianca was a chaste, good girl who was not interested in any boy. She didn't leave her parent's home in the middle of the night to practice sin and corruption. Instead, the poor, helpless girl was led out from the safety of her home and community under the influence of some supernatural force.

From her bedroom, Katrina could hear Miss Renee in front of the house defending Bianca's honor, while from the back she could still hear her mother's weeping. It was a supernatural force. At nightfall, she still wore her pajamas, still remained locked in her room.

She did not, could not eat or sleep that day. In her room, she realized the old woman *was* the trickster the old folks always warned she was. The woman was evil, and worse, she had Katrina's hair.

Katrina went to the old woman's little house the next day. Owing to what she had heard about hoodooing, she dragged a tree limb behind her to destroy her footprints and was careful not to walk across any signs drawn on the ground. Stepping carefully up the stairs, she knocked on the door, trying to be brave.

"I want my hair back!"

"Alla da hair ya own jus nah gurl, is on yur head. Wha cha gave is given, wha cha begot is begotten. Cain't go back."

Frustrated, Katrina's thoughts, for the first time in her life, turned to murder. She wanted to strangle the old woman or hit her in the head savagely, repeatedly with something. Katrina wanted to inflict pain, to make the wicked woman suffer. She wanted to watch the woman bleed and die! Knife gripped in her pocket, she thought she would slit the woman's throat. She imagined stabbing her over and over.

"You killed my sister!"

The old woman held a conjuring hand out before the girl, fingers posed rigidly, her eyes rolled back.

"Troubled ya are, gurl! An troubled yu'll be alla yur days!"

The chickens in the yard and in the coops became restless, clucking and squawking all around. Nervous, Katrina stopped her advance. Eyes returning, Madame Toussainte continued.

"It waz you come fount me out. It waz you schemed evil gainst dat gurl. Ya branged me her thangs when ya knows good well what Ah do. Ya gat everthang ya axed fa."

"I didn't want her dead!"

"Ya drop a ol hen's egg, ya gonna be surprised it break when it hit da groun? Rememba gurl, you come ova ta me ta do dis bidness, so don't be surprised if da cuss meant fa ya sista done fount a way ta come back on you!"

Her voice held a stern warning.

"Nah git out from ma door fa ya makes me mad."

Years later, after Deuteronomy became an inspector with the SFPD, Lafourche Parish authorities allowed him to revisit the Bianca Scott murder case. He took three weeks off work and went back to Thibodeaux to re-examine the events surrounding Bianca's death and to follow-up uninvestigated leads.

Twelve days into the research, Deuteronomy made a shocking discovery. Fifteen years after Bianca's death, a man named James Grant, one of the young men questioned by the sheriff after the incident, confessed to Bianca's murder before a preacher and two other witnesses on the eve of his execution in Livingston, Texas.

James claimed Bianca was his secret girlfriend, being he was ten years older than the girl and she was a minor. He said she lied, insisting she was pregnant with his child and she threatened to tell her parents and the community about the affair if he didn't marry her.

He promised to take her away to elope that night, and he would have gone through with the scheme, but he decided at the last moment he would not let her blackmail him into marriage. When he refused, she told him she was going to the sheriff to accuse him of statutory rape.

They argued and he, in anger, pushed her in the river. Diving in after her, he held her face under water until she stopped moving. He tried to leave town, but his money was short. He almost fell apart when a sheriff deputy questioned him about the girl. He was sure the man saw the scratches on his face, but the law let him go. Panicked, he went home, stole all the money from his mother's purse and bought a one-way bus ticket out of town, never to return.

Deuteronomy worked an additional four days to either corroborate or discredit Grant's claims. In the end, it seemed likely that Grant and Bianca *were* intimately involved and that he *was* at the river with the girl on the night she drowned.

When Deuteronomy presented the evidence to his wife, she became angry, rejecting any suggestion that her sister was engaged in an inappropriate relationship. Katrina insisted she would have known if her sister was involved with a boy. Instead, she accused Voodoo Priestess Madame Toussainte of putting a curse on the family. It was then that Katrina began to believe she had become the primary target of the *Voudoun's* curse.

She fumed as she walked away from the little house, dragging the branch. It wasn't fair. That *hoodoo* witch had killed her sister! And she had the nerve to make threats! If anyone deserved to die, it was that old black bitch! Katrina stopped in the yard, her eyes first training on the caldron suspended in midair and then on the crackling fire below.

The woman had her hair in that house. Because the woman was evil, she wanted the hair for a specific reason, for some wicked purpose. Katrina had heard the hoodoo stories. The woman had it in for her. What was there to lose?

The little wooden house was old and dry. It was isolated in the woods. Taking up a flaming brand, Katrina walked toward the house, hurled it onto the roof and turned her back.

"In the name of the Father, the Son and the Holy Ghost."

She walked away without looking back. The fire must have spread quickly, because she could hear the loud crackling of the growing flames as she reached the path that led to the main road. A minute later, she heard the screams and shrieks of the old woman. Closing her eyes, she prayed the old woman was still in the house. She prayed she was listening to the agonizing cries of the old woman burning on her way to Hell.

CHAPTER 27

"Don't ask me how I know, but I know. This killer has claimed from the beginning that he's already *dead*, that he is supposed to commit his seven murders from the grave."

Saint Claire forced a half-smile and glared over at Brady who shrugged, feinting astonishment.

Noting the exchange between the men, Captain Sanchez removed her jacket and, symbolically, her rank. Instead of meeting in her office, she asked Saint Claire and Brady to speak with her in the adjoining conference room. The three sat at the table as seeming equals.

"Come on, guys. We're all in this together. Now I'll forgive the fact that both of you chose not to share that essential, very meaningful fact with me if we can just have an open and honest discussion about where we are in this case, just the three of us."

The thought of the killer being already dead was of great relief to Sonia, if only it were true. If he really was dead, all she had to do was escape whatever trap he had pre-set for her over the next fifteen or so days. But for the moment, death lurked in the shadows and around every corner. Sonia counted her days, hours, minutes and seconds as precious, her every breath a blessing.

She was at her desk when Saint Claire called back to provide details about the Vang murder, which by his count was the third in the killer's series of seven. The death of Paul Vang came almost twelve days after the murder of young Father Sean O'Brien, which amounted to more than one-third of the killer's professed time limit. The killer had six days to commit the final four murders.

In his second letter, the killer predicted the violence of the Vang murder. He said, *I must apologize in advance, Saint Claire, for the lack of art in the next murder you'll encounter,* referring to the Father O'Brien murder, with frog poison on the rosary beads. But he continued, *the reality of my present condition exerts obvious limitations, but I promise at least two honorable mentions and one real masterpiece over the next six murders.* If the killer really was dead, then Sonia was convinced his killing Paul Vang in the way he did was his "honorable mention," if not his "masterpiece."

In the discussion after the Andrea Brady revelation, Sonia and Chief Leong agreed Sonia should question both detectives on the matter while attempting to gain Saint Claire's trust, and then Leong would conduct a follow-up interview with Brady in private.

Sonia, in a gesture Leong considered over-the-top, brought in coffee, orange juice and pastries for the meeting, and her instincts served her well. Both detectives expressed gratitude for the accoutrements and seemed to open to her, at least a little.

"Let's start with you, Saint Claire. Your assessment of the Vang murder? Why didn't we see this coming?"

Despite her tone, which was genial, the detective took the question as a personal affront.

"The thought of Vang did cross my mind. In fact, it more than crossed my mind, but tiny crossbows and darts in a tool shed? I knew he was going to change tactics, do something violent, but there were just too many possibilities."

Brady nodded in agreement, clearing his throat.

"You, you said you saw the hole in the wall behind the couch?"

"I saw it that first time. And when I looked at it the second time after Mary showed it to us, I realized only then it was irregular, and by that I mean it was too regular, too symmetrical. It was placed in the perfect center of the square made up by the studs behind the drywall. And the killer did the same with the large hole behind the headboard in the bedroom."

Sonia was pleased she had him talking. Leaning forward, her facial expressions and demeanor beckoned him to continue.

"To me it was a hole, and O'Brien, though he was a priest, he was still a kid. I figured he accidentally damaged the wall and rearranged the couch to cover it. I didn't know enough about him to think otherwise. For the same reason, there was no way I could have known that Vang did his own handiwork and that he had a tool shed under the house. Had I known those things, I probably could have saved the kid."

Brady cut in.

"But the killer knew those things."

"In three out of the four of the killings so far, the killer has managed to access the home of the intended victim. He studies his victims and in each case he's used knowledge of their personal habits and circumstances to set up the murders."

Brady continued Saint Claire's thought.

"And that's why he's always been a step ahead of us. Because he's always on the inside, he already knows what we never find out until after the fact. This guy is smart!"

Saint Claire frowned.

"He's smart, but not perfect. It was bound to happen. But with Vang he made his first mistake."

Eyebrows raised, Sonia tilted her head.

"Really? How's that?"

"He miscalculated. According to the killer's schedule, Vang was supposed to die a week before he did. Mary Vang told me her husband was estranged from his sister for years. She said she and Paul hadn't planned on going to the wedding in Minnesota until this sister called eight days before the event and begged Paul's forgiveness. The killer couldn't have predicted her last minute change of heart, or his. That's why there was a twelve-day gap between the second and third murder."

Brady looked up from his open book of notes.

"Okay, so what does that mean?"

"It means he's a week behind schedule, so what should have taken thirty days will now take thirty-seven. And if any of the next four murders are predicated on his original timing, they'll misfire. He was clever through the first three, but here is where it all starts to unravel. That is, if he's actually dead."

Sonia smirked.

"So you're telling us you don't believe he's really dead?"

"I didn't say that."

"You think he's alive?"

Saint Claire turned toward Sonia.

"At best we can conclude that either he's dead or he has some very specific reason to want us to believe he is. But again, this Vang murder gives us an in."

Brady closed the notebook.

"An in to what?"

"This murder was different than the others. With Mrs. Rosenthal and O'Brien, we know he at some time entered their homes. In Rosenthal's case, he tampered with her medicine. In

O'Brien's case, he put frog poison on rosary beads meant for a specific occasion, a funeral, which he knew in advance would happen. In those two cases, it wasn't necessary to know the victims on a personal level. He counted on them doing what they were supposed to do. Rosenthal had to take her heart medicine and O'Brien had to fill in for Father Gonzales at the wake and the funeral."

He sipped from the coffee cup and continued.

"But it was different with Vang. Facts suggest the killer knew Paul Vang on a personal level, certainly enough to know Vang did minor handiwork, and specifically drywall repair, when necessary. He had to know Vang had a tool shed under the house, and that he only opened it when he was doing the work."

Brady nodded, cutting in.

"I get it. Vang was a millionaire, a few times over. He could have hired... *most* millionaires would have hired a professional company to do the work. But this killer somehow knew Vang, after seeing the holes, would do it himself."

"Exactly. And the killer probably knew Vang only rarely had an apartment requiring the type of repairs he could do. Mr. Radiochenko's lived in his place for what, ten years? And Miss Bessie was in hers forever. That tool shed was covered with dust and cobwebs, meaning Vang hadn't opened it for a while. According to Mary, Vang never worked on any of the apartments unless a tenant moved out. That Painted Lady was his baby."

Sonia gestured toward Saint Claire.

"So what are you thinking?"

"I'm thinking the killer knew Vang personally, either because he rented from him or because he lived in the neighborhood."

Brady shrugged.

"But what do we look for? We have no idea what he looks like."

"Five-eight, five-nine, white, short blond hair, early thirties, fairly good-looking, usually wears dark glasses."

Sonia did not attempt to disguise her astonishment.

"How do you *know* that?"

"Interviews with various witnesses—you *have* those. Chloe at the Brocklebank Apartments, Maria Fuentes, other witnesses. Descriptions are vague, but they're consistent."

She sighed, crossing her arms.

"Let's just cut to the chase. I know it's a sore subject, but you think this is the same killer who murdered your son? Right?"

Saint Claire dragged the palm of his left hand down his face.

"All I know for sure is the killer knows *me* and he's got somethin to prove. No, let's just say it is the same guy, in a new incarnation. Couldn't be anyone else."

Sonia smiled. He was finally letting her in. She had never seen Saint Claire so willing to share spontaneous opinions and suspicions. It was exciting in an odd way. And yet to her disappointment, Brady interrupted.

"New incarnation? What does that mean?"

"Ten years ago, Slater assigned me to investigate a series of bizarre murders. The killer in that case had a fixation with identical twins. He would find a pair and study them over time, and then at some point he would murder one, and on the same day or night he'd murder the other."

Responding to the astonishment showing on the faces before him, he nodded.

"He would kill two identical people in exactly the same manner on the exact same day, usually a little less than an hour apart, of course 'just under an hour' being the average interval between the births of identical twins. It required an uncanny amount of planning. Anyway, after he killed them, he would strip them naked and place them in fetal positions resembling their probable womb position with the oldest facing south. It was the strangest thing I'd ever seen."

Sonia shook her head.

"Why twins?"

"At first we thought the killer was possibly an older or younger sibling of identical twins, but there was no evidence of anger or resentment in the murders. The killings almost seemed clinical. He didn't limit himself to sets of male twins or sets of females the way a slighted sibling might. Instead, he alternated male and female right through seven double murders."

Brady cut in.

"There's the number seven again. There something to that, right?"

"Always seven. Over time, we realized the killer had a religious upbringing. He wanted to be God, seven being the number associated with divine completeness. After seven, he would move to another incarnation, but we didn't know it back then. And the story got even stranger."

"How the fuck could it get any stranger?"

Saint Claire sighed.

"Well back then, I had a good friend on the force, closest thing I've ever had to a best friend. Joe Curry out of Park Station, Golden Gate Division. I know you've both heard the stories. I started out with him at Mission, but he had moved over to Golden Gate. While I was tracking my Twin Killer, he was involved investigating a killer who was murdering gang leaders on all sides, black, Mexican, Chinese, Vietnamese. In each case, the leader was stabbed in the heart with an ice pick and beheaded. Early on, no one knew what was going on. Gangs were blaming rival gangs, and we almost had Gang World War III in the city."

He sipped from the orange juice.

"But Joe worked hard to get the word out. He talked to the gangs, stopped the war. Of course in doing that good deed he got in hot water with the department. Chief complained that telling gang members there was a serial murderer stalking their leaders had placed the entire city and its police force in danger. He accused Joe of hyping up gangsters who would arm themselves and kill innocent people they'd mistake for the killer. No surprise, the black and Latino communities believed the killer was a cop."

His eyes shifted toward Sonia.

"By not revealing the existence of a serial killer, the department was willing to let the gangs shoot it out among themselves, just as long as they killed each other, just as long as they kept the violence gang on gang, black on black, brown on brown, *you* know."

Brady's face showed confusion.

"But the killer wasn't a cop?"

"No, he wasn't. When Joe and I started comparing notes, we realized we were dealing with the same killer. This serial killer was involved in two separate series of murders at the same time. I remember thinking back then if murder could ever be an addiction, we were looking at it. He was an addict, and he was prolific."

Sonia's throat felt tight, muting her voice.

"So what, what happened?"

"When he reached seven murders in each case, he stopped, presumably to move on to another series, another movement as he called them."

Brady spoke.

"And your son, when he was murdered, was he in a series of seven?"

"He was the fourth in a series of seven."

At the mention of his son's murder a second time, Saint Claire's disposition changed. He withdrew. He stopped talking and answered questions tersely. It was obvious he wanted to end the discussion and return to the investigation.

"So you're going to re-canvas that neighborhood?"

"I've got a composite drawing, and it's fairly accurate according to Chloe at the Brocklebank building. I'm going to interview every homeowner, tenant and landlord within a three block radius if I have to. If he's lived in that area any time recently, someone is going to remember him. And if that happens, we'll have a thread."

"A thread?"

He stood.

"A trail. Something to follow, something that'll lead us to a man, a grave, or both."

CHAPTER 28

He started knocking on doors at 10 a.m., beginning on California Street near Franklin. The elaborate Victorians were huge and stately, and many were occupied by a combination of owners and tenants. Because there was no way of telling how the living space was divided, Saint Claire knocked on all the doors. His progress was slow.

Most of the neighbors knew about Paul Vang's murder and a killer still-at-large, and so while some remained behind small cracks in door openings, the majority had at least as many questions for Saint Claire as he had for them.

The third woman on record said Paul was a visible and active member of the Neighborhood Watch program. He also knocked on doors as a realtor and broker, offering listing services to sellers and mortgage loans to buyers.

According to an old man at mid-block, Paul was polite, but nosy. If he saw a nice garden, he'd strike up a conversation about gardening to get a person talking. If there were children, he'd talk about the latest child psychology theory or schools in the area. The man said Paul was always trying to find and mash the buttons that got people talking, and when they were talking, he took it all in. He would talk to anyone, even bums passing through the neighborhood.

By one o'clock, a reporter had pulled up to a curb. She watched Saint Claire for thirty minutes before exiting the car to approach the detective.

"Kiyomi Yamakita, with the *Chronicle*."

She extended a steady hand.

"And you're Inspector Saint Claire investigating the Vang murder. Any luck on leads from the neighbors?"

"Not really. It's slow going."

Before he realized she had done it, she passed her card.

"Nice little neighborhood. Finding many people at home?"

It was a sunny day, and both reporter and detective faced eastward to shield their eyes.

"I've talked to a few."

"Someone called the newspaper and said you had a drawing of the killer, and she said you thought the killer lived in this neighborhood at some time?"

Saint Claire checked his watch.

"I'm sorry, Ms. Yamakita. I'm a detective. It's my job to leave no stone unturned, explore every possibility. I'm investigating here. I'm not suggesting anything."

She clutched his arm as he turned to walk away.

"What about the drawing?"

She smiled, adjusting her purse on her shoulder as he turned.

"Can I see it?"

He hesitated a moment.

"Sure."

She scrutinized the sketch, using her body to shade the paper from the sun.

"Interesting. Isn't this supposed to be the same serial killer who murdered Helen Rosenthal and Hector Fuentes?"

"Unknown. I'm in the neighborhood to investigate the *Vang* murder."

"Can I have this drawing?"

He reached over and tugged the paper from her fingers.

"I'm sorry. It's my only copy, and as you can see, I'm just getting underway."

He turned back toward the landmark home.

"I've got your card. If anything interesting turns up, I'll let you know."

It would be only a matter of time before the story broke and embellished, irrelevant details would make the public paranoid. Saint Claire halted his interviews after the *Chronicle* reporter started her car and drove away. The clock was ticking.

What troubled Saint Claire about the Vang murder also applied to the murder of young Father O'Brien. In order to set up each of the murders, the killer had to expose himself to potential witnesses. Yet no one he interviewed remembered any suspicious new residents or outsiders in the last year.

Father O'Brien's apartment in the Victorian was located above the apartments of Miss Bessie and Mr. Radionchenko. The only way to access the apartment was to pass in front of Miss Bessie's apartment, and Miss Bessie, limited to a wheelchair and walker, was always home. And anyone entering the building had to ring the intercom and gain access from one of the tenants.

O'Brien had invited some person into the apartment and that person had secretly made the holes in the walls. This meant it could have been someone from the church or someone who had befriended the naïve young man.

Upstairs in the apartment, the carpet and floors were cleaned and the walls were freshly painted in eggshell white. Kaholy had had the holes professionally repaired two days earlier. Yet, Saint Claire sat at the center of the living room for a contemplative fifteen minutes before going back to the Vang house to interview the young widow.

"Mrs. Vang, do you have time for a few questions?"

"Mrs. Vang is my mother-in-law. Just call me Mary."

He nodded.

"Okay Mary, how often were you over at the apartment before the murders?"

"Not often. I have a one-year-old, ya know."

"I understand. Do you remember any of your tenants ever entertaining guests? Any regular visitors?"

Kaholy crossed her arms and cocked her head, a little suspicious.

"Miss Bessie's daughter came by once or twice a week. Mr. Radionchenko is a little crazy, ya know, but he never had anyone come by. His family's dead, or back in Russia."

"What about Father O'Brien?"

"He was a priest. Whadaya think? Sometimes he had folks from the church, men only, but not much. Ya wanna sit down?"

She led Saint Claire back to the living room, where he sat on a couch adjacent to her.

"If the killer was ever at the house visiting O'Brien, do you think Miss Bessie would have seen him?"

"Miss Bessie saw everything. She was nosy cuz she had nothin else ta do, but she's dead. How would that help?"

"Did she ever say anything about any of O'Brien's visitors? Any complaints, comments?"

Kaholy sighed.

"Nope. Too bad she died. She probably could have helped you."

He grimaced.

"I know. What about Mr. Radionchenko? Has he ever said anything?"

"He's crazy. He don't talk, unless you speak Russian. I don't think he even knows anyone died."

Saint Claire opened the folder.

"You think if I show him this picture—"

"Wait! Who's *that*?"

Surprised, he handed the picture across to her.

"It's an artist's sketch of what the killer might look like..."

"I've seen him. Wait, he lived on this street. I always thought that dude was weird. He lived on the other side of the street, two houses down on the left, bottom apartment."

Saint Claire stood and walked to the window to identify the house.

"Right there? You know this person?"

"Paul knew im. The priest knew im. He was quiet, but his eyes were always goin. When he was around he was always *watchin*, like he was studyin things or somethin. I thought he was a thief."

"Do you remember the name he went by?"

She closed her eyes.

"John. His name was John. I don't know his last name."

"And when was the last time you saw him?"

She shrugged.

"A month, a month and a half I think. Hey, he was a wacko, but he's not the killer. I could tell ya that much."

"How do you know that?"

"Cuz he's dead. I think it was an accident, but he's been dead for at least a month. So unless dead folks can get back up and kill people, ya know like vampires an zombies, I think you're chasin after a dead man."

CHAPTER 29

A wide beam of morning sunlight slanted across the room, bathing a stack of books on the floor in a surreal gilded glow. The aroma of freshly brewed coffee pervaded the space as she sat next to the steaming cup, her fingers working the computer keyboard. Barefoot, she wiggled her tingling toes in another beam of deliciously warm sunlight. This morning, it felt great to be alive.

It seemed almost too good to be true. She was feeling so much better. It was like she had been relieved of a heavy burden. In an instant she had escaped the dark, heavy fetters that had kept her off course for the majority of her life. She knew her proper path and she knew the time had come to embrace a new destiny.

When she met with psychiatrists and a lawyer a day earlier, she didn't reveal how and why the change had occurred, but she assured the women she was cured of her affliction. Yet if she had told the doctors a *voodoo* priestess had come into her room and lifted an evil curse, she was certain the result would have been much different.

Mama Jezebel confirmed that the old woman, Madame Toussainte, had jinxed Katrina years ago in Thibodaux, and she admitted the spell was a strong one. To break the jinx, Mama Jezebel started by preparing a spiritual bath with hyssop, rue and a dozen other uncrossing herbs. After the bath, she burned two white offertory candles dressed with uncrossing oil and she lit the uncrossing incense.

Mama Jezebel instructed Katrina to read words from the 37th Psalm of the Bible, which began,

Fret not thyself with evildoers, neither be thou envious against the workers of iniquity. For they shall soon be cut down like the grass, and wither as the green herb.

According to Mama Jezebel, Madame Toussainte did die in the recent hurricane, and with her all the evil she had wrought. Her malevolent spell died with her, but Katrina still needed to be cleansed and blessed.

Katrina read from Psalms 37 as Mama Jezebel ladled the cleansing bath water over her head. She recited the psalm thirteen times before she rose from the tub. Standing naked between the candles, she recited the psalm a final time as the water dripped from her body. The *Voudoun* stressed that she would have to repeat the process for thirteen days in a row to break the spell completely.

That evening, the *Voudoun* directed Katrina to consume a strong alcoholic drink as she sat on the floor. Mama Jezebel had brought in a makeshift altar with candles and spread flour on the floor in a deliberate fashion. She wore a white tunic and a long white skirt with an uneven hem. A female assistant, who arrived after the bath, sat just outside the candles' glow, quietly beating a drum. Her name was Nani.

Barefoot, Mama Jezebel danced before the altar, shaking a rattle and chanting words in a foreign language. She danced slowly, languorously at first, but her movements increased in momentum and fervor as the drum, the rattle and the chanting intensified in volume. Then all at once, Mama Jezebel's body stiffened and she fell with a thud to the floor.

Her assistant explained through a thick *patois* accent.

"Her *ti bon ange* be done left her body and the spirit be takin control."

When Mama Jezebel rose, she seemed a different person. She looked down on Katrina with an expression that appeared ancient, wise and benevolent. As she spoke in an African tongue that Katrina could not understand, her voice was as a man's voice. She placed a hand on Katrina's head, pronouncing a blessing of some kind and gestured toward the *Rada* above.

Katrina had no idea how the women smuggled a chicken in, but Mama Jezebel's assistant quickly slit the bird's throat and clutched the chicken's struggling body as its blood spurted into a thick glass goblet. After stuffing the still flapping body into a large gunnysack, she presented the warm drink to the *Loa*-possessed priestess.

Mama Jezebel sipped at first, and then she turned the goblet up and drank heartily. Wiping her mouth with the palm of her left hand, she smiled, nodded and pronounced additional blessings. When she stopped, her face went blank and she sat on the floor, her head bowed.

The ceremony over, Nani began cleaning the room. By the time Nani finished, Mama Jezebel had awakened. The *Voudoun* seemed confused and a bit wobbly on her feet as she stood. Smiling sheepishly at Katrina, she adjusted her wet tunic and skirt, her color and demeanor returning.

"The curse is lifted. Your life is now your own to live."

To Katrina, they were the most precious words ever spoken. And yet, she realized she had not considered much beyond the thought of freedom itself. She felt like the disheartened slave, who suddenly granted emancipation, had no place to go, unable to conceive of freedom.

Over the next day, she imagined leaving the hospital and starting a new life. But how? She was still married. She wondered if she should go to live with Deuteronomy. He had sold their five-bedroom home in the Berkeley hills years earlier. He spent part of the proceeds on a condominium in the city, so it was community property. She had never seen the place, but after twelve years of separation, she wasn't sure if living with her husband would be a good thing.

She still loved him, but things had changed. In fact they had changed years before their son was murdered. It was something his mother had told her, something shocking. For years, Katrina was reluctant to believe it, but the seeds of doubt had sprouted and grown over the years.

For two nights in a row after the ceremony, she had taken the spiritual baths, reciting the psalm, and each day after, she felt better. So it was on the third morning that she sat at the computer, composing a prayer of thanks.

He tapped on the door before turning the knob and pushing it open. When he entered, he noticed the drapes were open and the sun was shining into the room. In twelve years, Katrina had never seemed so content. As she stood to greet him, she looked radiant, happy.

"Sit down, Ronnie. Have a cup of coffee with me?"

He nodded as he sat, skeptical.

"Isn't it a beautiful day out today? How was your drive over?"

"You're right. Very nice day to be in the city. Drive was good."

Deuteronomy took the coffee and sipped, sitting back.

"Okay, something's different about you. What happened?"

"You think I'm different?"

"Yeah, you seem different."

She smiled.

"I am. I feel different. I feel like I've been reborn. My spirit wants out of this place. I think I need to get back to my life!"

"I'm glad you're feeling better, and you look fantastic, but what's this about getting back to your life?"

"I want out, Ronnie. I came in here voluntarily, and I told my doctors yesterday I'm over the trouble I was having. I told them I want to be released within the week."

His frown was barely discernible, but it was there.

"You know, I can't begin to understand what it'd be like in here for so long. I know you want to try it out there, but I don't think it's a good idea. It would be very difficult for you out there."

"No more difficult than for anyone else! I can't stay locked up here forever. Do you want me to die here, is that what you want?"

"No! I want you to get better. You know what I'm talking about."

She bowed her head, searching for words to proceed.

"I am better. I'm cured."

"What do you mean?"

"The *Voudoun* came. She was here three nights ago. The curse has been lifted. I can get on with my life."

"A *Voudoun* came to this hospital? From where?"

"From New Orleans."

He scanned the surroundings.

"And she conducted her pagan ceremony in this room?"

"Yes. A *Voudoun* put the curse on me in the first place, so I needed another *Voudoun* to get it lifted. I had to balance the equation. You wouldn't help me, so I got someone else to do it."

"Who? Brady?"

She sighed, disappointed by his response.

"That's not important. What really matters is that I'm getting out of here. If you don't want me with you, I'll find a place of my own."

He crossed his arms.

"No, I think you're just oversimplifying things a little. I mean, you're right. You did come in here on a voluntary basis.

But after you were in, there was a psychological evaluation done on you and a court hearing, remember? And the court issued an order committing you to the care of the doctors here pending a future evaluation to determine when and if you're well enough to leave?"

"I am well enough to leave, and I've requested that hearing."

He stiffened a little.

"And I'll have to object to your leaving. This is too sudden. I think it's a little premature."

"I've been in this prison for twelve fuckin years! What do you mean premature?"

Profanity from Katrina usually predicated an outburst or a physical confrontation. His eyes darted toward the door, and then he caught her eyes. At least she was listening. He continued.

"Tell you what, I was against getting a *Voudoun* in here, but I'll meet you halfway. Give it two weeks, and if you still feel better, I'll go to the court and testify on your behalf. I'll help you get out."

She held her ground.

"If you're going to help me, then help me. I've been in here twelve years and I want out yesterday! If trying to get out now means you won't help me, then I'll do it without you. And if you want to testify against me, then do that. I'm sorry. I just thought I had a husband."

"Oh come on! You can't wait two weeks?"

"No, Ronnie. I really can't."

She lowered her eyes.

"If you're not willing to commit to helping me, I think this discussion is over. Now if you'll excuse me, I think I want to be alone."

When he opened the door to leave, an older woman stood in the doorway.

"Hello?"

"Deuteronomy Saint Claire, I know who you are. May I come in?"

Katrina nudged Deuteronomy aside and escorted the woman in. Remaining inside, Deuteronomy turned back toward the women, shutting the door behind him.

"You're that damned witch. You came here to take advantage of my wife!"

Katrina came between the two.

"She's my guest, Ronnie. And you were just leaving?"

"She has no power, Kate. She's a charlatan. How much you pay her?"

Mama Jezebel answered.

"She paid for tickets out for me and an assistant, and for the cost of a live chicken. No more than that. I don't work my gifts for money."

"Then why did you come here today?"

"I came to check on her before I go home. I have an afternoon flight. It's a follow-up."

She turned toward Katrina.

"Don't fret. He's a decent man. He means well."

She looked back at Deuteronomy and smiled.

"No matter where one goes, the problems are the same. If you really love your wife, you must open your heart and share everyting. Share your secret. And if she loves you, she will share hers. But more than all else, you have to help this girl get out of this place. If she does not, she will die. I've seen it. Secrets can kill."

Her eyes returned to Katrina.

"Remember everting I told you. A *Voudoun* can lift a mere curse, but not even God... not even God can change what's already passed or what destiny has designed."

"Do you keep any kind of books around here, a ledger maybe?"

"Yeah, somewhere around here. Why?"

"I'd just like to determine the date of his last transaction when he was here."

The white-haired man nodded and pushed his glasses back up the bridge of his nose.

"Always keep good records. Accountant for thirty-five years before I retired."

He opened a file drawer at his lower right and leaned left to read the tabs as his fingers sorted.

"There it is. I kept a file on him."

"What is his full name?" Brady asked.

Whitey opened the file.

"Jonathan Dough, and that's Dough spelled d-o-u-g-h. No middle initial."

Brady rolled his eyes.

"John Doe? Are you kidding me? Come on, you *had* to know it was a made-up name!"

"I thought so. That's why I checked and double checked his ID. I even made a copy of it."

"You have a picture of this guy? I need to see it."

"I tossed it already. The guy won't be renting from me again unless he's a zombie. Jonathan Dough has been dead for over a month."

"How do you know he's dead?"

"Police found the body, of course. Somehow, he musta fell on the BART tracks near midtown. Train dragged him a quarter mile. He was all mangled and burned, but they had his wallet, his keys and his jewelry. And he had a shoulder tattoo. I had to go to the morgue to identify the body."

"And you're sure it was him?"

Whitey nodded.

"It was him, all right. Him just as sure as I'm looking at you. Damn shame! He was a decent young man. Always paid his rent two weeks early."

Brady removed the composite sketch of the killer from his attaché.

"Is this your John Dough?"

"Was. That *was* him. But it's like I told you, he's been dead for a month."

CHAPTER 30

Sonia sat at the conference table, reports, pages and notes spread out before her. Her life was critical to the outcome of this case, one of seven pieces in a bloody puzzle, a secondary or tertiary plot in a bizarre mystery.

Beginning with the oldest cases, she worked toward the present. Of the earlier cases, the *Killing Artist* series was the most interesting. Seven years earlier, a serial killer in San Francisco had quietly recreated seven great masterpieces in death.

There was a brief reference to the series in the second letter when the killer wrote,

"You've seen my work. I showed at the DeYoung."

The killer was referring to the DeYoung Museum, the city's largest public arts institution. But while the DeYoung featured collections of American Painting, African Art, Oceanic Art, New Guinea Art and South American Art, the killer's work imitated the European Renaissance masters.

One morning, a DeYoung museum guard reported a double murder, discovered in the Koret Auditorium, just to the right of the main entrance. The bodies of a handsome young man and an older man with a beard were found arranged in a macabre homage to Michelangelo's *Creation of Adam*.

The county Medical Examiner concluded that the men had been killed in the early evening and the bodies positioned as rigor mortis began to set in. The killer used tiny sutures to sew the eyelids open and the skin was sprayed with a commercial tanning product that disguised the pallor of death. The doctors ruled asphyxiation as the cause of death in both men.

Over the course of several months, the Killing Artist, a designation he chose in a letter to the police, recreated *Madonna and Child* by Raphael, da Vinci's *Vitruvian Man*, van Eyck's *The Annunciation*, *Pietà* by Michelangelo and two others, though the artistic references became more subtle in subsequent killings.

As in the other two serial cases Sonia researched, the killing stopped after seven crime scenes, like Saint Claire said, and then there was little or no serial activity for two to three years. To Sonia, the killer wanted the police to know he was the same killer in all the series.

As she reread the second letter, a line stood out in her head. The killer wrote to Saint Claire,

"You have understood killers because you are genetically prone to kill."

Maybe it was all a game and Saint Claire was in on it. The top brass were still convinced he was withholding crucial information.

Her stomach started to cramp again. Over the last week, her appetite was missing, and when she forced herself to eat, it was difficult to keep food down. Maybe it was the meds. She hadn't been so miserable since she was pregnant with Tati. Doubled over with pain, she lunged for the door and staggered down the hall toward the bathroom.

When she returned, Brady was sitting at the table, reading one of the old files. As he looked up, his eyes widened.

"You okay? You're looking uh, a little stressed."

"I'm fine."

"And it looks like you're losing weight."

Self-conscious, she wiped the corners of her mouth.

"I'm fine, Brady. Where's Saint Claire?"

"On his way."

She eased into the chair across from him.

"What are you reading there?"

"One of his earlier cases, the one they called the Monozygotic Twins serials. Captain Slater and the Medical Examiner back then believed there was more than one killer. Slater was sure the killer had an accomplice."

"I know. Most of the victims in the series were stab victims, so the examiner commented on the wounds. And always one of the twins was stabbed by a right-handed person, while the other was stabbed by a left-hander."

Brady interrupted.

"What is Saint Claire?"

"Left-handed."

When Saint Claire arrived, he seemed distracted.

"Sorry I'm late. Working hard and getting nowhere."

He took a moment to reorganize his thoughts.

"Next murder on the killer's schedule is supposed to be a woman, but it won't be you, Sonia."

Brady pushed the file in front of him aside.

"How do you know that?"

"Killer sees himself as an artist, and art requires balance. Those reports you're reading, it's all there. Formal balance in art places equal or very similar objects on either side of a central axis, creating symmetry."

He had gotten ahead of himself. Standing at the window glancing out, he started again.

"Okay, the first three killings were men, and that means the next three will be women. Now I said the next killing isn't supposed to be you, Sonia, because I've scrutinized everything coming away from Vang. The ripples go out in many directions, but none go toward you. That means there has to be at least one and possibly two women between Vang and whatever the killer's got planned for you. I'm pretty sure of it."

He looked toward Brady.

"What did the landlord say?"

"Said our killer died a *month* ago, in a BART accident."

"You have the report?"

For reasons he didn't understand, Brady resented the question.

"Ordered it before I came in here."

He paused.

"Okay Saint Claire, I've got a question for you."

"What is it?"

"In two of the earlier cases, both the Medical Examiner and Slater said they believed the killer had an accomplice."

Saint Claire turned and looked toward Sonia, who affected indifference.

"It's true. They believed the perpetrator had an accomplice, but that was based on a limited understanding of the killer and his methods."

"Well, you can't argue facts. In almost all the cases where the twins were being murdered, one was stabbed by a right-handed person and the other by a left-handed person. In the North Beach cases, the victims were strangled, some by a right-hander, others by a left-hander."

"I understand what's in those reports, Brady. Remember, I was there."

Brady shrugged.

"Yeah, I can't argue that. You were there."

He waited until Saint Claire turned in his direction.

"And apparently you don't think there was an accomplice?"

"Impossible. I know this killer. He's a megalomaniac. His ego wouldn't allow him to rely on an accomplice."

Sonia chimed in.

"Then how do you explain the right-handed and left-handed stab wounds?"

Saint Claire sighed.

"I know it doesn't make sense. It threw me at first. That was his intention. But after examining the facts a little closer, the answer was obvious."

Brady wagged his head.

"Obvious? Well somehow I must have missed it. Can you uh, enlighten me?"

"The killer's ambidextrous. He was able to stab or strangle people using either hand with equal skill."

Brady groaned aloud in disbelief.

"Oh come on! That's as cheesy as John Dough being his name. There's no way you could know that!"

Saint Claire smiled. He had never shared, not even with Slater, how he knew, but the time had come.

"Okay, earlier I said the killer sees himself as an artist and that balance and symmetry were important to him. Truth is, he's obsessed with balance. I know this guy."

Walking over to the table, he located the twins' serial report.

"If you reread this report, you'll find nothing random about the stabbings. He alternates right and left consistently. The number of wounds to each of the twins and the general placement of those wounds are exactly corresponding... almost mirror images. If you read the report with that in mind, his pattern is exact, it's unerring. To him, it was art."

He pushed the report toward Sonia.

"It becomes even more evident if you factor in the time of death, which can be used to establish the alternating pattern."

Neither Sonia nor Brady responded as Saint Claire continued.

"And in that case with the strangled therapists, he alternated right-hand dominant and left-hand dominant in exact placement and order. Same person."

Brady interrupted.

"But there were seven. They're always seven. So why would a person so obsessed with balance choose the number seven? It's an odd number."

"Because he thinks he becomes God at seven. The seventh killing is always different. The seventh contains the twist. It's where he makes his statement. If you remember, the seventh set of twins was each electrocuted, not stabbed."

"Meaning what?"

Saint Claire was tempted to explain, but an explanation would have led to even more questions, and he could feel the clock ticking.

"What we really need to focus on now is preventing number four. Vang died five days ago, so I think we're running out of time. I've gotta go."

"Wait! Before you go!"

Brady rose from the chair, his frustration showing.

"If you know this killer so well, and you know the next three victims are supposed to be women, do you have any idea about who the seventh victim will be?"

Saint Claire stopped and turned.

"Of course I do. I've known it from the first day."

He smiled.

"I'm the first murder of the series, which of course means I'm the seventh victim."

CHAPTER 31

He insisted he had made a full recovery, but his hands were still a little shaky.

"It's me, only better. Ask Oksana. You know, with all that heavy metal stirrin around in my blood, I haven't needed the *Viagra* at all. And I swear it's grown three inches! One problem, though."

Saint Claire seemed concerned.

"What's that?"

"Damnedest thing! Never knew it before. When they reach this size, they turn *your* color."

Derrick Slater sat in the leather armchair in his upstairs recess, sipping a Jack Daniel's on ice from a highball glass.

"I've seen that look. Somethin's botherin ya. Ya wanna talk about it, but because you're an asshole, ya want me ta drag it outa ya. So let's just imagine I've spent the last hour naggin at ya and bitchin about how ya need to open up and share whatever it is you *don't* wanna talk about. Save me the hassle."

"It's Katrina."

"What about er?"

Saint Claire sat back on the sofa and removed his hat, something he had never done before in Slater's presence.

Slater took another large sip of the whiskey, making a face to disguise the degree of his surprise. But the ear wasn't nearly as mangled as he had imagined it would be. The top was missing, cropped off along a scarred, jagged horizontal line.

Looking at his friend, Slater saw something in Saint Claire he had rarely seen. Head bowed and shoulders slumped, the detective seemed vulnerable, almost defeated. The spectacle was sobering. Slater wasn't sure if he even wanted to know what had happened.

"Is she better? Worse? What is it?"

"She's asked the doctors to release her within the week."

"What? Is that so bad?"

"I just can't let it happen. Don't know what I'll have to do, but I have to make sure she doesn't get out."

"Why?"

Saint Claire began a response and stopped.

"It's not a good thing. Not now."

"What about the curse?"

"Claims she got a voodoo woman from New Orleans to perform a ritual in her room. Claims the woman removed the curse."

Slater still couldn't understand why there was a problem.

"What was her condition? Clinically depressed?"

"And schizophrenic. She's a danger to herself and others. That's what I told the court twelve years ago, and that's what I'll tell them now if I have to, for her own good."

Slater stood. Saint Claire had never been so irrational.

"Hey, I'm not trying to take a side, but I've talked to Katrina. Aside from her bein a little obsessed about that *voodoo* curse, I've never seen anything actually *wrong* with her. If she's over the curse, what's the problem with her gettin out?"

Saint Claire sighed and looked over at his friend.

"She's a danger."

"How?"

He closed his eyes for a moment.

"Katrina's always been fragile. I knew that from the beginning, and it was fine with me. The big change came about a year after we got married, when she was pregnant with Christian. Where she had been warm and loving before, she turned ice cold, for no apparent reason. She wouldn't let me touch her. When I tried to talk to her about it, there was just no reaching her."

He wagged his head.

"Anyway, she never wanted Christian. Early on, I thought it was my imagination, but I was sure she was doing things purposely to miscarry or lose the baby. She smoked and drank the whole time. I believed back then I had to watch her like a hawk to make sure she didn't terminate the pregnancy."

He looked toward Slater.

"But Christian was born in spite of her, a beautiful baby. I was happy, and I wanted her to be happy too, but she wasn't. She wanted nothing to do with him. It was at a time before doctors had any real understanding of perinatal and peripartum depression. Anyway, about two weeks after he was born, she left us. I was in graduate school. My sister called and said Katrina left the baby with her and kept going. I didn't see her again for two years. And we didn't get back together until Christian was four. And then a week after she got back, I think she tried to kill him."

His eyes watered as he remembered.

"Christian almost died. He had an allergic reaction to something she gave him, some herb she was taking. He went into anaphylactic shock. It was real dicey for about twenty-four hours. He barely survived."

He paused, hollowing his cheeks, blowing a sigh.

"She got pregnant again about a year later. She was religiously taking birth control and making me use condoms. We weren't even having sex much, but she got pregnant anyway. When she found out, she fell apart. She swore it was that curse."

Slater interrupted.

"She lost the baby?"

"I didn't think it would happen, but she carried the baby to term. Beautiful girl. We named her Geneviève. She was two months old when I found her dead in her crib. Doctors said it was SIDS, but I always thought there was more to it. I would have never been able to prove anything."

Slater raised his eyebrows.

"I'm sorry. I never knew anything about your daughter. I know from experience how painful it is to lose a child. I hafta ask though, would you really force Katrina to live the rest of her life institutionalized on a mere suspicion? You might be wrong. What if it actually was *SIDS*?"

Saint Claire nodded.

"You're right. Sure you're right, but it's not that simple. Some years later, we took a vacation to Spain. Christian was nine and I had just started teaching at Berkeley. We were there three weeks in all."

He took a large sip from the brandy snifter, finishing off the amber liquid.

"So uh, four days before we left Spain, we went to Portugal. We were on the beach that last day, a beautiful beach. I was just sitting there under an umbrella, reading a book while Katrina and Christian were out at the water's edge, digging up clams. I guess I got a little absorbed in the book, because I lost track of time. When I knew anything, a woman up the hill was screaming and crying. I couldn't understand what she was saying, but the sound of a mother's wail at the loss of a child transcends all language."

Slater replenished the cognac in his guest's glass.

"It obviously wasn't Christian?"

"No. It was a four-year-old boy. Up the hill, there was a little thatch-roofed cement building with a shower and a toilet. The woman found her son's still warm body on the floor by the toilet. He'd been strangled to death."

"And the locals accused Katrina of it?"

"No. Exactly the opposite. The mother thanked Katrina for being so helpful. One of the men said a group of gypsies had camped at the beach couple of nights before, so in no time they were all blaming a gypsy man who straggled behind for the killing. But I knew the killer wasn't the gypsy."

"And you knew this how?"

Saint Claire tensed the muscles at the base of his jaw, and drew a breath. After taking another sip from the snifter, he began.

"We were the only ones on the beach, Katrina, Christian and me. We saw no gypsies. The man they accused was a crippled itinerant asleep in a tent a mile away. The man could barely walk."

Reflecting, he shook his head.

"I was at the base of the hill the entire time. And the little building with the shower and toilet was just up the hill behind me. So the beach was in the front there, then there was me and the building, and behind it a small village where all the people were related in some way. And I know for a fact that Katrina visited that building behind me at least twice to use the toilet. She claimed she was having stomach problems, TD or something."

Slater stared at Saint Claire for a moment. He nodded.

"Okay, I can understand you havin your suspicions. With your daughter, you were a father lookin to make some sense of a loss just like I was. I went through that. But with this boy at the beach, there are just too many other possibilities. You were in that village for what, a day or two? You have no idea what may have been goin on there before you got there. You don't know what was goin on in the boy's life. There could have been a sexual predator in the community, any number of things."

He sighed, setting down his glass.

"I think you've chosen to ignore all the other real possibilities because it's been more convenient to blame Katrina. You've created a rationale that allows you to sleep at night when you know there was probably no valid reason to have her institutionalized in the first place."

"I haven't finished."

But Slater continued, perturbation audible in his voice.

"I'm not a psychology professor like you are and I'm not takin a side, but do you think it's at least possible this might be more about resentin her ditching you and Christian? I mean, she left you. And the fact that she changed on you? Maybe a part of you wants to *punish* her for cuttin out the sex. I'm just not seein how she's a danger to herself or anyone else."

"After the incident in Portugal, she wasn't the same. She was even more withdrawn. When we got back to Berkeley, she took a leave of absence from her job for depression. The leave was supposed to last a month, but she kept extending it until a year had passed. She began seeing a psychiatrist after that first year and she got better. Then she went back to work at the hospital."

His eyes stared straight ahead, fixed on an invisible scene in the distance.

"I thought everything was better, but then I discovered she had become addicted, off and on, to a few of the medications she was taking, the *diazepam*, the *fluoxetine*, the haloperidol and maybe one or two other exotic psychotics. As a psychopharmacologist, she had access to any drug she could ever want."

He paused.

"A visiting professor from New York University had a son about Christian's age. His name was Sage. He was thirteen, and he was over just about every weekend. The boys played well together, and we had become good friends with the professor and her husband. You know, after what happened in Portugal, I was reluctant to let any of Christian's friends spend the night."

He cringed at the memory.

"It worked for a while, but then one night Christian came into my study and told me he couldn't wake Sage up. I rushed to his room and tried, but the boy was barely breathing. He didn't respond to CPR or anything else I tried. By the time the ambulance arrived, he was dead."

"What killed him?"

"Medical examiner said it was respiratory depression and hypoxia, but he couldn't explain why a healthy, thirteen-year-old boy would all of a sudden stop breathing."

He sipped, pausing to take a breath.

"Katrina said she thought the boys were experimenting with drugs, inhalants. As it turned out, the toxicologist noted Sage was hypoglycemic at the time of his death. But even after a full autopsy was performed, there was no finding or evidence of drugs in his system."

Still standing with the highball glass in hand, Slater held up his hand in a halting motion.

"Hold on. Hypoglycemic? Why was the boy hypoglycemic?"

"Examiner couldn't explain it. There was no prior history of the condition."

Slater pulled over a chair and sat across from his friend, speaking after a pause.

"And you think Katrina somehow killed the boy?"

"I was hoping the toxicology report or autopsy would turn up something in the way of evidence, one way or the other. Sage's parents were devastated, but they had a good support system in their church. They accepted the unexplainable loss as the will of God. But yes, I think Katrina killed the boy. She's a drug expert. She used a drug she knew couldn't be traced."

"And what do you think her rationale is for all these killings?"

Saint Claire looked into Slater's eyes.

"I never told you this, but her grandfather was a killer, though no one in the community ever realized what he had been doing until many years after his death. That was because he targeted travelers, people just passing through town. The longer their journey, the better for him. He was clever, like her. He would kill people between points A and B, north and south, east and west and so on so that when police started investigating, they had to search the length of the entire line rather than focus on any specific point."

He shrugged.

"He buried them in graves in a fenced off plot he owned by the river. About ten or so years after he died, a geologist with the Thibodeaux Public Works Department discovered one of the bodies while surveying for natural gas. By the time they finished digging up corporal remains, there were more than thirty people buried in that plot. Her grandfather was a killer, a pathological killer. And as far as anyone could tell, there was no rationale. He killed for the sake of killing."

"And that makes Katrina a killer?"

"Well, the whole idea of murderers genetically passing down their propensity for killing to successive generations is scientifically inconclusive so far. It can't be proven, but in my experience I'm convinced it happens. Show me a killer and I'll show you a family history rife with violence and death distributed throughout. If there is such a thing as a killer gene, I think she inherited it from her grandfather."

Slater realized Saint Claire was revealing personal information and opinions that were painful to share, but he disagreed. Based on his own experience with people and criminal minds, Katrina was no killer. He sighed, sitting back in the chair.

"Tell me somethin. You really believe one of the ways you can recognize people with thisth killer gene is because throughout their entire lives they're surrounded by violence and death? Even if nothin can be proven conclusively?"

"Yeah, to a degree."

Slater half-smiled, his eyes glazed his speech slurred.

"Then let me be the first to say I think you must have that killer gene!"

"Excuse me?"

"Look at your life, Saint Claire. All those murders you're accusing Katrina of, you were there! And you've been surrounded by and involved in a lot more death than Katrina could ever be."

He sipped the last of the whiskey from the glass and sat it down forcefully.

"Come on, there was that first woman in Louisiana, and your college roommate, and your son, and your partner Joe, and the former Berkeley students and all the murders in all the cases you've worked. Death is your lifelong companion. It's your obsession. It's why you've never gone back to teachin. You can't exist without it."

He stood, wobbling a little.

"I'm sorry. Too much booze while I'm on medication, I guess. Maybe *you're* a killer, Saint Claire. You've been my best friend for a long time now, but do you think it's never crossed my mind? I've always thought if anyone was smart enough ta pull off all these murders for all these years and get away with it, and not just get away with it, but ta be so smart that all the San Francisco Police Department could do is hope and pray he'd stop or move on, if anyone could do that, it would be someone just like you."

CHAPTER 32

"Bobbie, can I see you in my office for a minute?"

Eyes moving from the computer screen to the speakerphone, she cringed, knowing what was coming.

"I'm working on that report you wanted out this afternoon. You want me to stop?"

"This won't take long."

Barbara Stevens had worked for the county of San Francisco for sixteen years, ten of those years with the Board of Supervisors, seven in the Clerk's office. She began with Rusty when he worked for the Office of the Legislative Analyst. His personal assistant for over nine years, she could almost read his mind.

Rusty Mullholland was not the sort of boss you wanted to make upset. *Berserker Rage*! That's the way associates and staff members described it when he lost his temper. After a public eruption, he would occasionally apologize in private, but this only happened with individuals he respected. Fortunately, Barbara was one of them. But on three occasions, his criticism had been caustic enough to engender letters of resignation from her.

She actually quit one time for two weeks. It took him two dozen unreturned phone calls, a bouquet of roses, the concession of a larger office with a window and a raise to win her return. He was wrong for the terrible things he said in that incident and he knew it. But this time, it was Barbara who had screwed up. If Rusty found out, he would have good reason to "tear her a new one."

She wondered how she could have been so stupid. After a college degree in Public Administration and sixteen years of experience in the trenches, she should have known better. Now, the reputation she had built, her position in county government, her retirement and even her marriage were at risk.

It would have been better if Saint Claire hadn't come by to interview her at work. Not that she minded answering questions. She had nothing to hide, but it raised eyebrows when a detective from the police department came to meet with an employee on the job, and it was worse when he came that second time.

Rusty noted the visits, but he said nothing either time. What he did comment on was the change in her demeanor. Over the week, she was irritable and short-tempered with subordinates. She had trouble concentrating on tasks and avoided the usual one-on-ones with him. So when he called her into his office, she knew he would want to have that heart to heart, not as her friend, but as her boss.

"Okay, I'll be right in."

She had dreaded the moment, but she knew it was coming.

"You wanted to see me?"

"Close the door. Sit down."

The psyche war had already begun. He was reading something, or more likely he was pretending to be reading some damning document in an attempt to force a defensive slip on her part. If he really had something, he would have come right out with it. She smiled nervously and sat, crossing her legs. Her best feature, they were always on display in stockings and high heels.

She and Rusty had history. He met her on the day he started in the Analyst's office and hired her right away, on her twenty-ninth birthday. Rusty was older, almost fifty, though he looked more like sixty. Over the years, the two spent many a night getting snookered in one bar or another. They had been to Vegas and New York together. And that one time in Cabo they woke up in bed together naked, but that was the only time and they never talked about it.

He looked up, his expression severe.

"I've been hearing things about you, and frankly I'm concerned. Is there anything you need to talk to me about?"

Indifference was not an option. She had to display firm non-culpability.

"Your wife has no idea about the *casita* you just bought on Gonzaga Bay. Other than that, no."

He reclined the seat back, staring across the desk.

"That's not it. Come on. Tell me, what's goin on with you? Why the cop?"

"Part of a routine follow-up. He said he found my number in a cell phone and he was just investigating all possible leads."

"And for that he had to come back twice?"

"Yes. The first time was questions, the second was follow-up. Pretty typical."

He nodded.

"And this person, who has you in his cell phone, is he under indictment?"

"He's dead."

Pursing his lips, Rusty shrugged.

"Dead? Anyone I know?"

She didn't want him to find out at some time in the future that she intentionally misled him. She had to come clean, but only to a point.

"Not directly. His name was Paul Vang."

"Paul Vang, the real estate developer?"

"Bingo."

Rusty's eyes narrowed as he tossed the mock document onto the table.

"Yeah. Wasn't he murdered? Some weird kinda Chinese mob hit, wasn't it? What was he into?"

She hesitated. If she denied any knowledge of Vang's questionable business dealings and then Rusty learned of her involvement, her career was over.

"The detective I talked to said the murder was random."

"Random? Well I hope nobody just randomly decides to put stakes through my throat. Come on, there's something else to it, isn't there? What was this business going on between you and Vang?"

"There was no business. I met him at a few county functions. We were acquainted, that's all."

Rusty's eyes studied her.

"Yeah, he was a big contributor, wasn't he? Wasn't he involved in political campaigns? For the supervisors and county measures?"

"I believe so, yes."

"And you work in this office? And you were in his cell phone? And the cops and maybe the feds are out there looking in at this wondering why? Right? You stupid shit!"

She sighed.

"You're reading too much into it. Vang was murdered. The detective said a Catholic priest was murdered on the same street a week or so earlier. He thinks there's a connection, a killer in the area."

Rusty grinned.

"You and Vang were doing the horizontal Macarena, weren't you? Don't lie."

"I'm married."

"And when did that ever stop you?"

Since he was making sexual innuendoes, it was obvious he had no idea about her actual arrangement with Vang. He had been bluffing earlier. Sometimes he was just plain obtuse.

She spoke in a whisper.

"Okay, you got me. Vang and I were having a steamy affair. Hot, incredible sex. Did it right on top of this desk more times than I can count."

He stopped smiling. Turning toward the window, he spoke without looking at her.

"Okay, you say it's just a routine investigation, and I'll accept that for now."

He turned on her, his voice quivering on the verge of anger.

"But if there's any goddamn mother fuckin bullshit goin on, and I mean anything screwy or un-kosher, as they say—if you've done anything that might come back to bite me in the ass, I don't think I have to tell you what'll happen to you."

His eyes were intense.

"You fuck me, and I won't just fire you. You know me. If you fuck me, I'll destroy you. It'll be scorched earth. I'll destroy you, and I'll fuck your family."

Brady had known for a week that she was coming, though she never gave him her complete itinerary. Was she going to stay with him or would she be at a hotel? Her flight was scheduled to arrive sometime on Monday, but she hadn't asked him to pick her up from the airport. No matter. He took the day off. It was about time, since he hadn't taken a whole day off work in the last two weeks.

The apartment was coming together, though the décor still seemed a bit sparse and the refrigerator held only a half-case of Bud in bottles, pre-sliced salami, milk, orange juice, a half-eaten calzone and several Chinese take-out boxes.

He was uneasy about her visit. She was different than most of the women he dated, older and much more direct. On Monday a week and a half earlier, when he mentioned that he left his wife, she responded by announcing she was coming for a visit.

Since his trip to New Orleans, they talked on the phone every night. In some ways, she reminded him of Andrea. She was an intelligent woman with a successful career, but she was more real.

When she wasn't working, the walls came down so that her personality emerged. Her sense of humor was wry. She had comical insights about the President and his cabinet, about vain celebrities and their problems, about her co-workers and about race relations. She was sexy, exciting and unpredictable.

Brady didn't tell Saint Claire she was coming, but Saint Claire was her "favorite relative," so it was inconceivable that she hadn't. Brady hadn't answered his partner's cell phone on the three occasions he called, unsure how the "traditional" detective would react to news.

She called at 2:00 that afternoon from a rented car on the way in from San Francisco International to tell him she had made 6:30 dinner reservations at her favorite restaurant in town. The place was not far from Union Square, on Bush at Powell. She asked him to meet her there for a cocktail at 6:00 and reminded him to wear a dinner jacket.

Saint Claire and Mignon were at a coffee shop on Powell when she told him who she was meeting for dinner. "Uncle Doodie" did not disguise his disrelish with his niece dating Brady. When he insisted that Brady was a married man with two daughters, Mignon said she was aware Brady had separated from his wife.

Frustrated, her uncle further reminded her that, according to the Catechism, separation did not end the marriage, and that he'd still be married in the eyes of God even if he divorced his wife.

"Old fashioned rules like that, Uncle, make me feel relieved I'm no longer Catholic."

Saint Claire told her Brady had the reputation of being a ladies' man and that his morals were base and impure.

"Your problem, Uncle, is you need to get laid. How long
has it been? And what ever happened to that Brazilian woman
you were dating? Tell her she needs to give it up."

"I'm not dating her. She's just a friend."

"You're in love with her. You can lie to everyone else, but
you can't lie to me. Come on, God'll forgive you. Auntie Katie's
been fucked up for a long time now. It's okay to find love when
you need love. It's human."

Unwilling to concede, Saint Claire told her that beyond
the fact that he was married and immoral, Brady was not a nice
person. When she pressed him for details, her uncle said he
couldn't share his reasons.

"Trust me. Go back home and don't speak with Brady
again. He'll disrespect you and he might hurt your son."

Saint Claire's words still playing in her mind, Mignon
left her hotel room, took the elevator down and caught a cab
over to the restaurant. Brady was waiting in the bar, fingers
peeling at the label on his beer bottle. He stood upon seeing her.

"Wow! You uhm, you look really stunning. What would
you like to drink?"

"Cream sherry, chilled and up, twist."

She wore a red V-neck cocktail dress with black figuring
all over it and black velvet high heel stilettos. She had pulled her
long wavy hair back into a bun with a dangling, large ringlet on
her right side. Her fingernails were sculptured, lacquered in
shiny red.

Drinks before them, the silence was uncomfortable. And
to think the phone conversations had been so lively and
exciting! He was nervous and she was having second thoughts.
Finally he reached over, placing his hand on hers.

"I'm glad you came."

"I was coming out to see my uncle anyway. Figured I'd
see you both on this trip. I love San Francisco."

Brady nodded, though he couldn't agree with the
sentiment.

"I like the restaurant. You've been here before?"

"It's my favorite restaurant of all time. I'm here every
time I come to town."

He angled his body toward her.

"How'd you discover this place?"

"My uncle brought me here for the first time. I'm not sure if you know this, but his big hobby is going back and trying to solve unsolved murders, the really tough cases. And the guy who first started this restaurant, I know it's French, but I think he was Japanese. Anyway, about a year after he opened it, they found him dead in his apartment—trauma to the head, someone murdered him, and the killer was never found."

"And did your uncle find out who murdered him?"

She shrugged, sipping the sherry.

"I don't remember. All I know is he brought me here when he was working on it, and I've been hooked ever since."

After they were seated, wait staff converged on the table and, seconds later, the stage was set for the nine-course tasting menu that Mignon was intent on enjoying.

Using a small ivory spoon, she scooped up a bit of the *Osetra* caviar, carefully arranged it atop the potato *blini*, added a little *crème fraiche* and placed it in her mouth. She sighed with delight and took up her champagne glass. If she had been uncomfortable earlier, now she was at ease.

"If I didn't say it earlier, you look very handsome tonight."

"Thank you. This is a wonderful restaurant. You did the ordering. I didn't see any prices."

"Oh you pay for what you get here."

She laughed.

"One time I brought my daddy here. Now, he was old school. He always brought it. When he saw the menu, he called the waiter over and whispered, 'For this kinda money, the food better melt in your mouth, digest itself and wipe your *ass* on the way out!'"

With that comment and subsequent laughter, the tension of their first date was broken. Their chemistry was even better at close quarters.

"So you're an oncologist, and that's a cancer doctor?"

"Yes, but I'm more of a professor. I teach at the Stem Cell Transplantation and Molecular Therapeutics Program at Tulane."

"So should I call you Dr. Saint Claire?"

She laughed.

"Now that would be my uncle Doodie, I mean my uncle Ronnie. I'm just Mignon."

"Uncle Doodie?"

"I'm the only one he's ever let call him that. You mention it to him, and I'll kill you if he doesn't."

"You have to know your uncle's a legend around here. He's caught a lot of killers in his time."

She shrugged, thinking of her uncle's words earlier.

"Did you come here to go on a date with me, or did you come here to work me for information about my uncle for your chief?"

She saw Brady blush.

"No, I came here for you. No more about your uncle. I promise."

Three hours after sitting down for dinner, they sipped coffee at the table.

"You're a good looking man. I'll bet your wife really misses you since you left."

"It's an adjustment."

"Do you miss her?"

Eyes focused on the table, he traced the relief design on the coffee cup with his fingertip. He shrugged without looking up.

"No. I'm sorry if it sounds callous. I don't miss her. But I miss my girls."

"Do you see them often?"

"Not as much as I'd like. I'm still getting my apartment together."

Mignon smiled.

"Tell me about your wife. It's Andrea, right? What is she like? Where did you meet her?"

"I met her at my sister's wedding. She approached me, and she's just one of those people who won't stop till she gets what she wants. Schemer from day one. Before I knew any better, she was planning our wedding."

"So were you in love with her?"

He sipped from the porcelain cup.

"I liked her. I think I really liked her, but I was never in love."

"But you married her?"

He bit his bottom lip, cocking his head, nodding.

"Yeah, I did. I was really into my career back then, and I was getting to that age where it seemed like marriage was the next logical step. Besides that, she had a great job with a huge firm, six figures."

"Then you're a gold digger man? You married her for her money?"

"I went through with the wedding because I agreed to marry her. I thought it was the honorable thing to do."

She studied his expression.

"But then you left her. So either you learned to dispense with honor over the years or you learned to use the vertebrae you were born with?"

He did not answer. He just looked at her, his face showing equal parts confusion and irritation. She held a serious expression for a few seconds longer before a mischievous smile broke through.

Laughing, she nudged him.

"I'm just messin with ya. I'm sorry about your marriage, but not too sorry. I'm sure you and the girls will adjust. It takes time. That actually works in our favor."

"What do you mean?"

"Over the next few months, we can have a long distance love affair. You've got your job and your children and I have mine, 2,300 miles apart. We'll each have our space and our own lives while we try to create something new and lasting."

Brady smiled, lingering on the words.

"A love affair? What about your uncle?"

She harrumphed, slightly snaking her neck.

"What *about* him? I believe in equal partnership. I'm perfectly capable of dealing with him on my end. The question is: can you deal with him on yours?"

CHAPTER 33

Saint Claire knew it was inevitable, but the timing could not have been more inopportune. He was so close. He knew the next victim's name. He knew where she worked and where she lived. He had even interviewed her twice. She was hiding something.

The story first appeared in the early morning paper under Kiyomi Yamakita's byline. She quoted the most lurid passages of the killer's unabridged letters to Saint Claire. Someone who had access to the letters had leaked them to her. The article named Saint Claire specifically as the killer's adversary and the last three paragraphs contained questions.

What was the relationship between the city's most celebrated homicide inspector and this killer? Was the killer really as brilliant as he claimed to be? What was the murder count to date? Could anyone murder seven people from the grave? And how was the killer, already dead and rotting, going to force Saint Claire to tell the world and history whatever he knew about him?

Even while Deuteronomy read the story in the *Chronicle*, his phone rang with calls from the press. As the television and radio stations got wind of the story, news of the killer's claim swept through the city and across the state. By mid-afternoon, the story would air on the national news stations and the Internet. Sitting in his car on Bryant outside the Hall of Justice, he focused on the horizon, an approaching whirlwind in the distance.

Anxious tapping on the driver's side window startled Saint Claire. One of the reporters outside the building spotted him sitting in the car and approached with a phalanx of colleagues, cameras and microphones. He forced the door open, and swatting at a camera, shoved a reporter aside as he made his way inside. Entering the building, he headed for the chief's fifth floor office to determine who had leaked the story and how.

Chief Rebecca Leong was expecting his arrival. The mayor's press conference was scheduled for 10 am, with Chief Leong standing by to participate in the Q and A. The mayor's aides had already compiled a list of questions that were "most likely to be asked" by reporters, though most of them could be evaded by reminding the public that the investigation was ongoing.

Chief Leong asked Saint Claire to stand beside her at the conference so that he could respond to questions specific to the investigation. Seated at the table across from her, he marked the five or so questions he thought he should handle.

It was going to be a long day for Rebecca Leong. She sipped her latté.

"Vang was murder number three, right? But if you count Gladys Rosenthal, he's actually killed four from the grave."

"If he's really in the grave."

"You going to go on record saying you think he's still alive?"

He shrugged.

"What could it hurt? If he's really dead, what does it matter? He won't hear it. But if he's alive and he's watching all this, his ego will force him to provide proof of his death. So if we all of a sudden get that proof, we'll know he's still alive."

He sipped his coffee.

"I just get the sense that anyone who's gone through the trouble to plan all this would want to *know* if he was able to pull it off. And in order to know, he'd have to be alive."

"A little convoluted, but it makes sense."

"If the murders go off the way he planned, maybe *then* he'll devise his own death, and he'll find some way to make his audience believe he was dead all along."

Saint Claire surprised the chief with his openness. Two months earlier, he would have never shared such a theory. She wondered what had changed Saint Claire, though she was irritated he didn't turn the killer's unabridged letter over in the first place.

"This isn't your private investigation, Saint Claire. It's a police matter. Sanchez specifically directed you to turn the contents of that envelope over."

"She asked me to turn the killer's letter over to her, which I did. Turning in two separate letters would have only confused things and changed the focus of the investigation."

"That wasn't your call to make."

He rose from the chair.

"At the time, it was. If you want to make that a criminal matter, just remember I'm trying to save lives here. We're only at three of seven, so there are four more murders planned, Sanchez among them."

He sighed.

"Look, I'm sorry if it seems I've affronted your authority by not turning over both letters, but you have to trust me enough to afford me *one* discretionary call, which I made. As a result, I know who the next victim is, and chances are I would have never come close to knowing if I had turned over the other letter."

"I really don't think that's true."

"Really, after this morning you don't think it's true? I shared that letter directed to me with only two people, persons I completely trusted, and someone still leaked it to the newspaper within a month. Can you imagine how fast that would have happened if I had given the other letters to Sanchez?"

Leong closed her eyes and nodded, mentally changing direction.

"You said you know who the next victim will be. Is that something you're going to share with us?"

"Yes. Her name's Barbara Stevens. She works for the County Board of Supervisors as assistant to the clerk, Rusty Mullholland. There was some connection between her and Vang, but it's something she's been disinclined to discuss, at least so far."

"Does she know she's next?"

He returned to his seat.

"When I talked to her before, there were limits to what I could tell her, but now that the story is out, I imagine she might feel a little more like talking."

"Do you know *how* the killer is planning on getting to her?"

He sat back in the chair, crossing his arms.

"No I don't. Don't have a clue yet. I'll talk to her this afternoon."

Leong massaged her scalp and sighed.

"We could place her in protective custody for the next few weeks?"

"I don't think it would do much good. If the killer's set a trap, it'll just wait the weeks out and kill her when she gets back to her life. Vang's murder was a week late because he went back to Minnesota on a fluke, but it still happened."

Leong was tired.

"Would you mind leaving me a copy of your notes on this?"

"I'll have them copied on the way out."

Saint Claire started to leave, but he hesitated at the door.

"Chief Leong, I have a question for you."

She sat up, a little surprised.

"Okay?"

"You knew. You and Sanchez *both* knew days ago about the killer's claim that he was going to murder from the grave. I only made two copies of my letters. One I gave to Slater and the other to Brady. Your information came from one or the other. Which one was it?"

She could have answered, "neither had provided the letter," but that would have been only half-true. The letter had come from Brady and a Brady had copied it for her, but it had been Andrea Brady, not Tom. In exchange for the letter and other information, Chief Leong had agreed to consider re-assigning Tom as an inspector in a department away from homicide.

"Do you trust me, Saint Claire?"

"Yes."

"Well, to quote a well respected inspector on this force, 'you have to trust me enough to afford me one discretionary call, which I'm making.' Believe me, telling you how that information came to me would only confuse things and interrupt your focus."

She stood.

"And right now, we need to let you do what you do best. Beat this killer at his game. Save the life of that fourth victim."

CHAPTER 34

"Katrina Scott Saint Claire, after reviewing exhaustive reports and opinions written about you and after today's testimony, the court has reached a decision on the matter before us. Do you have any additional information or any statement you'd like to add before the final decision is delivered?"

Her voice shook.

"I do, your Honor."

Outside of her hospital room, Katrina seemed smaller, almost mousy. Her note cards shook in unsteady, clammy fingers. She wore a conservative, burnt umber pantsuit with low brown leather heels. Her hair was pulled tightly back into a bun. Pouting bronze painted lips, she took a breath and began.

"Your Honor, professors, doctors, students and friends, twelve years ago I relinquished the reigns of my life, trusting and hoping that the doctors and staff at St. Mary's would guide me, comfort me, and most importantly, possess the insight to understand me as I worked through challenges and faced great demons created by circumstances beyond my control."

She stopped. Closing her eyes for a moment to calm herself, she focused on slowing her speech.

"I came to the hospital at a very difficult time. My son had just been murdered and my husband and I had recently separated. As many of you know, I'm a doctor of psychiatry, a psychopharmacologist and an author. You also know I've been in the subject of more than a few studies here at the hospital. And while I wasn't required to, I cooperated in those studies. In fact, Dr. Khouri wrote that working with me was like having a psychiatrist on the inside of a patient's head."

She looked toward the doctor, who nodded.

"I was pleased to be of assistance to Dr. Khouri and many of the other doctors at St. Mary's, but the time has come for me to reclaim my life, at least what's left of it."

Eyes leaving her notes, she looked toward the judge.

"I want to renew my license if I can, but I don't know if I'll ever be involved in another practice. Maybe I'll work in research, and I know I'll continue to write. I just think it's time for me to leave St. Mary's. I've resolved my issues, so there is no reason for me to continue there."

She scanned the room, searching for her husband.

"As for my state of mind, I'm as rational as *most* people, for whatever that says about most people."

There was mild laughter from among the ranks of colleagues attending.

"Life has made me cynical, and yet I continue to be inspired by the human mind. I believe I still have much to learn and to contribute, so I beseech your understanding and indulgence, regardless of what my husband wrote to you about me."

The judge smiled.

"Your husband? Are you saying you want me to disregard what he wrote in his affidavit to the court?"

"He's non-objective, your Honor, and not well suited to make any recommendation about me."

The judge removed her glasses.

"I happen to disagree, Dr. Saint Claire. Your husband, the *other* Dr. Saint Claire, knows you better than this court does, and he's been right there with you through all this. As I understand, he's visited you a few times a week from the time you entered St. Mary's until now. For twelve years? Is that true?"

Katrina nodded.

"Yes, that's true."

The judge laughed.

"Don't look so disappointed, doctor. Your husband indicated that the basis for which you were admitted no longer *exists*. He recommended for your release."

Katrina' cupped her nose and mouth in her palms, crying.

"Thank you. I'm sorry. I had no idea!"

"I sincerely wish you the best in all you wish to accomplish. And doctor—"

Katrina looked pleadingly toward the judge.

"Yes?"

"Cut your husband a little slack. Records show he's been there for you in the really important ways. Your petition for release is hereby granted."

Barbara called him even before he could get out of the room, within a few minutes after the press conference ended. Her voice was shrill and desperate.

"I need to talk to you, Saint Claire! When can you meet me?"

"Thirty minutes. Where?

"Not here. Let's meet at a bar, any bar. I need a fuckin drink!"

The press conference had been the standard affair, with the major and Chief Leong carefully managing what information they gave out. But when Saint Claire was asked how he expected to go up against a genius who was already dead, his face showed disapproval.

"Well, first of all, I think labeling this guy a genius is an overstatement. In his letter, he attempts to call himself a genius, but I haven't seen any real genius evident in the murders. He poisoned three people and booby-trapped another. Over the years, I've been up against some very smart killers, and this guy doesn't rank in the top five. He's not even clever. Conniving, I'll give him that."

Unrecognized, a smartly dressed woman standing to the right of the stage interjected.

"Do you believe he really *is* killing from the grave?"

Saint Claire smiled.

"I'm not willing to believe he's dead just because he wrote it in a letter and then that letter was irresponsibly printed in a newspaper. It follows that if he's half as smart as he wants you all to believe, he would have provided *proof of death*."

No one followed up.

"What I mean is the location of his body maybe, a cemetery and a name! If he really is dead, what should he care if we were to dig up his body to confirm his claim?"

He took a breath and sighed.

"I'll believe he's dead when I see his corpse. Otherwise, the investigation will proceed under the assumption the killer's still out there, alive."

Another older man in the front row motioned, raising a hand. He spoke in slow, careful syllables.

"Are you willing to stake your reputation as the city's great sleuth on that position?"

Saint Claire bowed his head for a moment and looked up.

"Yes, I'm willing to stake my reputation on that."

He had expected the call from Barbara after the broadcast, though he hadn't expected it to come so soon. Throughout two interviews and three phone calls, she had been taciturn and guarded.

The newspaper article, however, had frightened her. When she called an hour before the conference, she asked if she was the killer's next victim. Saint Claire would neither confirm nor deny her suspicion, but he asked her to call him again if she thought of anything that might lead to a break in the case.

They met at a quiet dive bar in the Lake Merritt area across the bay, in Oakland. When he arrived, she was seated at a table along the right wall, away from the bar running along the left side. She was in the process of ordering a second Bombay Sapphire gin and tonic as he sat. Glancing across the table, she offered to buy him a drink.

"I'm on duty, but you go ahead. Club soda, please."

She clutched a black, oversized leather purse in her lap, her right hand reaching for what was left of the first drink.

"Okay, what's the rule?"

"I don't know. What rule?"

She leaned toward him.

"If I tell you something, will you be obligated to report it to the authorities and get me in trouble? I mean, if I'm still alive?"

His voice took on a compassionate tone.

"I'm just a detective. I'm not the DA, but I will say this much. If you tell me something that's going to save your life and the lives of other people, whatever you say will never go past me. You have my word on that."

Barbara's watery blue eyes were pink, puffy and denuded of make-up. She forced a smile as the server delivered the drinks.

"Thank you. I've done something bad."

"What's that?"

Turning away, she swigged from the glass.

"You asked about the relationship between me and Vang?"

"Yes."

This time she polished off the drink, and signaling the server, ordered another. Turning back toward Saint Claire, she took a breath.

"About two years ago, Paul Vang approached me and offered me a job as a private consultant, you know, under the table. He said he'd pay me almost as much as I was making with the county. My job was to poll the board and staffers, informally of course, and let Vang know how I thought the supervisors would vote on issues relating to his business interests."

She tried to read the detective's face.

"You think I'm corrupt, don't you? But it gets worse. The arrangement worked for a year, and then one day Vang asked me if I would deliver a package to one of the supervisors. The next month, he asked me to deliver another, but I'm not dumb. I realized the packages contained money. They were pay-offs not only for the member's vote, but for that member's influence on the rest of the board."

A tear rolled down Barbara's cheek.

"I've always considered myself an honest person. I would have never thought in a million years that I'd be involved in a bribing operation. But before I knew any better, I was delivering a package for Vang every month. The packages came by courier to my house, a nine by twelve inch box with a brown paper wrapping."

Saint Claire interrupted.

"But then Vang was murdered..."

She looked back to make sure no one was listening.

"Yes. About a week before Vang was murdered, I got another package. I hadn't given it to the supervisor because it was early, and I didn't think the supervisor would expect it until the end of the month. And then, as you said, Vang was murdered."

Saint Claire's expression was blank.

"Okay. Did you deliver the package to the supervisor?"

"No. When Vang was murdered I got scared. I felt like everyone was watching me. You were calling me and coming by. And besides, it was a bribe from Vang, and Vang was dead."

Saint Claire sat back as the server delivered Barbara's next cocktail. Server gone, he leaned back in.

"You wouldn't happen to know how much money was in those packages, would you?"

"I do. I was nosey. I always peeked at the supervisor's adding machine tape when the supervisor left the office. Thirteen thousand, five hundred dollars! Same amount every time."

On hearing the amount, Saint Claire rechecked his notes, though he already knew. After a half-minute, he looked up.

"Where is that package now?"

Barbara tugged on the purse strap.

"It's right here, in my lap. I didn't know what to do with it."

"Give it to me."

She handed him the purse, confused.

"What *is* it?"

He held the purse at arm's-length, gently removing the package.

"The other packages may have contained money, but I don't think this package does."

He moved it closer, testing its weight and examining the wrapping. Then he walked it outside the building and placed it in the parking lot near the dumpster. The midday sky was gray, threatening rain, though the air was warm. Barbara followed Saint Claire, drink still in her hand.

"What are you doing, Inspector? What is it?"

Cell phone to his ear, he had already dialed the number.

"Police emergency! Get me dispatch."

Barbara continued to approach him, but he held a hand out.

"You have to stay back. No, go back inside, get your keys and leave. Things are gonna get crazy here, and you don't want to be anywhere around when that happens."

A small voice responded in his phone's earpiece.

"Yes, this is Inspector Saint Claire with the San Francisco Police. I'm out at Lake Merritt and I've discovered what I believe is an explosive device. I'm going to need you to send the Bomb Unit."

The cocktail glass shattered on the asphalt. Barbara's palms covered her mouth, terror in her eyes. Saint Claire's voice was insistent.

"You better go. Go now, Barbara! I'll call to let you know what happens next."

CHAPTER 35

By three o'clock a light rain began to fall, and as the barometer dropped, the sky began to squall. Something was coming. In the parking lot, the bomb unit of the Oakland Police had been at work for thirty minutes.

The captain confirmed for Saint Claire that the package did contain an improvised explosive device. Because immediate detonation would destroy evidence that might lead back to the perpetrator, his unit would gather as much information about the device as possible before placing it in the mobile blast chamber, brought over from the station.

The restaurant and a perimeter extending out two blocks had to be evacuated before the package could even be moved. A large crowd had gathered on the other side of the yellow caution tape.

Saint Claire was still in the parking lot at four, detained by Oakland police officers, when the Oakland chief insisted he return to the bar for questioning.

Inside, two black men sat at a table they dragged to the center of the room. The dark-skinned detective on the left seemed meek, while Nelson, his lighter-skinned, freckled partner was aggressive. Nelson was standing, his arms crossed.

"Deuteronomy Saint Claire, good that you could make it. Sit down."

Saint Claire knew the type, the self-cognizant asshole. He could have decided not to sit, but he conceded, aware that a verbal sparring match with the Philistine would waste precious time. He sat.

"What can I do for you, detective?"

"You can tell me what you were doing with a bomb in our jurisdiction. Nigga, ya need ta keep your shit in San Francisco! We got enough of our own problems here. Where'd you get the bomb?"

Saint Claire sighed. The man's belligerence stemmed from insecurity.

"It's exactly like I told the captain earlier. I came across a suspicious package and I did the responsible thing. I called it in."

"Bullshit. We interviewed the bar manager. And he said he watched you walk outside with that package in your hand. You put that package out there. He said you were sitting with a blonde at that table over there, a blonde slammin down Bombay gin. Where is she?"

Saint Claire shrugged.

"Don't know her. Just met her here, had a drink with her, asked her out, but she said she wasn't interested."

"You had a drink with her? A club soda?" He sighed, disgusted. "No wonder she turned you down."

Nelson's partner had answered a cell phone call. He interrupted to whisper into the detective's ear. Nelson nodded as he listened, and turning toward Saint Claire, he grinned.

"Looks like I'm gonna get a chance ta spend some time with the blonde bitch who turned you down. Officers arrested someone matching her description for DUI four blocks from here an hour and a half ago. Said she hit a parked car. I think maybe you're gonna wanna come down to the station."

"Are you nervous about leaving here?"

"Petrified. But then I can either face what's out there or live the rest of my life in here like a laboratory rat. I've wasted twelve years. I don't know if I can survive out there, but I have to try."

Brady sipped coffee from the delicate cup, gently returning it to the saucer.

"And you're telling me you couldn't have done this ten years ago?"

"I was jinxed, hexed! Not until Madame Toussiante died in the hurricane. Not until I could get a *Voudoun* in here to uncross me. For that, I'm in your debt, and for the same reason, I'll never forgive Ronnie. He could have helped me, but he wouldn't! I'd rot in here if it were up to him."

Brady wagged his head.

"Not true."

Katrina rolled her eyes.

"I am so fucking tired of hearing how much he's been there for me. Prison inmates get fed and checked on a regular basis. Keeping me in here was his way of punishing me for leaving him."

Brady laughed.

"Come on. You really believe that? The man is still totally in love with you. I don't think he's been laid during the entire time you been gone. I respect that. If that's not dedication, I don't know what is."

"You're talking about his dedication to God, and that has nothing to do with me. It's his weakness. He can't help doing the right thing—regardless of how much it hurts the people he's supposed to care about. It's just Ronnie."

She wiped angry tears from the corners of her eyes.

"He never came here because he *loved* me. He came out of a sense of duty, but love and duty are two very different things."

She spoke without looking at him, trying to hide the emotion.

"I'm not young anymore. I need someone who's going to love me, not someone who just feels a scriptural or marital obligation toward me. He will never understand that."

Brady stood, uncomfortable with her anger.

"So where will you go?"

"I don't know. Ronnie thinks I'm coming back to him, but I won't, I just can't. I haven't told him that yet."

"Do you still love him?"

She hung her head a moment before answering.

"Of course I do, but not like a wife should love a husband. It's hasn't been that way since Christian was born. It's a different kind of love. It's more familiar."

Brady nodded, pretending to understand.

"Tell me about Christian."

"He was our son and he was murdered. What else do you want to know?"

"What was he like? Was he more like his father or you?"

Katrina turned away, discomfort reshaping her posture. She did not want to discuss Christian, but she felt an obligation to Brady. He was the one who got the *Voudoun*, after all.

"From his father he inherited the ability to be cold and detached, no matter what he was doing. He could just turn his feelings off when he wanted or needed to, even when he was a baby. It was almost, inhuman."

She cringed.

"From me he got his instincts. He could read people, and he could be charming. He could usually get them to do what he wanted them to do. But while I've always tried to help people, he was cruel."

She looked over at Brady.

"Why are you so interested in Christian? He's dead."

"I know, but there's just something about him. I mean, he's part you and part Saint Claire. And I have to tell you, you are two definitely dysfunctional people. He couldn't help being fucked up."

He heard the words before he even realized he had spoken them.

"Oh, I'm sorry. Please forgive me."

Katrina only sighed.

"No, you're right. *And some have dysfunction thrust upon them.* He didn't stand a chance."

"What happened?"

"Well let's see, when he wasn't unplugged emotionally, he hated his father."

Eyebrows raised, Brady seemed skeptical.

"Hated?"

"Yes, hated. When Christian was young, Ronnie was his hero, but when he turned thirteen, the bristles came out, the testosterone and all. It wasn't just Christian, it was both of them. After about a year of arguments every night, I think Ronnie got tired and gave up on Christian. He was busy in his work and he just couldn't afford the emotional investment. He turned off."

She paused, reflecting

"Christian didn't handle that well. As much as he tried to turn off his own emotion, he really resented his father giving up, turning off. So finally, about a month before he was murdered, he called his father on it. He was angry. They went at it, but not physically. It was a battle of wills. They argued and staked positions. Both of them were so stubborn."

She closed her eyes, glimpsing back into time.

"In the end, the will of the father was too much for the son. Christian broke down, weeping, crying like a baby. He said all he ever wanted was for Ronnie to see him, to hear him. Once again the little boy who idolized his father, he begged Ronnie to explain why he gave up on his son in a time of need."

She wiped the corners of her eyes with a tissue.

"For everything else Christian said earlier, Ronnie had an answer, but when he asked that, Ronnie broke down. It was the first and only time I ever saw him cry. Oh he cried, and he begged Christian to forgive him. And he swore to Christian that he would never give up on him again, no matter what."

She sighed, looking over at Brady.

"A month later, Christian was murdered. We had to go down to identify what was left of his body and his personal effects. The rest had been burned."

She shrugged.

"Ronnie was consumed by guilt. He felt helpless to do anything. He felt he had failed Christian again, and I think he believed the only way he could keep his promise not to give up was by finding Christian's killer."

Brady sat back in the armchair.

"And now he's convinced the killer he's after is the same person who murdered Christian?"

"Your guess is as good as mine. I never know what Ronnie is thinking. Says one thing, does the complete opposite."

Glancing over at a stack of folded cardboard boxes, Brady nodded.

"Where will you go?"

"I don't know. You have any ideas?"

"I'm hardly ever at my place. You're welcome to stay there until you figure something out."

She laughed wryly.

"I don't think that'll work."

"Why's that?"

"Because I told Ronnie you and I were having an affair."

Brady sprung to his feet.

"You did what? When, why would you tell him that? He doesn't even know I've ever been here!"

"Of *course* he knows. He's shrewd if nothing else, and I'm sure he hasn't let on. Remember what I said about him being able to turn off emotion? I told him the story of you fucking me before the two of you went to New Orleans."

His face flushed, Brady felt warm.

"What! Why would you say that?"

He paused.

"Did he believe you?"

She smiled.

"I don't know. You tell me. You work with him."

She laughed.

"He didn't believe me. You're funny. You act like you're afraid of him."

"No, I'm not afraid. I just respect him as a man and I don't want any problems. Besides that, I'm interested in his niece."

"Who? Let me guess. Mignon?"

He nodded after some reluctance.

"Yes, and if you have an opinion about her, I don't want to hear it. I don't like these games you play."

"I understand, and I'm sorry if you'll feel uncomfortable now around Ronnie. But you did say you were coming over here to show me something and ask me something. What is it?"

Standing, Brady took the folded paper from his pocket.

"One thing Saint Claire has always says: if he's smart, he knows at least one person smarter, and that's you. I was hoping you could look at something and tell me what you think."

"What is it?"

Unfolding the paper, he reached over and placed it in her hand.

"It's the killer's first letter to Saint Claire. What you want to look for is at the bottom of the second page. The numbers down there, three sets of three. Saint Claire couldn't figure out what they meant. I was wondering if you might take a guess."

She looked up.

"Can I read the whole letter?"

He glanced over his shoulder toward the door.

"Well yeah, I guess."

She flipped to the first page and began reading. While waiting, Brady noticed Saint Claire had left him three text messages in addition to three phone calls that morning. Sooner or later, Brady would have to return the calls.

After five minutes with the letter, Katrina handed it back to Brady, who motioned.

"Those numbers? What do you think?"

"Well first of all, I think Ronnie is acting if he's telling you he hasn't figured them out after all this time. I'm fairly certain he knows what they mean."

"Okay, and what do you think they mean?"

She shrugged.

"I don't know. I'm looking at them for the first time. But if I had to guess, being that the letter was to Ronnie, I'd probably say they're scriptures."

"Scriptures?"

"Yes, but then that's just me going on instinct at first glance. I could be wrong."

CHAPTER 36

Saint Claire had just sat in his car when his cell phone started ringing again. From the prefixes, he knew some calls were from the newspapers and television stations. Local talk radio commentators, after reading the letter, had already dubbed the murderer the *Undead*. One anonymous caller even phoned in to express his hope that the killer would be successful.

Saint Claire had turned left on Madison when he recognized Sonia's distinctive ringtone. Two weeks earlier, he asked her to call him if she noticed anything suspicious, especially in her daily routine.

"Sonia?"

"Is it true?"

"Is what true?"

"I heard it on the radio. They're saying you stopped the killer! You won! They said you discovered a bomb meant for the fourth victim and the Oakland Police exploded it."

Instinctively he knew, but he wanted to make sure.

"I'm on Washington almost at the Oakland Police Station. Who's sayin all this?"

"There's some woman in custody with the Oakland police. I don't know, but I think it was the Stevens woman you were telling us about. She's saying she was the killer's fourth victim and you risked your life to save hers. It's all over the news!"

As he pulled into a parking spot on 7th, a throng of reporters converged around his car.

"Stay where you are, Sonia. I need to talk to you. I'll be there in about an hour. Stay put."

He could not hear the chirping of the automatic door lock over the reporters' shouted questions. He tried to go around the vehicle, but his path to the building was blocked.

"Congratulations Inspector! You're a hero! How do you feel?"

"How were you able to identify the fourth victim, Saint Claire?"

"Do you think you've won? Is this thing over?"

Two officers on the stairs in front of the station recognized Saint Claire and made their way through the crowd as he moved toward him.

"Whatdaya think, Detective? Is it *over* now?"

"Do you still think the killer is alive and at large?"

"What about this woman Bobbie Stevens? How does she fit in?"

Flanked by the officers, Saint Claire entered into the building where he faced another wave of reporters and questions. Ignoring faces and microphones pointed toward him, he entered the elevator with the officers, who blocked journalists from pursuing further. With the closing of the doors, he enjoyed the sudden sensation of silence.

"Congratulations Inspector. This whole story is hella interesting. I watched you at that press conference. I think you won. That killer wasn't such a genius after all."

The young officer on Saint Claire's left had removed his hat before speaking. He smiled, proud for the unexpected honor of conducting San Francisco's prominent Inspector Saint Claire up to the chief's office.

"I think I'd like to be a homicide detective one day."

The other officer remained silent, though he glared in disapproval toward his younger counterpart. Saint Claire thought for a moment and turned toward the young man.

"I don't have a wife to go home to, no family, no friends. I work sixteen-hour days. I can't share what I did at work with anyone. I live alone in a dark apartment. I look at dead bodies, women and children sometimes, sometimes bloody, mutilated or molested. I have vivid, scary nightmares, but often what I see in the day is far worse. I have to put myself in the sick, twisted minds of killers, I have to think their thoughts, indulge their cruel perversions. If I couldn't turn off my feelings and detach, I wouldn't be sane. Is that really the kind of life you want?"

The officer backed away, uncomfortable.

"Well, I don't know. Is it really that bad?"

"Take a moment sometime. Think about what you really want to do, and follow your heart. If my son lived to be your age, it's the advice I would have given him. Thanks for seeing me in."

Chief Chapman stood for the introduction, and then he directed his assistant to clear the room so he could speak with

Saint Claire in private. Chapman was a squat older man. His graying hair, still high and tight, had discernable remnants of black. A former Marine officer, he was muscular for a man in his late sixties. Seated behind his desk, he began.

"Saint Claire, when I watched you on television this morning, I would have never thought in a million years you'd be sitting in my office this afternoon. The media out there, I had nothing to do with that, but now they're asking questions. You think you could help me out here?"

Saint Claire relaxed a little, easing back into the seat.

"I can, but you have to catch me up on everything. Who's talking to the media?"

"The woman you were with over at Lake Merritt, Barbara Stevens. By the time my officers got there to arrest her for DUI, she was already talking to reporters. She said you suspected over a week ago that she was the fourth victim and made her check her house. She said she discovered a strange package planted under her bed, and then she brought it to you at the bar. Quite a story! But I'm not sure if I believe it. I'm guessing you know what she's hiding."

Saint Claire checked his watch.

"If she's hiding something, I don't know what it is yet, but that's what I've been trying to figure out."

"I talked to your chief. She told me you probably wouldn't tell me anything. Any suggestions about how we're going to handle the press out there?"

"We?"

Chapman smiled.

"Oh, being you know so much about this case and you're keeping critical information to yourself, Chief Leong offered your recently proven public relations services to the Oakland Police Department. You don't want to talk to me, you go deal with them."

Saint Claire nodded toward the chief.

"That's fair. I'll do whatever you need me to do, but I think it would be in all our best interests if you let me talk to Barbara Stevens in private. And whether you believe me or not, I don't have all the facts yet."

The chief sighed.

"Do what you have to do, Saint Claire. Just be ready to feed those vultures in forty-five minutes."

Barbara Stevens was being held in a meeting room on the eighth floor of the building. The detective presented ID to the guard and opened the door.

"Saint Claire!"

Rushing toward him, she attempted to throw her arms around his shoulders, but he caught her wrists, stopping her advance.

"Are you okay?"

"I'm so glad to see you! It was a bomb, wasn't it? They told me it was a bomb."

He waited for her excitement to wane and released her wrists while backing up.

"It was an improvised explosive device, yes. A bomb."

Her hands went to her face as she groaned.

"My God! What the fuck! My husband and I have slept for the last two weeks with that goddamn bomb under our bed! My kids played in that room! We could all be dead!"

Saint Claire spoke to soothe her.

"You did the right thing by coming forward with it. You're no longer in danger."

She was crying.

"Yeah, thanks to you. Oh my God!"

She sank back into a leather armchair.

"Do you know how close I came to tearing that package open? I figured Vang was dead. I couldn't give it back to him. And fuck, what was I supposed to do? Give a supervisor a bribe from a dead man? I thought I had thirteen and a half thousand dollars in cash under my bed. If it hadn't been for you, I'd have opened it. I'd be dead right now!"

Saint Claire sat in a chair at the table.

"We need to talk."

"What is it?"

"You spoke with reporters. I need to know what you told them and what you plan on telling them when they get to you again, because they will. And when they do, they're going to dig."

She approached the table, her face concerned.

"I don't know. What should I have said?"

"You shouldn't have talked to them. What did you say?"

Nervous, she sat.

"I told them I found the package planted under my bed. I said you came by my job twice, and you told me you thought I was the killer's next victim. And I said I called you when I saw you talking on TV about the killer, and I brought the package to you."

"That's all you told them? Nothing about Vang?"

"Are you crazy? I would never do that! I'd be in so much trouble."

Saint Claire nodded.

"Okay, I can't tell you what to say, but if I were you I wouldn't say any more than what you've already said, and I mean nothing else. Play the victim if that's what you need to do, but don't give them a way in. You understand?"

"Yes."

"And I need you to tell me the name of the supervisor Vang was making his payments to. I know it's one of the three women on the board. Which one is it?"

Barbara turned her body away from the detective.

"Why is that important? Vang's dead. Besides, you gave me your word you weren't going to tell on me."

"I won't. I just need the name of the supervisor. Just some follow-up investigative work I have to do."

She stood, her voice trembling.

"Why? The bomb's exploded. It's over. You saved the fourth victim, me! He said you'd save that life and the lives after! You beat the killer at his own deal. I'm not going to give you a name."

"Barbara—"

"No! As far as I'm concerned, that chapter's closed. Please, I just want to go back to having a normal life. I swear I will never get caught up in anything like this again! Thank you for saving my life, but no, I can't."

While the sound of the door being pushed open startled Barbara, it halted the detective's rebuttal. The woman who entered seemed familiar. In her early fifties, she was attractive.

"Miss Stevens? Hi, my name is Destiny Mitchell with the *Aegis Foundation*. Your boss asked me to come over here to make sure you were okay."

She turned toward the detective.

"Inspector Saint Claire, I take it you were interviewing Ms. Stevens?"

"I was, on a matter unrelated to the crime involved in her arrest."

Destiny walked toward the table.

"Doesn't matter. Ms. Stevens, when you were arrested, were you properly informed that you have a right to have an attorney present for any interview conducted by law enforcement?"

"I, I guess. Are you a lawyer?"

"I'm not here in that capacity. *Aegis* operates in an advocatory capacity for women who are victims of violence. You've been through quite an ordeal today. You may even be suffering from shock trauma without realizing it. I'm here to help you work through the overwhelming emotions and get you to a place where you can rest and understand what's happened today. That work for you?"

Barbara nodded as Destiny continued.

"The police in this building and the reporters out there, you don't say one more word to any of them, including this one here, you understand?"

"Yes."

"I've made arrangements for us to use a private elevator and exit through the rear of the building. Your husband's already picked up your children. You'll be coming with me to a recovery facility owned by the foundation. Ready?"

Barbara hesitated.

"You mean I'm being released? What about the DUI?"

"We talked to the DA. There won't be any charges. According to statements on record, you got in your car and drove because you were ordered away from a dangerous area by a law enforcement officer. You did what he told you to do."

She smiled, turning toward the detective.

"And for that little gift we thank you, Inspector Saint Claire."

"You know, Chloe, it seems you're about the only one who's ever got a good look at this guy so far."

She rolled her eyes.

"Yeah, but it cost me my job. I had to quit this morning, between reporters calling me and weirdoes showin up to ask me questions about him, not to mention the thought of this sick freak bein still alive! Brocklebank wasn't payin me enough."

"You said the *Today* show called and offered you money to come on and talk about him?"

"Did I say *Taday*? I dunno, I don't watch those shows. Yeah, anyway it was one of em. Said they'd fly me out to New York, put me up and pay me pretty good to come on. I started packin this afternoon."

She sipped a caramel *machiato*.

"Always wanted to live in New York. I'm shoppin! I won't be comin back, ya know."

Brady's eyes examined the police artist's sketch based on Chloe's description. He tossed it onto the table.

"When you look at this drawing, does it look like him?"

"Well yes, and no."

Brady sat back.

"Let's start with the eyes. How does it look like him?"

"The eyes, I only saw them once when he raised his sunglasses to get a better look at me, but the eyes are almost right, only they were set a little farther apart. And the jaw, it seems about right."

"Okay."

"The mouth is all wrong, too big. The nose is wrong, cheeks. No, I think it's the whole shape of his face."

Brady leaned over to examine the sketch.

"What? The artist wasn't listening to you? Why didn't you tell the artist that?"

"I did. I kept on askin her to change things till it seemed like she got frustrated, then I got frustrated and we just settled on that, what you have there."

"What about the make-up?"

She shrugged her shoulders, a sense of confusion blossoming on her face.

"What are you talkin about?"

"When Saint Claire interviewed you right after Mrs. Rosenthal was murdered, you said you thought the suspicious man who came in twice was wearing make-up."

Chloe laughed.

"I don't remember. I don't remember sayin that."

"Just try'n think back. Did he have on foundation? Was it lipstick? Eyeliner?"

She furrowed her brow as she struggled to think back to the time.

"Mmmh, I think I would have to say foundation."

"Okay. Really noticeable?"

"Naw, not really. But I think I remember now thinkin it was nicely done. You know, there, but not really there?"

Brady nodded. He glanced toward the window at the fading sunlight outside the coffee shop.

"Yeah. What about his hair? What color was it?"

"Brown. Light brown."

"Straight or curly?"

She squinted, remembering.

"Straight. Moussed up, a little spikey."

"How tall was he?"

"Not tall. About my height. Handsome, kinda clean-cut guy."

Brady picked up the sketch, turning it ninety degrees to view it from a different angle.

"What about his lips and his nose. Notice anything in particular about those?"

"Nice lips! I had forgotten. Yes, he had nice lips. Nicely-shaped."

"Thin?"

She laughed.

"I said nicely-shaped. Skinny lips've got no shape at all."

CHAPTER 37

By the time Saint Claire got to Sonia's apartment, the sky was dark and he could feel the weeks of starvation and sleep deprivation beginning to tax his mind and body. It was his *modus operandi* during major investigations. He starved his body, avoiding solid foods and denying himself any more than four hours sleep a night. He did this to induce a diminished self and a mind state from which he could better understand the killer psyche. It had been two weeks.

Sonia offered him the remainder of the *mole poblano* with chicken she had for dinner, but all he accepted was a glass of *piña-guava* juice. His body burning with fatigue, he sat across the table from her, her visage blurry in his eyes.

"Sorry it took me so long to get over here. I was stuck in Oakland."

"I know. I saw you on television."

He took a sip from the glass.

"Today's been a long day. I got a lot to share. You up for it?"

She smiled.

"You, wanting to share? Now that's a change. Sure I'm up."

He nodded.

"Well, first of all, despite all you've heard today, Barbara Stevens wasn't the fourth victim."

"Not the fourth victim because you stepped in and saved her life, right?"

"No, she was never the intended fourth victim. She was just a conduit to the fourth victim."

Sonia stood, agitated. As she turned toward the window to mask her disappointment, her hands began to fidget. Rising, Saint Claire guided Sonia toward the couch, insisted that she sit and took a place next to her. He spoke softly.

"Vang was paying off one of the county supervisors through Barbara Stevens. He was making monthly payments in the amount of thirteen thousand five hundred dollars, which was the exact amount Maria Fuentes received—she thought— from Gladys Rosenthal. Obviously, the killer intercepted Vang's last payment, took out the money and left it for Maria to set the trap for his first murder, Hector. Then, he replaced the money with an improvised explosive device, thinking Barbara Stevens would deliver it to the supervisor on Vang's payroll."

He tightened his fingers around Sonia's to make sure she was still listening.

"The problem came when Vang unexpectedly went to Minnesota for five days. Because he was gone and died the day after his return, he never gave Barbara Stevens delivery instructions, which he always did by cell phone."

Aware of his fatigue, he wasn't sure if he was making sense.

"If Vang hadn't gone to Minnesota for his sister's wedding, he would have died one week sooner and the corrupt supervisor would have died in an explosion a few days after his death. Barbara Stevens told me she expected Vang's call on the weekend of the wedding, but Vang's cell phone had no coverage in Hutchinson, where the ceremony took place. He died before he got a chance to give her the instruction."

Sonia's mind was racing.

"No matter what, by discovering the bomb, you stopped the fourth murder. That means this whole nightmare's over, right?"

"If he was telling the truth, I would say yes, but I don't think we can afford to make the mistake of trusting him. Until I find him, dead or alive, this will never be over for me."

Sonia's eyes welled with tears. Uncomfortable with the proximity, he rose, but she followed.

"So now what? I just have to keep on living like this? I can't keep on living like this!"

In the emotion of the moment, she hugged him hard.

"What am I going to do?"

Saint Claire stood there in virtual shock. It had been at least a dozen years since he had allowed anyone to embrace him. All along, there was a part of him that craved to be touched by another person. Standing there, Sonia's arms around him, her body touching his, Saint Claire remembered how wonderful it was to be close to another person. He could feel her heart racing, so near to his.

Awkwardly, he put one and then the other arm around her and pulled her close, yielding to the need. The left side of her face was pressed against his chest and his chin rested atop her head. For a minute neither spoke.

Throwing her head back, Sonia looked up into his eyes. He could feel his own heart racing, wanting. He could feel her firm warm body, relinquishing. Slowly their faces drew together until they reached a deliberate stop, lips less than an inch apart.

He could feel the heated breath from her nostrils, could smell the coconut and spice tropical oil smoothed onto her neck, could sense a sort of mild current flowing from her smooth skin, tingling in all the places where their bodies touched. Her eyes were soft, warm. Something in those eyes caught him and, while holding him in place, poured her vulnerable soul into him.

Their lips barely touched at first, with both pulling back slightly. And then a slow, warm kiss. Their bodies pressed against each other as his hands ran down her body, clenching her hips and pulling her against him. Her hips gyrated in preparation for surrender. Suddenly, he backed away.

Still trembling, she looked into his eyes and hung her head.

"I don't know why that happened. I'm sorry."

He clasped her shoulders, and then with the fingers of his right hand, he raised her chin. His eyes had welled with tears.

"No. Please don't be. That was the most wonderful thing that has happened to me in a long time. I wanted more, but I didn't want to ruin the moment. I don't know if it makes any sense to—"

She put her fingers on his lips.

"I understand. It was wonderful for me too. Just hold me for now?"

He sprang up from the couch an hour later.

"I think I fell asleep. What time is it? Eleven fifteen?"

She opened her eyes, squinting in the light.

"We both fell asleep. It's almost midnight. What? You have to go somewhere?"

He sat, bending over to retrieve his shoes.

"Unfortunately, yes. Something I've been dreading for weeks."

"Police business or personal?"

"It's personal." He nodded sadly.

She reached over, caressing his back.

"Is it something I can help you with?"

He stared straight ahead, his expression blank.

"No, Sonia, this is something I would never share with anyone I care about."

Sergeant Sean McCarthy was doing the driving. He cruised along Fell through the park and somehow ended up on Kezar, which in turn became Lincoln. No left turns! There was at least a little logic to the way streets were set up in Boston, but San Francisco was a mess.

"We're almost there."

McCarthy made a sharp right without signaling, the cigarette almost tumbling from his lips.

"Just about a half mile up the road."

The terra cotta faced restaurant/brew house was located on the far west end of Golden Gate Park. The view of the sea from the café's large window could only be had on the edge of San Francisco.

Outside, the chilled wind whipped foamy white caps atop waves that crashed onto the rocky shores. At dusk, ominous black clouds descended on water and land, seeming to stop just beyond arms' reach. Just then, driven rain began an assault on the window, obscuring the picturesque view.

"This is uhm, Officer Angelique Curry. She works in Richmond district, right? Her father, as you know, was Joe Curry. He was Saint Claire's partner for a long time, and Saint Claire's supposed best friend at the time of his death,"

McCarthy cringed.

"...or murder, more precisely."

He turned toward the woman.

"So Angelique, this is Inspector Tom Brady, he's Saint Claire's present partner. Part of what he's doing is checkin Saint Claire out, for the chief, of course. And I just thought it would be good to get the two of ya tagether. I figured ya might be able ta, ya know, help each other out."

Guarded, Angelique smiled and nodded.

"My father's death has been hard on me, but years ago I decided to put it in the past, to let it go. There's nothing I or anyone could do that would bring my father back."

She recomposed herself.

"Look, I agreed to this meeting because the chief asked me to do this as a personal favor to her. Make no mistake. I don't want to be here, so let's just get this over with."

McCarthy sat back in the chair, extending his arms as he shrugged.

"Oh come on! Have a beer. Have an appetizer. I'm buyin. Ya drove all the way out here!"

She tightened her jaw.

"No. If you have questions, ask. I'll answer, and then I'm leaving."

Brady nodded.

"That's fine. Well Angelique, you know the story. The chief told me your father was killed by a bullet from Saint Claire's gun. She also said Saint Claire had an ironclad alibi. He was with Slater in a public place when your father was killed. I'm just wondering what you think."

She batted back tears.

"I met Saint Claire when I was only twelve. He was always nice to me. I thought of him as a second father."

She looked away.

"Until my father was killed."

She took a breath.

"My problem with this whole thing is my father was a good man. He never did anything wrong to anyone. No one had any reason to kill him. So when he was dead and it was Saint Claire's gun, and there was no suspect in sight, I just don't understand how they cleared Saint Claire so fast and easy. Maybe it was because he was friends with Slater. I don't know."

Brady reached over, patting her clasped hands.

"I'm sorry. But tell me, Angelique, do you personally think Saint Claire murdered your father?"

"I don't know. I think it's possible."

She pursed her lips and swallowed hard.

"You know how he does that thing? He gets unsolved murder cases, and a lot of them he solves."

She paused.

"So if he *didn't* kill my father, why hasn't he tried to solve that case? Why hasn't he tried to find my father's killer?"

She bowed her head, weeping.

"Is there anything else? I just want to go home."

Angelique gone, McCarthy swilled a mouthful of dark, micro brewed beer as he studied the menu.

"She's right, Brady. I was there at the time. Half the department thought Saint Claire at least had somethin ta do with Joe Curry's murder, and maybe Slater was in on it too."

CHAPTER 38

The storm intensified to full force. Gusts of wind from far out over the ocean crept in, stirring and roiling the Bay, driving the surge, pounding the gates of the city. Freezing rain whipped about in all directions, strafing structures and the surrounding landscape alike. Downtown Oakland seemed deserted. The parking lot near Jack London Square held a few scattered cars. Deuteronomy fought his way against the drafts to the restaurant in solitude. Right hand holding down his hat, he wiped his eyes with his left, staring out at the agitated water.

Inside, he was in another world. The room was warm, dimly lit and peaceful. He could smell the grilled chicken and hints of the salmon he liked so much. He heard her voice from the club as he removed his overcoat and gloves. She was singing a sassy Cole Porter tune with her intriguing, subtle Portuguese accent.

"Couldn't sleep, and wouldn't sleep, when love came and told me I shouldn't sleep..."

His regular spot was taken, so he took a table on the right, a little farther away from the stage, nearer to the window. She probably wouldn't see him until after the set, but she would know he was there.

"Romance finis, your chance finis, those ants that invaded my pants finis..."

It had been a difficult day. It was nonstop since he left Sonia's apartment, straight to the prison and then a failed attempt to see Katrina. Since her day in court, Katrina neither answered nor returned his calls. And on the three occasions he went to the hospital, the front desk indicated she was meditating and did not want to be disturbed.

He called Barbara Stevens' boss, Rusty Mullholland, to set up an interview. Saint Claire wouldn't reveal Barbara's secret, but he was counting on Rusty to clue him in on the back stories and habits of the three women supervisors. Rusty agreed to a one o'clock appointment, but he pushed it back to two thirty due to an emergency. At two o'clock, Rusty phoned with a hurried apology and a request to move the meeting to the next morning at nine, no more postponements, no more excuses.

During the day, Brady finally returned Saint Claire's call, explaining he took two days off to deal with child custody issues.

He admitted he saw Mignon, but he provided no other details. He suggested a noon meeting at the station, after Saint Claire's appointment with Rusty.

Sitting at the table, Saint Claire sipped the *paradis* cognac, thinking of Sonia. She was his captain, his direct supervisor, but she had become a friend. Despite their working relationship, the kiss did not feel inappropriate. It felt natural. No words or explanation had to be spoken. When he next saw her at the station, neither would be uncomfortable. It was a kiss, nothing more.

The set over, he ordered Gisele's drink and waited for her to come to his table. As his eyes stared out the window, he was lost in his thoughts.

"Is this seat taken?"

He smiled.

"Well, I was saving it for the first *pretty* woman who came up, but you can have it."

She laughed.

"How was your day?"

"Not one of the best. Not one of the best for *either* of us I'm sure."

Gisele tried to find his eyes, but they had returned to the window. She sighed.

"*Assim sao as coisas.*"

"What's that?"

"It is what it is."

He nodded.

"Yes it is, but how do you feel?"

She sat back.

"How *can* I feel? It's over. It's over at last."

He reached over and patted her hand before he realized what he had done. He never touched her in public, except to shake her hand. Her skin felt so soft, wonderful. Recoiling, his voice was almost apologetic.

"Are you okay?"

When she raised her face, she was crying.

"I'm singing. Singing makes me feel better."

For a few minutes, neither spoke. Uncomfortable, Saint Claire broke the silence, though without making eye contact.

"I'm here if you want to talk."

She opened her eyes.

"What's wrong?"

He shifted his weight in the seat, glancing over.

"Nothing's wrong. Why?"

"You're different today. Why are you looking out there so much? I'm here! Not out there."

He tried turning toward her, but he was thinking of the event he witnessed earlier in the day. The spectacle would not leave his mind. He felt sullied, unworthy of her goodness and grace. But there was something else bothering him, something that threatened to undo the wonder and magic of whatever he and Gisele had created over the years. He accepted he was in love with Gisele. For that reason, he could not look into her eyes.

"I'm sorry, but I'm here to talk if you want to."

Her voice was angry.

"I came here to sing to *forget* about it. I don't wanna talk about it. I can't! I gotta go."

When she reappeared on stage ten minutes later, she had regained her stage composure. She even smiled during the piano introduction. The song she chose to start the set was one Saint Claire, over many years of following her, had never heard.

> *Look out the window at that rainstorm,*
> *I've let the wind blow up a brain storm*
> *And now I'm wondering whether weather like this*
> *Gets you too...*

She glanced out to the place where she knew he was.

> *It may go on like this for hours,*
> *Too late in Fall for April showers*
> *So while we're caught here*
> *Got a thought or two*
> *I need to share with you*
> *Here goes...*

Words could not describe what he felt when she sang. He rose and fell on her voice, was transported to another world through her lyrical interpretation. For a brief instant, all was right.

Darling, tell me now
Have I done wrong somehow
That you won't look at me
Need it pointed out
Can't keep my wits about
When you won't look at me
Is there something I oughta know
You're finding hard to say
Well, there's just a trace
Hiding on your face
And I've learned it that way.

He arrived at San Quentin Prison a few minutes after midnight. By then, a crowd of protesters were assembled at the main entrance, shouting expressions of condemnation, displaying defiant banners and placards, raising candles skyward, appealing for divine mercy.

Guards directed him through a visitors' center where he joined other observers. Circumspectly, he acknowledged Stefano Rossi's mother and brother. He recognized the victims' family members, a couple East coasters, several reporters, the defense attorney, the prosecutor and a few other faces from the trial, and possibly a juror.

A guard led the group down to the basement room where inside they saw a pale green octagonal metal box, six feet across and about eight feet high. There were five glass windows facing the area where the observers would sit or stand. Through the glass they could see the rubber sealed steel door where Stefano Rossi would enter.

A sense of discomfort pervaded the darkened room. No one spoke for the ten or more minutes they waited. Then they saw two guards lead Stefano to one of two identical metal chairs with perforated seats. Somberly, the guards strapped him into the seat marked "A," binding his upper and lower legs, arms, thighs and chest.

The moment seemed surreal, absent of sound, carried out in artificial light within the bowels of Earth. Finally, guards affixed a long stethoscope to Stefano's chest so that a doctor on the outside could monitor his heartbeat and pronounce death.

Stefano was stoic throughout the process, but a sense of panic seemed to set in when the guards left him and sealed the door shut. Eyes widened, he tried to turn around to see the door, and then he tried to look down at the chair. His head snapped back and forth as he checked the floor on his left and right, looking for the gas. Several times he stopped, his eyes straining to pierce the darkness of the observation room, as if hoping to see a familiar face.

He responded in panic at the hissing sound of the chemical reaction under the chair once the gauze bag containing the pellets fell into the bowl. As the hydrogen cyanide gas began to rise through holes in the chair, he instinctively held his breath, sheer terror filling his eyes. A few in the observation room cringed, waiting for the inevitable moment when he would have to draw a new breath. His mother began to weep aloud. *What was she thinking? Why would any mother want to watch the death of her baby?*

After seventy-five seconds, Stefano heaved, exhaling, and tried to take another breath. Instantly, he began strangling. Over the next four and a half minutes, he bucked, his muscles tensing, confronting the restraints. He squirmed in the chair, violently snapping his head back and forth. His pain contorted face became blue and he jerked and coughed, choking on the drool that trailed from his mouth. His eyes began to move independently of each other and to protrude from his face.

Then he seemed to lose muscle control. Still heaving and gasping with a twisted mouth, he began to twitch all over. His face was dark. His lips seemed black. The twitching synchronized to become violent convulsions and finally, the seizure began.

"God help him! I can't watch any more of this!" The mother of one of the victims rose, hurried to the back of the room and faced the wall. "I think I'm going to be sick."

She was followed by Stefano's mother and about three-quarters of the observers. Only a mesmerized Saint Claire, a few reporters, the defense attorney and two other men continued to watch as Stefano's body began to slump in the chair. Foam oozed from his mouth as his body had spasms for another two minutes. Finally he stopped moving, an expression of horror contorting his face, his twisted mouth and eyes frozen open.

The images from Stefano's death were branded into Saint Claire's conscious mind. Stefano had died a horrible, painful death. He was a man who loved Gisele, and Gisele had loved him. He was her husband. She had vowed before God to be loyal to their marriage unto death, and death had come. She was free.

Saint Claire on the other hand, was not free. Katrina would leave St. Mary's soon. True to his vow, he would have to welcome her home if she decided to come. He would have to live with Katrina as man and wife, forsaking all others. He would have to forget Gisele.

Sadly, as he watched her sing the haunting song, his heart ached with the knowledge he might be watching her sing for the very last time.

Just another soul
That really knows my soul
And you won't look at me
Does that take the prize?
How much I love those eyes
And they won't look at me
Now the rain has gone
But something lingers on
There's certain sadness here
Now that the sky is clear
And it's all so clear
Yes, it's all so clear... to me now
And I can't help but fear
That certain sadness here... to stay.

CHAPTER 39

After a stint in the Peace Corps and a tour with Amnesty International in Guatemala, where her husband was killed by a death squad soon after their wedding, Nancy Thackeray Pearce arrived in San Francisco with bona fide liberal credentials. A Kennedy School of Government graduate, she got a job in the mayor's office and bought a place in the Castro neighborhood off Market Street. Over the ensuing years, she was involved in the Castro Street Fair, the San Francisco AIDS Foundation and the San Francisco Bay Area Homeless Project.

In the late 1990s she took a job at the California State Association of Counties, where she worked as an advocate for CSAC sponsored legislation, spending much of her time in Sacramento and traveling the length of the state for meetings. The mayor suggested that she should run for the county supervisor seat being vacated by the representative in her district. Nancy was elected easily and had been a popular activist in her neighborhood and the district for many years.

Two years earlier, Nancy got involved with a Human Rights Watch organization that launched a campaign against the trafficking of women and girls, and what began as a concern evolved into a cause and then an obsession. She donated over two hundred thousand dollars from her personal inheritance to an organization dedicated to extracting women and girls from dangerous and degrading circumstances, and she became active at fundraising events for the organization and others like it.

When Paul Vang, representing a group of San Francisco developers, approached Nancy and explained the group wanted to make monthly donations to her cause, she told Vang her vote and influence were not for sale. But Vang insisted that the group was not attempting to influence her vote. He said they had approached her because, according to their records, she was the supervisor on the board who *best* voted her conscience.

Nancy was shocked when she received a cash donation from Vang via Barbara Stevens. She told Barbara to pick up the package and to return it. But when another package came the next month, Barbara had sufficient time to rationalize accepting the money. A check would have to go through the organization's fundraising apparatus, where half the funds would be re-appropriated to pay salaries and corporate expenses. Less than

46 cents of each dollar would go to help the needy women and girls.

She knew a few key individuals within specific organizations who could use regular donations of cash to make a real difference, so she kept the money and sent it where she thought it would best be employed. Her contacts reported little difference in the first few months, but by the fifth month, they began to document real and quantifiable progress. Abused women and girls were benefiting. The money was making a difference.

When Vang's group asked for a meeting to discuss pending legislation, Nancy agreed merely to hear their concerns. But the case they presented to her made good sense. When the vote came up, she supported the legislation because it was good for San Francisco, and she even managed to bring two colleagues over to her side.

The money came regularly, the women and girls reaped the benefit, and Nancy continued to vote her conscience. But upon Vang's murder and the discovery of a bomb in a package delivered to Barbara Stevens, Nancy realized instantly she might be one of the killer's targets. The big question: was her life still in danger?

"Inspector Saint Claire?"

The detective looked up from the worn and tattered paperback copy of *Hamlet* he was reading.

"Yes?"

"Sorry for making you wait. Mr. Mullholland is ready for you now."

Ode to Yorrick still on his mind, Saint Claire closed the book and rose.

"This won't take long."

Upon seeing the detective, the city official rose, excited.

"Inspector Saint Claire! Berkeley professor! Thanks for coming. I've been dying to meet you. I hear you can read minds."

"Read minds? Someone told you wrong. I hardly get a chance to read the *paper* in the morning."

Rusty laughed.

"You mean when you're not on the front page?"

He paused as the detective took a seat across the desk.

"But to the darker purpose of your visit. How was Barbara involved?"

"Unwittingly. She thought the killer was out to get her, but he was only using her to gain access to his actual target."

A sudden flash of fear flooded Rusty's face.

"Me?"

Saint Claire suppressed an urge to laugh.

"No, not you. As far as I can tell, he was after one of the supervisors."

"Really? Which one?"

The detective raised his eyebrows and shrugged.

"Don't know. It's one of the women."

"Three of the supes are women. So that narrows it down to three?"

Saint Claire reached for his notebook in his jacket pocket and readied his pen.

"Tell me about them."

Rusty furled his brow, concentrating, and then he reared back in the chair, his paunch rising above the surface of the desk.

"Well first of all, there's Cordelia Martini, the former mayor's daughter. She's a real bitch. I could probably see someone wanting to kill her. What's this killer's motive?"

"It has nothing to do with the victim. It's more of a personal, art motivated thing for him, art and irony. Who else?"

Rusty seemed to stop himself from asking another question.

"Nancy Thackeray Pearce, real smart, but she can be a bitch, you know, standoffish. Came from East Coast old money, liberal as they come, Harvard graduate, MPA from Berkeley, probably the smartest of all the supes."

Saint Claire nodded as he wrote.

"And Shenita Williams?"

"*Definitely* a bitch. She's just got this gigantic, black, bitchy chip on her shoulder. Know what I mean? Like the whole world's in this vast conspiracy against her. In all the time she's been here, I think I've had maybe one real conversation with her. Her husband's a lawyer and some kind of a sports agent, you know, money. Shenita's problem, she's little outa touch with the people she represents in my opinion."

Saint Claire closed the notebook and looked toward the supervisors' board clerk.

"Thank you very much, Rusty. You've been a great help."

Rusty sat forward, confused.

"What? That was it? You don't have any more questions? You're done?"

Saint Claire stood.

"Yes. You've been very helpful."

Rusty stood and came to the corner of the desk.

"I don't get it. We spent all this time planning this meeting and it's over in two minutes? You shot your whole load in two fuckin minutes! You were out in the lobby longer than you were in here."

"I was early."

"Well all the same, can I ask you a question?"

Saint Claire checked his watch.

"Sure."

Rusty sat on the desk, his fabric covered stomach hanging between his thighs.

"Okay, do you think this killer's alive and he's still planning on murdering one of them?"

"We have no proof he's dead, so we can't rule out that he isn't. One of your supervisors was definitely a target. If she still is, I'm just hoping I can get to her before he does."

"And Barbara? Was she involved in something she shouldn't have been?"

Draping his overcoat across his forearm, Saint Claire did not flinch.

"Barbara helped to delay if not prevent murder number four and the other murders that might follow. She was the lucky break we needed to turn this thing around. That is, if it can be turned around. But then, you obviously know your assistant better than I do."

He checked the watch again.

"You know Rusty, I actually have a little gap in my schedule today. You don't mind if I sit in your lobby for a few minutes? I figure I could catch up on some reading."

Rusty motioned with a nod, skeptical.

"Knock yourself out, Inspector."

"And I can call you if I have any further questions?"

Rusty sighed, shaking his head.

"Yeah. When you need another two minute interview, you know where to find me."

It was a long shot, but he hoped it would be worth his time and effort. He hadn't expected Rusty to provide much in the way of new information. He had already examined the backgrounds of the woman supervisors. The meeting with Rusty was a device. Saint Claire just needed to be visible and available.

Of the three women supervisors, he figured the killer would choose Martini. According to rumors circulated at City Hall, her husband, Tony Madruga, had a gambling problem that caused cash flow concerns. In the previous year, the couple had to sell off three investment properties. And, like her father, Cordelia wasn't above playing dirty to achieve her aims.

In the last election, Cordelia's opponent accused her of threatening to reveal the questionable legal status of her husband's parents to immigration officials. And when Cordelia fired her campaign manager for being involved in a scheme to pay a prostitute to seduce her opponent's husband, many believed the supervisor was actively involved. If front man Vang was looking for an unscrupulous supervisor, Cordelia Martini seemed the obvious choice.

Saint Claire didn't expect to be approached by a supervisor, but he was certain the supervisor in question would be nervous and would want to talk.

"What are you reading?"

"*Hamlet*, Shakespeare play."

The young woman wore jeans, tennis shoes, a hat and sunglasses.

"Oh, I read that in college. Everybody *dies* at the end, right?"

Saint Claire closed the book, pretending to be shocked and disappointed.

"I can't believe you just told me the ending! I was in the final Act."

Her hands went to her mouth.

"Oh, I'm sorry! I don't know what I was thinking! I'm sorry."

Saint Claire smiled.

"It's a tragedy. Everyone always dies at the end of his tragedies."

The woman sat back, embarrassed, smiling.

"I knew that."

She pulled the glasses down the bridge of her nose to make eye contact.

"You're Saint Claire, right?"

He nodded.

"Yes."

"If you give me your book, I'll look at it and I'll slip a note in the pages in the middle. It's a private phone number from someone who needs to talk to you. Can I see the book?"

Saint Claire scanned the room for anyone who might be watching. No one suspected her. Leaning toward her, he handed her the book. Note pursed in her palm, she examined the book, opened it, and slipped the folded scrap of paper inside. Nodding approval, she handed it back to the detective.

"Call her at six o'clock. She'll be waiting for your call."

CHAPTER 40

They sat at the bar in the upstairs recess in Slater's home. Brady had called earlier to request a private meeting with the former captain and asked him not to mention it to Saint Claire. Slater seemed hesitant to meet until Brady reassured him the discussion was not part of a campaign to smear the inspector.

Slater as usual, was *hittin the Jack* as he waited for Oksana to finish at the spa. He told Brady he didn't have much time because he was taking his wife to a play and a late dinner in the city.

Brady arrived with a sealed case of Slater's favorite whiskey and a box containing a dozen *syrniki* for Oksana. In an attempt to break the ice, he challenged Slater to a game of nineball, which he lost miserably. Game over, they sat at the bar to discuss Saint Claire.

"So what's the real story about Joe Curry? The bullet in his head was Saint Claire's, fired by Saint Claire's gun. According to the record and your testimony, he had an alibi, but doesn't the whole thing raise a red flag for you?"

Slater thought for a moment.

"Well maybe if I wasn't *sittin* with im at a crowded funeral service at a church at the exact time Joe was shot, and maybe if we weren't twenty miles away from the crime scene, and then maybe if he actually *had* transportation, because he wasn't ridin with me, maybe *then* I'd see that red flag you're raisin."

"I, I just think it's a little strange, that's all."

"The world's a strange place, Brady. I stopped tryin ta figure it out a long time ago."

Brady rose from the bar stool, walked over to the couch and plopped down.

"Saint Claire saved the fourth victim, that Stevens woman. Do you think it's over?"

"Is Saint Claire actin like *he* thinks it's over?"

"No, not really."

Slater sat in the leather chair across from the detective.

"Then it ain't over."

The meeting wasn't going as well as Brady thought it would. He just couldn't find a way to make a connection with the older man.

"Tell me something, do you think Saint Claire might be a little prejudiced?"

"About what?"

"About white people. Do you think he secretly doesn't like white people?"

Slater sighed.

"That funeral we were at, it was my son's. Saint Claire was like a second father to my son, Stuart. Stuart admired Saint Claire because Saint Claire saved him from prejudice and hate. He helped Stuart find redemption. Why would you think he's prejudiced?"

Brady started to answer, but he hesitated. He sipped again to build resolve, motioning with the drink.

"He has this niece, Mignon, and I think we have something that works, you know, romantically. We have chemistry. Well anyway, he told his niece he didn't want her having anything to do with me."

He looked into Slater's eyes.

"He said he'd never approve of us being together. What do you think *that* is?"

Slater chuckled, looking toward the ceiling.

"That's funny."

"What's funny?"

Slater looked toward Brady, shaking his head.

"You! Saint Claire doesn't want you going out with his niece and you think he's prejudiced? Truth is you're a sleaze! Who do ya think you're foolin?"

The sound of music from downstairs meant Oksana was home. Finishing the last of his drink, Slater smiled and leaned toward Brady, almost whispering.

"Listen, I'm white. My ass has been white a lot longer'n yours, and I wouldn't want ya goin out with *my* niece."

Busy though he was, it bothered Saint Claire that Katrina hadn't returned his calls, and worse, that she made excuses to avoid his visits. Deuteronomy had readied his condominium for her. A huge vase of freshly cut white irises, her favorite flowers, sat on a low table in the living room. There were two bottles of champagne in the refrigerator and sun-ripened nectarines and white peaches in a bowl on the kitchen counter.

He fixed up the extra room to resemble hers at the hospital. There was a couch, a chair and a new computer for her writing projects. He hadn't included a bed because he imagined she would be sleeping in his room.

The thought of sleeping with Katrina again was strangely exciting. It had been so long! Over the previous couple of nights, he imagined making love to her again. He thought of being on her, over her body, her thighs spread open. He remembered what it felt like to be inside her, the softness, the warmth, the wetness. She would be looking up at him as he moved in and out with deliberate slowness.

But he realized Katrina was having a difficult time with the thought of being outside the hospital for the first time after twelve years. He understood her well enough to know that. She was stressing out over the idea of being on her own, without the security, without the safe regular schedules and routines she had grown accustomed to at St. Mary's. It was a big step for her. And she was capable of playing elaborate mind games to mask her insecurity, not just from others, but from herself.

He studied her face, prepared for the worst.

"Hi Ronnie. I'm sorry if it seems like I've been avoiding you. I've been thinking. I've had a lot on my mind."

Seated in the leather chair in her hospital room, he smiled, attempting to put her at ease.

"I realized you would have... mixed feelings about leaving and starting out again. It is a big step."

"It's not that big a step. I can do this. The curse was removed. I could have done this a long time ago if you—"

Noting an angry edge in her voice, he raised his hands in surrender.

"Look, I'm sorry we disagreed about that. I'm just happy that, for however it happened, it worked out. Okay?"

She sat back, relaxing.

"Okay. I don't want to fight anymore either."

She dropped her head, sadness overcoming her.

"You know, Ronnie, I really adore you. I love you. And whether I've shown it or not, I know you've been there for me through all this. You've been my best friend."

"Well, I love you. You're my wife and partner for life." He rolled his eyes. "Even if that *did* rhyme."

He leaned toward her, taking her hand.

"You don't know how I've longed for this moment. I was beginning to think it would never come, but you're leaving this place. You're coming home."

She blurted out the words.

"I'm not coming home, Ronnie."

He could not find a sound to respond.

"It's not because I don't love you, because I do. And it's not because I don't want to live with you, but going home to you would be wrong."

It was as if someone had punched him in the stomach really hard. He hadn't seen it coming. He sat back, barely able to breathe.

"Why?"

"I don't want to tell you why, Ronnie. I thought I should, but I don't think I can do that. Will you just trust me on this one, please?"

His body and disposition tensed.

"Oh please! I've waited twelve years for you, been there for you. And then on the day you're getting out you up and tell me you're not coming home to me?"

He stiffened his jaw.

"No I can't just trust you on this, believe me. You have to tell me. Is there someone else?"

"No."

"Then what is it?"

Katrina closed her tearing eyes and crossed her arms.

"You really don't want to know, Ronnie. Trust me, you don't."

"Yes, I do. I'm listening."

She fell silent, unable to begin at first.

"Do you remember when we were dating? Do you remember how your father was staunchly against it and your mother was all for it?"

He nodded.

"Yes?"

"Remember after your father died and your mother *lived* with us, when you were in graduate school?"

"I remember that, too."

"Well, when you were in school and at work, your mother and I used to talk a lot. We talked about everything, about the way you were so attached to her as a boy, and the naughty things you and your brothers did, and local gossip in the community, Miss Annabelle, everything."

She closed her eyes, nodding.

"And she talked about her earlier life, her parents, her Auntie Rose, about going out to see Louis Armstrong in New Orleans and the floods of 1947."

Reaching over, she took his hand.

"Well, one night, she told me a story about a beautiful girl and a handsome boy who were in love. The girl was young, maybe seventeen. He was a year older. He had light skin and green eyes, and he fell in love with her. They used to sneak off after school and lay out in this vast alfalfa field looking up at the clouds in the sky, making big plans.

"He was supposed to go to college to become a doctor and she was going to be a professional nurse. After college they were going to move up North to a big city, maybe Chicago or New York, and they were going to live like George Brent and Bebe Daniels in the talking movies they watched."

Deuteronomy had no idea where the story was going, but he wouldn't interrupt.

"They had one wonderful summer together, living in a world that they made their own, and then the rest of the world came crashing in. When he brought her home and introduced her to his family, they frowned on her. They were rude, nasty to her. And it was only because her skin was darker.

"His family was a bright-skinned family, and they weren't about to let some pussy-whipped boy pollute their family bloodline by marrying someone darker than a brown paper bag. They told the boy they'd disinherit him if he didn't take her home to her people and never talk to her again. Your mother said the boy protested at first, but after that day, he was never the same. According to your mother, a young man didn't go against his family back then, especially if he wanted to go to college."

She sighed.

"Anyway, a few years later this boy met and married a woman so light she was damn-near white. But the boy and girl met again years later, after *both* were married and both had kids. By that time, he had a pretty good career. And he wondered what if, he wondered *what if* he had been brave enough to go against his family? You see, in all that time, he never stopped loving her, and she still loved him."

Her eyes welled up until a tear trailed down her cheek.

"So they had this secret affair. They agreed to meet on one day a year, one day only. They'd go somewhere, usually out of town, and they'd spend the entire day making love. And after that day, they'd go back to their unsatisfying, compromised lives, counting the days until their next encounter."

Her smile was bittersweet.

"Problem was, one day she got the feeling she was *pregnant* with his child, and when the baby came, she was convinced it was his. Her husband was suspicious, but he never confronted her about it and raised the child as his own, along with his own."

She stopped.

"You're an intelligent man, Ronnie. You know what I'm getting at."

He was defiant.

"I don't. You'll have to tell me."

"You want to know why things changed after I got pregnant with Christian? It's because your mother told me that story when I was pregnant with Christian. I can see it in your eyes. You already know. The girl in the story was your mother, and the boy was my father."

Next came the words he did not want to hear.

"So the reason I can't go live with you, the reason I can never make love to you again, Ronnie, is because that child they had together was *you*."

Her words overwhelmed him. He shrank in the chair, unable to respond.

"You understand it now, don't you, Ronnie? I can't be with you because you are my brother. You're my *brother* by blood. We have different mothers, but my father is *your* father. I love you, but I can't be with you. It just wouldn't be right."

CHAPTER 41

During their fifteen-minute phone conversation, a police detective told her to beware of things that seemed odd or out of place. If that was the case, she was worried the killer could attack from anywhere. Everything seemed out of kilter. She got the distinct impression someone had been in her house, in her bedroom even. Over the last day or so she felt she was being watched, lined up in the crosshairs. As long as she stayed in San Francisco, she felt vulnerable.

No one knew about the cabin. Her name was not on title or listed on any of the public records in Placer County. There she would be invisible, off the killer's radar. She would be off everyone's radar. It had been years since she had taken the time out to be truly alone, and four months since she had been at the cabin. She didn't see her decision as the act of a desperate, frightened woman. It was an opportunity to reassess her life.

She decided to stay in a hotel in Berkeley for the night and head out to Lake Tahoe at the first sign of light. She would stay at least two weeks or longer, if she thought the threat to her life still existed. The seat on the board was just a job. It wasn't worth dying for.

No one knew about the relationship either, though many had made accurate assumptions about her sexuality. The cabin was actually a result of that relationship. It was a private retreat, stocked with food, wine, a pot stash, links to the outside world and everything else she would need, except her lover.

She met Barbara Stevens on the very first day she started with the Board. She thought Barbara was attractive, but Barbara was married and seemed unavailable. That didn't stop a furtive friendship from developing, however. Early on, they just had extended, tantalizing phone conversations. Through those, she learned Barbara was unhappy in the relationship with her husband, Bob.

According to Barbara, Bob was intelligent and attentive, but he lacked ambition. His reluctance to take risks condemned Bob and Barbara to a life of mediocrity. Barbara wanted out of the marriage, but she stayed for the kids. There had been a couple of illicit friendships, but nothing serious.

When Barbara admitted she was attracted to power and people in powerful positions, the affair began in earnest. It had to be covert, but it was passionate from the beginning. The risk was exciting.

When Paul Vang approached Barbara to find out which county supervisor might be willing to work with his group, Barbara gave him two names, Cordelia Martini and Nancy Thackeray Pearce. The developers paid Barbara one hundred twenty-five thousand dollars for the referrals and for other sensitive information she provided about board members.

Barbara wanted to invest in real estate, but she didn't want Bob to know. A financial advisor helped her form a closed corporation so that she could purchase and hold the property under a corporate identity. When she was ready to buy, she asked her lover to help find a good deal. The cottage in South Lake Tahoe was a steal, a hurried, undervalued sale resulting from a divorce. Barbara made $120,000 in equity by the close of escrow.

It was a little after ten in the morning when Nancy arrived at the cabin a little ways up the mountain. All was quiet as usual. She pulled into a parking space behind the house, hiding her car under the branches of an overgrown tree. Luggage and bags in the living room, she sighed with relief as inside, she locked the back door. No one, not even Barbara, knew where she was. She was safe.

Saint Claire didn't mind that Brady called to push their meeting back thirty minutes. It gave him time to think. Katrina couldn't have been telling the truth. She was reinventing reality to cope with the stress of leaving Saint Mary's. Sitting at his desk, his thoughts kept returning to the night she left him twelve years earlier.

They were sitting on that swing in the backyard at their Berkeley home, the white, wooden swing they had ordered in Louisiana. They had just gone through the ordeal of Christian's murder and funeral, with all its sadness, pomp and ceremony. Katrina was crying. She told Deuteronomy she needed to tell him something important, but she never did. Instead, she placed her hands in his and told him she loved him, but she could no longer live with him.

When he thought about it, the timbre of her voice earlier in the day was reminiscent of her tone on that evening twelve years earlier. She even incorporated some of the same phrases and facial expressions. It was bizarre, an eerie *déjà vu*. But Katrina was clever. If anyone could regress and recapture the poignancy of an old memory, harnessing it to reshape reality, it would be her.

If Katrina didn't want to live with him when she got out, she could have just told him. He would have eventually understood and accepted her decision. The elaborate story and the gross suggestion that she was his sister was unnecessary, unless her objective was to alter the relationship to achieve a separate objective.

As his sister, she would still have his loyalty and devotion, and yet she would not be burdened with the pressures and responsibilities of being his wife. He wondered if her leaving the hospital was a mistake. Maybe she wasn't ready.

But there was one other memory that kept coming back to him, something he had forgotten until Katrina told her story. He must have been maybe six or seven years old, back in Thibodaux, walking home from school in a large group of children. Two of the Williams boys, the twins, had started threatening him. Deuteronomy remembered how Bianca Scott stepped in that day. She was smaller than they were, but she took on the twins. She kicked one of the boys in the balls and had the other on the ground, choking him, when a grown-up came over and pulled her off.

Shamed for being beat up by a girl, the Williams boys complained she cheated by kicking, and crying, asked why she was taking up for Deuteronomy.

"Because he's my *brother!*"

Deuteronomy thought she said it only to justify protecting him. As he recalled, Bianca was always very nice to him, sometimes overly nice. And while she never made any further mention about being his sister, he always felt a special connection to her.

Deuteronomy knew his mother and Benjamin Scott courted in high school. But the suggestion that Benjamin Scott was Deuteronomy's real father! The logic failed. If his pious, religious mother believed Deuteronomy and Katrina were brother and sister, she would never have encouraged them to date, let alone marry and have children. It went against God!

Katrina claimed his mother did not mention the affair and her suspicion about Deuteronomy's parentage until Katrina was pregnant with Christian.

"In Bible times," she remembered Bernadette saying, "brothers and sisters marryin served to strengthen the family line." Bernadette repeatedly reminded Katrina that Sarai was Abram's half-sister.

It wasn't until four months after the baby was born, about a year after Bernadette's revelation, that doctors diagnosed the old woman with delusional disorder. Neurologists said Bernadette could have been suffering from delusions for years. And they suspected the slow growing tumor detected along one of the medial temporal lobes of her brain would bring about more fantastic delusions.

Katrina initially dismissed her mother-in-law's story as the prattle of a lonely, demented woman. When Christian was born, however, she fancied she saw her own father's face in the boy's face. Worse, she began to think her *husband* manifested facial expressions and gestures similar to those of her father and grandfather. It was why she stopped having sex with him.

Deuteronomy begged her to explain why she had changed, why she had become so distant, but she did not have the strength to talk to him about it, especially after Bernadette's death. After Christian's murder, she thought she had worked up the nerve to tell him the story and her suspicions, but she was unable to speak the first word.

Over the years, she succumbed and allowed him to make love to her on rare occasions, but she was always miserable afterward. The thought of having sex with a man who might have been her brother was repulsive. With each occasion she became more convinced her mother-in-law got it right.

After Christian was murdered, she determined she could no longer live with Deuteronomy, and yet she was unable to tell him why. Three weeks after she left, she had a nervous breakdown and checked herself into Saint Mary's, where she "escaped from everyone and from herself." Now she believed, with her admission to him, she was finally free. It didn't matter whether he believed her or not. She had conquered the demon. She had liberated her soul.

CHAPTER 42

"You talked to one of the county supervisors? How'd that come about?"

"One of her aides gave me her phone number and asked me to call her, which I did at six."

It had been three days since Brady met with Saint Claire. He seemed a little nervous.

"Which one was it?"

"Cordelia Martini."

"So she *was* on Vang's payroll? You were right."

They met at the station. Brady sat in a chair across from Saint Claire, who sat at his desk, re-ordering his notes. It was late, and the darkened room seemed empty. Saint Claire adjusted the light at his desk.

"Martini and maybe one or two of the others. But it wasn't an admission. Martini contacted me to talk only because she was sure she would be the next victim."

"Why so sure?"

"She claims someone's been following her. She said she had private dealings with Vang prior to his murder, and apparently Barbara Stevens was the liaison between the two."

Brady nodded.

"So the bomb Barbara Stevens brought to you was really meant for Cordelia Martini?"

"Martini thinks so. I think it's possible. A couple of minor details still bother me, though."

"Details you might want to share?"

"Not yet. Not at this time."

Saint Claire despised playing games. He wanted to broach the subject from the moment Brady entered the room. Unlike Brady, he could not pretend all was well.

"Did you think you were going to get some dirt on me from Slater?"

Brady became defensive.

"I don't know what he told you, but that wasn't why I went there."

"Let me guess. You thought because you were white and *he* was white you could somehow get him to give you something on me? Maybe you think you're still in Boston!"

"No. But what does Boston have to do with anything?"

"Why don't you tell me, Brady? What *does* Boston have to do with anything?"

"You brought up Boston. If there's something you want to say, why don't you just say it?"

Saint Claire stood, contempt on his face unmistakable, as he looked down on the younger man.

"We both know why you came here, to spy on me for the chief, but still I was willing to give you a chance. And it was almost working. Turns out I was wrong about you."

Brady stood to challenge the detective.

"And the chief was right about you. You don't share! How do you expect anyone to trust you? And who are you to interfere with our access to information? We're supposed to be on the same team. You tell us only what you want us to know!"

Angry, Brady said it.

"And you resent white people."

"I resent *some* white people. And I resent some black people."

The men locked eyes. After a moment, Brady broke the gaze.

"You resent me."

"Yes, I resent you! Not because you're white, but because you represent all the smug bigotry, injustice and arrogance black people and many others have lost lives trying to overcome in this country. You have no respect for black people."

Brady turned, getting in the detective's face.

"Fuck you, Deuteronomy! Fuck you and all your secrets. I don't have to put up with this shit!"

Saint Claire called out as Brady spun around to leave.

"No, no Brady, you're not leaving! You started this. What about *your* secrets?"

Brady stopped and turned.

"I have no secrets."

"Think about Boston."

Brady shrugged.

"Okay, what about Boston?"

"Reginald Walter Perry, the fourteen-year-old black kid you shot and killed in Boston. But I doubt if you even remember his name."

Brady bowed his head. His jaw clenched, he raised his head, nodding.

"Of course I remember the name. How did you hear about that?"

"*You* didn't tell me. It's a secret, right? A big secret?"

Brady extended his hand in a halting motion.

"You've probably only heard part of the story. It's not what you think."

"Let's see, fourteen-year-old black kid, walking home from the store after getting long matches for his grandmother's stove, you're chasing a group of black kids who allegedly broke into a candy machine, a vending machine! The group disperses and gets away. So you see this lone black kid in the distance, and thinking he's one of them, you tell him to freeze. When he turns to hear who's talking, you shoot him because you think the matchbox is a gun. Did I miss anything?"

Brady sighed, ill at ease.

"Those are basically the facts, yes. It was a horrible error in judgment, but that doesn't make me a bigot. I probably would have made the same mistake if the kid was white."

"I doubt it. But let's just say we give Tom Brady the benefit of the doubt. Let's say it was an honest mistake. Then why the cover up?"

Brady's face showed confusion.

"What are you talking about? There was no cover up."

Saint Claire huffed, disgusted.

"Okay, innocent fourteen-year-old black boy gets shot by a white cop—he was an *A-student* in case you didn't know. Newspapers don't report it because editors don't want to stir up racial tensions in the city. And we all know Boston's history with racism. Television news won't report it because they're cozy with the police. Kid's grandmother is all he had. She's devastated, but hers is just a tiny voice no one wants to hear. And so the gunning down of a fourteen-year-old black kid in the street gets ignored. Why? Because to people like you, nothing significant had happened. No big deal, it was just another dead black kid."

Crossing his arms, Brady tried to defend himself.

"Look, I'm, I'm not sure where you got your story, but what you *didn't* hear is how bad I felt about it!"

"Oh sing me the blues! I'm just about sure Reginald Perry felt worse. Don't you think?"

"You didn't hear how I made it my responsibility to take care of his grandmother until the day she died. I got her a nice apartment in a good neighborhood. I provided support for her and I saw to it that Reggie's younger sister's college tuition was paid right through grad school."

Saint Claire took a deep breath.

"That's all well and good. But why did you participate in the cover up?"

"There was no cover up!"

"Well, why isn't it in your record?"

Brady was unprepared to respond.

"I don't know. Honesty, I don't know."

Saint Claire crossed his arms.

"Stop being such a hypocrite, Brady. Why didn't you share? The incident isn't in your record because a judge sealed the record and you didn't bother to mention it to anyone here. So what were you trying to hide? The fact that you're a racist?"

"Fuck you, Saint Claire! That's *exactly* why I didn't mention it! So people like you wouldn't make it into a racial thing. I am not a bigot."

"Spoken like a true bigot."

Saint Claire smiled, sarcasm coloring his voice.

"And who were you to interfere with the public's right to know? And the chief's right to know? And your partner's right to know?"

He paused for a moment, sneering.

"I can accept the shooting may have been an accident, but the cover up? You knew what you were doing."

"It was damage control. I made it up to his family."

"But you didn't take responsibility for his death, even if it was an accident. If the boy's life meant anything to you, you would have accepted responsibility for taking it, but you didn't and you haven't. That means you're either racist or dishonest. You tell me which one it is."

Brady was silent.

"So the next time you want to judge me and berate me for having secrets, just remember what you're covering up."

A half-minute later, Brady spoke without emotion.

"So what are you going to do, Saint Claire? Tell the chief and everyone else about the shooting? Paint me as the bigot you think I am? Ruin my career?"

Saint Claire had returned to his desk and his notes. He answered without looking up.

"Don't worry, I won't say anything. That'll be just one more *secret* you'll be able to condemn me for not sharing."

Nancy awoke disoriented, unable to discern whether she was viewing the sunrise or a sunset. For a moment she forgot where she was. She must have drifted off to sleep. Her memory slowly returned.

She spent the previous day reading over sections of her will, something she had been promising herself to do for five years. It wasn't as bad as she imagined, just matter-of-fact language involving what would happen in the event of her death, but the thought of being dead and gone was depressing.

Fortunately, she brought a couple cases of wine and some of her favorite snacks. Eating always made her feel better. The food took little preparation. Smoked salmon and capers from the refrigerator, cream cheese and thinly sliced baguettes. Judging by the vintage date, she feared the oak-aged, amber colored chardonnay was a little past its prime, but it ended up being the best California white she ever had.

After the food and wine, she was feeling better. San Francisco and the idea of a killer seemed a world away. She took a deep breath and exhaled all the stresses of the past week. As her eyes scanned the interior of the cottage, she fancied living the rest of her life there. Lake Tahoe was beautiful all year round. Maybe she would never go back to San Francisco. At once, she realized the one thing that would make the experience even better.

She packed the bowl with the tip of her index finger. She and Barbara kept their marijuana stash in an expensive, lacquered mahogany humidor intended for cigars. Barbara called it *Pandora's Box*. When she opened it, the skunky aroma from two bags of sticky green bud wafted into her face.

But she was really after the Thai stick in the right corner of the box, premium buds of seedless marijuana skewered on marijuana stems. Just one bowl would be more than enough.

Minutes later, pure bliss! The world was beautiful and warm, with a soft buzz playing in the background. The reds and browns in the bedspread were deep and vibrant, the cotton fabric feather-soft against her bare, tingling skin. She lay there, paralyzed for the moment, noticing the metallic flecks dispersed about the ceiling. Feeling deliciously excited, she began to touch herself.

She could feel chills and waves of pleasure traveling from her epicenter to the farthest reaches of her body, to the tips of her fingers and toes, to the roots of her hair. She thought of Barbara's body and re-lived some of their most passionate encounters in the bed. And finally, release. That moment of intense pleasure was the last thing she could remember from that night.

Looking over at the clock, she bolted from the bed. It was 9:30 in the morning! She was supposed to call her assistant at 8:00. She felt hungry. Eggs and bacon sizzled in separate frying pans as she pressed down the plunger of the double cup French coffee press. Breakfast done, she headed for the home office. Something told her she should have called Barbara for *her* computer password. The detective told her to stay away from anything routine. But she would be on the computer for less than ten minutes, just enough time to remotely check her email and to respond where needed.

Steaming coffee on a coaster at her right, she pressed the on switch and waited. The computer began its standard opening procedure, but one of the screens was different. Her computer was doing something different! She froze in the seat. What was happening?

It seemed the computer was making a phone call, but to whom? Then she heard a sudden vibrating sound from the underside of Barbara's desk, its back edge lined with the back edge of her own. By the time she looked back to her computer screen, it was too late.

The explosion was violent and fiery. In that fraction of a second, she realized her end had come. The spool of her entire life zipped past her from nothing to nothing, with moments of happiness and grief, joy and pain, birth and the events leading to her present predicament.

She saw the twin towers crashing down, the fall of the Berlin Wall and the election of the first African American president. She saw the look on her father's face as she was born and the agony of her brother that summer afternoon when he broke his left arm. She watched as she made love for the first time. It was as if she had all the time in the world to go back and forth wherever she wished in the tapestry of her life, and when she could want no more, she knew it was over.

The end seemed too sudden, too abrupt. In slow motion, the desk and computer disintegrated, replaced by an ever expanding plume of heated wind, black smoke and red-orange flames—and along with them, one shrieking and terrified San Francisco County Supervisor.

CHAPTER 43

It was a major news story. Reporters and camera crews converged on South Lake Tahoe as investigators sorted through the damaged portions of the cabin. The fire station down the hill had responded in time to save portions of the cottage and prevent a widespread fire.

The supervisor's legs and pelvis were charred beyond recognition. Her upper torso had been blown from her body between lumbar segments three and four. When the fire crew arrived, Nancy's blackened upper torso rested against the wall farthest from the desk, its cooked flesh smoldering and on fire.

Duck taped to the underside of Barbara's desk, firefighters found a cell phone, still plugged into one of six outlets in a surge protector. It was modified with a makeshift board that trailed two long lead wires. According to a munitions expert on-site, the wires ran from the underside of Barbara's desk to the underside of Nancy's, where they were attached to a blasting cap.

The battery of the cell phone was 3.6 volts at 1.2 amps, or roughly 5 watts of energy, just enough power to detonate the blasting cap. The blasting cap detonated a substance one investigator called *PBX*, or plastic bonded explosives, better known as *C-4*, which is 1.34 times more powerful than *TNT*.

Someone had altered Nancy's computer logon protocol so that during the process, the cell phone taped underneath Barbara's desk received a call. When it began to ring, the vibration circuit, a small motor with an unbalanced cam, produced the electricity required to detonate the blasting cap in 1.25 pounds of *C-4* in an open-ended steel box, bolted to the underside of Nancy's desk. The killer installed the heavy box to direct the blast forward. At the moment of explosion, the *C-4* decomposed to release nitrogen, carbon oxides and heat, expanding at a rate of about 26,400 feet per second. Nancy never stood a chance.

When local law enforcement ran the plates from Nancy's vehicle and learned she was a San Francisco County Supervisor, they contacted the Anti-Terrorism Task Force of the US Attorney's Office, Northern District of California. The ATTF immediately sent over its own investigators. All the major

American news agencies sent correspondents to San Francisco and other crews came from as far as Australia and Japan.

It was a huge news story, and since the killer could not be interviewed, Saint Claire became the biggest target for reporters. His photo and life story, including the account of his son's murder, his wife's time at Saint Mary's and his work as a detective were in newspapers across the country.

He refused interviews and avoided reporters, dreading the mayor's press conference in the morning. Chief Rebecca Leong called that afternoon to tell him about the 10 o'clock media event and to advise him the mayor wanted to meet with him that evening.

He drove to South Lake Tahoe during the day to get a look at the cottage, thinking the whole way about Katrina. That morning, he had given her a cashier's check for seventy-five thousand dollars, enough for her to rent and furnish an apartment and have some money in the bank. Still hopeful, he told her there was a vacancy in his building. Gently, she explained she had already found a place in Sausalito and she would invite him over for dinner once she got settled. He considered asking her to volunteer her DNA for testing against his to settle the question, but he realized it didn't matter. Her feelings toward him had shifted permanently.

He thought of Gisele on the way back to San Francisco. When she called him earlier to tell him he looked handsome on television, she was on her way home from Stefano's funeral. Though he still talked to Gisele on the phone, in the past week their conversations had been short and superficial. He promised to call when he left Lake Tahoe so they could talk all the way back to the city.

He decided to wait to tell her in person about the development with Katrina, because he wanted to speak with the archbishop about how to proceed. An annulment didn't seem right for a marriage of such length, but surely the church wouldn't force a brother and sister to remain married. With an annulment, there was at least a chance for him and Gisele. But sister or no sister, he wasn't sure he could forsake Katrina after she had been his wife for so many years. He still had feelings for her, husbandly feelings. He had vowed before God to be bound to her for life. He couldn't just walk away.

Gisele was pensive at the beginning of their phone conversation. Try as she might, she could not abandon the emotion and guilt evoked by the day's big event. She had touched Stefano's cold, bloodless face as he lay in the casket, her fingers tenderly tracing the outline of his lips. Standing beside him, she remembered how those lips smiled so warmly, how they felt kissing her neck. Sometimes, when she told a joke to cheer him up when he didn't want to smile, the laughter tried to escape from the right corner of those lips.

She touched his hands. They were hands that guided her from life as a silly girl to the splendor of womanhood. Those hands had caressed her face in times of joy and sadness, wiping away a thousand tears. They were manly hands that had clutched her shoulders to pull her close, hands that gripped so tightly when he was making love to her. It was hard to imagine those same hands had killed so many people.

As Gisele stood beside him, his mother approached the casket, never looking over. Scowl gripping her face, she told the woman consoling her that her son's wife, her immoral daughter-in-law, was a selfish and disloyal whore, that she was never a good wife to Stefano, and as he rotted and suffered in that prison, the little bitch was having an affair with the same black cop who had fabricated evidence against her son to get him convicted.

When *Suocera* began with details about how her son coughed and gagged so in that gas chamber, Gisele could take no more. She left the church, insisting the limo driver take her home immediately. Sitting alone didn't make things better, and neither did two shots of rum in quick succession. By the time Deuteronomy called, she was hurting, crying in the dark.

They talked for three and a half hours. After an hour, Gisele opened enough to repeat the awful things *Suocera* said about her. She was insulted and angry, adamant that she was never disloyal to Stefano in her heart as well as her body. She insisted she and Deuteronomy had been no more than friends and wanted to hear him repeat the words. But an hour and a half later, she was back to her happy, sarcastic self.

She found it amusing that the priest who did the eulogy spoke as though Stefano was a church martyr, a saint. She didn't think the cleric had ever even met Stefano and wondered if her husband's mother had flown the poor man in from New Jersey without telling him her son was a convicted killer who was executed in California's gas chamber.

Gisele was intrigued by the love affair between the supervisor and Barbara Stevens. She wondered if Barbara's husband was in on it. She mused that maybe the husband was a schemer who somehow found out about the affair.

"Oh yes, maybe it waz a crime of passion and all those news yahoos got it all wrong? Maybe that huzband made the bomb blow up, knowing those guys would love to have again that story about this *Undead* killer. Ya think?"

"The whole thing just makes me sick to my stomach. Of *course* it's the same guy, and I'm next! I know it."

Brady looked across the desk at the captain, who aimed the remote at the television.

"I can't watch this!"

Serial murder pundits were chattering non-stop as she scanned the channels of the television cable news circuit. Armed with texts of the killer's first and second letters, experts ventured to explain the mind of this serial killer as well as serial killers in general. A composite profile and description of the killer began to emerge as the coverage wore on.

The killer was male, probably white and possibly bisexual. While most serial killers were either doctors or nurses, and it seemed this killer had a medical background, he was neither. Rather he was more likely a graduate student or a scholar.

By forensic definition, he was the *organized* type of killer, meaning he was above average intelligence. He planned his crimes methodically, scheming to maintain a high degree of control over crime scenes. He had a solid knowledge of forensic science, which enabled him to predict where investigations were going and how to elude law enforcement for so many years. If he was alive, he probably monitored police communications regularly and was watching with great interest as the story unfolded before him on television.

Experts guessed the killer chose to challenge Saint Claire because he believed this Berkeley professor-turned-detective was the most intelligent cop on the San Francisco police force.

Or it was possibly because Saint Claire had, sometime over the years, come close to catching him. Or maybe the killer was one of Dr. Saint Claire's former criminal psychology students, pitting himself against his teacher.

Whatever the case, he was fixated on the inspector. And the mayor's 10:00 am press conference promised to be the biggest news event of the day.

"Sonia, it's not just me, but everyone's noticed how things have changed between you and Saint Claire. Some people think you two have a *thing* going on, you know, like an affair."

She smiled.

"And?"

"Do you? Is there something going on between you two?"

She laughed.

"If there was, do you think I'd tell you?"

"Well, you used to complain he didn't share information with you, but now apparently he does. I'm his partner, and he shares more with you than he does with me."

"I'm his captain. What's wrong with that?"

Brady puffed his cheeks to blow out a sigh.

"Okay. But when he's talked to you, has he ever mentioned anything about me?"

"Anything like what?"

"I don't know. Just anything. Has he told you what he thinks of me or anything else?"

Sonia squinted her eyes, trying to read Brady.

"What? Does he have something on you?"

He smiled, though not with his entire face.

"No. I was just wondering. You know how he is."

She nodded, still skeptical as he explained.

"It's just that, I'm not sure if you know this, but I'm kinda dating his niece."

"What do you mean kinda dating? You mean *sleeping* with his niece?"

"No! I mean, not yet. But she told me he has a problem with it. I think he has a problem with me because of it."

She shook her head.

"Brady, I wouldn't want you dating my niece. You're definitely handsome, but you're a pig, and you're married."

He stared, contemplating whether he should reveal the truth about his marriage. It was useless. He returned to his seat and bowed his head.

"Has anyone spoken with Barbara Stevens?"

"She's a basket case, still under a doctor's care. And if we ever finally get a chance to talk to her, she'll be surrounded by lawyers who won't let her say anything. It's fucked up! I mean, we're talking about people's *lives* here, and they're more interested in protecting the feelings of that slut bitch who—"

She stopped.

"I'm next, and we're running out of time."

"Why are you so sure you're next?"

Her hands were shaking as she raked strands of hair from her face.

"He's already killed four out of seven. That means there're three left, and Saint Claire is sure he's number seven. That leaves five and six. I'm five."

"Well, maybe you're supposed to be number six."

She swallowed.

"No."

"You seem sure, but if something about each murder he commits is supposed to set off the next murder, that means you would have to have some kind of link to the supervisor. There would have to be a connection, if you were going to be next?"

She nodded, pursing trembling lips, her eyes watery.

"That's just it. There *is* a link between me and the supervisor."

CHAPTER 44

The mayor kept pushing the time of the meeting back until by 11:00 p.m., Saint Claire construed there would be no meeting until morning. He was surreptitiously checking the progress of Katrina's move into her Sausalito apartment when the mayor's secretary called, insisting the mayor was expecting to meet with Saint Claire at the city hall office in fifteen minutes.

Traffic was light, but it still took Saint Claire forty minutes to reach City Hall. He expected Chief Leong to be at the meeting, but when he entered the room, it was just Mayor Douglas seated at the conference table. The mayor's tie was loosened and the top two buttons of his shirt were undone. He seemed exhausted, though he smiled.

"Let me apologize if Jessica was short with you when she called. It's been a long day for both of us. I had to push this meeting back because I had interviews with Larry King, MSNBC and two of the other networks. It's been a circus, but this is an election year. I had to make myself available. Of course you understand."

Saint Claire's nodding signaled the mayor to continue.

"Chief Leong wanted to be here for this meeting, but it got late and I told her you and I would talk and we'd fill her in on what we'd agreed to put before the public prior to the press conference. That work for you?"

"I suppose it has to."

"Good. Of course, you know the press and the public are eatin this up, the national press, the overseas press. It's one of the biggest stories of the year!"

Saint Claire made up his mind about the mayor in that instant, but he hoped to appeal to the man's humanity.

"The important thing, at least to me, is saving the life of the next victim. Whether this killer is dead or alive, I just want to see that no one else is killed."

"Of course you do. But you were at a disadvantage from the start. No one's going to blame you if another person dies or two more people die for that matter. We all know you're doing the best you can under the circumstances. And you almost prevented the fourth murder. There's no way you could have known about Supervisor Pearce and Barbara Stevens. I don't think even her husband knew. Idiot fuck."

Saint Claire studied the mayor's demeanor, focusing his thoughts to hide his disapproval.

"I appreciate your understanding, Mr. Mayor, but we're in a position here where we still can save lives. I don't think this killer is dead like he claims he is. He's out there watching all this. We just can't let him get to seven. We don't want him to get to five!"

The mayor nodded.

"Of course we don't. What's important at this juncture however, is tomorrow morning's press conference. I think we need to get on the same page, so I'm going to share what I'm thinkin."

"I'm listening."

"Okay, at this press conference, I'm going to introduce this whole situation. You know, the same shit that's been on television all day, except I can do it first-hand cuz it's my city. I'll tell em we've been reactive and responsible throughout this whole situation and make sure they know San Francisco isn't the only city with this problem of serial killers. I just need to be decisive and show a sense of carin. It worked very well for Giuliani."

"Will I be able to talk to Barbara Stevens before the conference?"

The mayor sighed, his expression derisive.

"And what do you think that will accomplish?"

"Well, did you ever think Supervisor Pearce's killer might be Barbara Steven's husband? The husband is always a suspect, and he had a motive, with the affair and all. If it's the husband, maybe the killer's already out of the picture."

Mayor Douglas glared his displeasure.

"Are you shittin me? You don't honestly believe that!"

"It's a possibility. I think it would be very embarrassing to you if we made a big deal about this killer just to find out it was the husband. Just a matter of being thorough to save face."

Mayor David Douglas always dressed in expensive dark suits with suspenders and white shirts. His shiny black hair was slicked back and his face was clean shaven. He was good looking and in shape for a man in his mid-forties.

Douglas grew up in the Barbary Coast, one of the roughest neighborhoods in the city, the son of a longshoreman father and a social worker mother. His father was a union boss with the ILWU until he was murdered by a disaffected dock worker, which left his widow to raise their six children, all boys. During the election four years earlier, Douglas played up his tough homegrown street reputation.

"What are you, tryin ta toy with me, Saint Claire? You know fuckin well it wasn't the husband. It's this *same* fuckin killer you left your job at Berkeley tryin ta find. This is the same fuck who killed your son, right? You think I don't know? When we have this press conference tomorrow mornin, I'm not gonna let you lead this whole city and this investigation down that dead end road. You're not even gonna mention the husband, you *feel* me?"

"No, I don't think I'm feelin you."

"Let me put it this way: tomorrow mornin will be a scripted performance. You're gonna say what I tell ya ta say. You're after the *Undead*, you think he killed your son, and you've been after him for twelve years. This is the final showdown, you against him. He's dead, but he's set up ta commit three more murders and you wanna stop im. End of story."

Saint Claire stood.

"I'm sorry. I didn't realize this was an audition, but I'm not an actor."

"Of course you are. Everybody saw that press conference last week, mattera fact, both of em."

The detective shrugged.

"I stand corrected. I'm not a paid actor. You want a talking puppet, call an agent. Either I'm going to answer questions the way I want to answer them or I won't be there. You feel *me*?"

The mayor got in the detective's face.

"Who do the fuck you think you're talkin to? I'm the mayor, your boss. And you're gonna do what I tell ya ta do or—"

Saint Claire didn't let him finish.

"Or what? I'm fired? Come on, if you've been properly briefed about me, you have to know I'm quitting after this is over. You can't threaten me. I'm playing this my way or no way."

He smirked as he watched realization transform the mayor's face. He didn't blink.

"Look, you brought this circus to town and you sold the show, and I'm willing to bet the bank you're not going to fire your star performer, not to mention the only one in this city who can stop this bastard."

He looked away.

"It might cost you your precious election."

"Fuck you, you pompous, self-righteous asshole! I care about my city."

"Then help me save the life of the next victim."

The mayor stared with contempt into Saint Claire's eyes. After a half minute, he turned away and went to his desk.

Seated, he motioned for Saint Claire to sit. Douglas leaned back in his brown leather seat, changing tactics.

"You want me to help you save the next victim? How can I do that?"

"Get me in to talk to Barbara Stevens. If you can do that for me, I swear I won't mention anything about her or her husband at the press conference. I'm just trying to save a life."

The mayor studied Saint Claire's face.

"I don't get it. Why so desperate? Is this next victim someone you know? Is it you?"

"We know it's a person. It's a life! I have to end this. Can you get me in to speak with Barbara Stevens?"

Douglas shrugged.

"I think I can."

"The sooner you can do it, the better."

The mayor nodded.

"I'll make a couple of calls."

"Thank you."

He called out as Saint Claire stood to leave.

"If I get you in to talk to her, we're gonna do this press conference my way, right?"

Saint Claire stopped, his words succinct.

"I won't mention Barbara Stevens or the husband, but as for the rest, you do the job you have to do out there, and I'll do the job I have to do."

Katrina paid the movers to stay overtime in order to get the furniture just right. Rather than wasting her own valuable time, energy and creativity decorating the apartment, she coordinated with an interior design company to do the preliminary work so that in the space of one day, it was as if she had been there for months.

Everything about her living room was soft, warm and earthy, from the overstuffed brown cloth upholstered sofa with large fluffy pillows to the lacquered rounded edges of the rosewood lamp stands. Lush greenery sprung from the seams of the room in frills, fronds and fans. There were no hard angles, no corners. The plush cinnamon colored carpet sunk soothingly under her bare feet. The recessed lighting, sconces and mirrors added to the soft feel of the twilight lit room. Votives flickered beneath aromatherapy warmers filled with vanilla oil, while separate candles contributed traces of wild blackberry and piña colada.

A soprano sang from symmetrically spaced speakers, the orchestra barely perceptible between the phrases, as if an angel was singing from the open heavens. The song, *Ava Maria*, sung in Church Latin, brought peace and blessing to her new home.

Katrina sat at her computer desk in the candlelit bedroom. She revised the day's work as she waited for the tub to fill. For the first time she could remember, she was happy. She felt complete, without Deuteronomy or even the thought of him. And the bath, foam and tiny bubbles filled with the fragrance of lavender, brought contentment and relaxation. Taking a deep breath, she slipped naked into the warm water.

He had been in the building for more than twenty hours. Two days earlier, he followed her to Sausalito and cautiously monitored her as she visited three apartment buildings. He knew which she would choose. He was outside the building the day before she moved in, watching the people who left and entered, determining the security protocol, studying the personalities on staff.

On his laptop, he was able to acquire a schematic of the building from a hack into the county planning office, though he didn't really feel it would be necessary. Still, he was careful by nature. Under the building, a seven-foot space housed the water heaters, the cooling and heating system and the telephone/communication panels and interfaces. He entered the building at 5 a.m. posed as a city-employed telephone line inspector, and he never left. Inside the basement, he waited.

The building security system featured door entry monitoring via a micro video camera in the entry access panel, along with a micro modulator that allowed residents' televisions to display images of calling guests. The structure was also equipped with a video surveillance system, cameras that displayed activity in the hallways and lobby to screens in a security office with two guards.

Notwithstanding, security at the building was easily breached. The system was in the basement, mounted next to the telephone unit. And the guards in the office were overweight, older men, with a limited understanding of technology.

When he shut down the cameras in the circuit operating on her floor, the guards called the problem in to the security company, but neither ventured down to the basement for a physical inspection of the unit. The building had a low security risk. There hadn't been an incident in years.

In the darkness of the underground room, he waited. If he ever possessed any virtue, it was patience. Waiting was something he did well because it afforded him the opportunity to think, and so he thought. Keen to check his watch, he left the basement a little after 11:00.

Locked doors had never been a problem. Dressed in a black body suit, he knelt with the pick and torque tool, manipulating the tumblers, raising the cuts on each pin stack to the shear line, one by one, until the plug turned freely. In a half minute he was in, pulling a black ski mask down over his face.

He could smell the scent of the vanilla oil and blackberry candles, as well as the lavender fragrance from the bath. Soft operatic music played in the bedroom where she slept. Something odd on the dining room table caught his attention. Breathing quietly, his eyes monitoring the slight opening in the bedroom door, he went over.

On the table lay a shiny silver dagger atop a leather sheath. It appeared medieval, perhaps Spanish in style, maybe from Barcelona. The polished tapered blade was stainless steel, the hilt was brass and the handle was smooth, polished hardwood. He lifted it, a black Isotoner glove covering his hand, and he tossed it a few times to test its balance. Excellent weapon.

Replacing it in the exact position that he found it, he moved around the table to the place her purse lay open next to four prescription medication bottles. *Haloperidol,* an anti-psychotic? Obviously, Katrina Saint Claire still had issues. The *Fluoxetine* he expected. It was an anti-depressant, but she wasn't using it. The seal was still intact.

Her purse contained an envelope stuffed with cash, *100s,* *50s* and *20*-dollar bills. There was a second envelope containing a plane ticket to Brazil, with a one-week layover in New Orleans. The capped end of an unused syringe jutted from the far corner of the purse. He checked his watch one last time and trained his eyes on her door.

CHAPTER 45

Timid, Sonia knocked on the door. It was late and she was nervous. After a moment, she heard footsteps approaching from inside. When the door opened, she cocked her head, peering in.

"You're here? I was afraid you hadn't made it home yet."

The door widened.

"I just got here. Come on in."

She sighed with satisfaction as she stepped over the threshold. She never imagined he would invite her to his condominium. According to talk around the station, Saint Claire had never invited anyone over, except Slater. He had never invited Brady.

As her eyes darted about the room, she was impressed with his taste in decor. The wood framed *Louis XV* sofa, seatee and *sette canape* replicated French antique classics. The pieces were nice to look at, but not exactly the type of furniture anyone would want to lounge on.

There was a good oil reproduction of Picasso's *La Chute d'Icare* on one wall and a replica of a work of the same title by Matisse on another. On a separate wall was an enlarged photo of an older black woman, probably Saint Claire's mother. Otherwise, the room was spartan, no rugs on a hardwood floor, no plants, no accents.

There was however, an oddity on a table next to the sofa.

"What's that?"

He was in the adjoining room, the kitchen, sorting through the day's mail. He leaned into the doorway to see what she was referring to and vanished again, calling out.

"Oh, think B.B. King. It's my version of Lucille. My brother Sam bought the first one for me."

"I never knew. Can you play this thing?"

Saint Claire re-entered the room, letters in hand, and walked straight through to his study before returning, shutting and locking the door behind him.

"Can I play it? Been in a band since I was thirteen."

"What kinda music do you play with it?"

He was amused at her naivety.

"Zydeco. You know what that is?"

"It's jazz, right?"

"A kind of jazz."

He sat in the chair across from her.

"I asked you to come here because I *did* get in to speak with Barbara Stevens tonight."

Sonia's face flushed with fear.

"What did she say?"

"Please don't worry. She didn't say anything about you. My problem is she didn't say much at all. She was still in shock and she was with a lawyer."

The frustration was evident in his expression.

"I tried."

"I know you did. It was a miracle you even got in there."

He nodded, his face solemn.

"Yeah. Well, I invited you over today because I'm afraid we're running out of time."

He hesitated and continued.

"I wanted to ask if you'd stay here for a week or two, until I get a better indication of where he's going next, or until I get a break, any kind of a break in the case. If he's dead, this condo would be the last place he'd have predicted you would be, given our history."

He struggled against the gravity of fatigue

"But then if he's alive, it comes down to the two of us against him, and he'd have to come through me to get to you. That being said, we both have to be prepared for an attack that could come at any time. If he's alive, he might figure out you're here."

She was confused.

"I don't understand. You're asking me to move in with you? Tonight?"

"Stay here and out of sight for a while. Take a leave of absence and disappear. Of course you'd have to let the chief know, but no one else. Call it in right now, from your cell phone."

After the disappointing meeting with Barbara Stevens, Saint Claire had gone to a jazz bar on Fillmore Street to have a brandy, to settle his spirit. As he sat alone in a dark corner, trying to determine where the killer would go next, his mind kept returning to a thought that had been bothering him all day. What if Katrina really *was* his sister? That would mean her father was his father, and by extension her murderous grandfather was his grandfather.

All Saint Claire had assumed about Katrina's personality and inclinations as a result of being that killer's granddaughter now applied to him as a grandson. Maybe the killer was right about him. It made him wonder why he had stayed in homicide for so long.

He remembered the killer's claim from the second letter: *if you are going to stop me, you'll have to be true to your nature, you are going to have to kill someone.* He wondered if the killer knew about this possible grandfather's legacy. If so, the killer would have to have been in New Orleans at some time, or in some relationship with Katrina, or with someone Katrina knew.

If you are going to stop me... you are going to have to kill someone. If Sonia, through her relationship to the supervisor, was number five, and Saint Claire himself was number seven, then perhaps the killer would set him up to kill number six to save his own life.

He had called Sonia from the bar, asking her to drive to the supermarket, enter the store and pretend to be shopping. After a few minutes, she was to go to the back of the store and exit through a door next to the truck loading bays where a cabbie Saint Claire knew and trusted would be waiting. This cabbie would take a less than direct route to Saint Claire's condo and make sure he wasn't being followed.

Saint Claire would spend a half hour surveying the area to determine if the killer was watching the building from somewhere in the neighborhood. Satisfied no one was watching, he would give the cabbie instructions to bring Sonia to a building side entrance, where Saint Claire had rigged the door to remain unlocked. From there, Sonia followed his directions to his door.

"I can't stay here, not just like that. I need to go home. I need to get some things."

"I'll get you whatever you need from the stores. If the killer's still alive, he would be watching your house."

"So you still think he's alive?"

Saint Claire nodded.

"He's alive, and he's out there watching, planning."

She crossed her arms, glancing toward the window.

"And you think I should stay here for how long?"

"A week, two weeks. He's the one on a schedule. Time's on our side. In two weeks it'll be almost sixty days since that first letter where he indicated he'd kill seven people in thirty. That letter's out there. He's trapped himself into time constraints."

"Why would that stop him?"

"All the sensation of this story, this genius label they've given him, is all based on him killing from the grave as he predicted in the letter. If it takes more than double the timeline he gave to kill the seven, no one will believe he's dead, and he won't reach the greatness he's trying to achieve."

Standing, he lifted one of the blind slats, peering down on the street in front of the building.

"If he set up your murder around something or someone in your life, and he has to link it to the murder of the supervisor, he couldn't possibly pull it off with you here, especially if he doesn't know you're here. And that means in order to get the seven killings done within a believable time span, he'll have to select another victim five, and you'll be safe."

A smile erupted as she nodded. He took a breath.

"Of course this alternate victim five will have to have a link to the supervisor as well, meaning I still have a chance to catch this asshole."

Sonia scanned the room.

"A week, two weeks here? What would I do?"

"Read a book. Lay low and stay alive."

"Where will I sleep?"

"You can have my bed."

"I'm not comfortable sleeping away from home. You gonna sleep with me?"

He smiled.

"Well, being you're my supervisor, you could order me to, but then that would be sexual harassment. I'll sleep on the sofa."

"That sofa looks uncomfortable. Hey, I didn't say fuck me. Unless you think you can't lay in the same bed as me for a week or two without *wanting* to fuck me. I understand if you can't handle it."

He laughed.

"What is this? Some grade school version of reverse-reverse-reverse psychology? I can sleep in the bed. Fine, that works. We'll just be sleeping, nothing else."

She nodded, undoing the top button of her blouse.

"And what will I be sleeping in?"

"The bed, of course. Isn't that what we agreed on?"

"You're being silly. I mean what am I going to wear? You got any women's pajamas lying around or a negligee I can wear, or should I sleep in the buff?"

He went to his bedroom door and pushed it open.

"You can wear my pajamas, top dresser drawer, might be a little big for you. And there's a robe on the right side of the closet. Make a list of anything else you need and I'll get it in the morning after the press conference."

Minutes later, Sonia came out of the room in large black silk pajamas, neckline falling over her bare right shoulder.

"Toothbrush, hair dryer, curlers, make-up, Oil of Olay? How long have you planned on hiding me here?"

He bowed his head.

"Those were actually for my wife. She decided not to come here. She got an apartment."

"I'm sorry to hear that. You coming to bed?"

He cringed at the sound of the words. He hadn't heard that question in over twelve years. He remembered the tone, the poetry of the words. The voice was Katrina's. His answer was always the same. Closing his tired eyes, he responded.

"You go on. I need to spend some time getting reacquainted with myself after this long day."

From a zippered shirt pocket, he withdrew a dark vial filled with four ounces of a clear liquid. After unscrewing the cap, he set the vial on the table. Gloved fingers reaching into a pant pocket, he tugged out a neatly folded black cloth napkin. Then taking up the vial with his right hand, he doused the center portion of the napkin with the liquid.

Vial returned to his pocket, he stood. Napkin folded in his left hand, he tipped toward her door, stopping twice to check the room. He always had good instincts in dark places, like a vampire. Somehow something didn't feel right.

He was going inside the room where she slept for a look around. If she began to stir, he would cover her face with the napkin he had soaked with the *methyl ethyl ether* from the vial, and then conduct a thorough survey of her bedroom. When she awoke, she would remember nothing, save a slightly pungent odor, if that.

He chose his subjects carefully, and he always found a way into their homes to conduct his research. His believed his method was similar to the way Michelangelo and Da Vinci took great pains and effort, going beyond the rest of the field, to perfect their respective arts. It was the way of the great artist.

The door to Katrina Saint Claire's room was slightly open, allowing him to peer inside. He could detect the shape and position of her body beneath the comforter, could see the back of her head, face turned away from the door.

One day, students and scholars would study and admire his work and technique, his assiduous dedication to merging murder with art. He was a modern master. No mind on earth, including all the killers who had come before and those who would come after, could ever come close to his singular achievement, *seven murders from the grave*!

Gently pushing the door open ahead of him, he stepped into the doorway.

"Surprise."

At first, he didn't realize what had happened. There was sudden, searing pain at the back of his neck. He didn't remember falling to the floor, but he found himself looking up at the ceiling before feeling the pain again, this time at the front of his neck. Dazed, he tried to move his arms to defend himself, but they, like the rest of his body were unresponsive. Someone was shocking him with a handheld device, and the sensation of electricity seemed to go on forever. Something was very wrong!

Then he saw her face. It was Katrina Saint Claire. The shape in the bed was not her at all. Too bold, he had underestimated her. She had set him up. She had out-planned and out-smarted him. He should have known. He hadn't been in such a helpless position in all his adult life, had never felt so vulnerable.

Before her mocking face, she held an unsheathed syringe. In terror, he realized she was going to stick him with one of her drugs, one of her poisons. He would probably never awaken, and she would secretly dispose of his body somehow, cutting short his bid to become the greatest serial murder artist of all time, robbing him of his destiny, committing his life and his work to obscurity, sending him to Hell unknown.

As the drug took hold of his body, sheer will kept his eyes open, and the last sight he saw was Katrina, with the shiny dagger from the table in her right hand, prepared to do her business.

CHAPTER 46

The mayor's press conference had been the usual meaningless media circus. Nothing the reporters asked could surprise Saint Claire anymore. But then, near the end, a uniformed officer approached him from behind and whispered into his ear.

Minutes later, he sped toward her apartment, his mind conjuring scenario after scenario. Was it really the killer or just another one of her games? He was angry that he let himself believe she was better, helped her escape Saint Mary's.

Katrina had called *911* at 10 a.m. just as the press conference got underway to report she had been attacked in her apartment. Saint Claire found it a bit coincidental that she timed the call so that he would not be available for first response. Instead, it was Brady who went over. Brady, the same person who had arranged for the *Voudoun* to come to San Francisco.

Saint Claire was sure Katrina saw Brady as a pawn, not intelligent enough to be considered as a paramour. She was using Brady to control the allocation of information. According to briefing he'd received, Katrina wasn't injured, but she was shaken up and under a doctor's care. She had fought off and managed to wound the attacker before he escaped through her front door, leaving blood and "other" evidence at the crime scene.

Katrina was up to something, and the introduction of this "other" evidence was key to whatever she was scheming. What was it? Semen? Another letter? A murder weapon?

He managed to lose the two press cars following him in Golden Gate Bridge traffic and proceeded north on the Redwood Highway at better than 75 mph until he reached Sausalito. When he got to her building, several reporters were waiting. Ignoring their questions, he rushed inside and up the stairs to her apartment.

The Sausalito police officers who stood on either side of the door were expecting Saint Claire. Removing his hat, one of the officers opened the door and nodded before the detective could identify himself.

Brady and the doctor stood in the living room of Katrina's apartment, speaking in low tones, while three Marin County crime scene investigators crowded around a stained area of the carpeting between the kitchen and the hallway. Saint Claire went for Brady.

"What happened?"

Brady backed.

"Hold on. Katrina was attacked, I think by the killer. If that's the case, he's alive like you've been saying all along. Everyone's got to believe you now."

"How convenient."

Saint Claire looked toward the doctor.

"Is she okay?"

"Traumatized, but stable. No physical injuries save a cut on her arm and a bruise on her face. She told me she had been institutionalized for twelve years. It's just terrible she gets out and her first night she's got to go through something like this!"

Glancing at the investigators, Saint Claire turned back toward Brady.

"What they got over there? Blood?"

He nodded.

"Yeah, blood, signs of a struggle. She said she used a stun gun initially, but then he came to and tried to kill her. She fought him off, you know. Saved herself."

"Besides the stun gun, was there a weapon?"

Brady took a breath, nodding.

"Now that's what's odd. Apparently he had a knife and she managed to get it from him and injure him with it before he got away. There's a sporadic blood trail that leads to a curb outside where he probably parked his car. We asked around. No one saw anything. They have the weapon over there."

Saint Claire rubbed his eyes, fighting tinges of fatigue.

"Okay, and this 'other' evidence Leong mentioned, what's that?"

"Well, she had the knife and they were fighting..."

"Yeah?"

Brady's eyes glanced toward the left side of Saint Claire's hat.

"And somehow she... well, she cut off his ear, at least the top portion of it. Investigators found it in a small puddle of blood next to the sofa."

Brady and the doctor exchanged looks.

"At least now we know we're looking for a guy with a mangled ear."

Saint Claire ignored the comment.

"This doesn't make sense. *You* interviewed her, Brady?"

"I talked to her, for about ten minutes."

"What did she say?"

"She said when she woke up this morning, she heard someone fidgeting with the lock on the front door. She wanted to call 911, but she was afraid he would hear her, so she hid and waited. She used the stun gun on him, which slowed him just enough for her to get his knife. They obviously struggled before she cut him, but I think she saw his face."

"And so why would you think it was our killer?"

Brady shrugged.

"Doctor, can you excuse us?"

The detectives moved to a corner of the room, where Brady spoke in a quiet tone.

"I'm not exactly sure why. I mean, this is her first night outside Saint Mary's, so I had to think, who would know she was out and where she had moved? And a woman locked up wouldn't necessarily have enemies? Except herself, right?"

Saint Claire nodded, as Brady continued.

"But if *you* had an enemy, he might try to get to you by stalking or maybe even killing your wife, and this killer definitely has it in for you. Now, if he's been dead for over a month, he couldn't have predicted Katrina would get out of Saint Mary's and move to Sausalito. So he's got to be alive, right?"

"If an attack ever really took place. You don't know Katrina. She's capable of staging all this, depending on whatever her motive might be, whatever game she's playing."

Brady sighed.

"No, that's impossible! With all the blood, and the ear?"

"Did you check to see she had both hers?"

"The doctor checked her out thoroughly. She's got a bruise and that's it. Come on, you're really being paranoid. Your wife was the victim of a violent crime here. She could have been dead. She didn't stage this."

Brady peered toward the bedroom door.

"I told her you were on your way. She wants to talk to you."

Saint Claire turned away.

"I can't talk to her, not till I find out what's really going on. Tell her I got called away on an emergency."

Brady grabbed Saint Claire's shoulder.

"Wait! I don't believe this. Your wife just got attacked and you're going to leave? Just like that?"

Saint Claire turned around, his tone serious.

"Whatever she or whoever is up to, I'll play right into it if I go in there."

He closed his tired eyes, taking a breath.

"Look, I care about Katrina so I am emotional, but I can't behave the way they expect me to. I can't just react."

He stiffened his jaw, dark circles of fatigue showing under his eyes.

"I'm so close now. I have to think my way through this."

He glanced in the direction of the bedroom.

"Tell her I'll come back to see her tonight. And make sure someone stays here to guard her. If she leaves, make sure someone follows her."

Brady called out as Saint Claire reached the door.

"Waitaminute! Have you heard from Sanchez? I haven't been able to get a hold of her all day, and the chief doesn't know where she is."

Saint Claire stopped and turned.

"I've been caught up in that press conference and avoiding reporters all day. No, I haven't talked to her."

"Maybe she's hiding out. I mean, if she was dead we'd know about it, right?"

Saint Claire's tone was dismissive.

"Yeah, that's right. I'm sure she's fine. She'll turn up."

Brady seemed skeptical as he scrutinized his partner's demeanor.

"And you have *no* idea where she might be?"

Saint Claire turned, looking into Brady's eyes.

"If I hear from her, I'll let you know."

CHAPTER 47

"I don't know. I really don't think it's a good idea. We still don't know if he isn't involved somehow."

"I really trust him now. He cares about me. Remember? I was worse about him than you ever were! Yes he's involved. His son was murdered. This whole thing is personal for him, but he's on our side. And he's trying to save my life!"

"I hope so."

Chief Rebecca Leong was amused by the cloak and dagger measures she had to play along with in order to have the face-to-face meeting with her friend and captain. She had never been told to "dress Latin" before, nor had she been to that enclave off Mission where hybrid seeds from Central and South American grew so lush in fertile American soil. Tropical flowers blossomed all around.

Sonia chose the restaurant's location to be discreet. It was a low-key establishment where she and Rebecca were just two among a sea of tan faces. They sat at a table in the corner, away from the window.

"Just in case someone was watching the building, I got one of the domestics to trade clothes with me and slipped out the back. Then I took BART over here."

Rebecca stared at Sonia, her mouth open.

"Wait a minute! You traded clothes with the maid? What were you wearing?"

Sonia squinted, remembering.

"Oh, you know that cranberry Austin Reed blouse I wear, the silk one with the high neck?"

Rebecca sighed.

"Ah, I loved that blouse!"

"That and the long burgundy cardigan and lace skirt, the Valentino."

"Yeah, I know that skirt."

Rebecca looked to Sonia's feet.

"Okay, and don't tell me you traded your shoes too. Which ones were they?"

"Black, open-toe heels—Dolce Vitas. Forget where I got em."

Rebecca gave Sonia the once over and turned back toward her coffee.

"Somewhere in this town a well dressed maid is telling one hellava fashion story."

"Oh no! I showed her my badge and gun. I warned her she would be arrested if she told anyone. And she definitely believed me."

When she talked to Sonia on the phone that morning, Rebecca tried to talk her captain out of staying with Saint Claire, offering to sequester her in either San Jose or Sacramento in a safe house or hotel. Sonia countered that if the killer could get to supervisor Thackeray Pearce in South Lake Tahoe, he would have no problem getting to a target in cities much closer.

Rebecca inveighed upon Sonia for an hour, begging her to come out of Saint Claire's condo for a short meeting. She promised protection from the condo to the restaurant and additional police attention to Saint Claire's building commencing forthwith. Rebecca didn't come right out and say it, but Sonia knew the reason her friend was so desperate to see her. Rebecca feared it would be the last time she would see Sonia alive.

They also had to discuss Tatiana. She was staying with Sonia's sister, but Sonia wanted Rebecca to finish raising her daughter in the event of Sonia's death. With that in mind, she made Rebecca the beneficiary on two life insurance policies amounting to $750,000.

"So I've heard rumors, but I've never heard it from you. Tell me, how exactly is it that there's a link between you and supervisor Thackeray Pearce. In all the time I've known you, you've never let on that you even knew her."

"I don't. I've never met her formally."

"That's what I thought. So what gives? Where's the link?"

Sonia bowed her head. Taking a breath, she looked up.

"I told you about my ex-husband, Antonio? How he left me for a man?"

Rebecca nodded as Sonia went on.

"Yeah, after he left, he never called me or the kids, except one time about three years ago. He called to say he got re-married. He married a twenty-one year old when the mayor was doing the same sex marriage thing here, a white boy named Zachary, he said. Well, after the supervisor died in that explosion, I saw Zachary for the first time, on television."

She batted back tears.

"Zachary Pearce. He was the adopted son of Nancy Thackeray Pearce. Antonio is the link between us."

"Oh my God!"

Sonia eyes beckoned Rebecca to contain her reaction. She scanned the room to make sure no one was watching before continuing in a quiet voice.

"It gets even more bizarre. After hearing from Antonio only once in over five years, three days ago he calls me and says he needs to see me. I asked him what about, and he says he'll tell me when he sees me."

"That's insane! You didn't agree to meet him?"

"No, I hung up the phone, and I haven't answered any more of his calls. He's called my phone twenty, thirty times since. I'm sure he knows where I live."

She stopped and sipped from the water glass.

"That's why I thought staying with Saint Claire might not be such a bad idea. He's so private, it'd be hard for anyone to get to me there."

"I understand, but I'm still not comfortable with you over there. Do me a favor?"

Sonia answered cautiously.

"What's that?"

"If you sense anything wrong, anything you're uncomfortable with, or you think Saint Claire's going to do something to you, no matter what time, day or night, dial my phone and punch in 911. I'll have someone over there in a couple minutes max. Will you do that for me?"

Sonia nodded as she stood.

"I can do that."

Tears spilled from her eyes.

"Rebecca, I just wanted to say I love you. You're the best friend I've ever had."

The women hugged, sobbing. Rebecca kissed Sonia's cheek.

"I love *you* too. You're my best friend. I just don't want anything to happen to you."

Breaking the embrace, Sonia backed up and adjusted her shirt.

"I'll be fine. I'm gonna get through this like I've managed to get through everything else. You *watch* me."

Her composure broke as she wiped away the tears.

"I love my children. Just in case something happens, make sure they *know* that."

Brady took the girls to dinner at *Bubba Gump's* on Pier 39 and then over to see the band. The Bayou Boys Zydeco Band was playing at a ballroom on Geary, and he had managed to get one of the opera house style balconies with gold-framed arches that overlooked the dance floor and stage. Andrea had to work late, so she missed dinner and met up with the family for the music.

From the balcony, Brady pointed Saint Claire out to his wife and daughters.

"The black man down on the stage with the hat, suspenders and the accordion, that's him."

Saint Claire, rapt in his element, had no idea the Brady family was in the audience. Brady had only discovered this clandestine musical life during the interview with Angelique Curry, the daughter of Saint Claire's former partner. Also on the stage was a tall, skinny light-skinned man playing a vest *frottoir*, a rubboard worn on the chest and played with spoons. A white man alternated between the upright bass and the fiddle while a fourth band member, an older black man, played drums and sang.

The music was unlike anything Andrea or the girls had ever heard, a fast paced heavily syncopated mixture integrating waltzes, shuffles, two steps, blues, rock and roll and reggae, with shades of hip hop and dance music. The dance floor was full from the first song. Haylie danced by herself, turning circles, in the balcony. But while Andrea and the girls focused on the band, Brady's eyes wandered to a table at the bottom right corner of the stage and the two women seated there. The darker skinned woman seemed to be thirty-five at best, while the younger was hard to make. She looked like a woman, but she moved like a girl.

Brady knew about the thirty-something woman. When he and Saint Claire were at the House of Blues in New Orleans, Saint Claire had left his cell phone on the table during a trip to the bar. Seizing the opportunity, Brady scrolled through his answered calls. He was quickly able to find the call from the night before, the call from the woman who was not Saint Claire's wife.

When Brady got back to San Francisco, he ran the number through the reverse directory and found the name of the caller, Gisele Ferreira, the wife of convicted murderer Stefano Rossi. Gisele had four or five albums on Amazon and a *Wikipedia* article. Online he easily found *Rio*, her boutique on Sacramento Street, and a mention of her stepdaughter, Carlotta, who was probably the younger woman at the table. Gisele checked out clean, but her relationship with Saint Claire was the mystery.

After spying for a few weeks, Brady concluded there was no sex. But Brady could see it in her expression as she sat there, smiling, staring up at Saint Claire as he performed. There was a definite sense of longing in her eyes.

It was good to see Saint Claire down there, loosened up, laughing, dancing. He seemed a different person, someone it would be fun to have as a friend. Haylie even asked her father if she could meet him.

For ninety minutes, it was a great party, and then members of the press corps began to show up. Upon seeing the cameras, band members politely thanked the crowd and excused themselves for the evening. Another band took the stage and began playing, but the quality was lacking and it was getting late. Besides, it wasn't Saint Claire.

Brady took his daughters' hands and led them from the balcony. Along the way, Andrea inserted herself into the chain and the four discussed music and Saint Claire on the way to the car.

CHAPTER 48

"You're way late! He tried to kill me! I could have been dead! I don't want to see you now. Please just go!"

"I was working and then I had a concert. I told you about it a week ago."

"And I still could have been dead. Shows where I fit in your list of priorities!"

Saint Claire stood in the hallway next to the guard, still wearing his suit.

"I'm sorry, Kate. I came by earlier and talked with your doctor. I was here, but I got called away."

When he stepped toward the door, she pulled it to near-closed. He sighed.

"This is exactly why I wanted you to come home with me, so I could make sure you were safe."

"The same thing could have happened at your house, when you were out working, or at your concert, or wherever you go!"

Over the day, he had been rethinking his earlier suspicions. Brady might have been right about him letting resentment get the best of him. And so Deuteronomy went to her apartment to apologize for begrudging her decision to live alone. He wanted to tell her he would still be there for better or for worse, in sickness and in health, right to the end.

But there at her apartment he could see the irrational hate and anger in her eyes.

"Why did you even come here? What, are you trying to look good for the reporters?"

Saint Claire looked toward the guard.

"Can you excuse us please?"

"Sure, boss."

He watched the guard walk down the hall and enter the stairwell.

"Kate, I know this isn't easy."

"All you know, Ronnie, is your duty. I'm just another *project* to you."

"You're wrong. I'm here because I love you."

The door opening widened and her face appeared.

"Deuteronomy Saint Claire, you have no idea! You don't have a clue about how to love me. You haven't loved me since

Geneviève died. You always blamed me for that, but it wasn't me. You just wouldn't see it."

She reacted to his approach.

"Back off, mother fucker! After our baby girl died, you always looked at me with that pious sense of suspicion in your eyes. Yeah! Like I murdered her or something! It drove me crazy! Yes, you're the reason I was on all that fuckin medication! You're the reason I was in a sanitarium for twelve years! I will always hate you for that! You stole the best part of my life!"

She was weeping.

"Do you really think I'm such a monster that I would kill my own baby daughter? Do you!"

She answered her own question before he could respond.

"No, you're a criminal psychologist. You would say did it because I was sick and needed to be institutionalized. So what are you going to say when you find out I didn't kill her? You're going to be one sorry bastard. You're going to realize that you fucked my life up because you had no faith in me. You coulda *loved* me instead! You fucked up my life for no reason!"

"Katrina?"

"Shut the fuck up! I don't want to hear you anymore. You put me in there, that hell I went through! And you have the nerve to tell me you love me?"

She spat into his face.

"You don't know me! You're not capable of loving me or anyone!"

She laughed, derisively.

"Not even that *Latin* girl you sneak around with! You're the one who needs to be locked up. You're the killer. You killed that poor little boy in Portugal! And if that wasn't enough, you killed Christian! *You* did it! You killed our son and ever since, you've been obsessed with murder and killing. I swear I hate you! I swear we'll never be together again!"

He could smell it in her spit. He could hear it in her voice.

"Kate, what have you had to drink?"

She looked straight ahead, her body sagging.

"Life is short, no promises. I have no one to love me."

"*I* love you."

She took a breath, trying to compose her face before breaking again. The anger had returned.

"You can't love anyone. But I'm going to find someone to love me. It's not too late. And when I do, I'm going to tell him ta go over and *kick* your sorry ass for lettin em lock me up for twelve years!"

Andrea had the space fixed up like a model home. She probably hired an interior designer and wrote a blank check, because she had the money to do that kind of thing. But the view from the condo in one of the huge twin towers on Rincon Hill was what made it worth the nearly three million dollars she spent on it.

The window overlooking the Bay Bridge seemed like a living, blinking postcard, while other windows offered spectacular aspects of the city from America's tallest residential building west of the Mississippi. Andrea's had conquered the corporate world. She literally had San Francisco at her feet.

Seated at the bar next to a huge window, Tom Brady did not feel at home. The condo felt more like a restaurant or some Las Vegas luxury theme hotel. Maybe it was the sophisticated lighting. All he knew was the space didn't feel lived in.

Andrea poured a Budweiser into a frosted pilsner glass, placed a napkin before him and sat the drink down.

"Much more comfortable than that little hovel you live in, isn't it?"

"Now I understand why the girls won't come to my apartment. You're spoiling them up here."

He looked toward Andrea.

"That hovel down there is real. This... this is pie in the sky. It's not normal. They shouldn't get used to living like this."

Andrea sipped her port from a chilled martini glass.

"And why not? It's just a condo. I think I'll buy another in Manhattan."

Obligatory small talk out of the way, Andrea got right to business.

"Just how long do you plan on staying in Palo Alto, in that apartment?"

He sipped the beer.

"I don't know. Few years, maybe longer. I know it ain't much, but I like it there."

"You're lying. Are you seeing someone special?"

"No."

She tossed a picture onto the bar.

"What about her? Isn't she Saint Claire's niece? The doctor from New Orleans?"

He shrugged, looking at the photo of him and Mignon at the restaurant on Bush Street.

"We went out to dinner. I'm investigating her uncle. No big deal. You watching me?"

"She's pretty."

"Yeah she's pretty, but she's his niece. So what's this really about?"

Andrea put on her best-practiced smile.

"I want you to move home. I realize you want to grow and you want something more substantial. I'm willing to make some changes."

Her smile disappeared.

"I'll give you anything. What's it going to take?"

It wasn't often he had such an opportunity. He had to find out how far she would let him take it.

"Well, I'll just go for broke. I want to have sex with my wife. I want to finally consummate my marriage after sixteen years."

She laughed.

"Surely you must be joking!"

He sighed.

"You weren't serious. The hovel suits me fine."

"You'll never talk to Mignon Saint Claire again? *And* you'll move home?"

He hesitated.

"It can't be a one-time thing. It has to be regular, reasonable but regular, like a real husband and wife. Yeah, a regular piece of ass."

She forced a smile.

"Yes. You still can have your casual girlfriends, and I can have mine. And just like before, nothing serious for either of us."

For him, it was Thursday poker night.

"I'm going to work homicide for as long as I feel like working it."

He reflected on the night in the restaurant a year earlier, the night she had emasculated him.

"And I want my *mother* to come visit us for a month every year, and you'll be nice to her."

She grimaced.

"*That's* as far as I'll go. Any further and I'm content to let you stay in Palo Alto. You can pay start paying for your truck, let your job pay for inferior medical and dental benefits, and living down there, you should probably get better life insurance,. You can finally be the Stanley Kowalski you've always wanted to be, but without my money."

He smiled.

"You're really going to have sex with me?"

She sighed.

"If I have to, yes, but don't think I'll enjoy it."

He raised his glass, toasting the compact.

"I'll move home, but we'll have to wait until after I finish this case. There's no way I could begin to move in the middle of all this madness."

She took a seat next to him at the bar and smiled, pleased at her accomplishment.

"Then you'll wait for the sex."

CHAPTER 49

"What the hell happened to you? What's wrong? You look like you could use a drink."

Deuteronomy looked around the condo. It was... different. The oil paintings seemed to hang straighter, and someone had dusted and polished the picture frames and furniture. The light fixture above had been washed and the annoying silhouettes of insect bodies were gone. The wall next to the calendar was clean. The dining room table was cleared and waxed. The air around him held a subtle citrus odor.

He forced a weak smile, glad to see her.

"Let me guess? You hired me a Mexican maid?"

"I was bored. I'm not used to having nothing to do all day. And I clean when I'm nervous. I would have cleaned your study, but the door was locked."

She took the accordion case from his hand and set it next the closet door.

"Oh that's heavy! And I hope you don't mind. I found your booze. I'm having a drink."

"*Mi casa es su casa.*"

She located her brandy snifter and sipped.

"*Bueno.* I opened some of your good stuff. I figure you owe me for leaving me alone here for so long. I really need to find a hobby if I'm going to be here for a while."

His face was different. He seemed vulnerable, injured. Two hours earlier, she watched him on the local television news grinning, laughing and singing on stage with his band. Something painful must have happened to him since that time. He was no longer capable of disguising his sadness; he was home.

She went to the kitchen.

"I'm not even going to ask again. I'm pouring you a drink. If you feel like talking, you can talk and I'll listen. I understand you're private, but sometimes it just helps to say what you're feeling, just to get it out there. And guess what? If I don't make it through all this, I won't be around to tell anyone your secrets."

She handed him the glass.

"That was a joke, a bad joke! You're supposed to smile, groan, something!"

He smiled.

"Well, depending on how it happens, maybe we can have a double funeral? Save the city a little money?"

She took his hand and led him to the living room.

"Not great, but it's a start. Let's sit down."

Seated next to him, she looked into his eyes.

"Drink your drink, relax, talk to me."

She took his left hand in her hands and began massaging his palm and fingers. Soft Latin jazz played in the background. After a minute or so, she could feel him begin to relax. His neck and shoulders, tense from the time he entered, began to loosen. And with each sip from the snifter he came closer to verbalization.

Ten minutes later, she got up and retrieved the bottle from the kitchen, refilled the snifters and began with his right hand.

"I'm sorry."

She was surprised by his words.

"Sorry for what?"

"I'm sorry we got off to such a bad start. You're a good person. I wish I had gotten to know you sooner. I'm sorry I kept us from becoming close. It was nothing personal, my fault."

She smiled.

"I know. You're private, and you're private because you don't trust many people. But when it comes right down to it, the real problem is you're afraid."

"Afraid?"

She drew a quiet breath.

"Well, it's just my opinion, you know, my take on things."

"What do you mean?"

"You're very smart, but you feel vulnerable, and that's why you block everyone out. You don't want anyone to figure you out cuz you're afraid they won't like what they see. That's why you hide."

She stood.

"I'm gonna try somethin, and because it's late and we're drinking, you're gonna let me."

She reached toward his face and took off his hat.

"There. I see it, and I'm not freaked out. I'm not running away."

With her right hand, she caressed his cheek and then his scarred ear.

"It's only a part of you, but I see *all* of you."

She smiled.

"It's the same thing with what's on the inside."

She leaned toward him and kissed his ear.

"Not so bad, is it?"

He reached up and caressed her cheek, his hand guiding her face toward his. Her mouth was warm, the kiss soft, delicate and tantalizing. This time was different.

Hands grasping his shoulders, she leaned back so she could look into his eyes, and upon some cue therein, she rose. She leaned close and kissed his forehead and then she was gone.

Deuteronomy sat there, consciously attempting to dismantle the barriers and defenses that had kept him safe for so many years. Katrina was right. Locked within the intimacy void, he could neither love nor be loved. A pitiful existence!

And she was right about Geneviève. He *had* blamed Katrina for their daughter's death. He never said it outright to her, but it showed in his eyes when he looked at her. He believed she was a killer, and he worked to have her committed because he believed a hospital, however confining, was preferable to a state prison. He believed he was protecting her, but he wondered, for the first time: *what if he was wrong?*

Katrina said it so many times, but he never heard her, not until that very moment. She said, "If you loved me, you'd believe in me, and you'd show me by giving me what I tell you I need." He had always given her what he *thought* she needed because he thought he knew better for her. For twelve years, he never believed her, he never really heard her.

Finally, he believed he understood Katrina and he realized at last the marriage was over. If he wanted her to remain in his life, he would have to work at being her friend.

He also realized that by suppressing his physical needs, he had lived the past twelve years in a distorted reality. After struggling for more than a decade, he was battle worn and vulnerable. It was inevitable. At last, those repressed carnal, needs and the opportunity to express them converged before him.

She wore a long red silk gown as she stood in the doorway, her form silhouetted by the light behind her. She was so attractive that night! He scarcely recognized her. Her dark eyes were the eyes of a goddess, deep, consuming, otherworldly. He had never appreciated her face before, but it was the very form of classical beauty. When she smiled, he could barely breathe.

Slowly, deliberately, she slipped off the gown and let if fall to the floor.

He stood there in wonder as *Actaeon* had before *Artemis*, a mortal man before the awesome ancient power and divinity of woman. Her neck was delicate and her soft, bare shoulders beckoned touch. Her skin, smooth and uniformly brown, needed no enhancement. Her plump, full breasts were as ripened fruit, ready to be enjoyed.

Resisting the urge to clutch her in his arms, he approached and inhaled a deep breath of her perfumed essence. His nose found a warm place behind her left ear where he kissed gently.

They moved toward the bedroom in a gentle, unhurried dance. He removed his jacket and shirt, exposing his muscular chest, shoulders and arms. She reached up from the bed, gently tracing his quivering abdominals with a finger. He tenderly kissed her neck and throat, and then her shoulders. Her stomach fluttered and had spasms as his lips and tongue dragged across her bare abdomen and then circled her navel. He knew what he was doing to her. It was carnal torture, and she sighed with pleasure.

Her fingernails dug deeply into the flesh of his back. She could feel him bumping into her thigh, her stomach and her wetness while he clasped her hips in his strong hands. In the darkness of the room, her sudden groan marked the end of one movement and the beginning of another.

"What happened to your ear?"

Her face rested on his chest, her left ear listening to the sound of his heart. For hours their entwined bodies had risen and fallen, searching for a rhythm unique to that rare moment. Arms around her, he tapped the top of her head with his chin.

"Why is it important for you to know that?"

"Because I want to know you."

He slid his hand lightly along her shoulder.

"As my captain or as my... friend?"

"As your lover. For whatever this means, last night felt right. It was *supposed* to happen, I think."

He nodded.

"I forgot how incredible it is to really touch another person. I've never felt it like that before, never in my life."

She laughed, embarrassed.

"Really?"

He paused.

"Absolutely, and I wouldn't just say that."

She smiled, her fingers tracing the contours of his chest. When she met Saint Claire, she really detested him. Lying there, Sonia realized all the anger, scorn and resentment she once felt for him had become concern, compassion and yes, love, with the same intensity.

His phone rang in the dark, flashing on the nightstand next to him. Startled, he reached over and flipped it open.

"Hello?"

He sat up in the bed.

"Okay, but it's six o'clock. Is it something that has to happen now?"

He nodded.

"Okay, give me uh, thirty minutes. I'll be there... Yes. I'll see you then."

He began the explanation as he closed the phone.

"That was Katrina. My uh..."

He paused.

"It was my wife."

Sonia nodded.

"I know who Katrina is. What does she want so early?"

"She wants me to come to her apartment. She says she has information, about the killer."

Sonia bowed her head.

"You still love her, don't you?"

He sighed.

"Okay, we just spent the night together. This time I *will* share. Yes, I love her."

He closed his eyes, building resolve.

"But I found out just recently that Katrina—"

He took Sonia's hand.

"Katrina is my *sister*, flesh and blood. It's a long story. Don't even wanna try to explain it now."

Sonia tried to play down her shock.

"Wow! That's deep."

"Yeah, it's deep. And as long as I'm sharing—the missing part of my ear—Katrina took it. She cut it off with a knife, the exact way she cut off the killer's ear this morning."

"Oh my *God!*"

He was already up, dressing.

"I always said she was smart. I think Katrina knows who the killer is, and if she doesn't start playing games with me, I might be able to end this, today."

CHAPTER 50

He started calling at 11:00 the previous night, but when Oksana answered, she was unwilling to disturb her husband. She told Brady the former police captain was always up by six and he should call back then. When he called at 6:15, Oksana said her husband had gotten up early and was already taking his morning walk. Brady was waiting in his truck, his window down, when Slater returned.

"My, my, you're up early, Inspector! Doin your best *Colombo* impersonation?"

Slater walked past the truck toward the house.

"You practicin at bein annoying, Brady, or were you just born that way?"

Brady slipped out of the truck and followed.

"Tell your wife I'm sorry for calling so late."

"And orderin her to wake me up? Come on, Brady, nothin you're doin is that important."

"You're right, I'm sorry, and please tell your wife I'm sorry. It's just, I need your help with something."

Slater's eyes darted toward the inside of the house where he was certain Oksana was listening. He spoke loud enough for her to hear.

"Look, I'm retired. I gave up all that stuff so I could have a real life, a life I really enjoy, with my lovely wife. I go to help Saint Claire and I end up in the hospital. I almost died. My wife coulda been a widow with the likes of you around. So I'll tell you just like I told him: I'm through with all police business. I'm through! A visit is fine, but absolutely no police business, you got that?"

Slater winked at the detective, who finally understood.

"I understand. No police business. Just a visit, and maybe a couple games of nine ball?"

Sipping orange juice in Slater's recess, the men started up a game. But when Oksana left for work during the rematch, Slater's demeanor changed from accommodating to insistent.

"All right, Brady, now tell me, what's your big emergency?"

The detective tried to be direct.

"I don't know if you know this, but someone broke into Katrina Saint Claire's apartment the night before last. She said he tried to kill her."

Slater sipped his orange juice, playing down his interest.

"I take it he didn't succeed, since she lived to tell about it."

"No, she said they struggled, and somehow in the middle of this struggle she managed to cut off his ear, I think his left ear."

Slater approached Brady at the table.

"Well no, I hadn't heard about that yet. You said it was the left ear?"

"Yeah, cut off in almost exactly the same place Saint Claire's ear was cut off. I was thinking maybe you could tell me if you think it was just a lucky coincidence or there's something I'm not seeing here."

Slater laughed.

"You're dealing with Saint Claire, times two. There's a lot all of us aren't seein."

"Well, maybe if we all put our separate pieces together, we'll get a better picture?"

Slater nodded.

"Tell me more about this break in. Any witnesses?"

"No. Saint Claire's first suspicion was that she set the whole thing up, except for the ear. He couldn't explain the ear. It had to come from a person."

Slater found his cue and scanned the table.

"You're his partner, for what it's worth. Has Saint Claire ever told you what happened to his ear?"

"Well, it's been crazy lately with this publicity and all. We haven't had a chance to bond or even really talk in this last week. You're his friend. Would you mind telling me what happened?"

"You're a detective. You gotta learn ta trust your gut. You already know what happened."

Brady looked at him.

"So it was Katrina? But how and why?"

Slater tapped the cue ball with tip of his stick, causing a chain reaction ending in the sound of a ball dropping into a pocket. He smiled.

"Ego. Pure unadulterated ego."

"What do you mean?"

"It's like Richard Burton and Elizabeth Taylor in that *Virginia Wolfe* movie. Saint Claire and Katrina always have some kinda game goin."

Brady seemed embarrassed.

"I didn't see the movie."

"Battle of brains, wills and balls. Katrina won. Happened about three months after he had her committed. She was supposedly heavily sedated, but somehow she managed to get out of the hospital and find her way to his apartment. I think she drugged him, cuz he slept right through from one night to the next. When he woke up, half his left ear was missing. He couldn't prove it was her, but it was. It was her way of demonstrating her intellectual superiority."

He stood the cue on its end, re-chalking the tip.

"She was really pissed when he had her committed. She could have killed him and they both knew it. It was more a humiliation to let him know that she could have, but didn't. Mind games."

"Okay, so why the ear?"

"Beats me. Saint Claire once told me croppin the ears was the punishment for hog thieves, the lowest of all petty criminals. Along the line of public humiliation for life."

Brady wagged his head.

"She's definitely a little crazy, but I didn't think she was violent."

"How violent do you have to be to cut off a sleepin person's ear? Saint Claire's always thought she was capable of worse, but I've never bought that. She's basically a good person who's gotten fucked in life. When she's mad, she can be a real bitch, though."

Brady leaned on the pool table, blocking Slater's view.

"So you don't think she's the killer?"

Slater took a breath and blew it out in a sigh.

"Apparently she's a mutilator, but she's not the killer we're lookin for. If she got the guy's ear, then she probably knows who he is, and I'm sure she'll eventually tell us, but she'll do it in her own time. Can you get your fat *ass* off my pool table?"

Leaning into the next shot, Slater changed the subject.

"Saint Claire ever tell you who *he* thinks the killer is?"

"The same killer who murdered his son, right?"

It was a long shot, but the yellow-striped nine-ball fell in. Brady groaned.

"This game's not for money, right?"

"What kinda chicken shit you think this is? It's always for money."

Brady pulled his billfold from his jacket pocket and resentfully slapped money on the table.

"It's not the killer who murdered his son?"

"Oh it's the same killer all right, but Saint Claire thinks he knows who the killer is."

"By name?"

Slater half-nodded as he placed his cue stick on the table and went back to the bar.

"Not exactly. Not long before Christian was killed, he started hangin out with another kid, probably in his early twenties. This was a rich, spoiled kid who Saint Claire said took his class under a made up name, but he definitely remembered seein the kid in the front row at lectures. Thought the kid was stalking im."

Slater sat on the stool, facing his guest.

"He was registered under the name *Kain Behram*, but I think Christian knew him as just Kain. He was a white kid, European I think, with short blond hair.

"Saint Claire said the name was made up. He got the last part from some guy in India—name was *Thug Behram*, I think. He strangled people. Anyway, this *Thug* character is listed as the world's most prolific serial killer ever, bout a thousand with his own hands. The *Kain* part Saint Claire said came from some the Bible, the first murderer in human history."

Brady took out a notepad.

"Can you spell those names for me?"

"I can't *spell* em! Your guess is as good as mine. I'm not even sure if I can say em again."

Slater went behind the bar and poured himself a drink. He offered one to Brady, but the detective refused.

Slater, seated on a stool, sipped and made a face.

"Saint Claire, after gettin a little irritated with the weird kid, went to admissions to investigate the name and his status as a student. A week later, the kid stopped showin up. And then a year later, Christian brings the weirdo home for dinner."

He watched as Brady scribbled in the pad.

"Yeah, he was at their house. Met Katrina, sat at their dinner table, a few times. And one of those times, he tells the family he was arrested for murder, twice, two separate occasions, and then he seriously hit on Katrina. Oh, he really had it bad for Katrina. He was obsessed with her, swore he was in love with her."

Slater shrugged.

"Of course, that was the end of him havin dinner at the house. After that, both Saint Claire and Katrina tried to keep Christian away from im. But Christian was fascinated by this kid and his wild and gory stories. Didn't listen to his folks. So one night he gets in a fight with Saint Claire and he moves to this Kain kid's apartment. It was somewhere on Mariposa if I remember right."

He grimaced.

"A month later, Christian is dead in the apartment and the kid's vanished into thin air. The apartment was rented out to 'John Doe' and we're stuck with no leads. Joe Curry, my lead detective on the case, interviewed Saint Claire, but a month went by we we're not gettin anywhere. Cold from the start. So one night Curry brings this cocky Berkeley professor into my office and tells me the teacher wants to be a cop. I went outa my way to discourage it. It took a few months, but he was determined to get on, and as you know, he's been there ever since."

He smiled, remembering.

"He would go to a murder scene and read it like a book, real quiet though. Sometimes he'd stay at an especially gory scene for hours, just sittin in the middle of it all, takin it in. He never said how he figured it all out, but he'd tell us where ta go and the killer would be there. Then he'd lay out the evidence.

"And then sometimes he'd *play* with em, get in their heads, force em ta make mistakes, tell on themselves. He's been in the newspaper a hundred times. In San Francisco, he's the best there's ever been, maybe in the whole country."

Brady stared ahead for a half-minute, and then he shrugged.

"Well, if he's so smart, why has it taken him twelve years to catch this guy? Here you got this super smart Berkeley criminal psychology professor going up against this kid? I mean, if he's that smart he should have caught this guy years ago."

Slater stood, ready to refresh the drink.

"Yeah, you're right. Cept one thing."

"What's that?"

Slater raised his drink, toasting the thought.

"The killer's grown up now. I'm beginning ta think he might be even smarter'n Saint Claire."

"How long have you been here?"

Upon hearing Katrina's voice, he closed the notebook and stood, watching as she turned and locked the door.

"Since six-thirty. I came right over. You made it sound like an emergency. Where have *you* been?"

"Out. Took a little longer than I expected."

"Where'd you go?"

She stopped unbuttoning her jacket, shooting him an angry glare.

"In case you haven't noticed, I live *alone*. I don't answer to you."

"Look, you called me over here, and then you wasted forty-five minutes of my time after I got here. I think I'm allowed to ask a few questions."

"You can ask."

He sighed.

"You sent the guard home?"

"I don't need someone monitoring everything I do. Let me guess. He was giving you regular updates? So once again, you never learn. You feel this need to control me. Well guess what? I'm free. I'm free of that hospital and I'm free of you."

The anger and the attitude this morning, he concluded, were affected. She was up to something. The rage and hatred were much more intense, much less contained, the night before.

"You called me over because you said you had something important to tell me. What is it?"

She took a deep breath.

"I called you over because I was feeling needy. I was *missing* you. I felt bad about some of the things I said last night."

"No, you said specifically you had something to tell me about the killer. I'm running out of time here. What is it?"

She turned away from him.

"The killer is dead."

"You killed him? By cutting off his ear? Where's the body?"

"I don't know. You wrote about serial killers as vampires. Maybe he's risen to kill again."

He clenched his jaw in anger.

"I should have never helped you get out."

"Why, Ronnie? Are you afraid you've loosed the Devil? Does it bother you that much you can't control me now?"

He focused on his breathing to better suppress his anger.

"I'm just trying to save a life here."

"Whose life are you trying to save, Ronnie?"

"The next victim's. Murder number five."

"And just who is this next victim? Do you know?"

He was wary.

"No, there's no way I could know who it is for sure. Why?"

"You're lying. You're the erudite Inspector Deuteronomy Saint Claire, remember? You've figured it out by now. Of course *you* know who the next victim will be. So why would you lie to me about it? Now there's the real question. Is there something between you and this fifth victim?"

There was no way she could have known he and Sonia had succumbed to sex the night before. Twelve hours earlier he himself never would have imagined it. But Katrina had a way of reading people. The choice of a word, a moment's hesitation— she'd find some vulnerability or inconsistency and she'd get inside the head. It was uncanny. She had called when Sonia was in his arms, bodies locked in sweat.

On the way over to Katrina's apartment he'd decided his working relationship with Sonia was over. No matter how it all ended up, the direction of his life had changed. Maybe Katrina heard it in his voice.

She made sure she could monitor his face as she continued.

"Is it possible this fifth victim is that *Latin* woman you've been sneaking around with for the last few years? Is that why you're so anxious to stop the killer at four?"

Without raising an eyebrow, he answered.

"I'm not sure what Brady's *telling* you, but I'm certain he'd say anything he'd think you'd believe in order to gain your trust. I figured you were too smart for that."

The staring match continued as he approached her.

"Now I came over here because you said you had information about the killer. You saw his face?"

"He had on a mask. I saw his ear, but then, so did Brady and the crime scene investigators, and you too if you saw the photos."

"Was it Kain? Did you see him?"

She turned away.

"I didn't recognize his face. It could have been him. I don't know. I was nervous."

"Why was he here?"

She looked back at him, her voice sarcastic.

"He broke into my apartment. I assumed it was for no good reason, so I didn't bother to ask."

"Did you drug him?"

"Of course I did. He wasn't going to just pose for me and let me take his ear."

"You had him. Why didn't you *kill* him?"

She turned toward him, her voice insistent.

"Because I'm not a killer."

"He killed our son!"

"*You* killed our son!"

"I can't believe you let him go!"

She crossed her arms.

"I'm just a helpless woman. It's really not in my job description to go around catching serial killers and murdering them for the police. But the police should thank me. I made it easy. If they want to find the killer now, all they have to do is look for the man with the missing ear."

His cell phone rang and, recognizing the chief's phone number, he answered.

"Saint Claire?"

Her voice was weak, shaky.

"Saint Claire, where *are* you?"

"I'm at my wife's apartment, checking on her."

She took an audible breath.

"When did you last see Sonia?"

His eyes flicked toward Katrina, who was ear hustling.

"About two hours ago. Why?"

"Because Sonia's *dead!*"

Saint Claire was speechless.

"Did you hear me, Saint Claire? I said Sonia Sanchez is *dead*, in your condominium, in your bed. Investigators are there and the outside of your building is crawling with reporters. You and I have a meeting with the mayor in fifteen minutes. Get your ass over here!"

CHAPTER 51

Brady arrived at the crime scene at 8:15. He knew the building where Saint Claire lived, though he had never been invited up. Reporters were standing outside, shouting questions as he brushed past them. He saw Kiyomi Yamakita, who he knew broke the story with a copy of the killer's first letter, clandestinely passed to her by Andrea.

Inside Saint Claire's condo, the mood was somber. Sonia's body was still on the bed as police photographers captured every detail. An examiner told Brady she had been shot at point-blank range in the face, the barrel of the nine millimeter placed on the bridge of her nose. She was nude and her body and the surrounding area showed no signs of a struggle, meaning she was probably shot as she slept.

Brady glanced sidelong into the room, avoiding the bed and the body as examiners began to cover it with a sheet. He spotted the silken red lingerie and an empty brandy snifter on each nightstand.

He got the call earlier as he was leaving Slater's house at 7:30. Chief Leong, overwrought, told him she got a *911* call from Sonia's phone at about seven o'clock. She had rushed over to the condo, where she found the front door wide open. She called for backup, and then she discovered Sonia's body in the bedroom. At the sight of Sonia's ruined face, Rebecca vomited and had to be escorted from the scene.

Leong explained to Brady that Sanchez was staying at Saint Claire's condo because, given her troubled history with the detective, it was the last place her ex-husband or the killer would look for her. It was a gamble that hadn't paid off. Something had gone terribly wrong.

After the examiners transported the body to the van outside, Brady checked the bedroom floor for a condom or condom wrapper. He knew Saint Claire was aware that Sanchez was HIV positive. If the circumspect inspector had sex with her, it wouldn't have been without a condom. Investigators were busy removing the blankets from the bed, collecting clothing and shoes for later examination. Brady watched as a woman poured the contents of the trash can into a white plastic bag. No condom wrappers, not even a tiny torn off foil or plastic corner.

He checked the space under the bed and between the box springs and mattress. Nothing!

Another investigator had collected a bag of flowers. She said that when the team arrived, an assortment of flowers was carefully arranged about the body. She recognized the daisies, buttercups, the violets and poppies, the scattered purple and yellow pansies, but the other long purple flowers she wasn't sure about. She showed Brady a single white orchid, dipped in blood, found next to the decedent's shoulder.

The television in the front room was on and the news channels were airing the story. Sonia's photo filled the screen as a reporter revealed what few details from the crime scene police were willing to disclose. Criminologists, crime scene experts, psychologists and pundits across the country weighed in on the special significance of the Sanchez murder. Unlike the previous murders, the Sanchez murder involved an active participant. Some living person had come into the room where she slept, put a gun to her face and pulled the trigger.

Yet many were unwilling to summarily dismiss the idea of a serial killer so clever that he could commit seven murders from the grave. The prospect was just too lurid a story to drop. Several commentators brought up the possibility that the killer had somehow created circumstances that had forced Antonio Sanchez, Sonia's ex-husband, to commit the crime.

An anonymous source at the police department reported overhearing three phone calls from Antonio to the police captain, during which the captain called her ex-husband by name, refusing to meet him and demanding he stop harassing her. And Mrs. Getz on the first floor of Saint Claire's building said she noticed a man who fit Antonio's description loitering around the front door during the previous night and earlier during the previous day. She subsequently identified Antonio from a photograph. Detectives arrested Antonio and took him downtown for questioning, identifying him as "a person of interest."

To Brady, it was amazing how quickly the news media could put a life in perspective. Producers provided insights and a photographic record beginning with Antonio's childhood, complete with quotes from a cousin, his fifth grade teacher, the girl he took to the prom, from deceased Supervisor Nancy Thackeray Pearce, his mother-in-law, and finally from shocked friends who confessed his behavior had changed dramatically since the supervisor's death.

Still others suggested the killer might have created circumstances that forced Inspector Saint Claire to commit the murder. Reporters didn't have to search long to find police officers, speaking anonymously, who could provide detailed accounts of an acrimonious and strained relationship between Saint Claire and Sanchez that had endured over many years.

Brady watched for a few minutes, impressed by the scope of the case. His grandfather had been a Boston cop whose involvement in the Great Brink's Robbery was vicarious at best, though the case was huge. But here was the grandson, a detective in San Francisco, a player in one of the greatest murder cases in history.

Two days earlier, television reporters interviewed Brady about his role in the investigation. He was the first detective to arrive at the Rosenthal crime scene. He was standing next to Saint Claire when the detective got the call about the Hector Fuentes murder, and he was at the chapel seated near Father O'Brien when the priest fell over dead. Brady and Vang had met for Dim Sum on Stockton Street six days before Vang was killed, and Brady spent numerous hours with Sonia Sanchez, working on the case, most recently two days before her death. He was *definitely* a player.

And yet, Brady was just a supporting player. Saint Claire was the real star, the personality, the super sleuth ex-Berkeley professor they all respected for being so intelligent. He was clever, but he didn't share.

Saint Claire, along with the killer, had created a sense of mystery and awe that had captured the world's attention. It was a classic confrontation. They were point-and-counterpoint, good-versus-evil, the aging, principal master forced to do battle with the more formidable and ruthless apprentice.

Saint Claire had an advantage. He had the hidden script. It's why he understood the killer so well. It's why he knew where to look for the cyanide that poisoned Gladys Rosenthal, and why he knew the killer used ricin-laced drugs to kill Fuentes. And the slow poison, lead compound dissolved in the Jack Daniel's at Slater's—Saint Claire had some inside understanding of even that! It's why he knew Vang would die after the priest and why

Saint Claire just happened to be available to Barbara Stevens so she could turn the bomb over to him.

True, he was working from clues contained in letters from the killer, but there was more to it. There was the set of three numbers at the bottom of the first letter. Katrina was certain Saint Claire knew what they meant. Then there was the ear. Saint Claire was missing the top portion of his left ear, and after breaking into Katrina's apartment, the killer was also missing the top portion of his left ear. There had to be something *else* that tied them together!

Brady scanned the condo, noticing many of the investigators had concluded their work and were headed back to the lab. It was an opportunity. The condo had to contain clues and maybe even a scene or two from the hidden script. He lingered in the living room for a moment, and then slipped unnoticed into Saint Claire's study.

The professor-turned-detective obviously liked books. They were everywhere, old books, new books, books on every subject. The glossy desk was clear, except for a copy of the Holy Bible on the inside left corner and a couple of books on the outside right. He read the titles without disturbing the tomes, realizing the old books were related to the murder of Police Chief Biggy, a hundred years earlier.

He went around the desk and sat in Saint Claire's chair, imagining himself as Saint Claire, sitting there with all his secrets, reading from that hidden script. He opened the bottom desk drawer to the right. It was filled with notebooks marked by chronological and alphabetical tabs. He withdrew a notebook, opened and examined it. It contained Saint Claire's handwritten notes about the correlation between the vampire paradigm and the serial killer.

The drawer contained files from M-Z. He was looking for B, so he replaced the file, closed the bottom drawer and opened the top drawer. B, *Brady*. He was almost afraid to open it, but when he did he was surprised at once, shocked. Saint Claire had secretly met with his wife, Andrea! They had lunch together at an Italian place on Sacramento Street. Behind his back! No wonder he knew about the Reginald Walter Perry shooting in Boston!

"Get the *fuck* out from behind my desk!"

Brady slowly raised his eyes as the fuming detective neared.

"And get out of my home!"

Brady didn't try to explain. The drawer was open and he was holding the notebook in his hands. He was certain Leong said Saint Claire would be gone meeting with her and the mayor. The meeting couldn't have been over that fast!

Brady dropped the notebook into the drawer and tried to make eye contact, but the detective stared right through him, his jaw clenched in anger.

The condo was quiet and empty on the way out, the investigators gone. Wagging his head, he knew he was right. There *was* a separate behind-the-scenes drama in action, and he hadn't had time to discover it.

In his car, he reflected on the morning's television news stories. Unnamed police officers and community leaders were suggesting Saint Claire should be considered a suspect in the murder of Captain Sanchez. If Saint Claire was arrested, then Brady would be able to go in, under the color of law, and read the hidden script without interruption from its lurid beginning straight through to the upcoming finale.

"Still no Saint Claire?"

"No."

The mayor sighed on the other end, fuming.

"And you've called im?"

"He just called in. He said he had to stop by his condo to secure it before coming over. Should be here any minute."

"Asshole! When he gets there, you bring im over. We're gettin a late start on this."

Chief Leong nodded, setting the handset down. Her eyes were red and swollen. In her lap, trembling fingers fidgeted with a moist white handkerchief. She could not get the image of Sonia's tortured face out of her mind, the bloody wound, the dark, sunken eyes and the fetid smell from her friend's loosened bowels. Sonia was a corpse! And to think she sat and talked with Sonia less than a day earlier. Poor Sonia! She was so confident she would survive.

Rebecca struggled to control her emotions. She wanted to mourn her friend, to get a good cry out, to find and console her friend's children. She promised that much to Sonia. Tati would be devastated. But duty required Rebecca to remain at City Hall. And then, there was the guilt.

The phones were ringing non-stop with calls from all over the world, many of them anonymous tips and suggestions. There was even a call from the director of the FBI in Washington D.C. In a brief conversation with Rebecca, he wanted to make sure the San Francisco police were putting the National Crime Information Center database to its full use. He gave her the phone number and email address for his best researcher.

Rumors buzzed about the building. According to one source, Sonia and Saint Claire had been "hookin up" for months. The arguments and friction between them was just an act to throw everyone off-track. Another person said a friend in the medical examiner's office reported Sonia had sex within three hours of her murder.

Antonio Sanchez admitted to loitering in front of Saint Claire's condominium building during the previous day and to being at the crime scene shortly after the shooting, but he insisted Sonia was already dead when he went into the condo. A friend of his spotted her at a Mission Street restaurant on the previous morning and followed her to the building.

Antonio said he was desperate to contact Sonia because he was afraid his husband, Zachary, would be the next target. He indicated that when he and Zachary went to the supervisor's house to put her affairs in order, they found several enlarged photographs of Zachary that someone had used for target practice. He said a bull's-eye was drawn over Zachary's face.

They found the posters folded and left on a shelf in the garage. Antonio had gunpowder residue on his hands and clothing because he and Zachary had both purchased guns for self-defense, and they were learning to shoot at a gun range on Utah Avenue in South San Francisco.

"You going to be okay?"

Her head snapped up.

"You're late. The mayor's looking for you, and he's pissed you've kept him waiting."

"Mayor's the last of my concerns. Is this just me or the two of us?"

She stood.

"He wants to meet with us both."

She led the way, but she stopped and turned back before opening the door.

"Sonia was my friend. I have to know something. It wasn't you, was it? You didn't kill her?"

He closed his eyes, taking a breath.

"Chief, you of all people know Sonia and I didn't get along in the beginning, but that changed. Sonia was my friend too. I really *cared* about her."

"Enough to have sex with her last night? Cuz that's what they're saying's going to come back from the lab. Were you two having an affair?"

"I don't know what to call it. It was only one time, last night. And it was, it was the beginning of something, something special."

He batted back the beginning of tears in his eyes.

"I can't believe she's gone."

Awkwardly, he extended his arms toward Rebecca, who seemed to need a hug. The embrace was brief though intense. Rebecca affected a smile as she adjusted her blouse.

"We better get over there before he blows a gasket."

Saint Claire expected the mayor to be angry, and he planned to resign his badge at the meeting. His own mood was foul. After Sonia's murder and Brady's intrusion into his study, it didn't matter that he had a badge. Being a cop offered no real advantage. He no longer wanted it.

Sonia's murder confirmed the killer was still alive after murder five. But Kain always made his statement at number seven. Cop or no cop, Saint Claire knew he would come face to face with Kain then. Maybe he'd let the idiot mayor and Brady deal with number six.

The mayor didn't seem angry when Saint Claire and Chief Leong entered the office. Rather, he was cordial and accommodating. First he sought to console Rebecca for the loss of her friend and captain, and turning toward Saint Claire, he nodded.

"You tried, Inspector. You did the best you could under the circumstances."

The smile disappeared.

"But we've got some real PR problems we gotta deal with. It's why I've been trying to get you over here. Let me see your gun."

Looking first toward the chief, Saint Claire withdrew the gun from his shoulder harness and handed it to the mayor.

"Have you fired this gun recently, Inspector?"

"About two months ago at the shooting range."

The mayor placed the gun on the desk.

"That's funny, but not really."

"Why's that?"

"Because the bullet that killed Captain Sanchez was fired from the nine millimeter Ruger pistol issued to you by the department. Any comment?"

Saint Claire looked over at the chief, wondering if she knew.

"I don't know. Are we at the part where you need to let me know anything I say can be used against me in a court of law?"

The mayor was quick to reject the suggestion.

"No, no. The *chief* here doesn't believe you would kill Sanchez, and neither do I, but the public out there and the media are another matter. It's just a matter of time before some of the more inconvenient facts about this Sanchez murder case become public knowledge."

Saint Claire sat back in the chair.

"Well I thought that was my gun. It's the only weapon I had in my possession at the time she was shot, and it hasn't been fired. At some point he must have switched it out so he could use it on her this morning. He's done it before."

"Were you fuckin her?"

Again Saint Claire glanced briefly toward Leong.

"No."

"Lab says you were. Said she musta had sex an hour, two hours earlier."

"Bullshit. There isn't a test in the world that could come back with a result like that. Those tests are based on the presence of sperm cells, which I know weren't there."

"Okay, but she *was* in your bed, and nude, with red lingerie on the floor, brandy glasses on the nightstands. Where did you sleep last night, Inspector?"

"Where did *you* sleep, Douglas? It's irrelevant where I slept. What? You think I had sex with her and then turned around and shot her in the head? In my bed in the middle of all this? Now why would I do that?"

Mayor Douglas shrugged.

"It's happened before. Okay, so what do we got here, Saint Claire? We got this killer, and his name is *Kain*? One of your former students, right?"

"I never said his name. How do you know it?"

The mayor smiled, standing near the large window.

"I'm a good guesser. And let's see, his ear is cut off in about the exact same place yours is cut off. Am I right?"

"It's possible."

"You *know* this killer, don't you, Saint Claire? And I'm guessin there are alotta things about the killer you know that you just don't wanna share. I'm wonderin why that is? The rest of us aren't as smart as you, so you give us these little tidbits to impress us, but no, you're not lettin us in on the real deal, and I just keep havin ta *ask* myself, why?"

Saint Claire spoke without looking.

"You're such a good guesser. Guess."

The mayor looked toward Rebecca.

"What I tell ya?"

Back at his desk, the mayor sat.

"Inspector, I said earlier we had some PR issues we had to address here, and the biggest one of those is that a slug from your gun found its way into Captain Sanchez's face. How do we deal with that?"

"Mr. Mayor, I'm sure you've already figured that out."

"And then, proof or no proof, the Captain *was* found nude in your bed, with lingerie and brandy glasses and all that shit, and with a receipt in her purse from where she bought a six-pack of condoms earlier in the day. Seems like an inappropriate relationship to me. What do you think, Chief Leong? They went through the entire six-pack!"

Rebecca seemed distraught.

"I'm, I'm not up for this, David. Just do what you're going to do."

"All right."

Douglas smiled toward Saint Claire as he activated the intercom to his secretary.

"Jessica? You wanna send Inspector Brady on in?"

Saint Claire knew what was coming. He stood, turning toward the door to face it. They were *all* in on it. There he was, Brady, doing what Saint Claire knew he would do from that first meeting in Gladys Rosenthal's bathroom. His eyes unable to return the detective's gaze, Brady spoke with his head bowed.

"Deuteronomy Saint Claire, you are under arrest for the murder of Sonia Sanchez. You have the right to remain silent. Anything you say can and will be used against you in a court of law. You have the right to speak to an attorney and to have an attorney present during any questioning..."

Saint Claire raised his hand.

"Stop! I know the routine. I already know what's going on. You think I didn't see this *coming*? Problem is, while you're busy playing this game with me, the killer's going to get to number six, and maybe that doesn't matter to you now, but it will."

He looked toward Rebecca.

"Because she's a real person, just like Sonia was a real person. And because of you, mayor, she's going to die. By arresting me you're playing to his hand because, believe me, he's had this planned for years. None of what you see is random."

CHAPTER 52

"Wake up."

Katrina tapped the left side of his cheek.

"Are you awake yet? Open your eyes."

His eyes did not want to open. His mind struggled to remain asleep. His body felt unusually relaxed. He wanted to sleep on and on, but he was losing his grasp, being ripped away, a babe torn from a warm bosom. *Something* was bringing him back. The light crept into his barely cracked eyes. Slowly, they opened.

It was two fuzzy faces at first, twins, and then they converged, becoming one huge, blurry countenance. He had no idea what had happened or who this person was, but he felt vulnerable, afraid. He blinked his eyes to better focus them.

"Can you see my face? I'm sure I'm the last person you expected to see."

He recognized the voice. It was her. Somehow, she had found him! In twelve years, no one had ever been present when he slept. He could feel it in his throbbing veins and unresponsive muscles. She had drugged him again.

Sleep made him vulnerable. It was why he slept in a tiny locked closet with no light in a locked room in an inconspicuous locked apartment, miles outside the city. It was why he went to sleep at dawn, when the rest of the world was just beginning to stir. When he slept, he never had a dream he could remember, not in many years, not since he was a boy.

But now she had dragged him out into the middle of the room where a bright light shone into his eyes.

"Awake yet? You're probably wondering how I found you."

She spoke slowly, enunciating, a sense of scolding in her voice.

"Of course you don't remember the last time we talked, or more accurately, the night you talked and I listened. You told me about this place, about the apartment, about the room and the closet. You even told me how to get in. You told me *everything*, about all your vampire secrets. You've been a very bad boy."

Even before his eyes adjusted, he could see she had her black case with the drugs and needles.

"That night, before you woke up and tried to kill me, I gave you a little cocktail, a little morphine with a side of scopolamine. It took a few minutes, but you really opened up. You shared until it hurt, and I mean hurt. You cried like a baby. And when you were all done, I warned you."

He was looking at her face, straining to remember. She raised the knife into the light so that he could see it.

"Your muscles want to move, but they can't. They think you're still dreaming. This time, for your protection and mine, I gave you a very special GABA agonist. Your mind is fully awake now, so I know you can hear me, but your body is still asleep. When you wake up, this will seem like just a horrible nightmare. I should kill you, but killing you doesn't bring Christian back, does it?"

The knife disappeared, he felt a distant tugging on the side of his head and he watched as she held up the bleeding sliver of flesh. Then she cut the front buttons from his shirt and opened it, exposing his chest.

"I could have just as easily plunged this knife into your heart and ended it all for you today. Right now, I have the power to send you to your grave unknown. At this moment, I am your god."

With the knife tip, she gently scratched a cross onto his pale chest, a shallow serration that slowly began to fill with blood. She spoke deliberately.

"Now, I'll tell you today just like I told you the other night. Stop this shit! Leave this town. Go someplace else. I mean it!"

She rose.

"Because if I have to track you down again, it'll be to put a *stake* through your heart."

Saint Claire sat alone in the small room examining his fingertips, comparing the patterns. An hour earlier, he was formally booked. They handcuffed him, paraded him down a busy hallway, fingerprinted him and unceremoniously snapped a mug shot. They removed his hat, exposing his cropped left ear. Yesterday he was a hero, today a spectacle.

As he walked the hallway, he got the distinct impression that some of the officers reveled in his humiliation. Many felt private vindication, seeing the arrogant detective taken down a peg, put in his place. Instead of showing support, some even joined voices with the detractors. After twelve years, it was sad to see how few friends he had on the force. In the hallway, the sergeant even slowed the procession in order to allow media photographers to take pictures, ear and all. He resisted feeling bitter, but he couldn't help thinking he would have been treated differently if he was white.

He knew the arrest was purposed to put him on ice while Brady searched his condo. He suspected Brady convinced the mayor he could solve the case if he had access to Saint Claire's notebooks in his library. Saint Claire wasn't sure how much Brady learned before he was discovered, but the younger detective had read at least enough to tell the mayor the killer went by the name of Kain. Once again, Saint Claire was forced to admit Brady was smarter than he let on.

He called Gisele early on to advise her things would be dicey for the next day or two. He predicted he would be arrested, but he swore to her that he had Sonia Sanchez at his condo to protect her. He had nothing to do with her murder, regardless of alleged evidence. He warned her against believing the lies and innuendo she would see on the news. Gisele, in a show of fierce support, swore she wouldn't even watch the news.

He was right. The media made an *update-at-the-hour* evening of his arrest, beginning with photos and videotapes of Saint Claire in handcuffs on his way to being booked and fingerprinted. Careful not to over-commit, news channels cautiously ventured theories and scenarios featuring Saint Claire as the brilliant detective/psychotic serial killer, like a character in a nighttime crime/suspense cable television series.

The analysis of his fingertips was a deliberate distraction, to keep his mind working. There was no window, no books, paper, pens, nothing to keep his mind occupied. Though no clock or watch was present to mark the hour, he sensed the impending showdown. Time was running out for victim number six. He tried to sleep to pass the time, but his stomach was upset and his spirit was agitated. Sonia was dead. He failed her. She was gone.

Maybe it was his own arrogance? He was certain the killer could not get to number five. The logic was flawed! Saint Claire knew that if nothing else, this killer's logic always worked. If the killer shot Sonia, the iota of uncertainty he expected from Saint Claire about him murdering from the grave was gone. So why the big boast about being this "undead" killer? Why the letters? It didn't make sense.

If the police continued to blame Sonia's murder on Saint Claire, then the killer would not get credit for murder number five, and his ambition to murder seven from the grave would be impossible to achieve, much less to have his audience believe.

At some point the killer would have to claim responsibility for Sonia's death. But he could not claim to murder seven from the grave, while admitting he was alive to kill Sonia. Had Kain made such an uncharacteristic and glaring error in logic? Was it possible? Or was he playing games with the meanings of words?

When Saint Claire awoke, Chief Rebecca Leong was entering the room, escorted by a guard, who she sent away. She nodded toward Saint Claire and took a seat on the other side of the table, a little nervous.

"How are you doing?"

He glanced around the room and sighed.

"Now that's got to be one of the most asinine questions I've ever heard!"

She nodded.

"For the record, I argued against your being arrested. I don't believe you killed Sonia, and neither do they. They just wanted you out of the way so they could—"

He interrupted.

"So they could search my condo. I know!"

Frustrated, he stood.

"And did you argue we still have a killer out there? A killer who's running out of time to make this whole show believable, and who's just dying to get number six on the books?"

Hands folded on the table, Rebecca nodded again.

"Yes, I did."

"You brought Brady here. You brought him here specifically to do what he's doing now."

"Oh come on, Saint Claire, let's be fair now. A lot of this you brought on yourself. For all these years this department has paid you to investigate murders in this city, and you've sat over there with your private agenda and with your private set of facts, information that could help us, but you've been unwilling to share. The mayor was demanding why, and who can blame him? What's this big secret no one but you can know?"

The detective crossed his arms and breathed, trying to control his temper. He turned his head away from her to hide the ear.

"I have a right to a private life, and that includes private facts that only I need to know! Now, I have no knowledge about whether or not you put out for your husband last night, Chief. I don't know how many times if you did it or *how* you did it, but they sure as hell don't have it on the news!"

He returned to the table and sat.

"By letting them arrest me, you're helping them put graphic details about my private life, some totally false, in the newspapers and on television. That injures me."

He sat back.

"And then you want to allow Brady and that racist idiot McCarthy to trample through my house, invading my privacy to make me share what I have a *right* to consider private? Because this department pays me, I don't have a right to privacy?"

Rebecca extended her palm, halting the detective.

"Saint Claire, you know as well as I do they haven't gone into your apartment, yet. You've had your lawyer downstairs opposing the search warrant since even before you were arrested. All it does is slows things down, and it means you'll be spending the night here."

"Fine if that works for you. Lock me up, let the killer run free, put your life in jeopardy."

"What? Is that supposed to scare me?"

"I don't know. I'd be a little nervous if I were you."

"That's good, cuz I'm not."

Saint Claire let his head fall back, closing his eyes as he spoke.

"Don't tell me it hasn't crossed your mind, Chief. I saw it in your eyes when Brady was arresting me. You know the killer knows who you are. And you definitely know each new victim has some connection with the previous victim."

He looked across into her eyes.

"Now I'll admit the killer surprised me with the last two, but if I had to guess on a number six, I'd say you're a likely target."

She stood.

"You know who this killer is, don't you, Saint Claire? The *Undead*, his name is *Kain* something?"

"Something, yeah."

"I'll level with you if you level with me. Do you honestly believe he's targeted me as number six? That I'm next?"

He stood.

"I wish there was another possibility. I've been after him for almost thirteen years. But yes, I honestly believe you'll be next."

Her eyes watered.

"Okay."

She stepped back, shoulders slumped and swallowed.

"Thank you, I guess. They've been watching your wife. Brady thinks she might be working with the killer. She's the only one who's seen him, and no one believes she cut his ear off in a struggle. She had him and she let him go."

Rebecca shrugged.

"And then she couldn't account for where she was when she went out this morning. They've had her under surveillance since this afternoon. As for you, they'll let you go as soon as they search the apartment."

She checked her watch.

"I have to go."

She extended a hand.

"Well, thanks for the warning."

He shook her hand and backed away.

"What are you going to do?"

"What do you think? I'm getting the hell outa town, tonight."

He followed her to the door.

"Are you sure you want to do that?"

"I'm not telling anyone that I'm going, not where, not when, not how! I'm just getting out, and I'm staying out until this thing blows over."

She tried to pull the door open, but he held it shut.

"If we know he's coming after you, we might be able to trap him."

She sighed in disbelief.

"Are you crazy? I have a family. No one's going to use me as bait!"

"You're the chief of police. He won't be able to get to you."

She moved his hand and forced the door open. By then, her eyes were flowing with tears.

"And who's going to stop him? You? *You're* going to save me? Well, I had a friend named Sonia Sanchez, and she trusted you to save her, but all you did was fuck her and let her die. No thank you, I'll take my chances watching to see what happens from someplace far away."

Wiping her eyes, she turned back to look on the detective for a final time.

"And if you think you're number seven, maybe you better follow my lead."

CHAPTER 53

It wasn't the first time Gisele noticed. With Carlotta gone in Santa Barbara, nothing should have been moved when she came home. It was a peculiar habit she picked up as the owner of a boutique. She would arrange things to lay in a particular way, lining up an outside corner of an object or garment with a corresponding inside corner of the room. And it bothered her when Carlotta moved things or left them out of line, but Carlotta was gone and would be staying the next six months with her birth mother.

She checked her jewelry and her valuable documents on hand, but nothing had been disturbed or stolen. The towels in the kitchen had been moved and someone had opened and altered clothing in her chest of drawers. Her panties in the dresser and in the laundry bin were all accounted for. But in the closet, someone had pushed the clothes back, randomizing the spacing between her silk hangers and garments.

In her bathroom, someone had gone through her medicine cabinet and make-up station. Whomever it was tried to replace items in the way they had been arranged, but the phasing was just a little off. It happened on more than one occasion. There was no other explanation. Someone was doing something inside her apartment when she was away.

Angry, she called the property manager and complained that one of the maintenance workers had gone inside her apartment without her permission. The manager, however, assured her the keys to all the apartments in the building were kept in his office in a locked safe. No one, he said, had been given her key at any time.

She assumed the manager was giving her a story to protect his job and the building owners from a lawsuit, and with good reason. One of the perverted maintenance workers was obvious about ogling her and went out of his way to always get in her face, grinning. She remembered a couple of very uncomfortable elevator rides with the gross, smelly man.

If the property manager had been careless and let him or someone else get her key, he wasn't about to admit it to her. So Gisele put the manager on notice, warning him if the incursions continued, she would take her complaint to the building owner, and then her lawyer. She took his name and advised him to remember hers.

She never considered that the creepy intrusions had anything to do with the killer in the news, not until a customer in the store mentioned that a police captain had been shot in the condominium of Inspector Deuteronomy Saint Claire. The moment she considered it, she broke out in a sweat. What if the killer was the person visiting her apartment, disturbing her things? At once, she was afraid to go home.

From a girlfriend's house, she called Deuteronomy, but she couldn't reach him. She even called the jail, but they wouldn't let her through. As a last resort, she called *911* and explained her situation to an operator. After repeated requests, Gisele revealed her name and admitted she was a friend of Inspector Saint Claire. She said she couldn't go home because she was worried the killer had been secretly visiting her apartment and might hurt her in this game he was playing with the detective.

The operator told her the police wanted to investigate her report and asked if she could meet a captain at her apartment in an hour. The operator assured Gisele she would be safe going home because the police would be waiting outside her building to escort her inside. True to the operator's promise, three squad cars were idling in the parking lot when she approached and turned off her vehicle. Across the street, reporters, like vultures, had begun to gather.

"Ms. Ferreira, I'm supervising Captain Brett Schneider from Metro division, field operations, and this is Sergeant Sean McCarthy, also from Metro. Because the intrusions you reported may involve the *Undead*, the chief thought I should personally come over here to oversee the investigation. Can we go up?"

Once upstairs, Gisele felt silly describing what probably seemed like imperceptible changes within the apartment. Hearing her own words, she admitted to being a little anal-retentive, owing to years managing a high-end boutique. One of Schneider's teams dusted the bathroom, her bedroom and the kitchen for fingerprints, but none but her own were found.

McCarthy struck up a conversation with Gisele as the teams worked, but Gisele thought he was creepy, even for a cop. It bothered her that he tried to become too familiar right away. Then there were his eyes, set too close together. He tried to be sly about it, but she caught him staring at her breasts, and he made a comment about her perfume, sniffing in her direction. She was unnerved by his eyes. She thought he looked like a rat.

"Ya know, the lead inspector in that case, that black guy Saint Claire, did you hear he's in jail accused of murder?"

"You know, I am a very busy woman. I do not have time to follow all those things. They do not interest me."

She turned away from McCarthy, hoping to discourage further conversation. Yet he continued.

"That Saint Claire was never the great detective he tried to make people believe he was. He's a liar and a murderer."

She looked back over her shoulder.

"Your opinion does not matter to me."

"They found that woman in his bed, naked. He had sex with her, and then he killed her."

Gisele was smart enough to know McCarthy wasn't making casual conversation. He knew about the friendship and he was trying to get a reaction from her. And he was trying to make her doubt Saint Claire.

"Why are you telling me that? What is your name?"

"Sergeant McCarthy."

She made the connection. This was the ugly police sergeant Saint Claire described weeks earlier. She stared straight ahead.

"I know who you are. You are that swine cop he told me about. *Tome cuidado*! Stop talking to me or I will make a complaint to your superiors."

"Whatever you say, sweetie, but watch yourself. He's supposed to by your boyfriend, but he was screwin the cap'n? I'd be worried if I were you. He's in jail for killin her and who knows, you might be next."

Brady felt a tinge of guilt as he turned off the car. It really was an invasion of privacy, after all. The search warrant was issued on probable cause that the murder weapon was in the condo, but he wasn't after the murder weapon. Based on Saint Claire's character and the events of the case, Brady was positive the black nine millimeter Ruger handgun issued to the detective was not in the library or anywhere else on the premises.

He waited downstairs, warrant in hand, for the building concierge to arrive. The harried man had called twice to assure the detective he was on his way, but it had been almost twenty minutes. Through the window, Brady saw McCarthy approaching the lobby door. Throughout the day, a light rain fell over the city. Once inside, McCarthy took off his hat and holding it tight, flung his wrist toward the floor to remove the water.

"Still waitin?"

Brady checked his watch.

"He's on his way. It'll be just a few minutes."

McCarthy nodded, drying his face.

"Think you'll find the gun up there?"

Brady eyed the sergeant.

"There's no *gun* up there. The killer has it. He switched guns with Saint Claire at some point and I'm guessing Saint Claire's wife, Katrina, probably helped him. She probably has it."

"Well, what do ya think you'll find?"

Brady checked to make sure no one was listening.

"I'm going to find out everything Saint Claire knows and everything he's thinking. There will be no secrets between us, at least not on *his* side."

McCarthy laughed.

"I don't believe it. I knew all along you were crazy, just like a fox. You came to this town and knocked im off that high horse, knocked im right on his black ass. He thought he was better cuz he was supposta be so smart, but you showed im. You showed *everybody*."

He smiled.

"Told im ta go ta hell and had him lookin forward ta the trip!"

Brady was embarrassed by the praise, but he did feel a sense of pride and accomplishment. Within a little more than a month, he had impressed the entire department.

"What happened over at Gisele Ferreira's place?

"God, that woman has the sweetest ass!"

Brady looked over.

"That's good. Did you talk to her?"

"That Saint Claire is one lucky son of a bitch! Gisele's as fine as fuck. An that *Sanchez* wasn't half-bad!"

"What she say?"

McCarthy sighed and began.

"Said um, said someone's been breakin into her place, hangin out, movin things."

"Anything stolen?"

"Nope, and no sign of forced entry."

Brady eyes were focused on the parking lot where a tall, thin man was approaching the building.

"Saint Claire told me it's what the killer does. He breaks in and cases the living quarters of his victims to set up the murder."

"What does that mean? Gisele's next?"

The concierge was making apologies as he came in the door.

"Inspector Brady, I am so, so sorry to keep you waiting! I'm Robert. Please forgive me. We've been short staffed. And the weather, oh God, you see it!"

Robert sneezed into a cloth handkerchief, extending his limp left hand.

"How are you today?"

"Fine."

"Oh yes you *are*! And I trust you have all your paperwork in order? I hafta admit, this is the first time I've been served with a search warrant. Ooh, it's a little exciting for me! But you probably do it all the time. Oh, and I see you even brought along a gruffy little side-kick."

McCarthy guffawed.

"Who, Tinkerbell?"

"No, you look more like the *Thing* if you ask me, except the Thing's a little better looking. Come along boys, I'm taking you on an *elevator* ride!"

Standing outside the condo door, Robert examined the documents for proper signatures before opening it.

"I'll be in the building for the next hour. You have my cell if you need me."

In at last! The condo seemed unchanged since Brady left it, except the door to Saint Claire's study was closed and locked, which meant he had to call for a locksmith. In the meantime, he and McCarthy went through the condo, checking cabinets and closets.

Sitting alone in the living room, Brady's conscience began to bother him again. Saint Claire could be arrogant for sure, but despite knowing Brady was hired to betray him, he had extended himself in friendship. He shared his family in New Orleans, his friend Slater and even a few poignant details from his personal life. Brady felt that Saint Claire, deep inside, was finally starting to like him, despite feeling Brady was inappropriate for his niece.

"There's no gun. Maybe we oughta just get outa here."

"Locksmith just called. He's downstairs. Come on, you gotta finish this. We're all countin on ya!"

Brady nodded, his eyes scanning the periphery. He found the art on the walls interesting. It made him think of Andrea and then of the bit he read about her and Saint Claire sneaking off to lunch together.

The idea of it made him angry. Andrea and Saint Claire had a lot in common. Andrea probably thought he was handsome, sophisticated and educated. She always said intelligence really turned her on. If Andrea was going to settle for a man she respected, it would have probably been someone more like Saint Claire. Sitting there, Brady was anxious to tell her of his day's accomplishment.

The locksmith admitted it was a tricky lock, and that's why it took him twenty minutes to disengage it. The study opened, Brady dismissed the man and entered the room. It was Saint Claire's private sanctuary, and it was ready for sacking.

"Does he have enough books?"

McCarthy scanned the shelves, but Brady went to the desk and sat.

"Turn up the lights. Pull up a chair."

Savoring the moment, he reached over and opened the top drawer on the right. In the instant he pulled on the handle, he knew something was wrong.

"*Goddamned mother fucker!*"

McCarthy flinched, standing.

Brady pulled out the bottom drawer.

"Fuck! It's empty!"

He yanked open the top drawer under the desktop.

"The whole desk is empty. He cleaned it out. He must have *known* this would happen!"

Suddenly, Brady thought of the mayor and all his supporters at the police department who had bragged him up all day. When they found out, he would go from being Saint Claire's clever nemesis to being the king of fools. He would be humiliated. McCarthy stood, scanning the room.

"He may've hid em. Did we check all the closets?"

"No. It's obvious he knew I'd be coming in here. They're long gone."

Brady took the phone from his pocket and dialed.

"Slater! It's Brady. I need your help, please! Fuck!"

He sighed, listening, and began.

"Okay, I'm at Saint Claire's, in the library. The stuff from his desk, did Saint Claire happen to give you all the stuff from his desk?"

Brady activated the speaker option on his phone to play Slater's response aloud.

"He's in jail, you asshole. How could he do that?"

"Yeah! Did he give you the files from the desk before he met with the mayor?"

"Are you askin if he gave me the *murder* weapon? Didn't you get the search warrant to go in there to look for the murder weapon? What other stuff are you talkin about?"

Brady shook his head.

"The notebooks! His notes. All the fuckin stuff from his desk!"

The answer was immediate.

"Shame on you, Brady! You're a false friend and a liar. Is that how you played it in Boston? Is that why you're here?"

Slater's voice reeked with anger.

"And shame on *me* for trustin ya."

CHAPTER 54

"Isn't this all a little ironic? It's funny, actually."

"What's that?"

"A month ago, I was locked up and you were coming to see *me*. Who would have ever thought the tables would turn so fast. Now I'm here visiting you."

Seated in the prisoners' visitation area, he wore a bright orange jumpsuit and tennis shoes.

Uneasy, Katrina forced herself to smile, uncomfortable with seeing him incarcerated.

"Bet you didn't know *Lady Day* was once sitting where you are."

"Lady Day? How's that?"

"I read it this morning. Back in 1949, corrupt cops raided her hotel and said they found opium. Locked her up in this jail, right here. It was an easy set-up since she was a known user, but the jury didn't buy it. Jury said she'd been framed and let her go."

She bowed her head for a moment. When she lifted her face, her expression had changed.

"I really am sorry about the other night, Ronnie. I said some mean things to you. I know you went out of your way to be there for me, and duty or no duty, you were there."

She daubed the corners of her eyes with a tissue.

"And that meant everything to me."

She looked into his eyes.

"We've been through life together, Ronnie. I love you."

A tear trailed down his face.

"I love you, too."

Finally the past, with all its history, suspicion, pain, betrayal and passion, was past. And the future was equally irrelevant. In the present, they loved each other, and that was all that mattered.

A guard screaming in an inmate's face ten feet away was enough to remind both where they were, and why. From the time Katrina arrived, Saint Claire had wanted to ask the question.

"What's going on between you and the killer? It is Kain, right?"

She nodded.

"It's Kain, but it's complicated. The important thing is that it's over now."

"What do you mean? Did you kill him?"

She glanced toward the guard.

"Trust me. He's gone. The game's over. He's left town."

"How do you know that?"

"Motivation. He's got nowhere to go. I burned his apartment with everything in it."

Saint Claire reared back, frustrated.

"I don't get it. If you knew where he lived, why didn't you just tell us? We would have gone in and got him!"

"You would have killed him, and that would have ruined you. Believe me."

"What are you talking about? He killed our son!"

She took a breath.

"Remember what the *Voudoun* said? You have to let go, Ronnie. Do you want to be a killer too? Nothing you can do now is going to get us Christian back. He's gone. Killing will only make you resemble the monster you hate."

He bowed his head.

"I promised Christian. I promised him I'd never give up on him again. I promised I'd never be too busy to follow through for him. I can't just give up. I have to finish this."

She reached toward him.

"You don't. Let it go. It's time to rejoin the living, Ronnie, for both of us."

He shook his head.

"I can't. I've spent the last twelve years doing this."

"And that's *enough* for Christian. You didn't give up on him. Looking down on you from wherever, I'm sure he knows that now. Maybe you can go back to teaching?"

He would not allow her to change the subject.

"He killed Sanchez. Do you realize the police think you and Kain might be working *together* in these murders?"

"It doesn't matter now. He's gone."

He realized the risk involved in the question.

"Did you help him murder Sanchez?"

She smiled to lighten the mood.

"No, but I should have. Could have called it a crime of passion. She was, after all, *fucking* my husband."

He was learning not to respond to comments and innuendoes about Sanchez. She cocked her head, sarcastic.

"At least I'm not one of those wives who will have to worry if you're going to sneak around with her again."

He ignored the comment, pressing on.

"Whatever you think you have on him, you can't make him stop. You don't know him like I do. He's going to finish this thing."

She shrugged.

"I know him. I really don't think he will."

She sat back.

"Since you brought up Christian and I'm free of the curse, I think it's time I shared a suspicion with you."

"What's that?"

"You remember Portugal in the village, the day that little boy was murdered?"

He answered warily.

"Yes?"

"You never said it, but you suspected for years that I had gone in that bathroom and strangled that four-year-old boy. You're acting now, trying to deny it with your eyes, but I know that's what you thought."

He nodded.

"Okay?"

"And I thought for years it was you. You've always been so controlled and quiet, but I know you have a dark side. You've always kept your Mr. Hyde locked away and out of sight. You even try to pretend he isn't in there, scowling out at us, but that monster has always been there."

Her eyes examined the two men visiting on the left before she leaned forward.

"Well I just thought it got to be too much for you. You were out of town, out of the country. No one knew you. We were in a village full of poor, naïve peasants. The idea of it was sexy. Murder has always been a turn-on for me, you know that. When I saw that little boy, alone, the thought crossed my mind. I fantasized about it. So I thought you went in there and strangled that boy to appease the fiend you'd kept imprisoned for so long, just to get it out of your system."

She sat back.

"I suspected you for years, just like you suspected me, but I think we were both wrong. There was a possibility neither of us considered, until now."

"What's that?"

"What if it was Christian? We were the only three people down there that day, you, Christian and me. He was only nine years old, but what if it was Christian who went in that bathroom and strangled that four-year-old boy?"

Saint Claire grimaced.

"That's impossible! He was nine years old!"

"Is it? If I saw dark in you, I saw pitch black in Christian as a boy. Back then you were too busy to see it. Like you, he could be cruel and detached. His eyes scared me. It made me remember what your mother told me. If you really *are* my brother by Benjamin Scott, then we both inherited our grandfather's killer trait on one side, but that would mean Christian got it from *both* sides."

He dragged his hand down his face, thinking.

"No."

"Well, if it wasn't you and it wasn't me, what does that leave us with? What other possible explanation could there be? There were no gypsies."

He shook his head.

"There were no gypsies."

"And little Sage, who died in Christian's room, unable to breathe, asphyxiated. I was on a lot of drugs back then, but I remember finding a soaked rag in that room, and I'm just about sure now I found a can of solvent under the bed the next day."

Her eyes began to water again.

"I think Christian covered Sage's face with that rag until he stopped fighting. And then he checked to make sure the boy was barely breathing before he called us."

Her voice broke.

"And Geneviève, our daughter. I don't even want to think about it! But he never liked her, and he never showed any emotion when she died. He sat there smiling at her funeral. I wanted to strangle him. I wanted to kill him."

She closed her eyes, taking a breath.

"When Kain killed Christian, you had your guilt to live with, and that's why, whether you realize it or not, you've been planning a murder for the last twelve years, obsessed with murdering Kain. I had no guilt, only grief to think that old black bitch back home had cursed my life, even out here in California."

She looked into her husband's eyes, her own showing resolve.

"I didn't feel sorry or sad when Christian was murdered, and I think it was because deep inside I already knew. Justice was served. Our son, a killer, simply crossed paths with a better killer. Whose fault was that? The only one to blame was Christian. He deserved it. That's why you have to let it go."

Deuteronomy drew a breath, overwhelmed by a flood of new thoughts and emotion. It was the difference between man and woman. He remembered Christian as a boy, but only superficially. He could not remember a single meaningful conversation he had with his son until Christian was fourteen, and by then they were arguing all the time. Katrina knew him in a different way. She saw inside the boy. She knew his thoughts, his weaknesses, fears, vulnerabilities and this dark side.

"It's over, Ronnie. Can we get back to living life? A new beginning, together?"

He leaned across the table.

"Do you mean that?"

"I needed a little time to myself on the outside. I needed time to sort things out, but blood or no blood, I believe we belong together."

He nodded.

"Yes, I agree."

"Counseling, we're going to need some serious counseling."

"Okay."

"And no DNA or paternity test. I don't want to know at this point. Do you?"

"No. But you can live with that? You know, sexually?"

She smiled.

"I don't know. Give me enough counseling, chemicals and alcohol and I can live with anything."

A guard approached and stood next to Katrina, telling her the thirty minute visitation was up. In his presence, the conversation could only be superficial.

"I love you, Kate."

"I love you too, Ronnie. We'll work on the details when you get out."

He watched as she walked to the door, and true to old form, she turned around in the doorway to look back at him, smiling.

Two hours later he had a surprise visit at his cell. It was a girl he hadn't seen in nine, ten years, when she was a teenager. Superficially, she looked like her mother, but there was something in her eyes, something deeper that was definitely her father.

"I'm sure I'm the last person you expected to see."

His eyes we're still adjusting to the light as he sat up in the cot.

"Actually I'm not surprised. Your father's been on my mind lately. Anyway, I've heard great things about you. Your father would be proud."

Angelique Curry bowed her head.

"What's happening now? This killer you're after, is all this somehow connected to my father's murder?"

He nodded.

"Yes it is, Angel. I've been after the man who killed your father for ten years, and now it's almost over. Either I'm going to get him or he's going to get me, real soon."

Ronnie was the unofficial uncle who had gone to all her ballet performances, who took her fishing and taught her how to box. He brought her pralines and the Nectar Soda all the way from New Orleans, and he even let her go onstage to sing zydeco songs with the band. He was her favorite uncle and the object of a childhood crush.

She was sixteen when her father was murdered. By that time, he had stopped being Uncle Ronnie's partner. And while Saint Claire and Joe Curry had still had regular phone conversations and rare meals together, there had been a rift.

Joe's funeral was difficult for Saint Claire. He felt estranged from the family. Joe's wife, Twyla, fell apart and poor Angelique, she didn't understand what had happened. All she knew was that her father was dead, and the bullet had come from the gun of her favorite uncle.

"Well, I hope you get him. This will never be over for me until I know."

Hesitant, she glanced away before continuing.

"Everyone's saying you were sleeping with Captain Sanchez."

"That's not true. She was at my condo those last two nights because we were assuming the killer wouldn't ruin his series by physically murdering someone. All that crap about his murdering from the grave, he blew it by killing Sanchez."

Angelique's eyes became teary.

"It's like I'm living it all over again. Your gun was switched again? How does that happen? It was no secret you and Sanchez had your share of problems, and she was found with your bullet in her head just like, just like Daddy."

Saint Claire began to respond, but she stopped him.

"Don't! I don't want to hear an explanation. You don't share, and not sharing is lying! No one around here believes anything you say. So if you say you're going to catch this killer when you get out, I'll believe it when I see it."

She wiped her face.

"But that's not why I came. I didn't come over to cry for you or dredge up the past. I just thought there was something you probably needed to know."

"What's that?"

"Of course you know Gisele Ferreira. They're saying she's your girlfriend."

"She's a good friend. What's going on?"

"She called Metro division last night, all panicked. Said someone's been hanging out in her apartment when she's been at work, checking her medications, going through her mail. Only thing missing was two pages from her cell phone bill, the call logs."

He stood.

"Where is she? They didn't let her stay in that apartment, did they?"

"She's staying with a girlfriend in Pacific Heights. They've been checking on her every couple hours."

"She must be at work by now. I've got to get out of here!"

Angelique studied her one-time uncle, wagging her head.

"You have no idea what's been on the news out there, do you?"

"No."

"I don't believe it. *You're* the big story across the country! Newspapers, television, the Internet! And this killer, Kain? In his first letter? He tells you he's going to make you *kill* someone before it's all over. They're saying Kain had something on you, or he somehow forced you to do it, but they're saying from the grave he made you *kill* Sanchez. No one else knew she was there. I heard the mayor talking about it on TV. Until they fully investigate this thing, I don't think you're going anywhere."

Brady was so frustrated he thought he should get drunk before dealing with anyone. He had promised the mayor and the chief if he were allowed to search Saint Claire's condo, he would "definitely" provide information and evidence that would blow the case wide open. Now he was publicly humiliated. Saint Claire had set him up. And Brady had betrayed a trust he valued more than he had imagined. Whatever friendship he had with Saint Claire and with Slater was gone, and for nothing!

Brady understood the irony of being angry with Andrea for leaking the copies of the killer's unabridged letters she discovered in his briefcase. By breaking into his briefcase and converting the letters to her own purposes, she had only done to him what he had attempted to do to Saint Claire, except she had been successful. He decided to go the condo to confront her.

She made sure to tell him the TV networks created a big build-up leading to the search of Saint Claire's condo, and then there was the big let-down, with a story about his betrayal.

He swigged the beer and set the bottle down, his speech slurred from hard alcohol.

"Well, maybe if you hadn't given copies of the killer's letters to Sanchez and Yamakita at the Chronicle, maybe I wouldn't be sitting here today, with egg on my face, with no one who'll trust me."

"I said it when you started here. Homicide just isn't your thing. You're more of an administration type. Your strengths are in leadership. You have to play to your strengths."

Maybe she was right. Maybe he had no business in homicide. Maybe he needed a change. Maybe he needed a big change.

"I've decided. I'm not going to come back home, sex or no sex. I need a woman who's going to be a real wife to me. Fuck this *sex by Geneva Conference*! I'm supposed to be married. I want a real wife. Is that too much to ask?"

She approached him and kissed him on the lips.

"No, it's not too much to ask. I said we'd have sex and we *will*, tonight."

"Really?"

"Really. But first I wanted to show you something."

She opened a folder that had been sitting on the bar.

"I've been home all day, so I haven't had access to my computer. But I did find a Bible so I could check the numbers you gave me against scriptures. You said Katrina Saint Claire said the numbers might have something to do with scriptures?"

She sat at the barstool next to him.

"Turns out the Bible I found was *Old Testament* only, so I tried it against the numbers. Here's what I got."

Brady took the sheet of paper from the folder and read.

After the number of the days in which ye searched the land, even forty days, each day for a year, shall ye bear your iniquities, even forty years, and ye shall know my breach of promise.

He looked toward Andrea.

"Okay, so what does that mean?"

"I don't know. Nothing at all, to me. I'm thinking maybe it'll mean something when you consider it with all the scriptures together. This is the second one."

He took the next sheet.

The LORD killeth, and maketh alive: he bringeth down to the grave, and bringeth up.

He dropped the sheet back on the bar, sat back and closed his eyes.

"*Maketh alive, bringeth up*? The killer said something in his first letter about resurrection. I think you're on the right track."

He looked toward the empty folder.

"What's the third scripture?"

"I don't know. It's in the *New Testament,* if I counted right. I don't have that. I was going to look it up tomorrow."

She nudged him, her voice taking on a sultry tone.

"You look tired, but I am a woman of my word. If you want me, I'm yours. You can have me right now."

He stood.

"That third scripture. I need to see that third scripture. You have no other Bible?"

"We live in twenty-first century Babylon. No."

His eyes scanned the room.

"Don't you have your computer?

"Left it at work, and the girls' computers aren't online yet."

"Then we need to go to your office to get online. If I can put it all together, I might be able to save the last two lives."

"Without Saint Claire?"

"*Including* Saint Claire's."

CHAPTER 55

Everyone at City Hall knew Mayor David Douglas *despised* waiting, especially on city employees. So it was no surprise when Jessica had a guard conduct Saint Claire to the mayor's office while the mayor was still in Los Angeles speaking at a meeting for the filmmakers union. The guard sat Saint Claire, shackled him to a table, and told him the mayor's flight would be departing Los Angeles in an hour or so. Hungry and thirsty, Saint Claire waited at the table over three hours before the mayor arrived.

"Saint Claire! What a surprise! You're on time!"

Douglas shielded his eyes as he examined the bright orange clothing and the tennis shoes.

"The color and style work for you. I think all you need now is a matching orange fedora. You could be the former mayor!"

"You're an ass! I hope you know that while you're standing there jackin yourself off, the killer's going to get to number six. That means you, Mr. Mayor, will be responsible for the next murder. When I get out, I'll make sure the city's voters all know that."

"You murdered Sanchez, Saint Claire! You're not getting out. You might be smart enough to make sure we never find the murder weapon, but we won't need it. DA says they collected a lotta damaging evidence from your apartment. Told me himself he thinks he's already got enough for a conviction."

Saint Claire smirked.

"And you believe that? Let me tell you how this whole thing's going to go down. It doesn't matter what they've collected. I'll be out of here in a day, by tomorrow at the latest."

The mayor laughed.

"What? You gonna break out?"

"No, the city's going to have to let me go. The *killer's* going to get me out. He needs me out there, to finish this thing. I'll admit, I don't know exactly what he'll do, but you can bet the farm on it."

He looked into the mayor's eyes.

"You just better hope no one dies before I get out, because if someone does, I'm going to make it a point to use it to trash your reputation from Candlestick Point to the Golden Gate."

The mayor stood over the detective.

"You think you can threaten me, you fuckin county inmate in an orange jumpsuit, you fuckin cop killer! How bout this? This is my city, and I'm gonna go outa my way ta make sure you get treated like the piece of shit you are for as long you're locked up. And I'm gonna make sure your guilty ass stays locked up for as long as I can make em keep ya!"

Douglas backed up, shaking his head.

"See what happens when you make me mad? Overnight, you've gone from highly respected inspector to highly suspected serial killer. Overnight! I hate arrogant fucks like you. You deserve it."

He sat at his desk, putting first one and then the other foot up on the surface.

"You realize how you're lookin at me? What, you wanna kill me too? And ta think I had you brought over here cuz I wanted to help you."

"I don't want or need your help."

"But you want outa here, don't cha? You wanna get out so you can go after your killer? Save a precious life?"

Saint Claire did not answer, but Douglas knew he was listening.

"You told Brady hours matter, you said *minutes* matter. What would you be willing to give me in exchange if I could get you outa here in an hour? Back on the trail of your killer? Who is it, Gisele that singer girlfriend of yours? Isn't that who you wanna save? Clock's tickin. She's runnin outa time."

"What about your DA and all that supposed evidence?"

"I was bluffin, but you already knew that."

"What do you want?"

The mayor smiled.

"I just want a peek into those notebooks Brady told me about. Just a peek for about fifteen minutes. It's personal. You can be right there watching me. An after that, I swear I'll have you outa here in an hour."

Saint Claire scowled.

"You really oughta have a *clone*, Douglas."

"A clone? Really? Why's that?"

"So you can do to yourself what I'm thinking you need to do, without the *KY*."

Douglas smiled wryly as he stood.

"Okay, have it your way, but just remember this: if your killer murders again before you get out, it'll be your fault for being unwilling to make a deal for that life. All that not sharing is finally gonna cost ya, Saint Claire."

He looked away from the mayor.

"You and the clone, just take it back to your office."

Douglas shrugged.

"Let me know if you change your mind."

The mayor headed for the door, but he stopped short, turning.

"You talked to Chief Leong last night? As a matter of fact, I heard you're the *last* person she talked to, but she didn't answer any of my calls this morning. And she's basically disappeared. Her husband says he doesn't know where she is, and no one else does. She's a missing person."

He stood in front of the detective.

"But I'd probably be safe bettin the farm *you* know somethin about it. Did she tell you where she was going, what she was doing?"

Saint Claire looked up.

"Nope."

"Husband's all panicked, worried about his wife. Kids are worried. Come on, she musta told you somethin. Help me put that poor family at ease."

"You could have done better by em if you hadn't arrested me in the first place. Haven't you talked to Brady? Hasn't *he* figured it out yet?"

"What?"

"Chief Leong is the killer's next victim. She's number six. So while you've had me in here, playing your games, the killer got Leong. And if she's already dead, it's your fault. Tell her family *that*."

Katrina noticed the unmarked police car behind her when she left in the morning. If some superior had ordered the young men in the car to remain circumspect, they were blowing it. The car followed about seventy feet behind, slowing when she slowed, stopping when she stopped. The plain clothed officers in it seemed nervous.

They followed her to the pharmacy, to the natural foods store, to the florist, to Deuteronomy's condo and then to the jail on Bryant. When she left after visiting her husband, they trailed her to Union Square, where at Neiman Marcus she bought a stained glass lamp and an African curio for her apartment. She had dinner on the way home at a restaurant on Bridgeway in Sausalito, seated at a table that offered a gorgeous view of Richardson Bay.

She had the *Cioppino*, made with fresh sweet Dungeness crab, mussels, clams and prawns. The savory tomato broth with herbs was just light enough to perfectly balance the flavors in the bowl. On a recommendation from the server, she had wine for the first time in almost fourteen years. It was a soft, delicate, delicious Russian River Pinot Noir, and she insisted on having just a half glass, though she paid full price.

Freedom felt beautiful, thrilling and sensual. As she looked toward the western horizon, watching the glorious sun setting on the bay, she appreciated a rare moment in which she had all the contentment a person could ever want. Life was good again, certainly better than it had ever been.

For as long as she could remember, that damned curse had hung over her head, and then there was the seeming endless imprisonment at Saint Mary's, but she had survived both, and she was wiser and stronger for it. Because of her past, she had an appreciation for freedom that most people never experienced.

In awe, she watched the movement of the darkening water, crystal edged ripples still glowing, reflecting the infinite energy of the shrinking sun. A gentle, barely perceptible breeze flowed inland from across the bay, carrying in it the ancient essence of the sea, the peaceful scent that made her want to rest, to be one with the tingling energy surrounding her.

The moon rising in the east was Eve's moon, it was the moon of Sarai, of Ruth and Mary. It was the same moon Cleopatra watched as the skies grew dark over Egypt, the same moon Harriet Ross Tubman relied on to illuminate her path, a moon that inspired generations of lovers to brave or foolish acts of beauty and passion. It was the beacon of dreams, and finally it was the moon overhead when Katrina and her sister Bianca walked home from the movies on warm summer nights, holding hands, both talking a million miles a minute.

Eyes lost in the black waters, she fancied she saw Bianca's delicate face, her pale blue eyes wide, her unabashed, uneven, contagious teenaged smile. Katrina missed Bianca more than ever. She needed her sister, and she wondered what her own life would have been like had Bianca never been murdered. Surely they would have been close. Bianca would have never forsaken her, or she Bianca.

Katrina's eyes welled with tears as she remembered the day she went to the *Voudoun*, foolishly seeking to humble her favored sister. Madame Touissante was an evil woman. She should have recognized Katrina was just a young girl who didn't understand what she was asking and how profoundly a single selfish and rash act could affect the future. The old woman should have scolded her for being jealous and sent her home chastised or whipped. Katrina only wanted Bianca to know what it felt like being Katrina. Bianca was her older sister, her dance partner, her best friend! Katrina only wanted Bianca to understand.

"I'm so sorry, Bianca. I loved you. I always loved you. I'm sorry if it was my fault that this happened to you. If I had known, I would have taken your place."

It was the first time Katrina had spoken to her sister in three decades, and it was only because she believed she felt the strong presence of her sister there in the darkness, reaching out to her from the water, which through its vast system of seas, rivers and streams running throughout the Earth, connected past with present, present with distant, surreal with life and life with death.

"We're both free now. I'm letting go. Not forever, just for now. I love you so much, but I have to let go."

Katrina's hands were trembling as she gripped the steering wheel on the fifteen-minute ride home. She wondered if anyone back at the restaurant witnessed or understood what she had just gone through. The tentative headlights edging up and falling back in the rearview mirror meant the police were still following her, but she didn't care.

Lamp in her arms, she walked past the guard and took the stairs for the exercise, two flights. Leaning against the wall next to her door, she aimed the key with shaking fingers and managed to open it while still holding the lamp.

Inside, the air smelled funny, and she usually left a light on in the kitchen, but it was off. Before she could turn to run or scream, she felt strong hands grasp her shoulders and she could not breathe. There was a terrycloth towel on her face. Cold! And that smell! The towel was soaked in ether. She held her breath, struggling wildly to escape, but she could feel her body growing weaker. He held his own body just beyond her thrashing elbows, writhing hips and stomping feet.

She opened her mouth to scream, but he stuffed the towel further in. Dizzy and terrified, she stared out into the darkness, wondering what ending he had planned for her. If she had suspected it in the least, she would have never let it happen. She thought she had won when she had him that last time. He had cried so pitifully. He promised her he would move on, but he lied. Ronnie was right!

Her body yielded, her legs, arms, shoulders and neck relinquishing their fight. A minute later, she was gone.

CHAPTER 56

"I'm sorry, Inspector, I'd like to help you, but my husband is not available."

Brady stepped forward, placing his foot in the doorway.

"You don't understand. This is a life or death situation for Saint Claire!"

When she looked up into his eyes, he realized he had only seconds to make his pitch.

"I went to the jail. He won't talk to me. Your husband's his only chance. Come on, Oksana, you've got to believe me. I'm trying to save his life!"

She glanced back over her shoulder and then toward Brady, narrowing her eyes.

"If you know this thing, why does my husband not already know this thing? Saint Claire told him everything. He told him too much!"

"No, I figured it out from one of the clues in the killer's letter. Saint Claire doesn't even know it. I figured it out, and we're running out of time!"

She contemplated for a moment.

"Okay, just a moment."

The door would not budge.

"Move your foot so I can close the door."

"You promise you'll come back?"

"No, I don't. You are going to just have to trust me."

When she returned ten minutes later, she opened the door only after having attached the chain inside.

"You are not allowed at this house. There is a coffee shop on Bridgeway near Filbert. It is early, so it will not be too busy. My husband is already on his way there."

Slater was seated and sipping coffee when Brady arrived. He nodded at the detective then looked away.

"Well look, if it isn't Judas Iscariot! Look, I don't have alotta time or patience for your crap, Brady. What do ya got?"

As Brady sat, he retrieved a folder from his soft briefcase.

"I figured out the numerical clues from the bottom of the killer's first letter. They were scriptures!"

He pushed the folder toward Slater so he could follow.

"In the first one, the main thing you want to focus on is what I have underlined there. It says, *each day for a year*. So when the killer says he's been gone for twelve *days*, which could really mean twelve years! Kain disappeared twelve *years* ago!"

He flipped over to the next sheet.

"Okay, now the second scripture says, *The LORD killeth, and maketh alive*. In that first letter, the killer 'thanked' Saint Claire for his 'resurrection,' for making him alive again."

He slid his chair to the left, so he could read as he explained.

"Cuz then it says, *he bringeth down to the grave, and bringeth up*."

Brady looked up.

"You get it, resurrection? Okay, it was starting to make sense, but then I looked up the third scripture and it all went out of whack. It said, *And they came again to Jerusalem. And as he was walking in the temple, the chief priests and the scribes and the elders came to him*. I just don't know about the third scripture. That just throws everything off."

He closed the folder.

"Does any of that mean anything to you?"

Thinking back, Slater remembered the killer from more than a decade before, from right after Christian's murder. Even then, the killer struck him as worldly, well-traveled, experienced and mature. And from what he had learned about the killer, who called himself *Kain Behram*, his ultimate ambition was to be smarter than Saint Claire.

According to Saint Claire, Kain's parents were of eastern central European descent, his father from a large town along the Carpathian mountain chain in Romania. According to Saint Claire, Kain's real name was Mihai Rădescu, and his parents had immigrated to the United States in 1989 when their son was still a teenager. He had an identical twin brother who died of mysterious causes at six-years-old. In Romania, Mihai's father was a prominent government official in Bucharest with a large estate. His mother was from a wealthy family in Băcia near Deva in Transylvania.

Three years earlier, Saint Claire took a trip to Romania and Hungary to research the family with the hope of finding Mihai or discovering some clue to his behavior, some particular vulnerability or information that would tip the scales just enough to trap him.

The wealth of his mother's family stretched back centuries. She was Hungarian, directly descended from an Ecsed branch of the renowned Báthory family. According to interviews and research, Mihai's mother Erzsébet was somehow related to the Elizabeth Báthory, the Bloody Lady of Čachtice, the most prolific female serial killer of all time. She reportedly bathed in the blood of her victims to retain her youth, inspiring the monikers Blood Princess and Countess Dracula.

Mihai began murdering people as a young teenager. Bucharest during the mid-1980s, was an ideal climate for killing. The people were poor and tensions were running high. It was easy to murder a person and drag the body to a secluded place. There was always someone else to blame—the mobs, political factions or the police.

Mihai's father was a deputy director of the Securitate, the corrupt secret police force of Communist Romania under the rule of Nicolae Ceauşescu. As such, he was a killer who recognized in early 1989 that a revolution and the overthrow of the Ceauşescu regime were looming. He got the family out of the country just in time.

Mihai continued killing when the family moved to Brooklyn, beginning with his parents, who suffocated when Mihai "accidentally" left the gas on before leaving the apartment one evening. His father had embezzled millions out of Romania before leaving, so Mihai, who had begun calling himself Michael Rad, inherited a vast estate.

Michael moved out west with his fortune. His first apartment was on Hartford Street in the Castro district. A year later he began at San Francisco City College, where he studied biology and chemistry. Described by former teachers as "extremely bright," he finished in just eighteen months and transferred to the University of Washington in Seattle, where he majored in organic chemistry and criminal psychology. He planned to go to medical school, where in his fourth year he could have opted to specialize in forensic science and pathology.

However, midway through his senior year at the university, Seattle police arrested him for the murder of his roommate in a Wallmont neighborhood apartment. Because the evidence was circumstantial, the court granted Michael's release.

However, suspicious police investigators monitored his activity from that point on and he was arrested a second time four months later.

This time one of Michael's college instructors, Professor Eugene McDermott, was found strangled in the trunk of his own Buick Park Avenue. Though Michael was released a second time for lack of evidence, the experience was enough to make him leave Seattle. He finished his undergrad at UC Berkeley.

As Slater sipped the last of the coffee in the cup, he remembered the time he and Saint Claire almost got Michael Rad, a name Saint Claire refused to utter. Slater remembered getting a brief glimpse of Michael's face when the killer turned, grimacing in pain after being hit by one of Slater's bullets.

"Waitaminute, do you still have the police artist's sketch of the man the concierge at the Brocklebank described? I saw it in the paper today, but I didn't really look at it."

Brady reached for it as he answered.

"Yeah, why?"

"Because I saw the killer's face for a second when I shot him."

Slater stared at the sketch.

"And this is him, Brady. It's Kain all right, also known as Michael Rad."

CHAPTER 57

Katrina pretended to remain unconscious as she assessed her predicament. She sat slumped in a chair from her dining room, the majority of her weight resting on her rump at the front of the seat, with the balance supported by her shoulders and upper back against the chair back.

Her legs were splayed, heels dug into the carpet, to prevent her body from sliding off the chair. Her head was back. She could feel a metal cuff, attached at her left wrist, anchoring her arm to the left back leg of the chair.

She could feel another person in the room, seated three or four feet away. He was watching her, waiting. She knew who it was, but she had to peek. He was there, watching her eyes move under their lids, signaling REM sleep.

He checked his watch. Leaning close, he nudged her shoulder.

"Wake up. It's time."

Straining, she sat up as best she could.

"Time for what?"

He turned away, avoiding her eyes.

"You already know."

"I think I know the what, but I don't know the why, or the how."

He nodded.

"I made a promise to you, and I'm breaking it, so I think I owe you an explanation."

"Okay..."

"You shouldn't have come and found me. You left me with no choice."

"Bullshit. You came into this apartment. You started this between you and me."

He wagged his head.

"I came by just to see you. You weren't supposed to be awake. You were just too smart for your own good. This was supposed to be between him and me. It had nothing to do with you, never with you."

Reluctant, he looked in her eyes.

"My plan was perfect, flawless, but you interfered. You forced me to rewrite the entire ending. You weren't supposed to be in it."

"But now I am, and the ending you're considering, it won't work. You didn't and can't murder seven people from the grave. It was an impossible premise from the start. Give it up and go somewhere else like you promised you would."

"I can't do that."

He stood, checking his watch.

"I'm going to finish this thing, and when it's over, I really will be the greatest serial murder artist of all time, the ultimate vampire. I just can't afford to have you interfering or spoiling it for me. You're the only one who really knows me."

"No, I think you're wrong there. He knows you."

"No, he thinks he knows. That's not the same thing as knowing."

She sat back, defiant.

"So what are you going to do? Shoot me? Poison me while I'm sitting here chained to this chair? You think that will make you the greatest serial murder artist of all time?"

"No, I wouldn't shoot you. I'm going to make you shoot yourself, *after* I'm gone."

He sighed, filled with regret.

"Number six was actually supposed to be Chief Rebecca Leong. She was going to disappear almost exactly one hundred years after the disappearance of Police Chief William J. Biggy, and her body was going to be found floating in the bay off the rocks of Angel Island with no apparent injury, an unsolvable murder, just like his was."

He opened the black medical bag sitting on the kitchen counter.

"Saint Claire's known about Leong from the start, but from the beginning I had planned for him to be in jail during the sixth murder so he couldn't act. If you watched the news earlier tonight, Chief Leong's missing. No one knows where she is, or if she's dead or alive, except me of course."

Katrina checked to see where the handcuff was attached to the chair. It was *under* the bottom rung. If she just tipped the chair up, she could free herself. But this killer didn't make amateur mistakes. He *meant* for her to be able to free herself. Nervous, she spoke.

"Okay, so you have Chief Leong and you have me. That makes two number sixes. If you've devised a way to make me shoot myself, what are you going to do, make her number seven?"

"No, I already have my number seven, but Leong figures into my new ending. I wish you weren't involved, but I know you."

He sat in a chair next to her, speaking into her ear.

"If I let you live, you'll come after me and you really *will* kill me, and like you promised, you'll make it a point to send me to my grave unknown. You'll punish me by condemning me to a future of obscurity. But I am the light of the world. That can never happen."

He bowed his head. As before, he wore a black long sleeved shirt with black pants and black soft-soled shoes. He wore black gloves and a black beanie knit hat pulled down over his hair and mangled ears.

"You could have killed me or turned me over to Saint Claire, but you let me live because you felt sorry for me. That was the only thing I had working for me during those two helpless, desperate moments where you had me, your pity. I had your pity and my destiny. If at murder seven it were to come down to me against you? Well, you said it. There'd be no more pity. You're too smart. You'd find some way to get me."

He nodded.

"I don't know what it is. You're psychic, at least about me. You think what I think *before* I think it. And while it makes me profoundly sad to overthrow such a noble, brilliant mind, I have no choice."

From the black nurse's bag, he withdrew a Velcro sealed removable compartment, and from that a syringe and a vial.

"I'm sorry I can't show you the same compassion you showed me, but I'll make sure you're remembered for it in this great opus."

Uncapping the needle, he inserted it into the vial, filling the syringe.

"I'm sorry."

Katrina cringed as he approached.

"What *is* that? What's in the syringe?"

From behind, he grasped a mass of her hair, pushing her chin toward her chest, exposing the back of her neck.

"Don't worry. It's a reenactment, for effect really. What I proposed to do to you, I've already done."

He presented the syringe, placing it on the table.

"It's filled with *Kainic* acid, which as you know is neuroexcitotoxic and epileptogenic. It produces lesions in your brain that lead to schizophrenia and epilepsy, permanent brain damage."

He looked into her eyes to make sure she understood.

"About ninety minutes ago, while you were still unconscious, I injected two vials of it into your spinal fluid. Even now, you can probably feel a little pain at the place where I inserted the needle, between L4 and L5. Your legs are still working, so I think I got it right."

Katrina arched her back slightly, acknowledging to herself that she had received an epidural injection. If he was telling the truth, it was already too late. Her head felt a little foggy, but she wasn't sure if it was cerebral edema or paranoia. She hadn't taken her meds. She hoped he was bluffing.

He checked his watch again.

"Right now, you brain is swelling and it will continue to swell until it's ruined. Before I leave, I'm going to dial 911 on your cell phone. When the paramedics rush up here, they'll probably be able to save your life, and after they do, you will never be able to take care of yourself, seizures all the time, pissing on yourself and crapping in your diaper."

He paused to let the images fill her mind.

"So you'll go back to a sanitarium, or a hospital, or some convalescent home where you'll be imprisoned for the rest of your life. You'll never be free again. You won't even be yourself."

He stood and went back to the black medical bag.

"Of course I love you and I'm not that cruel. I've left you a way out."

From the bag, he took a black handgun and placed it on the table before her.

"Based on the dosage, I would guess you have somewhere in the area of twenty-five minutes to decide what you are going to do, which is ironically just a few minutes less than it'll take the paramedics to begin work on you. But based on my experiments, you might be comatose when they arrive."

He leaned over and kissed her on the mouth, his tongue trailing over her lips. Then, flipping open the phone on the table, he dialed 911. He removed the handcuffs, went back around the table, recapped the syringe, returned it to its case, closed the bag and turned back to Katrina.

"Goodbye. I've always loved you."

She picked up the gun in her right hand even before she knew what she was doing. Standing, she pointed it toward him, trying to steady it in her shaking hand.

"You're an abomination! I'll kill you!"

He turned, calm as he extended his palm.

"You're smarter than me. Haven't you already figured it out? There's only one bullet in that gun. If you shoot me, there'll be nothing left for you! You'll be committing yourself to an eternal Hell you know all too well. So once again, goodbye."

Katrina laughed maniacally, pointing the shaking gun at his face.

"No, you only think it's goodbye. I'm still going to win. Haven't you learned by now? You can't beat me."

He stopped in his tracks, concerned as she came around the table, crazed look in her eyes, still pointing the gun.

Backing away as she approached, he wondered if she would pull the trigger or worse, if she had figured out his ending. He was overcome by fear of the unexpected. He knew there was a huge risk in waking her up. He knew she would get inside his head. She could possibly turn the tables, but he had to do it. It was the only way.

He cringed as she drew near. She smiled, peering into his eyes, seeming to discern his thoughts as he stood there trembling, pinned against the wall next to the door. She spoke, rage and hate radiating from her angry face.

"From the grave I'll spit my last *breath* at thee."

Once again, she had taken control of the scene. He felt helpless, terrified in her imposing, omniscient presence. In her hand, she held the power to end his life, and if she wanted to, she could make up a story that would condemn him to the realm of anonymity. If she pulled the trigger, she would render him insignificant. So once again, he appealed to the only weakness in her he understood, pity. He cried again, like a little boy.

"Please don't kill me! Please don't take it away from me!"

She turned away, her mind fighting a growing sense of dizziness.

"Go!"

He rolled past her along the wall, scrambled for the door, and seemed to vanish into thin air, leaving her apprehensive and alone with thoughts that were becoming increasingly irrational.

Katrina tried to focus straight ahead, but the room seemed to be turning, slowly clockwise. *Kainic* acid, she remembered, was derived from red algae. In rats' brains it caused lesions and permanent damage from swelling. Putting her hands to her face, she closed her eyes and took a breath, trying to calm herself, steady her nerves, restrain her imagination.

She saw the future. The ambulance would come and her life would be saved. Mental capacity diminished, she would be assessed and eventually placed in a facility where routine and schedules would define the rest of her life. Her internment would be in some dismal place where humans were treated like laboratory rats. Whatever mental ability remained, she would never be given credit or acknowledgement for thinking a single thought. In desperation, she would scream to be understood, but no one would hear. She would be the prisoner of infirmity.

Deuteronomy would be there. He would have her somewhere close so he could visit her regularly, four or five times a week. He would never marry or allow himself to love because he too would be a victim of the same routine. He would grow old without realizing it and die unfulfilled. He was a good man, and he deserved better.

Time had passed. She could hear the sound of footsteps out in the hallway. It sounded like at least a dozen men. She was becoming more and more dizzy, struggling to retain the dominant voice with all the sounds and voices swirling in her head. She loved Deuteronomy. She really loved that man, though he would never realize how much.

She couldn't tell if the knocking she was hearing was coming from the door or from someplace in her head. She didn't know if her merely *thinking* about someone knocking had created the sensation of sound she was hearing.

The physical door seemed to be in a cycle of backing and approaching, nearly touching her nose once and then retreating twenty feet away. Tilting her head back, she placed the gun barrel at the top of her throat, at the apex of her neck, aiming upward at an angle that would assure the greatest damage.

Love told her that she had to let him go. She had gambled and had lost. It wasn't fair. Her whole life had been one huge injustice, one big, *fucked up* travesty. Why were other people allowed to be happy, to take ease in love and life, to enjoy the freedom and exhilaration of being human and to feel communion with the universe?

And why were the wicked, Madame Toussainte among them, allowed to live such long and prosperous lives, while Katrina had been doomed from the moment she met the old woman, and perhaps from the moment she had been born?

Mama Jezebel said it back in her room at Saint Mary's: *not even God can change the past, and she was right. Not even God can change what destiny has designed.* Katrina realized at last the die had been cast. More than thirty years earlier, Katrina set in motion a series of events that caused her sister's death and doomed her to a life of sorrow and sadness, a life under a curse that could never be lifted.

It was her curse, but not his, and she was running out of time. If she really loved Deuteronomy and the idea of freedom, she had to put an end it to a lost cause. St. Jude had abandoned her long ago. She was not going back to a hospital. Perhaps there was a better life on the other side.

Someone was knocking with a greater sense of urgency and there were loud murky, voices on the other side of the door. Someone was calling her name. Slowly, she eased down to her knees, the cold gun barrel still pointed in her throat. And strangely, from that place of humility, she could see Bianca. Her sister was smiling toward her, welcoming her.

When the door opened, Brady stood there frozen, his eyes beckoning her to relent from her apparent course. He shouted something she could not understand. Too late. Not even God could change the past, but Katrina had seized control of the future, and not just her own. She smiled.

"Brady, listen carefully. Remember these words: *There, in the very middle, and I will punish him and escape from everyone and from myself.*"

She affected composure right to the last moment.

"Please tell Ronnie I love him."

When she pulled the trigger, the gun produced nothing more than a loud click in the silence of the room. Desperate, she closed her eyes and pulled again. The gunshot was sudden and loud, the bullet exploding through the top of her head, carrying her life and soul upward through a thin veil of bright red blood. Her limp body crashed to the floor below, her shoulders and hands twitching.

As officers began to crowd in from behind, Brady was only beginning to consider the significance of the event he had just witnessed. Katrina Saint Claire, for all her personality and her great intellect, was dead. But why? The *voodoo* curse had been lifted and she had won her release from Saint Mary's. She was an incredible, beautiful woman at the beginning of a wonderful new life. Why would she shoot herself?

Brady was beginning to understand what Saint Claire had been saying all along, that nothing was random. At breakfast earlier with Slater, he finally realized what was required to be Saint Claire's friend. It was trust, and it worked both ways. Slater was Saint Claire's friend because he trusted him and he respected his friend's right to privacy.

Overall, Saint Claire *did* share, but he shared nothing more than he needed to. A true friend, like Slater, had learned to accept his terms. Saint Claire's bizarre mind was always going in a dozen different directions. Sharing all his suspicions would be too much for most people to bear, so he kept them to himself.

Katrina's hand twitched a final time as the puddle of blood surrounding her head grew, resembling a nimbus, a halo of sorts. As he heard the siren from the approaching ambulance over the whispering in the room, Brady was struck with the most troubling thought: Who was going to tell Saint Claire?

CHAPTER 58

The mayor of Sausalito received a private phone call from San Francisco mayor David Douglas, who made an unusual request. As a result, the city was uncharacteristically restrictive to reporters who arrived at the scene of the Katrina Saint Claire suicide. Police extended the crime scene perimeter to the street in front of the building and to the property line along the sides and the back. No officer spoke with reporters. The silence only added to the sense of mystery.

After eight hours however, details of the story began to emerge. Katrina Saint Claire had indeed committed suicide. She had taken her own life by firing a bullet through her brain as San Francisco police Inspector Tom Brady, a special unit of the Sausalito police department and Sausalito city detectives looked on. But most remarkable was the fact that the gun used for the suicide was the same gun that had been stolen from Inspector Deuteronomy Saint Claire, presumably the same gun that had been used in the murder of police Captain Sonia Sanchez.

Anxious to put it all together, television news stories began to suggest Katrina, recently released from a mental institution, murdered Sonia after discovering the captain was having an affair with her husband. Experts suggested that Katrina should have never been released from Saint Mary's.

After hours of speculation, several media analysts advanced a general theory. Katrina figured out about the affair a month or so earlier, and that was why she so abruptly petitioned to leave the hospital. Shortly after leaving, she managed to get an exact match to her husband's gun and switched it out with his. When she called Saint Claire from her cell phone on the morning of the Sanchez murder, insisting he come over, she was actually outside his building. She watched him leave, and once the coast was clear, she went inside and shot Sonia in her sleep with her husband's gun.

No one had an explanation for the flowers strewn about the bed, but most concluded that she staged the break-in and attack at her apartment days before the murder in order to deflect suspicion away from her. The ear could have come from anyone.

During the two days after the killing, they added, Katrina began to feel guilty about what she had done. She had murdered a police captain, a mother of two, and framed her husband for the murder. She had exacted revenge on both, but at a painful price. The guilt eventually consumed her, culminating in the 911 emergency call and her suicide. She had taken her own life with the Sanchez murder weapon in order to free the man she loved.

Another theory suggested she was the *Undead* killer all along and had used her expert knowledge of drugs and poisons along with an accomplice on the outside to set up murders one through five. When analysts counted Gladys Rosenthal as murder number one, Katrina's suicide became the seventh murder, a self-murder.

At the jail, Saint Claire was isolated from other prisoners and the guards were instructed not to speak with him, lest someone mention Katrina's suicide. Saint Claire realized, however, something was amiss and began to press guards for answers. The defensive reaction he got from them only confirmed his suspicion. There was something rotten in the city of San Francisco.

Former Police Captain Derrick Slater had never been a big fan of the mayor, but urged by Oksana and Brady, he reluctantly agreed to the meeting at City Hall. News of the Katrina Saint Claire suicide had been hard to fathom. Two days earlier, he had lunch with her in Sausalito at the restaurant next to the spa. At a table by the huge window, Katrina gushed about how wonderful freedom felt, about the exciting things she looked forward to in her new life.

Slater felt for his friend, who had already lost a daughter and a son, and now a wife. He knew Saint Claire loved Katrina in a way most people could not appreciate or comprehend. Despite her rants, explosions and the games she played, she was his best friend, the only person alive who truly understood him.

Slater knew the mayor would ask him to break the news to the inspector, but he didn't anticipate Douglas' effort to manipulate the facts. The man seemed desperate.

"You have to let Saint Claire know the same thing could have and probably would have happened if he was out there. I mean, when Brady opened the door, she was still alive. He tried to stop her, but she was hell bent on doing it. No one could have stopped her! Let's face it, Katrina Saint Claire had problems. They should have never released her from Saint Mary's. That's who he oughta go after, the doctors who released her. She and Sanchez would be alive today if they had never let her out."

Slater nodded and stood.

"Okay, I've heard what you had to say. Can I go now?"

Douglas stood.

"You're his best friend. That is, if a guy like Saint Claire can *have* a best friend. You have to make him understand it wasn't my fault. As a matter of fact, I didn't even want to *arrest* him in the first place. It was Brady and that harebrained idea about goin after Saint Claire's secret notebooks. My mistake, I should have known better. You can tell him I *fired* McCarthy for that shit, and I'll fire Brady if that'll make him feel better."

Slater stared straight ahead.

"Is that all, Mr. Mayor?"

Douglas sighed and nodded.

"Help me out here, Slater, will ya? Help the *city* out. I'll *owe* ya."

"That's all well and good, Douglas, but all I can think about right now is my friend who just lost his wife and what I owe him."

The story of Police Chief Rebecca Leong's disappearance ran on the news concurrently with the story of Katrina Saint Claire's suicide and continuing details from the investigation. According to Sonoma county sheriff deputies, the chief's car was found outside a hotel in Santa Rosa, off Highway 12.

The front desk clerk said Leong had checked in at around 11 pm three days earlier. However, when the maid went in to clean the room the next morning, the bed hadn't been slept in, though the chief's luggage was still in the closet. After a second day and a similar report from another maid, the daytime manager's interest was piqued by a story about the chief's disappearance on KRON and he compared the chief's name against those on the guest register.

Detectives checking the room reported her luggage had never been opened and her purse, containing her wallet, cell phone and car keys was still on the bathroom counter, undisturbed. There was no sign of a struggle, but investigators could only conclude the worst. She had vanished from the room without a trace.

The last phone call she made was to Captain Brett Schneider from Metro division, field operations. At 8 pm, she had called and asked if he would oversee the inspection of Gisele Ferreira's apartment. Before that, she spent time meeting with Saint Claire. Mica, Leong's distraught personal assistant, said the chief seemed upset after her visit with the detective. After that encounter, Rebecca went to her office, called Schneider and then left without saying a word.

It took a while, but somewhere in the course of airing and rehashing the story, one reporter, while crediting Brady with the insight, alluded to the unexplained disappearance of Police Chief William J. Biggy and his unsolved murder. Sonoma county sheriff deputies searched the rest of the hotel and three mile perimeter for her body, but just as it had been in the case of Biggy, the police had no leads.

After Katrina committed suicide with the murder weapon from the Sanchez case, it become clear that Saint Claire couldn't have murdered Sanchez, unless the two were working in league. If Katrina really was the cold-blooded killer some were making her out to be, analysts argued that a guilt driven suicide would have been out of character.

However, in breaking news, details began to emerge from the search of her apartment. Police had found a vial containing batrachotoxin, the frog poison used in the Father O'Brien murder, in a box under her bathroom sink. They also discovered traces of ricin in a clear, square, one-inch, zipped-topped plastic bag in the same box. And in the kitchen drawer, there were four six-inch pine dowels similar to those used in the Vang murder, tucked away next to the steak knives.

Curious observers began to ask why Saint Claire was still in jail. Paul Perez, acting in the place of Leong, along with the mayor, answered that the inspector was in the process of being released. He said the department's sympathy went out to the detective, not just for the loss of his wife, but for the ironic realization that she could realistically be the killer he had been seeking for the last twelve years.

Though she promised Deuteronomy she would not watch the news, Gisele found the story of Katrina's suicide impossible to ignore. Deuteronomy was always evasive and uncomfortable discussing her. Gisele gathered that Katrina was intelligent and manipulative, but the thought that Deuteronomy's wife was a serial killer! It made her wonder if Katrina was the person who had been breaking into her apartment. The first break-in corresponded roughly with the day of her release. The very idea made the hairs stand up on Gisele's arms.

Eyes darting about the room, she looked for her markers. The doilies under the lamps—all on point. The magazines on the coffee table, on. The curtains and blinds, on. She rose and went to the kitchen. The settings on the dining table, on. But the sprayhead on the kitchen faucet was at six o'clock. By habit, Gisele always reset it to four o'clock. Someone had been in her apartment!

Rushing back to her living room, she found her cell phone and dialed 911, and then she dialed the number from the house phone, hesitating, afraid to speak aloud. When she went into her bedroom to grab her pre-packed overnight case, she peeked into the bathroom and noticed her medicine cabinet was not completely closed. Frantic, she checked her watch. The police were taking too long! She couldn't wait. What if someone was in the apartment, in the bathroom or a closet!

When she yanked the front door open and saw him, she gasped, unable to scream. Grabbing her right arm, he pulled her toward him, clutching her under his left arm while showing the gun in his right.

"Come on out and close the door."

She complied carefully, struggling to contain her emotion. She did not want to give him the satisfaction of seeing her afraid.

"If you plan on killing me, you might as well kill me now. I will not be a stake in some poker game."

He smiled as he guided her toward the stairs at the rear of the building.

"You underestimate me. If I planned to kill you, you would have been in the grave a long time ago. We're unlikely allies. If I get my way, you'll still be alive when this is all over."

CHAPTER 15

"Katrina's dead."

Saint Claire did not react to the words. He just stared straight ahead.

"Did you hear me? I said *Katrina's* dead."

When two solemn guards escorted him from his cell after telling him he was being released, the detective sensed the sixth murder had already occurred, but he was unprepared for this news.

Saint Claire froze, thinking of the last time he saw Katrina. Just before she left, when she had stood in the doorway and looked back at him smiling, it was as if for the first time in more than twenty years there was a real connection. He could still see her face, her smile, a longing look in her eyes. The thought of her being dead was unimaginable.

Spirit defeated, he looked toward Slater.

"What happened?"

"It was a suicide."

"Bullshit! She was murdered."

Slater took a breath.

"No, she committed suicide. Brady witnessed it."

"No, you're just not seeing this thing. Wait—why would Brady be there?"

Slater presented a report.

"She called 911, and Brady just happened to be in the area when the police responded. When they forced the door open, he was right there. She was alive, and then she pulled the trigger. She shot herself, through the brain."

Saint Claire wagged his head, tears swelling his eyes, blurring his vision.

"No, it couldn't have happened like that. If that's what she wanted, why would she call 911? Katrina would never have committed suicide... unless someone found some way to force her to do it."

Slater sighed.

"She was alone. Look, I know this is a shock for you. It was a shock for me, but you have to read that report. The gun she used to do it was the gun issued to you, the one stolen from you, the same gun used in the Sanchez murder. She had the gun."

"She didn't murder Sanchez. *Kain* did. I don't know how she got that gun, but the whole thing was a set-up. You know how he is! She was murder number six."

Slater felt sorry for his wounded and desperate friend. He wanted to be comforting, but he had to be honest.

"That frog poison used to kill the priest, very rare. They found a small container of it in a box under her bathroom sink."

"Are you hearing yourself Slater? Don't you think that's a little too convenient? You taught me that, remember? And I'll bet they found the ricin in the same box?"

Slater nodded.

"As a matter of fact, they did. And they found dowels like the ones used on Vang in a kitchen drawer."

"Are you *hearing* yourself? Leong and Douglas and the rest of those assholes might be stupid or hopeful enough to believe and follow those leads, but not you! This whole thing's been a set-up from the beginning. I'm here because he wanted me here, and I'm out because he wants to finish this thing today. You have to trust me on this!"

Slater thought for a few seconds.

"You're right. I think you're right. If he made her commit suicide the way she did, he is what he says he is. But what do you think he wants? Are you really number seven? Leong's missing. She's been missing three days now."

"I thought she would be number six. Is she dead?"

"No, just missing. Disappeared, just like chief Biggy in that case you've been tryin ta solve over the last few months. Brady pointed that out. It's all over the news."

Saint Claire sat and closed his eyes, thinking.

"First Supervisor Pearce, then Sanchez and then Katrina. He might have Leong, but she's not dead, not yet, not till after this thing's over."

Slater shrugged.

"I don't get it. What's goin on here? The killer framed Katrina so he could get you out, but what does he want from you? What does he want you to do?"

Saint Claire shrugged and shook his head.

"It all makes sense. He said it in the first letter. He's doing these killings and creating all this publicity to focus the world's attention on him and serial killers, with me right in the middle of the storm. He wants me to make him into some sort of messianic icon."

He dragged his fingers back over his head to smooth his hair.

"He made it to murder six. At seven, he wants to force me to raise him from the dead. He said in the letter he was going to force me to tell the world his story, to make him the greatest serial murder artist of all time. I have to find a way to stop him. If he wins, I have to give him greatness."

Tears spilled from his eyes.

"He killed Katrina, and I won't reward him for that. Whatever it takes, I'm going to make sure no one knows anything about him or about anything he's done. I'm going to destroy this asshole."

Slater stood, ready to leave.

"I'm right there with ya. How can I help?"

Saint Claire stopped before opening the door.

"Well, first of all, we have to go to your storage and burn all my notebooks."

Slater seemed confused.

"You do that you won't have any evidence against him."

"It won't matter."

"Why not?"

Saint Claire swallowed and bowed his head.

"Because after he's dead, I don't want anyone to know anything about him. In order for me to win this thing, he's got to go to his grave unknown."

He tightened his tie.

"Even if I've got to go with him."

CHAPTER 60

"I'm sorry about Katrina."

"Just cut it."

His throat was tight again. He sipped the brandy and swallowed to relax the muscles.

"Don't be mistaken. The only reason I'm talking to you is because you're the last person who saw her alive. You betrayed me, and for that I don't like or respect you. It's just ironic you keep popping up. If it isn't coincidence, I'd think he's using you, but I always figured you to be the wild card in this thing."

Looking away, Brady sighed.

"And I always thought you believed in God."

Saint Claire bowed his head, reflecting.

"I *do* believe in God."

"Well, if it isn't coincidence, it doesn't have to be Kain. Maybe it's *God*! Maybe it's divine intervention, divine justice. Maybe it's bigger than you. Maybe *God* isn't going to let him get away with this!"

It was a profound thought.

"Brady, in all the time I've known you, that's the first really intelligent thing I've ever heard you say. Maybe you're right, and maybe I needed to hear that. Thank you."

The men sat in silence for a moment.

When Saint Claire got out the jail, he tried to find Gisele, but she was missing, and Leong was still missing. Frustrated, he called Brady for a meeting at his local bar hangout on Fillmore. He had to know.

"Did she really commit suicide?"

"That's what it looked like to me. She was on her knees when I came in the door. She recognized me, and then she said something crazy."

Brady caught himself. He hadn't meant to use the word.

"I'm sorry. I would have stopped her if I could've, but it happened so fast."

Saint Claire stared at him.

"Do you remember what she said?"

Brady retrieved his wallet from his back pocket, and from that wallet he pulled out a white slip of paper.

"One of the detectives wrote it down. She said, *there, in the very middle, and I will punish him and escape from everyone and from myself.* I tried an Internet search, but nothing came back that made any sense."

Saint Claire nodded.

"Oh, it makes sense all right."

He stood and squinted at the tab before throwing money on the bar.

"Thanks Brady. Maybe it's divine justice *after* all. See ya round."

Headed north up the Redwood freeway, it made more sense to stop first at Slater's home on Wolfback Ridge Road, since Katrina's apartment on Sherwood Drive was miles further up the highway. Slater had driven him from the jail to his condominium, where he showered and picked up his car.

Katrina had apparently stopped by his condo when he was away. She had left white irises and a large tin of the almonds he liked. On the way out the door, Slater invited Saint Claire to his house, where Oksana had prepared a "healthy" lunch.

In the silence of the car on the way over, Saint Claire could only think of Katrina and feel a growing sense of desolation. There was a void in his chest, an emptiness reaching to the very pit of his stomach. He imagined her last thoughts.

Brady said her final words were, "tell Ronnie I love him." He wondered what Kain had said or done to make her feel *suicide* was the lesser of two evils. The line Brady repeated was from Katrina's favorite book, words spoken by a character whose intellect and desperation she understood.

When Oksana saw the detective, she hugged him long and hard.

"I am here if you need anything, Ronnie. I am sorry about Katrina. I really liked her after I met her."

At lunch the plates were artfully arranged and the food was well prepared, but Saint Claire could not eat. He felt numb and disoriented. When he tried to smile, he had no control over the muscles of his face.

Oksana tried to be understanding and supportive. She continually poured the *gewürztraminer*, which was about the only substance at the table he could stomach. Afterward, Saint Claire went with Slater to the recess for stronger libation.

Through all the despair, guilt and anger he felt, he really needed a friend.

"I'm turning over my badge today, so these are my last couple hours as a cop.

He leaned in.

"I'm going to kill that bastard even if it sends me back to jail."

"You said earlier you think he *wants* you to kill him, that he wants to make you kill im."

"He does, because if I kill him, I'll have to answer for it, and that means I'll have to tell the world his story, and that's where he's wrong."

Slater poured a brandy for his distraught friend, who continued.

"I could kill him and just clam up. Let them put me in jail for murder, but I don't have to say anything. I could do seven years standing on my head if it meant sending him to Hell without a nametag."

Slater shrugged.

"He's smart. You don't wanna admit it, but he's smart. Do you think he hasn't thought of that? He's gotta have a counter for you doin that. He's been ahead of you the whole time."

Saint Claire sipped from the snifter.

"You're probably right, and that's why we've got to burn the notebooks and all the evidence I collected against him. As a matter of fact, we need to do that right now."

Slater had stowed Saint Claire's files in a mini storage facility on Bridgeway. The facility was modern and well-guarded. Saint Claire parked in front of the office and rode with Slater inside, past two rows of garage-sized units, complete with roll-down doors. The truck came to a stop along a row on a diagonal across from the manager's office. The smaller units in this area were inside the buildings, with a common access door.

Slater unlatched the dolly in the truck bed and led the way inside, down a dark, musty, cobweb-infested hallway. He stopped at a whitewashed door on the right near the end with the number 112 painted at eye level. Sifting through his keys, he found the match, unhinged the lock and yanked the door open.

"Goddammit! I don't *believe* this!"

He closed the door and checked the number again, and then he checked the lock.

"I locked em in here just a few days ago. I didn't even tell Oksana! Who could have known?'

Both already knew, but Saint Claire had to see it with his own eyes. He stepped inside the empty room. All his research, notebooks and evidence were gone.

"It's the same problem I've had with him all along. He's always been just a step, just minutes ahead. And here we are in the final hour."

Saint Claire's frustration showed on his face and in his clenched jaw.

"Yeah he's smart. All things being equal, this hasn't been *fair* to me all along. If I ever needed to catch a break, Slater, I need to catch one now."

CHAPTER 61

The caked, rust-colored bloodstain was still on the carpet in the place where Katrina's head had fallen. Saint Claire froze just before it, imagining the scene. Had he been standing there a day earlier, he could have saved her. Together they would have figured it out, and together they would have prevailed.

But Kain had managed to divide them, and so for the moment, it seemed Kain had conquered. Saint Claire, however, did not believe Kain had outmaneuvered Katrina. There was more to her suicide than the obvious and she had hidden the answer somewhere in the apartment.

The last words she spoke, *there, in the very middle, and I will punish him and escape from everyone and from myself,* came from Tolstoy's Anna Karenina, Katrina's favorite novel from the time she was a teenage girl. Anna spoke the words just before committing suicide by throwing herself in the path of an oncoming train. The meaning, he supposed, was less cryptic and more literal.

Like her husband, Katrina valued books, venerable, tattered, physical works of art that always outlived their owners. She was fond of the say she had learned from her grandfather, "Whenever there is a quandary, dilemma or trouble brewin in the soul, the answer can always be found in a book.

He went to her *petite bibliothèque* to start his systematic search, beginning with scrapbooks and photo albums he had no idea she had stored away for so many years. There were pictures of his mother, and father; there was a photo of Deuteronomy at his kindergarten graduation, awkwardly bowing with his back to the audience; there were pictures of Christian as a baby and as a boy; there was another of Benjamin Scott and Bernadette Nicholas at the high school prom; there was that photo of Geneviève in her crib, the one that tugged at his heart. He couldn't even look at it.

And finally, there were pictures of Katrina at various stages of her life: as a baby, as a snaggletooth little girl, as a member of the seventh grade field hockey team, as she proudly posed with fellow eighth grade graduates, as class president during her junior year, as a college student and as a bride. Then there was the picture she cherished most, a photo of her and

Bianca hugging right after winning a dance contest. At first glance, they seemed like twins, though Katrina was slightly darker. Dressed in clumsy costumes they had sewn at home, both seemed so happy.

Many of the books planned for filling the empty shelves were still in boxes against the wall. Saint Claire knelt by a large box and cut through the tape with the blade of his utility knife. She had packed the box full to the top. He stopped. If she placed the clue in the middle of a book, it must have been from one of the already opened boxes, or a book that was not in the library.

Suddenly it hit him. Library aside, it was the one room in a home where books were revered. And that's where he found the Tolstoy novel, on a shelf in the bathroom.

He let the book fall open in his hands to reveal the pink, perfumed sheet of paper, folded neatly in half. Shutting his eyes for a moment, he took the note and unfolded it. He batted his eyes slowly, searching for desperate, scrawled words through warm, stinging tears.

Though most experts were convinced Katrina was either innocent of the *Undead* murders or had had an accomplice, the San Francisco police considered the Sonia Sanchez murder solved, as well as the murders of four other victims.

Sonia's funeral was scheduled for the following Monday. The mayor, the governor and a prominent Latina actor were scheduled to speak. There was also great public interest in Katrina's funeral, but inside sources suggested it would be a private service conducted at an undisclosed location at an undisclosed time.

The mayor remained low key throughout the media frenzy. From the moment the story broke about Katrina's suicide, Douglas stayed cloistered in his office, avoiding questions from reporters. He issued a statement through a spokesperson expressing relief that the killer had been stopped and indicating a need for a better follow-up procedure for recently-released mental patients. Rather than blaming Katrina, he condemned the hospital for failing her and other *troubled souls* like her.

Nevertheless, the prospect of an international audience held a seduction the mayor could not resist. He agreed to a press conference where he would speak on the Civic Center stage, standing between the governor and the congressional house speaker. Minutes before the event, however, the mayor grew concerned about the considerable risk he was about to take.

He asked the interim chief to station his most loyal officers around the stage with specific orders to bar any attempt by Saint Claire to approach, and he asked the governor to instruct the state police guarding the building's entrances to hold the inspector at the door if he tried to enter.

Despite the security, the mayor still appeared uneasy at the press conference. During a generous introduction by the state's chief executive, Douglas' eyes nervously scanned the audience.

"Citizens of San Francisco, and by extension my fellow Americans, in the last thirty days our city has undergone an ordeal, an ordeal that underscores an ugly aberration in American society. As cities grow and the world becomes a smaller, more closely-knit community, we *all* will have to face the scourge of the serial killer who, like the terrorists that plague us here and abroad, is a faceless, nameless enemy of society."

He took a deep breath, seeming to become more comfortable.

"In crowded cities all over the world, these monsters prey on us. According to sociologists, it's an epidemic that has resulted from population growth. In fact, numbers show we, in large cities, are more likely to lose our lives to our own serial killers and our neighbors than we are to foreign terrorists."

He raised his hands.

"So what are we to do? How are we to defend ourselves? There has been much study, and much debate. Some geneticists say one day these killers can be identified through DNA testing. Individuals possessing this killer gene and their families can be identified, and potential killers can be quietly monitored by law enforcement. But to many, that would be un-American, an invasion of privacy.

"Maybe it would be an invasion, and maybe we need to consider other solutions, but one thing is certain. This problem is going to get worse over time, especially with the world population and cities growing at unprecedented rates and the fact that the public has a fascination, or more disturbing, an unexplainable admiration for these sick individuals. Just look at what's happened in San Francisco. And it's the same sick obsession in other big cities all over the world. They're selling murderabilia on eBay for God sakes! And some of it is reportedly being sold by the killers themselves!"

He found the greatest concentration of cameras and stared directly toward them.

"My advice to the public is this: stop being part of the problem, stop contributing to these monsters, stop buying their books, stop watching the serial killer docudramas on cable television and stop going to movies made about them. Don't let the media give these guys the fame they're after, and by all means, don't finance the next series of murders by paying your money on *eBay*. We have to ignore these guys. They won't go away, but we should never, under any circumstances, give them the fame they're after."

He paused, nodding slowly.

"Things are far from wrapped up here in San Francisco. At this moment, we don't know for sure that the murderer of Police Captain Sanchez is this *Undead* killer, but police have collected evidence that indicates there is a strong probability the person who murdered Sanchez was somehow involved in the previous four murders. They're seeking a white male, possibly in his late twenties or early thirties, and who goes by the name *Kain*, as a possible accomplice. You can find a sketch of this individual on the front page of this morning's paper and at the furthermost exit of this room."

Once again, his eyes found the cameras.

"If any of you out there have any information about this individual or any of these recent murders, please contact the police department immediately."

He looked toward the congressional House Speaker.

"Now, I have as my very special guest today, all the way from Washington DC, but originally from San Francisco, one of our very own, a woman of great vision and indisputable integrity, a woman who has represented the needs of our city, our state and indeed our country with all the—"

"It's Saint Claire!"

The reporter who shouted the announcement shifted the focus of many in the room as well as several of the cameras to an entrance where the detective stood, flanked by state police officers belonging to the governor's security detail. The two at his sides faced backward, restraining the detective's arms, while the third stood in front of Saint Claire, weapon inconspicuously drawn.

The detective's gamble paid off. Much of the attention in the room shifted to the officers, who reluctantly released the detective. He advanced boldly to the center of the hushed room, shouting.

"Katrina Saint Claire is not the killer! She did not murder Captain Sanchez and she did not commit suicide! She was murdered."

He waited for the murmuring in the room to subside before continuing.

"Sonia Sanchez, I could not save, though I would have given my life in place of hers, I swear it. But Katrina Saint Claire, my wife, I could have saved her, if not for that man there."

He pointed toward Mayor Douglas, who flinched as if he had been shot.

"I wanted to save lives, and I literally begged him to help me do that, but that man does not care! He didn't care about Sonia Sanchez, he didn't care about my wife. They're both dead because of him. And make no mistake—he doesn't care about anyone in San Francisco, but himself."

Saint Claire had surprised even himself. When he forced his way past the guards, he had no idea what he was going to say to reporters and onlookers, if even he got the opportunity to do so. He hadn't counted on being allowed to speak publicly, let alone to a television audience. Finally, his luck had turned.

"We all know Chief Leong is missing. Now there's a life I can save, God willing. If her life can be saved, I'll save it, and in the process I'll prove Katrina Saint Claire was not a killer and did not commit suicide."

He reached into the inside pocket of his jacket.

"But I won't do it as a cop. I refuse to work for Mayor Douglas one minute longer."

He called toward the stage.

"So Mr. Mayor, I am formally tendering my resignation. I no longer answer to you. You *know* what you can do with this badge."

He relaxed his fingers, allowing the badge tumble to the floor, and then he held his palms outward, halting advancing reporters.

"I won't respond to any questions. You'll have enough to write about when this day is over."

CHAPTER 62

He recognized the smell of blood as he opened the door, a sharp, pungent, slightly chemical odor. It lacked the pheromones of menstrual blood, which he had always been able to distinguish, not by smell, but in a place above his hard palate, in a vomeronasal area just behind his nose when he crinkled it. No, this was venal/arterial blood.

Cautiously, he removed the key and peeked into the living room of his condominium. The lights were on, though he remembered turning them off before he left.

The room was still, and yet it had changed. On the table sat a huge mass of black curly hair and two half-filled wineglasses. A small gray speaker, topped with an antenna, likely a bi-directional baby monitor, sat on the lamp stand next to the couch. He could sense it. Kain was in the house, probably in his study.

He drew his gun and slipped through the front door. Twelve years! He had waited twelve years for this moment. The only exit was at his back, so the confrontation was inevitable. He would come face to face at last with the man who had murdered his son. It was down to two minds, two wills, man verses man.

He spoke, still scanning the room.

"I'm here."

"Welcome to Act Two, Scene Seven, my grand finale!"

The voice, rendered flat and modulated to a higher key through the small speaker, carried an unmistakable arrogance.

"I beat you, Saint Claire, and now I'm going to make you tell the world my story."

Saint Claire stared at the monitor in disbelief, studying the voice. Systematically, he examined the room. He wanted to hear more.

"I'd hardly say you've won. You predicted seven murders in thirty days. It's been almost forty-five. You said you were going to murder your seven from the grave. But if you're in my study, you're obviously still very much alive. There's nothing special about you. You're just a run-of-the-mill thug. Face it, your story isn't worth telling."

The voice was mocking.

"Oh! Ow! You hurt my feelings! You're just getting me so rattled with your insults that I don't know what to do. Who knows? Maybe I'll lose my temper and do something rash or stupid. Any more put-downs, professor? Your plan might be working."

Saint Claire finished checking the sofa and approached the monitor.

"I won't tell your story. That's something you can't make me do."

"Oh but I can, and you will."

The dark red liquid in the crystal glasses was not wine. It was blood, and an odd-shaped object sat at the bottom of one. Drawing closer, he recognized what it was. It was a pearl bracelet, likely the pearl bracelet Gisele always wore on her right wrist. The hair on the table and the blood in the glass were hers. Behind the door, she was Kain's bargaining chip. He continued to case the room as he answered.

"Okay, you're going to make me tell your story, but you've got to know, the story I tell won't be flattering to you. I mean, what am I going to say? Here's the story of the world's greatest serial killer ever? This is the genius who tried to make us all believe he was dead, but he wasn't? He's a murder mastermind so clever that he sneaks up and shoots women in their sleep? What story are you going to make me tell?"

There was no response. After fifteen seconds, Saint Claire spoke again, approaching the door.

"Are you still there?"

The voice sounded angry, articulating careful words.

"Maybe you could tell about how I killed your crazy wife, or rather about how I left her with no choice but to take her own life. Maybe you could tell about her last helpless, desperate moments."

The detective allowed himself to feel anger, though he knew it might work against him.

"Maestro at murder? Isn't that the silly term you used? Tell me, did you outsmart her or did you cheat and stack the deck while she was unconscious?"

The voice was unapologetic.

"Both. I told her I injected Kainic acid into her spinal fluid—yes, when she was unconscious. I attacked her intellect, and after I told her what I had done, she was pitiful. You should have seen your wife. She was convinced if she hadn't shot herself, her brain would have turned to mush and she would have been an incontinent, drooling idiot for the rest of her life. But then again, maybe I was bluffing. Maybe I injected her with a placebo. Either way, she made a choice, but more important, I left her *with* a choice."

Tears in his eyes, Saint Claire nodded. He knew all along Katrina hadn't committed suicide. The white irises she brought were still on the table. In the warmth of the condominium, the buds had opened, effusing redolent, sweet perfume throughout the room.

He had waited twelve years already. He wasn't going to rush the conclusion, and so, holstering his gun, he went to the bar, poured a brandy and savored the first sip. Feeling hunger for the first time all day, he went around the bar and got the tin of almonds Katrina had left him.

They were garlic almonds, his favorite. When he and Katrina were together, she would buy them by the four-pound container and he would go through the can in two weeks if Christian didn't raid his stash under the bar. He remembered having major arguments with his son, who would wipe out his almonds and leave the empty can in the cabinet.

He poured a large quantity of the nuts into a glass bowl and threw a few to the back of his mouth, crunching, reminiscing. He sat and sipped from the snifter.

"And with Sonia Sanchez? Did you leave her with a choice?"

"Sometimes in life there are choices and sometimes there aren't."

He looked toward the door.

"Admit it, your murder from the grave scheme ran out of steam at number four. You couldn't be clever anymore, so you just shot her."

"At five, I was forced by circumstances to change direction, but the conclusion will be the same. In the end, I will have killed seven from the grave."

Saint Claire shrugged.

"But I'm talking to you now! You're alive."

"Death is relative, and so is being alive. You can't tell me Katrina isn't alive, in your memory, and in mine. And by the same token, Christian is dead."

"I'm convinced you want to play a game about this, something I'm not going to do at this point. Come out of my study and let's finish this like men, face to face."

Just then, Saint Claire's cell phone buzzed with a text message. He took the phone from his pocket and furtively checked the screen.

> **From: Tom Brady**
> **Subject: RE:**
> **Msg: Saint claire – brady. Rite outside dor. Hear u talking inside. No whats going on. Plse let me in. Can help. Wild card! Remember?**

Saint Claire made his way to the front door, speaking to cover any sound of the doorknob turning and the door easing open.

"I'm going to make sure nothing about you leaves this condo today. I'll make sure the world knows nothing about you, make sure you remain irrelevant."

Brady slipped in, his gun drawn, as Saint Claire eased the door closed behind him. Pointing, Saint Claire directed Brady to an area along the wall to the right of the door of the study, where he would have a clear shot as the killer crossed the threshold.

"You coming out?"

Saint Claire heard tapping from the other side of the wall, just in front of Brady. When it stopped, the killer called out.

"Why so anxious all of a sudden? You trying to set a trap for me?"

Saint Claire knew right away the words weren't random. He should have expected it! His eyes desperately searched the room, but when he located the camera, it was too late. He yelled toward Brady.

"Get down!"

The shot, fired from the other side of the wall, exploded just in front of Brady's chest, striking him at center mass. He gasped and slid to the floor, trailing bright red blood down the wall.

"Did I get him?"

Saint Claire rushed over to his partner and knelt. Brady, straining to breathe, had fallen facedown. Saint Claire didn't want to turn him over, fearing he might drown in his own blood. Standing, he hurried to the picture frame where the camera was mounted, threw the camera to the floor and stomped on it.

"Come on out, asshole! Coward!"

The laughter was mocking.

"I'm smarter than you are. Who do you think I am?"

"What I think doesn't matter. You are what you are."

"This is the moment I've waited for. I'm coming out."

The killer unlocked the door from the other side.

"The devil hath power
To assume a pleasing shape; yea, and perhaps
Out of your weakness and your melancholy,
As he is very potent with such spirits,
Abuses you to damn you."

When the door opened, he stood there, smiling, his gun drawn.

"Surprise."

He raised his hands.

"You going to shoot me?"

Saint Claire lowered his gun, still in shock, not merely by what he saw, but by the reality that his twelve year ordeal was at its end. His questions and fears had been answered simultaneously.

Lowering his hands, the killer smiled.

"With secret joy indulgent David viewed
His own youthful image in his son renewed."

He walked toward the detective, effusing confidence.

"My father! Dad, you promised over a dozen years ago you wouldn't give up on me, and you haven't. For that, I thank you. And because of that, I knew this moment would come, my resurrection!"

Saint Claire's eyes checked the young man's left hand in disbelief. The pinkie was missing.

"Who are you?"

"You know who I am. I've bleached my skin and hair over the years, but it's me. Oh, I get it. You're thinking if you don't acknowledge me as your son it'll frustrate my plan? You don't want to play, but you have to make the next move. You have to play."

Still in shock, Saint Claire glanced toward Brady, who wasn't moving.

"Why?"

"Why do you have to play or why are we standing here today?"

"Yes, to both."

Kain smiled, walked to Brady's body, and nudged it with his foot. He reached down, took the detective's gun and tucked it in the back of his own waistband. Then he grabbed Brady by his hair and a back pocket, forcing him to stand, speaking all the while.

"Tom Brady, your new partner. This all works out. Now I have a witness, or leverage, however you want to play it."

Brady groaned. He was bleeding from a wound just below his right clavicle. Also, when the bullet hit him, Brady's teeth clamped down on his bottom lip with so much force that it split open and trailed blood down his chin. Gun still drawn, Kain pulled a kitchen chair to the center of the floor and forced Brady to sit, slumped in the seat.

Saint Claire shrugged.

"Maybe a witness, but he's not leverage by me. Go ahead, shoot him again. I never liked him."

Kain laughed at the look of betrayal on Brady's face. Turning back toward Saint Claire, he removed his black beanie.

"Matching ears, like father, like son!"

The smile disappeared.

"I'm a killer, you're a killer. You just don't know it yet, but you're learning. You want to kill me, don't you? You're going to kill me before it's all over. You're going to kill your own son. Don't cha love the irony? For twelve years you've been after your son's killer, and today you find out it's you!"

He turned, went around the wood framed sofa and sat.

"If you pour me a brandy, Dad, I'll let you know what you're up against."

Kain smiled, motioning with the gun.

"Come on, humor me."

On the way to the bar, Saint Claire re-holstered his gun. His left hand fingered the phone in his jacket pocket. He almost dialed 911 for Brady's benefit, but he realized police outside the door would only create a hostage situation. If they came in shooting, everyone inside would die, including Gisele.

He placed the snifter on the table and poured brandy for his son. However, instead of taking up the snifter, Kain reached for one of the blood-filled wineglasses, took a long sip and nodded.

"Ahh, that's good. That's *very* good! Excellent balance. A little iron deficient, slightly anemic. She must have had her period last week."

He licked his lips and sipped again.

"The perfect aperitif. I poured one for you. It's still a little warm."

Setting the glass down, he took the snifter and drank.

"She's back there in your study. Talks alotta shit for a hostage. I had to gag her. That's her hair and eyebrows there. You don't want to see her, believe me. Looks like uncle Fester."

He leaned forward and placed his gun on the table.

"Here's the deal. You kill me—you save your life and the lives of three, no, no, four other people, but you'll be forced to tell my story. Try and get clever, all six of us die and you still tell my story."

He smiled.

"You already know. I have your files, your notebooks, your notes and evidence, all safely stowed. And with them I've included my life story, ironically written by you, Deuteronomy Saint Claire, based on the evidence. And you said I was wasting my time majoring in Lit! It's a bestseller. But unfortunately, you won't be around to sign copies."

Saint Claire sat on the upholstered seatee to the left perpendicular of the sofa.

"You haven't thought of everything. What if it turns out I wound or otherwise incapacitate you and arrest you? You'll spend the rest of your life in prison, in solitary."

"You shoot me and I'll die, period. For the last two days I've been taking *coumadin*. It's a blood thinner. Took a high dose just before you came in. Even a superficial wound would be mortal, eventually. But I'd have enough time to shoot you and your lover back there. And naturally the three others would die."

Again the reference. Saint Claire shrugged, turning toward Kain.

"Who are the other three?"

"Two you already know. Your partner Brady here and Rebecca Leong, your chief."

He took a sip of the brandy.

"Early this morning, I took her out to Angel Island, to a remote rocky shoreline I know very well. There's a cave there, a cozy little spot, and it usually stays pretty dry."

He reached across the table and took the bottle, pouring first for his father, and then for himself.

"But today's a new moon, meaning at some point today, which is in roughly four hours, the moon and the sun will align. At that point, the envelope of the tide generating forces of the sun will augment that of the moon. The result—an unusually high composite tide, a spring tide. And that cave that's dry for twenty-eight days of the month will become completely submerged, with the police chief in it."

He sipped and smiled proudly.

"Her wrists, ankles and mouth are bound with water-dispersible, pressure-sensitive tape. It dissolves in seawater, but unfortunately for your chief, the amount I used will take about ten minutes to dissolve, and I don't think she can hold her breath that long."

He sat back.

"The force of the ebbing tide will wash her out of the cave, so they'll find her drowned, floating off the rocks in a week or so, and they'll have no idea how their chief of police met her end."

He looked up into his father's eyes.

"What do you think? Brilliant?"

Saint Claire stifled any reaction.

"Not really."

"Oh come on! When are you ever going to give me my proper credit for having a brain? I spent my life looking up to you, and you've spent yours looking down on me. We're eye to eye now, Dad. No, I'm taller. Now you have to give me credit. You can't have 'brilliant' all to yourself, professor."

Saint Claire studied the good-looking young man across from him. He had grown so much older, but there were certain things about him that had not changed. The edges of his eyes, his mouth! And he looked so much like Katrina!

"Is *that* what this about? You don't feel you ever got enough credit from me? You want to prove to the world how smart you are?"

"I'm the smartest killer ever. You can't deny that. You tell me. Has there *ever* been anyone smarter?"

Saint Claire sighed. In his own notes, documentation and memory, he couldn't imagine a killer more cold, calculating and prolific, but he wouldn't admit it. And with the thought, the implication of accepting this killer's identity was painful to consider. For years, when he thought of his lost son, he recalled images of Christian as a handsome little boy and as an intelligent though troubled teenager. Could this same boy have grown up and killed his own mother and so many others?

"You had the potential to be brilliant. You had the potential to be smarter than I could ever be, but you wasted it."

"No, *you* wasted it. You're a natural killer, a vampire. You thirst for blood just like me, and you satisfy that lust when you linger at your murder crime scenes, especially the gory ones. I've *watched* you do it. You're obsessed with blood and death just like I am."

He reached for the wineglass and finished off the deep red liquid.

"Ever hear the expression, *those who can, do, those who can't, teach*? You've sublimated it for all this time. You managed to find a socially acceptable way to indulge your thirst, as a teacher and then as a detective."

He lifted the second wineglass and set it in front of his father.

"Have a sip. It's delicious."

He smiled, sitting back

"Tonight, you're going to cross that threshold. Killing me will mark your unique rite of passage to becoming what you truly are, a vampire killer just like me."

"I'm not a killer."

"Oh but you *are!*"

Kain laughed, nodding.

"And you're just as vain as I am. I mean, you are my father, after all."

He leaned forward.

"In the book I wrote, the one by *you* of course, you don't quite come across as brilliant. I outsmart you at every pass, as in actual life. You're constantly in awe of me, and finally you plot to murder me because you envy me. I am the killer you wish you could be. But unlike you, I accept what I am."

"A killer by choice?"

"No, a killer by nature, a force of nature. Why do so many people accept the notion a person can be born with a genetic predisposition to become gay? We're humans! The most competitive species on earth! We've always killed and murdered our competition. So why is it so hard to understand and accept some of are born with a genetic predisposition to kill?"

He removed Brady's gun from his waistband, placed it on the table, and settled into the sofa.

"I know all about Percival Scott, my mother's grandfather, *my* great grandfather. When they counted all the bodies, he had murdered at least forty-three people, and that was back in the 1940s and 50s. I also know he wasn't just my mother's grandfather. He was *your* grandfather too. And that means I inherited the predisposition from both sides."

He looked over at Brady, who had slumped forward. There was a growing puddle of blood on the wooden floor in front of the chair.

"Did your partner ever tell you that, Inspector Brady? Did he ever tell you he was married to his flesh and blood *sister*?"

He laughed.

"My father is mine uncle. A little less than kin, a little more than kind."

Saint Claire pressed the interrogation.

"And Michael Rad?"

Kain smiled proudly.

"As you've figured out by now, when I staged my own murder, I needed a body. Michael was an incredible killer who taught me a lot, but I outgrew him. Besides that, there's only room for one at the top. He was in my way and he had access to millions of dollars. When I discovered how to convert that access to my purposes, I no longer needed him. He made two mistakes. He was overconfident and he was in love with me."

"So you killed him, burned *his* body in the bathtub and cut off your own finger to stage your murder?"

"I killed Michael Rad *and* Christian Saint Claire that night and became Kain, and since that time, I've walked the earth as a creature of the dark, nameless, cold, 'preying on humans,' as the mayor put it. It's a real hunger with me. I have to kill every few days. It's a thirst. I need to feed."

He picked up the second wineglass and drank, looking away.

"And that's why I need to die. When my story is told, the world's killers will better understand who and what they are. They'll understand their hunger and the nature of themselves as killers. Some will find peace and others, incredible purpose."

He looked back toward his father.

"All you have to do is raise that gun and shoot me. When I fall, you resurrect your son to glory."

He stood, spreading his arms.

"Into your hands, my father, I commend my spirit."

Saint Claire refused to react to Kain's blasphemous attempt at drama.

"I don't buy it. Who's the other person?"

"What other person?"

"You said if I didn't shoot you, three others would die. You said Brady and Leong would be the first and second. So who's the third?"

Kain's eyes flashed as he remembered.

"Oh! I thought you already figured it out. It's your friend, Slater. Don't you just love creatures of habit? After the ordeal with the mercury, after he almost died, he went right back to drinking his Jack Daniel's. He'd make a good laboratory rat."

He nodded.

"I went to his house last night and replaced the bottle up next in his queue. This one has three times more poison than the ones that made him sick. One drink from that bottle and he's dead. So if for some reason you don't walk out of here alive, your friend is toast. Okay, now our little chat is over."

He reached for his gun on the table and handed it to Saint Claire.

"Recognize it? You should because it's your gun. I broke in this condo and switched another gun out for it ten years ago. Look at it."

Saint Claire examined the black Ruger pistol as Kain continued.

"It's the same gun I used to murder your ex-partner, Joe Curry. But I only did what you secretly wanted to do. You knew he was in love with your wife, my mother... and aunt. You were relieved when he was gone. Check it. It's your gun all right."

He presented his chest, closing his eyes.

"And now you're going to use it to kill your son."

Saint Claire raised the gun, pointing it toward Kain's face.

"If it were only that easy. Nature is powerful."

He lowered the gun and put it on the table.

"But there is something more powerful than nature. Pour me another drink."

He went to the bar to retrieve the bowl of almonds as Kain, reluctant, refreshed the snifters.

Saint Claire placed the bowl on the table and sat on the seatee, taking a swig of the brandy.

"I'm working up the nerve, but I still have a couple of questions."

Kain raised his left sleeve, checking his watch.

"Your chief is running out of time, and so are you."

Saint Claire reached for a handful of nuts.

"You made me wait twelve years. If I'm going to kill you, you're going to answer my questions first. You can wait a few more minutes."

He ate a few nuts and took a sip of brandy.

"It's something that's bothered me for all these years. That summer we went to Portugal, your mother, me and you, you remember the four-year-old boy who was found strangled in the bathroom?"

Kain laughed to himself, remembering.

"Yes, I do."

"Was it you?"

"It was me! I watched that little boy come down to the beach alone. He was playing with a stick in the water, digging up shells and clams, poking little crabs, killing them. He was all alone."

Saint Claire could see Kain getting excited as he relived the experience.

"I watched him. I stalked him like a cat. And when he went to the bathroom, I followed him in."

His eyes seemed to glaze over.

"He was sitting on the toilet when I came in. I surprised him. He shouted something at me in Portuguese when I went up to him, but he was small and weak. I didn't know why I was doing it, but I pinned him to the floor and choked him hard. I was laughing. I didn't let go until he stopped moving."

Reaching over, Kain grabbed an ample handful of nuts.

"And when he was dead, I just walked away. I found the little stick he had and took it with me when we left as a souvenir, brought it all the way home, but yeah, I killed him. I was nine at the time."

He ate a few of the almonds, crunching quietly, savoring the flavor.

"I *love* these things. I don't think I've had em since I lived at home, but I love them. Irresistible!"

He ate a few more and reached toward the bowl again. Saint Claire watched him eat, resisting an urge to smile.

"The boy on the beach, was he your first murder?"

"No."

Kain laughed. He finished the last few nuts in his hand.

"I killed your best friend, Joe. I killed your lover, Sanchez. And I killed your wife, my aunt-mother, of course. I've ruined your life, and none of it has made you angry enough to kill me. But do you want to know who my first murder was?"

"Yes."

Kain stretched his neck as though it were cramped and sipped more brandy.

"You blamed my mother, but it was me. I was six. I slipped into her room and smothered her in her crib. I killed my baby sister."

He nodded, smiling, a droplet of blood showing at the corner of his lip.

"Yes, I murdered Geneviève."

As Saint Claire watched, refusing to react in anger, he saw Kain begin to realize something was going dreadfully wrong. Suddenly, Kain was gasping for air. He sat back on the sofa, clutching his throat, his eyes wide, staring at his father with an expression of incredulity.

"You! What did you *do*?"

Saint Claire backed away.

"Nothing. It's your mother, from the grave. She scribbled me a note before she shot herself, saying she put something in the almonds. She knew you'd eat them. She left another note in the flowers. Hold on."

He took the envelope from a plastic clip hidden among the irises, opened it and read a single word on a small sheet: *Echinacea*. He refolded the slip, still holding it in his hand.

By this time, Kain's distress had grown. His chest heaved as he struggled to stand, his eyes searching for Brady's gun on the table. But Brady, clenching teeth in his bloody mouth, lunged forward to take the gun from the table. He pointed it toward Kain with wild, shaky hands.

Saint Claire's voice remained steady.

"Calm down, everybody."

Gasping, Kain looked up at his father, who continued.

"Let me tell you what's going on. You probably don't remember it, but you almost died when you were four. It was right after your mother came back. I had no idea what had happened, but she says here she innocently gave you tea made from *Echinacea*, having no idea you would have a reaction to it."

He watched as Kain began involuntary hypoventilation.

"Turns out you're highly allergic to *Echinacea*. It's a very rare allergy. You didn't know about it, did you? I didn't. I guess it's something only a *mother* would know."

He went around the table and helped Kain sit back on the sofa.

"Try to steady your breathing. Apparently, she put powdered *Echinacea* on the almonds. You're going into anaphylactic shock. Just sit back, breathe."

"No!"

Kain tried to lunge forward, but he fell back onto the couch, clutching his throat.

"Help me! You can't let this happen to me!"

Saint Claire looked directly into Kain's eyes.

"Why? You said you wanted to die."

"I said I need you to kill me! You have to shoot me!"

Kain looked toward Brady.

"Someone shoot me!"

Saint Claire took the Ruger pistol from the other side of the table and backed away.

"I'm not going to shoot you."

Kain could barely speak.

"Don't, don't you dare call the fire department! You have to shoot me, now!"

Saint Claire only crossed his arms.

"Don't worry. I won't be calling the paramedics either. That choice is yours. You can use my phone to dial 911 if you want to. It might not be too late."

"No! No, I can't!"

Saint Claire's smile was barely perceptible.

"Then I'm going to stand right here, and watch you die."

"No!"

"And as you die, I want you to think about everything you've done, all the people you've hurt, the lives you've ruined. In the end, the only person who could successfully reach back and murder from the grave has been your mother. In the end, she beat you."

Anaphylaxis had set in. Saint Claire approached his son.

"You want to talk about a predisposition?"

He sighed. He hadn't thought about her for years, but Miss Annabelle Lee's image flashed for an instant in his memory.

"I don't want to hear about your needs or your hunger, because it's all bullshit. You were right about one thing. You were right about me. Because of you, I'm finally forced to confront an inner demon and memory I had locked away since I was kid. Maybe I *was* born with a predisposition to kill, and maybe I've been feeding it in my own way, but that doesn't mean I've had to go out and kill people."

Kain was wheezing. His chest heaved as his body struggled for oxygen. He coughed, his bulging eyes pleading upward.

"You're, you're my father! I'm your son, Christian!"

Saint Claire shook his head.

"You said it. My son Christian was murdered twelve years ago, and that's all anyone will ever know. There will be no resurrection."

Tears streamed down his face as he watched his son dying before his eyes. He wanted to help him, but he couldn't.

"No one will ever know your story. After you're dead, I'm going to dress you in old clothes and leave your body outside a homeless shelter in the Tenderloin. No one will claim you, so you will be cremated, nameless forever."

Kain's eyes were glazed over. He was beginning to lose consciousness.

"I'm sorry, Dad. Please don't! Please don't take away my name!"

Christian's eyes widened.

"Don't burn the book!"

Deuteronomy cringed, his heart aching. He was crying. He felt pity, not just for is son, but for himself.

"I love you, Son."

Loud, insistent knocking on the door startled Saint Claire from his mourning. Uneasy, he shot a glare toward Brady, but Brady was in no condition to respond. Standing, Saint Claire wiped the tears from his face, approached and turned his head so his ear was nearly touching the door.

"Who is it?"

"Police. Can you open the door, please?"

When he opened the door, two officers stood in the hallway. He didn't recognize either, but both obviously knew who he was. The shorter man, standing in the front, spoke up.

"We're sorry to bother you, Inspector. We know your situation. But we just got a call from one of your neighbors. She said she heard what sounded like a gunshot come from your unit. Is everything okay in there?"

The young officer tried to peek around the door, but Saint Claire moved into the gap, blocking his view.

"Everything's fine. I'm not sure what the neighbor heard, but it wasn't from this unit. Inspector Brady and I were just talking things out."

Brady called out.

"Hey guys! We're just talkin things out in here. Everything's fine."

The officer nodded.

"We saw his truck downstairs."

He seemed reluctant to ask, but he had to do his job.

"Inspector, do you, would you mind if we came in and took a look around?"

Saint Claire held a hand forward in protest.

"Yes, I would. I just lost my wife. This is not a good time."

The taller man in the back bowed his head, subtly nudging his partner.

"We understand. We're sorry to bother you, Sir. Sorry about your wife."

Saint Claire forced a weak smile.

"Thank you for understanding."

He closed the door. When he got back to the sofa, Kain had lost consciousness. Deuteronomy took his son into his bosom and watched as Christian's body struggled to breathe its last breath.

CHAPTER 63

For two and a half hours, search teams combed the rocky coast along Angel Island. Saint Claire had phoned the interim chief, indicating he had good reason to believe chief Leong was alive and was hidden in a cave near the water, bound and gagged. He also warned that the cave would be submerged at high tide, meaning if teams did not find the chief in three hours, she would be drowned.

Along the coast, the wind began to blow clouds and fog inland. The sky was growing dark. During his investigation of the disappearance and death of Police Chief Biggy, Saint Claire had spent many hours on the rocky shoreline. He gave specific details about where the cave might be located.

Rebecca Leong was weak, malnourished and dehydrated when she was discovered, but her vital signs were strong. Searchers carried her, dressed in a seawater soaked sweater and jeans, up to the road where a life flight helicopter waited. They flew her directly to the hospital.

Earlier, Saint Claire drove Brady to the San Francisco General Hospital emergency room. He told the attending physician Brady had been shot in a carjacking as he got into his truck outside Saint Claire's condominium building. Saint Claire said he heard the shot and ran to Brady's aid, but he did not get a good look at the perpetrator.

Saint Claire called for over an hour, but he got no answer. He tried the house phone a dozen times and the cell phone at least as many. He even tried Oksana on her blackberry and at the spa. The absence of any response was disquieting.

Gisele sat in a chair at the kitchen table, traumatized, seeming catatonic. Her head was bald, and her face, absent of eyebrows and make-up, was wan and tired. Hands palms up on the table, she stared at the slits on her wrists, each beginning to crust over in scabs. Saint Claire worked in the background, patching the wall.

Christian's body was still lying on the sofa, but his clothing had been changed. His form fitting black outfit was gone. Instead, he wore a pair of oversized brown corduroy pants and a tattered red and black wool plaid button up shirt. The filthy white patent leather shoes on his feet had lost their luster long ago.

Saint Claire didn't want to disturb her, but he couldn't leave her. She hadn't uttered a word since he found her bound and gagged in the closet of his study. She needed time to steady her nerves and regain her senses. He couldn't tell if she was still frightened or if she was angry as she sat there, taking deep steady breaths. He had to get to Slater, if it wasn't already too late.

"Gisele?"

Cupping her left elbow in his hand, he gently tried to nudge her up from the chair.

"You need to rest."

"Don't leave me!"

"No. No, I'm not leaving you. You're coming with me. We have to go now. We have to try to save my friend, Slater."

She stood, wobbly at first, leaning against him as they walked toward the door. He tried to keep his body between her and the sofa so she wouldn't see Christian lying there, but she stopped suddenly, staring at her antagonist. Saint Claire watched her eyes narrow just before she flew around him toward the sofa. She was pounding Christian's face and chest with her fists when Saint Claire dragged her off the body.

"Bastard! You better be happy you are already dead!"

"*Fique tranquilo*, Gisele, *fique tranquilo!*"

She was so angry she could not speak. Instead, she spat.

"*Pobre diabo!* He was drinking my blood! For two days he was drinking my blood!"

The lights were on inside the house. Slater's Jaguar, which he normally put inside after finishing his last errand, was parked in front of the open garage door. Saint Claire held Gisele's chin in his fingers as he spoke.

"You wait here. You've had trauma enough for the day. I'll be right back."

He entered the house through the garage, calling as he checked the kitchen and family room.

"Slater?"

He climbed the stairs, headed toward the recess.

"Slater? It's Saint Claire!"

When he pushed the door open, he could see the body sprawled on the couch. A newly opened bottle of Jack Daniels stood on the counter. Judging from the amount of space above the liquid, Slater had poured at least three good drinks from the bottle. Saint Claire felt an ache deep in his bowels as he turned toward his friend. Slater was either dead or dying.

But there was something odd about Slater lying there. He seemed too relaxed, too natural. Saint Claire approached the body, slowly leaning over his friend to see if he was still breathing. Slater's eyes opened suddenly. In an instant he was on his feet, coughing.

"Goddammit Saint Claire! What the fuck! What are ya, tryin ta scare me ta death?"

Saint Claire was at a loss for words, but Slater had ample to continue.

"What are ya doin, asshole? How'd ya get in here?"

"You left the garage door open. How much did you drink from that bottle?"

Slater shrugged.

"You're lookin at it."

Saint Claire examined his former captain. If the bottle contained three times more mercury than the previously tainted bottles, then Slater would have never awakened.

"Where'd that bottle of Jack come from?"

Slater yawned and looked back over his shoulder.

"Oh that! From Oksana. She said the woman next house over reported a suspicious person in the neighborhood three days ago, looking at our house."

He turned back.

"Then yesterday she said she thought someone had been in the house. And ya know, after that story about Gisele on the news, she just got suspicious—poured out almost a full case of booze. I was in tears. Told me I could only drink it one bottle at a time from now on, and *she* has to buy it. Bossy broad! Why'd ya ask?"

"Just wondering."

Saint Claire went to the bar and re-capped the bottle.

"You ever think about switching to a different brand? Ever feel like you're a laboratory rat?"

Rescued drink in hand, Slater laughed.

"What? Are you drunk? What are you talkin about?"

Saint Claire took a seat on a barstool.

"You might want to sit down for this. I'll give you the short version. The unabridged version, you don't want to know."

CHAPTER 64

Three men stood at the gravesite. It had been a long week of funerals. First Sonia Sanchez and then Katrina Saint Claire. Sonia's funeral had been a media event, with wide reaching public displays of sympathy, long flattering speeches, declarations of praise and several musical tributes by celebrities, local and international.

By contrast, Katrina's service was private and solemn. There was just a priest, Father LaRue, who handled a brief service along with the rite of Committal. Only Saint Claire, Slater, Oksana and Brady were in attendance. At the gravesite, Saint Claire, heart heavy and eyes filled with tears, read a poem she had written about freedom two nights before she died.

The burial on this day, however, was for neither. There was no service at all. It was just a burial, performed in an unceremonious fashion at dusk. After much deliberation and vacillation, Saint Claire decided at the last moment to claim the body of his son from the morgue. It was the right thing to do. He said the decedent was remotely related to him and he bought a coffin and a funeral plot.

But he quietly paid two graveyard workers five hundred dollars apiece to bury the coffin at the gravesite of Christian Saint Claire. After twelve years, his son's body was finally at rest, and with it a tired, troubled portion of his own soul.

"Besides sharin that flask you got in your jacket pocket, Saint Claire, have you decided what you're gonna do now?"

Saint Claire handed the flask to Slater.

"I don't know. I'd like to think I'm through with death, but I don't know if I can escape it. I'm starting to believe he was right about me."

Brady nodded emphatically.

"He was right. You can't escape it. That hunger's gotta be fed somehow."

He reached for the flask.

"Besides, you've seen the news. The city's mad at the mayor. He's not going to win reelection. And I'm sure Leong would welcome you back. You did save her life."

Saint Claire took a deep breath and sighed.

"I don't know. There's one more important matter I have to settle. Then I'll... then I'll take a little time and decide."

He raised the flask in his hand.

"To endings, and to beginnings."

He drank and nodded toward Brady.

"To the beginning of a friendship! After all this, I think I have two friends now."

Brady looked over, surprised. The week's ordeal had made him a little emotional. His face was at odds with itself, but the tears were impossible to control. He wiped his eyes.

"Goddamn you, Saint Claire! I liked you better when you hated me."

Saint Claire laughed, and then he became somber, bowing his head.

"I appreciate you two coming out, but would you mind? You can take the flask, but I think I'd like to spend a few minutes here alone."

He shrugged, daggers of pain stabbing at his heart, and looked up.

"I have to let go."

The fire burned brightly, topping the brim of the dented metal garbage can. Saint Claire had come down to North Beach that night with an entire shopping cart full of fuel. They were his notebooks and notes, representing years of painstaking research and documentation, but the question had been answered. Today they meant nothing.

He found them placed neatly at the center of Gisele's apartment living room. If he and Gisele had not survived the crisis in his condo, police searching for answers would have found all his notes where the killer had left them. In addition to the notes, Kain had left a hardbound, self-published book, titled *Murder From the Grave*, by Deuteronomy Saint Claire.

This book contained a glamorized account of every murder Kain had ever committed, complete with explanations, pictures, reasoning and documentation for his most illustrious murders. The book included a chapter for each series, including the *Song of Seven Sets of Twins*, the ambitious *Killing Artist Series*, and the three years he spent stalking and murdering serial killers. At the end, the author tallied the list: 948, not including the last seven.

It took Saint Claire three days to read the book. It was so graphic in detail that he had to put it down on several occasions and take an extended break. Murder after bloody murder! It was a book that required censure, a book that could never be read.

In the end, he reluctantly conceded its premise. Kain had written a book that addressed the needs of a latent sector of human society: the killers. They live in all our communities, at the schools, at the hospitals, in the military and within departments of law enforcement, disguised, often even from themselves, but killers nonetheless.

In the book, Kain made an attempt to speak to the killer existing in human society, an attempt to put individuals in touch with their often hidden, though murderous inclinations. In doing so, he sought to establish himself as the greatest serial murder artist of all time, a perfect paradigm of the killer genotype.

Saint Claire feared the book would find resonance in a society that was becoming ever obsessed with murder and death. Most obvious were the television shows, featuring crime scene investigations, murderous recreation in docudrama and likable serial killers, and the board games, video games, magazines and movies were no less obsessed with killing. Kain's book would probably have become a bestseller, and for that reason, it could never be read. As much as he revered books, Saint Claire had to destroy this one.

He had finished reading it an hour earlier. There were probably other copies, but as long as he was alive, he could deny their authenticity. With the last of the notes burned, he held in his hand the book, a very powerful and dangerous book, a book that would contribute to the ultimate erosion of human society.

Closing his eyes, he prayed for forgiveness and tossed the book into the flaming bin, relinquishing any connection to it. In a few moments, it would be over. He watched as it began to burn. But in that very instant, Saint Claire revisited the mind of his son, the killer. Kain *had* to know this ending was possible! He probably thought he would win, but ever thorough, he had to consider the possibility that he might lose.

In that event, he had to know Saint Claire would want to expunge him and his work from the sphere of human awareness. Books could attain immortality, lest *fire* should destroy them. But should the book ever be destroyed, death would come to the destroyer. Just then, Saint Claire reflected on its odd appearance and remembered his son's last words, "Don't burn the book!"

Glued to its bulging spine, just inside the outer cover, was a thin, six-inch long plastic slip filled with triacetone triperoxide, a powerful explosive, extremely sensitive to temperature change. In the fire, the book had become a bomb!

Saint Claire realized he might have been too close to escape. Turning away, he dived toward a cement bank of stairs behind him just as the metal can erupted into a violent, fiery explosion.

The heat and concussive force of the blast racked Saint Claire's body in midair, burning him and slamming him into the cement wall. The can, obliterated in the explosion, became shrapnel, piercing his legs, arms and torso. The explosion was heard all over the beach, and the resultant fireball caused the area to glow as flames exhausted the fuel.

ACKNOWLEGEMENTS

This book, and certainly no other book I could write, would not be possible if not for the incredible people in my life who have continued to put up with me. I won't pretend to be able to name them all here. But as the book goes to print, I can't help but reflect on a few who stand out for contributing ideas, helpful criticism, advice, support and inspiration.

As I began the book, I enlisted a few readers who patiently waited and read chapter by chapter as I wrote, lending comments and suggestions. There were others who read the completed manuscript and gave the earliest critiques. The readers group included Stephanie Beaver-Patton, my official proofreader, Amber Burnett, Jennifer Burnett, Shirley Ferguson, Tori Rhodes, Ken Regan, Marian Regan, Susie Steffes, Leslie Grant, Dr. Gregory Douglas, Jessica Douglas, Roger Brown, Mike LaBrada, Elisa Nicholas, Rinnetta McGhee, Ashliegh McGee, Sandra McGee, Richard McGee, Barbara McGee, Mark McGee and Natsumi McGee. I would like to give special mention to Steve McGee, who contributed to the conclusion. I thank you all for your contributions to the book.

Professionally, I would like to thank Jerry Chisum, former San Francisco criminalist and blood splatter expert, for providing background and comments; Dean McGee for providing background medical; agents Steve Kasdin and Jill Marsal, for believing in this book; the Sandra Dijkstra Literary Agency; editor Stacia Decker; eexpert Jamie Pride; my cousin Cornell Cotton for his energy and ideas; Nikita Cotton for help on the cover; and Denora Watts and Danika York from my writers' group.

In addition, I want to thank my extended family, which includes my parents, children, siblings, aunts, uncles, cousins, nieces, nephews and all the friends I have made along the way.

With the greatest humility, I thank God for allowing me the time, personal circumstances and disposition to write, and for providing me the great privilege of coming into contact with the people listed above.

LaVergne, TN USA
14 October 2010
200807LV00004B/12/P